YAACOV HERZOG
A BIOGRAPHY

YAACOV HERZOG
A BIOGRAPHY

Michael Bar-Zohar

Translated by Yael Lotan

HALBAN
LONDON

First published in Great Britain by
Halban Publishers Ltd
22 Golden Square
London W1F 9JW
2005

www.halbanpublishers.com

All rights reserved. No part of this publication or audio recording
may be reproduced, stored in a retrieval system, or transmitted in any form,
or by any means, electronic, mechanical, photocopying, recording
or otherwise, without the prior permission of the Publishers.

A CIP catalogue record for this book is available from the British Library.

ISBN 1870015 93 2

Original Hebrew title
The Life and Times of a Jewish Prince:
A Biography of Yaacov Herzog
Copyright © 2003 by Miskal – Yedioth Ahronoth Books and Chemed Books

Translation copyright © 2005 by the estate of Yaacov Herzog
Foreword copyright © 2003 by Shimon Peres

Michael Bar-Zohar has asserted his right under the Copyright,
Design and Patents Act, 1988 to be identified
as the author of this work.

Maps copyright © 2005 by Martin Gilbert

Audio compact disc
Copyright © 1961 by the estates of Arnold Toynbee and Yaacov Herzog
℗ 2005 by Halban Publishers
Recording courtesy of Sony/CBS
Compact disc reproduction by Lemon Media, Somerset

Typeset by Computape Typesetting, Scarborough, North Yorkshire
Printed in Great Britain by MPG Books Ltd., Bodmin, Cornwall

Contents

	Foreword by Shimon Peres	vii
	Maps	x
1	In the Thick of War	1
2	Two Worlds	31
3	War	49
4	The Secret Agent	71
5	Redeeming Lands in Jerusalem	86
6	At First Sight	108
7	Acting Foreign Minister	130
8	Birds Over the Cedars of Lebanon	153
9	The Challenge	175
10	The Duel	192
11	The Absent Father	215
12	Dr Davis and Mr Charles	225
13	Collapse	257
14	A Time of Flourishing	269
15	Six Days and a King	293
16	A Gift from Hussein	322
17	Decline	337
18	Epilogue	350
	Bibliography and Sources	353
	Notes	356
	Index	379

To Pnina Herzog *In Memoriam*

Foreword

Yaacov Herzog was a Jewish scholar by upbringing, and a statesman by aptitude. Scholarly knowledge requires talent, while statesmanship demands intuition. As a scholar you may reside in the grove of academe, you must be meticulous, painstaking, capable of absorbing entire systems of knowledge and familiar with every part of it. To be a statesman you must move among people, discern their true nature, assess their frame of mind and their intentions. You have to notice which way the world is tending, recognize dangers, discover opportunities, win hearts and, when necessary, fight.

Yaacov Herzog bridged the great divide between the introverted, intellectual, almost shy personality and the extroverted, industrious, always public personality, and did so gracefully, persuasively, and above all, with conviction.

He knew how to harness his intellectual capacity to strategic purpose. He had come to the corridors of power from the domain of the Torah, yet never needed to forsake one for the other. On the contrary – since morality lies at the heart of Judaism, it is faith which judges day-by-day moves.

'I was drawn from childhood to two worlds,' he wrote, 'to the world of the Babylonian Talmud ... and to that of international developments.' He went on to note that 'In today's Peking [Beijing], Confucius would be much like Plato or Aristotle in Greece ... all three great historical figures, but not necessarily part of the daily experience of the people among whom they had lived.

But I'm convinced that if Rabbi Akiva were to arise today, many Jews would speak to him, question him about his attitude towards the Bar Kokhba war, and what he thought about the destruction of the Temple. They would talk to him about the nature of the Jewish people, its dialogue with the God of Israel, and with the nations of the world.'

Ben-Gurion, with his innate shrewdness, soon realized that in Yaacov he had a person who knew the past and understood the present, who could envision the future and see the links between spiritual and practical spheres. Yaacov became one of Ben-Gurion's closest advisors – perhaps the principal one – in the intellectual as well as the diplomatic field.

David Ben-Gurion was deeply preoccupied with Jewish history. He saw it as replete with prophecy and poor in statesmanship. Jewish history was well endowed with prophets, which enabled the people to maintain their great spirit, but it suffered from a scarcity of statesmen and therefore underwent destruction and exile, conquest and Holocaust. We wished to be 'a light unto the nations', but were 'the least of nations'.

Ben-Gurion thought, as did Yaacov Herzog, that statesmanship was a dialogue not only with the present, but with history. But history is not a gift from heaven – it is written by mortal historians, and even the great ones are not supreme judges, nor even objective judges.

So it happened that Yaacov Herzog challenged one who was regarded as a foremost historian, whose historical philosophy had influenced many intellectuals the world over. Arnold Toynbee had pronounced a death sentence on the Jewish people. He had never been particularly impressed by Judaism, and from an historical perspective regarded the Jewish people as a fossil whose life was over and whose future was nonexistent.

Herzog engaged Toynbee in one of the most dramatic debates in the history of our people. Toynbee was universally regarded as an intellectual giant, while Yaacov Herzog's reputation was

Foreword

known only to a limited circle. Yet Herzog showed himself a formidable adversary to the eminent historian, and saved the honour of the Jewish people, showing that it was very much alive, active, building and fighting, and that the 'news' of its demise was unfounded.

Yaacov knew that modern wars are waged between nations, but that they are also contests of faiths. He built up a network of relations with non-Jewish religious leaders, with whom he maintained clear lines of communication. Yaacov realized that it was not enough to defend Israel's borders – the Jewish heritage, too, needed to be defended. Even when circumstances require Judaism's brawn, it must not be forgotten that it is first and foremost a religion of moral values.

It was Ben-Gurion who declared that 'The fate of Israel depends on her strength and on the justice of her cause.' Yaacov Herzog contributed justice to the strength, and strength to the justice.

Shimon Peres
Tel Aviv 2003

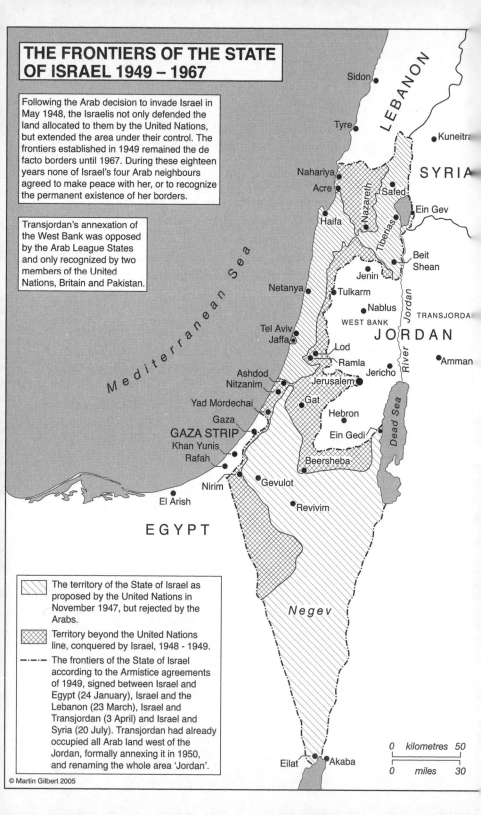

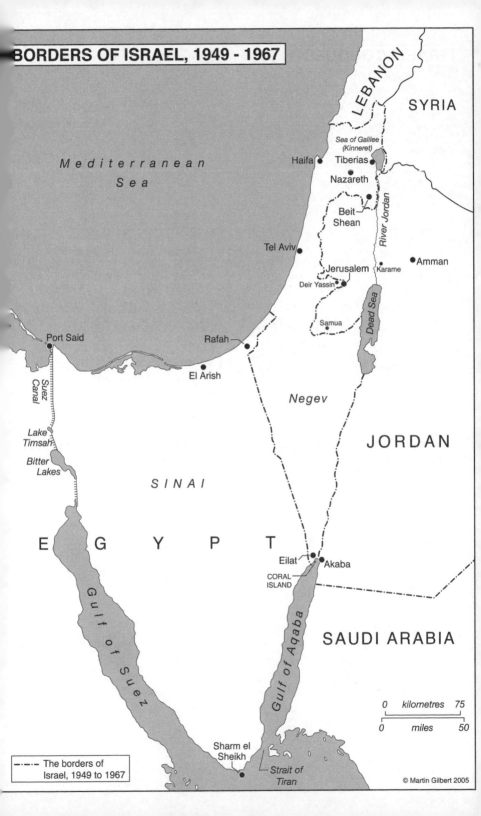

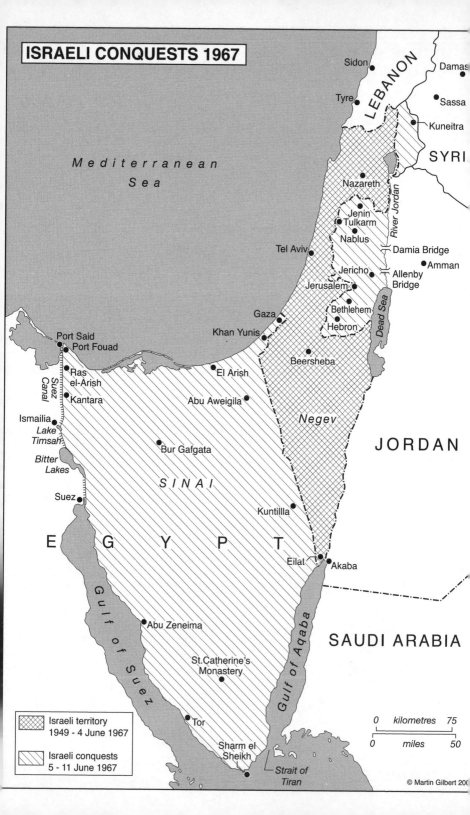

I

In the Thick of War

On the night of 26 October 1956 Yaacov Herzog was unable to sleep.[1] The son of Israel's Chief Rabbi, Yitzhak (Isaac) Halevi Herzog, Yaacov was then head of the United States department in the Foreign Ministry. He had been at the Foreign Ministry for only two years. Thirty-five years old, slim and bespectacled, with a high brow and smiling eyes, Yaacov was known to be a calm individual, not easily flustered. On this night, however, he felt very restless – a few hours earlier he had heard, almost by accident, the secret information that Israel was about to go to war.

That Friday morning, during a discussion at the Foreign Ministry about the Iraqi army's ominous movement towards the Jordanian border, he received a phone call from Teddy Kollek, then director-general of the Prime Minister's office. Did Yaacov know, Kollek asked, the significance of the mobilization that was taking place in Tel Aviv? The minister at the United States embassy had just telephoned to ask about it. Yaacov suggested that Kollek ask Yitzhak Navon, Prime Minister Ben-Gurion's political secretary, or his military secretary, Colonel Nehemiah Argov. But Kollek, offended by being left out of the loop, urged Herzog to ask them. Herzog phoned Navon, who replied that 'White [the US minister] must not be told anything,' and snapped that if White had not approached him directly, why should he make enquiries on his behalf?[2]

In the evening White telephoned Herzog's home and asked about the general call-up. There was no sign of the Sabbath in Tel

Aviv, he said, and the army was mobilizing vehicles and reservists. Herzog had no choice – he put on his Sabbath clothes and walked to Ben-Gurion's Jerusalem residence.

Yaacov had known Ben-Gurion since boyhood. Yaacov's distinctive personality combined the qualities of a skilled diplomat with that of a thorough and original scholar of Jewish history and Talmud. Ben-Gurion 'appreciated and encouraged' him, in his words,[3] and over the years they had held wide-ranging discussions about political matters as well as spiritual and religious subjects.[4]

Yitzhak Navon and Nehemiah Argov were both at Ben-Gurion's house, and at first they tried to dissuade Yaacov from pursuing the matter. They did not care to inform the US embassy about the mobilization, but he argued that if the Americans did not receive a satisfactory answer, they might draw far-reaching conclusions, and the next thing would be a message from President Eisenhower to Ben-Gurion.

Eventually Ben-Gurion's assistants relented and agreed to ask the Prime Minister for his response. Ben-Gurion came downstairs, heard the question and instructed Herzog to reply to White that the Israeli government had received information that the Iraqi army was massing on the Jordanian border, and Israel was taking precautions. Herzog hastened to pass the reply on to White, stressing that the mobilization was partial, and the American diplomat seemed satisfied. But Nehemiah Argov, who accompanied Herzog back home, told him in confidence that the purpose of the call-up was entirely different – Israel was going to attack Egypt in three days' time!

Herzog was very agitated, but succeeded in hiding the fact from his dinner guests – American leaders of the United Jewish Appeal.[5] Later that evening he told his wife Pnina, from whom he never kept anything, 'We're going to war against Egypt.'[6]

The following day Herzog saw the Interior Minister, Moshe Chaim Shapira, at synagogue, and noticed his tense, preoccupied expression. 'He probably also knows that we're facing momentous events,' he noted.[7] In the evening he went to a meeting at the house of the Foreign Minister Golda Meir with senior members of the Foreign Ministry – the director-general Walter Eytan, Arthur Lurie, Gideon Rafael, Emile Najar and Mordechai Shneerson. Golda informed them of the main points of the war plan and swore them to secrecy. Later that evening Herzog returned to her house and analysed the situation. The news about the Iraqi troop concentrations near the Jordanian border, he said, could be used for a short while to justify the mobilization. But as soon as fighting broke out the Egyptian President, Gamal Abd al-Nasser, would call on the United States to stop Israel; he might also seek military assistance from the USSR. Herzog assumed that the Soviets would not give Egypt military assistance, but the possibility that they might would cause the United States to put massive pressure on Israel to stop the attack. He advised Golda Meir to remain close to the Prime Minister in the next few days, as 'there will be critical political developments which will call for immediate decisions.'[8]

Herzog's assessment was borne out before the first shot was fired. On Sunday the call-up intensified, and American diplomats were no longer satisfied with Herzog's claim that it was partial.[9] At noon the US Ambassador, Edward Lawson, telephoned him to say that he had a message for Ben-Gurion from President Eisenhower and wanted to deliver it at once. Herzog called on Golda Meir and the two rushed over to the house of President Ben-Zvi, where Ben-Gurion usually lunched on Sundays. At these lunches, which had become a tradition, the Prime Minister would report to the President about the weekly cabinet meeting.

Having heard Golda Meir's report, Ben-Gurion instructed her to invite Lawson to his house in Tel Aviv at eight o'clock that evening. Golda told Herzog to go to Tel Aviv and accompany the Prime Minister at the meeting.[10] Pnina packed a small bag for him and he left.

Before driving to Tel Aviv, Yaacov stopped to see his brother, Brigadier General Chaim Herzog, at the Schneller army camp in

Jerusalem, where he was busy with the mobilization of thousands of reservists. Chaim told Yaacov that he had been ordered to attack the Jordanians at the first provocation.[11] Yaacov warned him not to shell the Old City, but Chaim assured him that he had a detailed map showing Christianity's holy places.

Yaacov drove on to Tel Aviv and reached Ben-Gurion's house on Keren Kayemet Boulevard (now renamed Ben-Gurion Boulevard) a few minutes ahead of the American Ambassador. From that moment Herzog became, albeit unwittingly, Ben-Gurion's personal foreign secretary and confidant for many months to come.

When he arrived at Ben-Gurion's house Herzog knew only a little about the secret 'Operation Kadesh' that would start the following day. Only a few of Ben-Gurion's closest aides were party to the preparations which had been going on for three months, and other than Golda Meir, most senior members of the Foreign Ministry were still in the dark.

Although Yaacov had not known about these preparations, he was thoroughly familiar with the background of the planned war. The previous year, 1955, had seen tension rise between Israel and Egypt. Nasser sent groups of suicide fighters, known as fedayeen, into Israel from bases in Jordan and the Gaza Strip. The terrorists attacked mainly civilian targets and murdered residents of border settlements – even deep within the country. Israel responded to these attacks with fierce retaliatory attacks on Egyptian and Jordanian military bases, and a vicious cycle of terrorist penetration and retaliation ensued.

But Israel had not contemplated launching a war against Egypt until the autumn of 1955, when the Egyptian-Czech arms deal became known. The information was that Egypt was about to receive quantities of matériel that were immense in Middle East terms – some 200 Mig-15 and Ilyushin-28 fighter aircraft, 230 tanks, 200 armoured vehicles, 100 mobile cannons, 500 other types of cannons, torpedo boats, destroyers and six submarines.[12]

The transaction upset both the fragile balance of power in the Middle East and the efforts of three Western powers – the US, France and Britain – to control the supply of arms to the Arab States and Israel. The Czech deal meant that the USSR had entered the region which had so far been seen as the West's area of influence and, in addition, given Egypt significant advantage over Israel. In November 1955, feeling greatly strengthened, Nasser announced the closure of the Straits of Tiran to Israeli shipping.

Israel felt its very existence threatened. 'The Czech deal caused us profound anxiety,' Herzog stated in a background paper about that period.[13] Having failed to get the transaction cancelled, the Israeli government began feverishly to look for new sources of arms, chiefly from the United States. But these efforts failed and in December 1955 Ben-Gurion raised the possibility, in a cabinet meeting, of launching a pre-emptive war against Egypt. The plan was rejected by a majority of cabinet ministers led by the moderate Foreign Minister Moshe Sharett, just as earlier that year, in April, they had not supported the Prime Minister's proposal to conquer the Gaza Strip.

Then, in the spring of 1956, a new source of arms became available. France had been embroiled in a ruthless war in Algeria since November 1954, when the Muslims rebelled against French rule. The Egyptian President had been very active behind the scenes, inciting, training and arming the Algerian rebels. France regarded Nasser as her chief enemy and naively believed that if only they could crush Nasser the Algerian uprising would collapse. The new French government, formed in early 1956 by the Socialist leader Guy Mollet, was hoping to deal Nasser a heavy blow and thereby destroy his support of the Algerian revolt.

Mollet's government was sympathetic to Israel's socialist leadership, and resolved to prevent a 'new Munich' in which Israel would be sacrificed to Arab aggression. Shimon Peres, then director-general of Israel's Ministry of Defence, held secret meetings with the French leaders, who agreed to dispatch large quantities of arms to Israel, mostly without coordination with the United States or other NATO members.

Israel was still hoping for a peaceful solution to the crisis, and this was the mission of President Eisenhower's personal representative, Robert Anderson, a former US Assistant Secretary of Defense. He came to Israel quietly in January 1956 and after extensive talks with the Israeli leadership, Anderson flew to Egypt, but his mission failed in the face of Nasser's intransigence. From that moment on, Israel felt more determined to launch a pre-emptive war. As a result Moshe Sharett felt compelled to resign from the Foreign Ministry and Golda Meir was appointed in his place. The likelihood of war increased greatly when, on 23 July 1956, Nasser nationalized the Suez Canal, infuriating the British government and giving France an excellent pretext to attack Egypt. A veil of secrecy was drawn over Anglo-French preparations, as well as over the Israeli-French dialogue.

Yaacov Herzog was involved in many of the diplomatic contacts that took place in 1955–6. He was close to Moshe Sharett and familiar with his concerns about the right policy to follow. He was the senior Foreign Ministry official assigned, alongside Teddy Kollek, to deal with Robert Anderson's mediation mission. In fact, many people regarded him as Ben-Gurion's 'political advisor', though he had no formal position. 'Yaacov had free access to Ben-Gurion,' said Teddy Kollek.[14] The rabbi's young son had impressed Ben-Gurion even before the War of Independence, in 1948, and when Yaacov was at the Ministry of Religious Affairs he would report to 'the Old Man' about Israel's relations with the Christian world, particularly the Vatican. In 1950, when Yaacov was only 28, they held long talks about Judaism.[15] During that year, as on other occasions, he advised Ben-Gurion about Israel's relations with the United States. He tended to be more optimistic than the Prime Minister about America's policies and Eisenhower's attitude towards Israel.[16] In the spring of 1956 he was one of the team that worked closely with Ben-Gurion to obtain arms from the United States.[17] Nevertheless, Nehemiah Argov's news about the imminent war took him by surprise.

'I found the Prime Minister in his armchair,' Herzog wrote in his diary after calling on Ben-Gurion on the night of 28 October.[18] While driving from Jerusalem he prepared some proposals concerning the necessary political moves. 'I put to him ideas about the imminent operation. He listened but did not react.' Yaacov had the impression that Ben-Gurion was unaware that he had been 'informed about the secret plan, if only partially'. Then Edward Lawson arrived, accompanied by his advisor Charles Hamilton, and delivered President Eisenhower's message. In it, the President responded to Ben-Gurion's expressed anxiety about Iraqi forces crossing into Jordan. 'I am not sure that I share your position in this matter,' Eisenhower stated, 'but in any case, as far as I am aware, there has been no Iraqi military incursion into Jordan ... I must frankly tell you of my concern about your massive mobilization, which I fear will only heighten the tension that you say you wish to defuse.' Further on, Eisenhower asked Ben-Gurion 'not to let your government launch an aggressive initiative that could threaten the peace and the growing friendship between our countries'.

Lawson then tried to get a clear answer from Ben-Gurion about the expected developments, but Ben-Gurion avoided giving an unequivocal response and only stressed the dangers to Israel's existence, especially the actions of the fedayeen. Finally, Lawson asked if he should start evacuating American nationals from Israel. A positive response would have amounted to an admission that Israel was about to go to war. Ben-Gurion replied that he could not express an opinion, nor even an assessment, regarding the risk faced by these American nationals.

When Lawson left, Ben-Gurion told Herzog that he was ill and had to return to bed. He had received the American Ambassador in spite of an attack of weakness and high fever (caused either by flu or, as Ben-Gurion was wont, due to intense pressure and stress). The fever, he said to Herzog, prevented him from replying to Eisenhower. Ben-Gurion then asked him to prepare a draft reply for the following morning.[19] He stressed that his message to the American President must not include an Israeli commitment to avoid military action.[20] Ben-Gurion wanted to complete the general mobilization and launch the operation before the governments of the world took steps to prevent it. At the same time, he did not want to mislead the American President. Yaacov hurried to the office of the Minister of Defence, where he met Shimon Peres and Nehemiah Argov, who revealed to him the real secret behind the projected operation.

Following the nationalization of the Suez Canal, they said, Israel and France had begun a series of confidential consultations, which peaked on 20 October 1956, when Prime Minister Ben-Gurion, accompanied by Shimon Peres and the Chief of Staff Moshe Dayan, visited France in secret. The conference, which took place in Sèvres near Paris, was attended by the French leadership, including the Prime Minister Guy Mollet, the Foreign Minister Christian Pineau, the Minister of Defence Maurice Bourgès-Maunoury, and senior military officers and advisors; the British government was represented by Selwyn Lloyd the Foreign Secretary. The meeting concluded with a decision to launch a tripartite attack on Egypt. The operation would begin with an Israeli attack near the Suez Canal, which would be interpreted as a threat to shipping, and would be followed by an Anglo-French ultimatum to Israel and Egypt, demanding instant withdrawal from the banks of the Canal. Israel would immediately agree, while the Egyptians would certainly refuse, as it would have meant withdrawing from the entire Sinai Peninsula and the east bank of the Canal. Britain and France would then attack Egypt, bombarding its airfields and land forces from the sea.

The agreement between the three states was formally signed. In

In the Thick of War

a separate undertaking France made a commitment to Israel, undertaking to protect her cities and shores from attacks by Egyptian aircraft and warships. French warplanes arrived in Israel, and French warships began to patrol not far from Israel's coast.

The cabinet had approved the operation that morning – Peres and Argov told Yaacov Herzog – but the members of the cabinet were not informed of all the details. The operation would begin the following day, 29 October, at 5 pm, when an Israel Defence Forces (IDF) unit would land near the Suez Canal. Yaacov was the only one in the Foreign Ministry, other than Golda Meir, who knew the truth about the forthcoming operation. 'The censor must be given clear instructions,' he urged. Peres and Argov summoned the chief military censor and the IDF press liaison officer. Meanwhile Herzog telephoned Golda Meir and told her about the meeting with Lawson. Then he retired into a closed office and spent hours racking his brain about public information and the answer to be given to President Eisenhower.[21] He caught a few hours' sleep at the Dan Hotel and returned to the office at 7.30 with the draft reply in his briefcase, only to be told that an official of the American Embassy had arrived at the office at 5 am and thrust a sealed envelope into the hands of the astonished guard at the gate. It was another message from President Eisenhower to Ben-Gurion, reiterating what the previous one had said, only in stronger language.

At 12 noon, after Golda Meir had approved his draft reply, Herzog went to the Prime Minister's house. Ben-Gurion was in bed, prostrate with a high fever and attended by his physician Professor Bernard Zondek. Paula Ben-Gurion at first refused to let the visitor enter her sick husband's room, but Herzog persuaded the doctor of the urgency of the matter and was allowed in. Ben-Gurion studied the letter, which described the growing threat to Israel: the Czech-Egyptian arms deal, the fedayeen incursions, and the creation of the joint military command by Egypt, Syria and Jordan, which Herzog described as a 'steel ring around Israel'. The concluding paragraph was phrased with extreme care: 'My government would be failing its principal duty if it did not use all possible means to ensure that the stated policy of Arab rulers to destroy Israel is thwarted. My government calls on the people of Israel to be both alert and calm. I am certain that you, with your extensive military experience, will appreciate the great and fateful danger in which we find ourselves.'

This was the passage designed to avoid deceiving the President of the United States – Israel was not promising not to go to war.

As soon as Ben-Gurion endorsed the draft, Herzog gave it to the Prime Minister's secretary to type and send to the American Ambassador. But when Herzog went downstairs he was told that the Ambassador had telephoned and asked to see him without delay. Herzog drove at once to the American embassy, having instructed Ben-Gurion's aides to send him the letter as soon as it was typed.

Lawson showed Herzog a telegram from the US Secretary of State John Foster Dulles ordering the immediate evacuation of all United States nationals from Israel. This meant that the US government was expecting war to break out at any moment. Lawson asked the Israeli government to assist with the evacuation, and Herzog promised that the IDF liaison office with foreign military attachés would help the US attaché in this operation.

The Ambassador was tense and wanted to know when he could expect Ben-Gurion's answer to the President of the United States. He must have assumed the delay was deliberate. Herzog replied that the letter was being typed, and indeed should have reached the embassy by now. To show that this was so, he telephoned Ben-Gurion's secretary and asked her in English – so that Ambassador Lawson could follow – what had happened to the letter. The secretary told him nervously that she had made a mistake in typing and, not having a suitable eraser, had sent someone to buy one, and was waiting for him to return. 'Never mind,' said Herzog. 'Correct it by hand and send it over.' But the secretary dug in her heels. She was not authorized to do this, she stated, 'and while I'm the Prime Minister's secretary, no letter of his will leave my hands with typing errors.'[22]

To pre-empt what might become a diplomatic crisis because of a simple eraser, Herzog patiently explained to the secretary that the American Ambassador would be transmitting the text of the letter by telegram, so that no one in America would notice the error. The re-typed letter could be forwarded later. But now, please, send the letter as it is, directly to the embassy. Finally she agreed.

Herzog proceeded to the Ministry of Defence, where he urged Ben-Gurion's aides immediately to wire Abba Eban, Israel's Ambassador to Washington, inform him about the approaching military operation, and ask him to prepare an official government statement in response.

Nehemiah Argov promptly rejected the first proposal. No ambassador needs to know about the operation, he declared, and no telegrams were to be sent about it, even in code, for fear that they would be intercepted and decoded by outsiders. The previous day Eban had sent a detailed report about a talk he had held with John Foster Dulles, who had emphasized that Israel should avoid making moves that would endanger the peace. Eban's message concluded with the question, 'What is going to happen?' But Ben-Gurion and his aides had decided to keep Eban in the dark. Accordingly, his question was left unanswered and he knew nothing about the imminent operation. (This led to an unfortunate sequel. On 29 October the still-uninformed Eban met the Assistant Secretary of State William Rowntree and did his best to convince him that Israel had no aggressive intentions. As they were speaking, Rowntree's secretary came into the room with a report from a news agency about Israeli paratroops landing in the Sinai. Rowntree read the report and said to Eban, 'Mister Ambassador, it seems that our conversation has just become academic...')

As for the official statement, Herzog discovered that no one had thought to prepare one. Nehemiah Argov told him that a meeting was scheduled for 4.30 pm at Ben-Gurion's house, and asked him to draft the main points of a statement.

The meeting around Ben-Gurion's bed included the Chief of Staff Moshe Dayan, the director-general of the Ministry of Defence Shimon Peres, the chief of the Security Services Isser Harel, the head of Military Intelligence Yehoshafat Harkabi, a representative of the Security Service, Yitzhak Navon and Yaacov Herzog. Dayan and Herzog argued about who should issue the official statement on the Sinai operation. Dayan wanted it to be the IDF spokesman, while Herzog argued that it should be the Foreign Ministry. Finally Ben-Gurion decided that the IDF would announce the military operation and the Foreign Ministry would issue an official statement. Dayan reported that the announcement of the IDF landing near the Suez Canal would be published at 8.20 pm, at which time the government statement would not yet be ready for publication. By the time Herzog finished drafting it together with Arthur Lurie, the deputy director-general of the Foreign Ministry, who then passed it to Shimon Peres and obtained Golda Meir's approval, and by the time it was translated into English, it was 10.30. In the two hours between the two releases the world was left to puzzle the significance of Israel's movements. The operation began on time, at 5 pm, when 395 paratroopers, commanded by Major Rafael Eitan (nicknamed Raful), landed on the eastern flank of the Mitla Pass, some tens of kilometres from the Canal. At that moment an armoured column broke through the Egyptian border and past the Quntilla police station and hurtled westwards to link up with the paratroops. Another column invaded Egypt in the Qsaimah area.

The IDF spokesman issued a laconic statement that Israeli troops had 'entered and attacked fedayeen units' at Ras al-Nakab and Quntilla, and 'had taken up positions west of the Nakhl intersection near the Suez Canal'.

The official statement, published two hours later, was a masterpiece of diplomatic acrobatics. It described the IDF operation in the Sinai Peninsula as an act of major retaliation, one of whose main objectives was to destroy the fedayeen bases, but it also spoke of Israel's right to self-defence, leaving an opening to continue the military operation. The cautious choice of words and the reference to the operation as an act of retaliation were designed to forestall moves by the international bodies to stop Israel in its tracks on the first day of the fighting, and to allow for the possibility that the French and the British would not live up to their commitment but would stay out of the region – in either case Israel could argue that it had intended to carry out only a short and limited operation.

The intense and eventful day concluded with a press conference held by Peres and Herzog at 1 am., in which they confronted some 'especially difficult' questions put to them by the international press.

Amid all this, a terrible event shook Israel's leaders and Yaacov Herzog – the massacre at Kafr Qassem. In that Arab village inside Israel, the border patrol shot and killed 43 Arab farmers, coming home from their fields, unaware that a curfew had been imposed on their village. 'We and the security men felt sick when we heard about the vile incident,' Herzog wrote a few weeks later. 'We must admit that there is something very wrong if young *Jewish* men are capable of such an act.'[23] (After the Sinai war the men responsible for the Kafr Qassem massacre were tried and sentenced to long prison terms.)

The following day the French–British ultimatum, agreed on in Sèvres, was made public. It aroused intense anger in the United States, as the Americans did not fail to perceive the connection between the Israeli assault and the French–British moves. France and Britain, America's closest allies, had made a secret pact with Israel behind Eisenhower's back. Such was the fury in Washington that the State Department in effect severed all diplomatic contacts with Israel for the duration of the fighting.

The following day – 30 October – caused Ben-Gurion the most

anxiety. On that day, Israel had to conduct the battle entirely on its own, and Ben-Gurion feared that the Egyptians would bombard Israeli cities from the air. He also feared that the Franco-British ultimatum would be delayed, and doubted the resolve of Britain's Prime Minister Anthony Eden.

But he need not have worried – except for a single Egyptian rocket's attempt to bomb a field in the south, the Egyptians did not attack Israel proper, and the British and French governments issued the agreed ultimatum to Israel and Egypt. At 10.30 pm Herzog turned up again at Ben-Gurion's house to show him the text of the ultimatum, which had been brought to him by the British Ambassador. It was time to formulate Israel's response, and Herzog had already prepared a draft for Ben-Gurion's approval. He found the Prime Minister in bed, though no longer feverish. At his side lay a book by Maimonides. Herzog asked Ben-Gurion to read the draft – it was late and every moment was precious. But Ben-Gurion was in no hurry. He invited Herzog to sit down and began to talk about the rules concerning slavery in Maimonides' *Yad Ha-Hazakah (The Strong Hand)*. Herzog was taken aback – the world was waiting, battles were raging in the Sinai, and the Old Man wanted to discuss slavery. He pointed out that the response to the ultimatum was 'extremely urgent',[24] but Ben-Gurion refused to change the subject and went on talking and asking questions about Maimonides. Herzog replied absent-mindedly, feeling tense and stressed. Again and again he asked Ben-Gurion to attend to the really important issue at hand, only to have Maimonides thrust at him. Feeling on tenterhooks, 'I answered his questions as best I could,' he related,[25] 'and kept begging him to examine the papers I had brought, but he simply ignored my urging.' After some ten minutes of this, 'a spark appeared in his eyes,' he sat up and became businesslike. He turned the book over. 'Give me the papers!' he said to Herzog, took them from his 'trembling hands' and carefully studied the ultimatum and the proposed response. Herzog understood that the talk about

In the Thick of War

Maimonides had not been without purpose. 'During those endless ten minutes he was trying to determine if he was sufficiently in control of the situation and able to read the documents calmly and serenely.'[26]

Herzog had personally savoured another dimension of the political crisis. 'Just imagine,' he later said to Yitzhak Navon, 'I'm in my office with the British ambassador, I'm wearing braces and my feet are on the table. Not long ago England was our occupier and ruler, and here we are, talking about a joint military operation, the meaning of the ultimatum and how we'll act afterwards ... I couldn't believe it. At that moment I felt that we really were an independent state!'[27]

And so, suddenly, Yaacov Herzog found himself at the heart of Israel's political and military circles. Throughout the Suez war and the difficult months that followed, he served as Ben-Gurion's advisor and shouldered the burden of the diplomatic campaign almost exclusively. Herzog became party to the greatest state secrets, and was catapulted overnight to a higher position than any other senior Foreign Ministry official. As head of the United States desk at the Foreign Ministry he had previously taken part in political discussions and decisions, but after only two years in the Ministry he was still something of a novice. Now, amid the turbulence of the war, he was promoted over older and more senior officials – the Ministry's director-general and his deputies and heads of other departments – to become the Prime Minister's confidant. Golda Meir remained in Jerusalem, took no part in the daily consultations, and left the field to Herzog's sole management, in spite of his colleagues' likely displeasure at his sudden elevation.

Herzog quickly fit into Ben-Gurion's inner circle. On the face of it, as a civilian and a well-dressed diplomat with Anglo-Saxon roots (he was born in Ireland), and a religious Jew to boot, Yaacov seemed like an oddity among the officers, activists and military figures around Ben-Gurion. In fact, the opposite was true – his pleasant manner, sense of humour, calmness under stress, and above all his sound advice, endeared him to the circle, which learned to trust and respect him. 'I can't remember an occasion,' said Yitzhak Navon,[28] 'when Ben-Gurion paid so much attention to a draft someone gave him as he did with Yaacov Herzog ... He would go over it, glance at it, usually confirm it with a little change here and there. He said many times, "This young man has brains. This young man is clever, he has a lot of sense." Later he would call him "an excellent fellow, a wonderful fellow" ... I liked him to have direct a connection to Ben-Gurion. We all preferred it, Ben-Gurion himself and I, who had to protect Ben-Gurion. But I didn't have to protect him from Herzog.'

Throughout the war Yaacov did not leave Ben-Gurion's side: he brought up the issues that needed immediate attention, initiated responses, composed public statements and diplomatic letters. Urgent letters and messages from world leaders and UN bodies went through him and he analysed them for the government. He did much of his work at night, after calling at the Foreign and Defence Ministries and Ben-Gurion's house, and finishing in his office in the Kiryah (Tel Aviv's area of government departments). Pnina remained in Jerusalem. 'I was alone with two babies,' she said. 'Once he rang and invited me to join him for a day in Tel Aviv. He had a room at the Dan hotel.'[29]

The international scene was stormy. France and Britain used their veto power to paralyse the UN Security Council while the military operation went on. But the UN Secretary General, Dag Hammarskjold, circumvented the Security Council by summoning the General Assembly, which discussed tough resolutions condemning Israel and its allies. Between the Afro-Asian and Soviet blocs and the disarray in the West, the UN General Assembly turned into an actively hostile arena for Israel. Herzog had to balance Israel's freedom of action with the political danger inherent in a torrent of condemnations and warnings emanating from the UN.

In the Thick of War

Herzog also maintained regular contact with the US Embassy. He had to formulate responses to various American pressures, which included direct and indirect messages from the US President via his aide, Sherman Adams, and the American Zionist leader, Rabbi Abba Hillel Silver. Ben-Gurion ignored these appeals, despite Abba Eban's repeated recommendations to respond to them positively.

When Herzog heard that the huge American Sixth Fleet was on its way to Israel to evacuate US nationals, he managed to persuade the American military attaché that such a display would cause panic in the United States. The message was passed on to the commander of the Sixth Fleet, who was persuaded by it and dispatched only two ships to Israel.[30]

These were turbulent and exciting days. The Israeli campaign in the Sinai was triumphant. It ended on 5 November 1956, when the 9th Division flew the Israeli flag in Sharm al-Sheikh. Not so the Franco-British operation, which advanced slowly and awkwardly. Their forces landed near the Suez Canal only on 5 November, after the UN General Assembly had passed a resolution demanding an end to the fighting and calling for the creation of a UN emergency force. They halted their advance after less than 24 hours, and their operation clearly failed.

Meanwhile Israel was celebrating, and even the normally cautious Ben-Gurion got carried away. On 7 November he made a victory speech in the Knesset, Israel's Parliament, in which he compared the Sinai campaign to Moses' stand on Mount Sinai. He declared that the armistice agreement with Egypt was dead and buried, and with it the armistice lines separating Israel and Egypt. Israel wanted to make real peace with Egypt, he said, adding that Israel had no quarrel with the people of Egypt. Israel was also offering peace negotiations with the other Arab countries, and undertook not to wage war against any of them if they did not attack Israel. He made no mention of his territorial aims, but stressed that Israel would not allow any outside force to be stationed within her own boundaries or in any territory under her control.

It was a triumphalist speech made by a victor who believed that his new position would facilitate making peace with his neighbours. Herzog regarded it as a tough speech and a 'gross error'. The day before the speech, when he read its main outline in Ben-Gurion's house, he tried to warn the Prime Minister that it would make a bad impression abroad. 'But Ben-Gurion was not receptive to arguments,' he noted sadly.[31]

Nevertheless, Herzog said later, '... the speech must be seen against the background of those days. Ben-Gurion, like all the people of Israel, felt it was time to put an end once and for all to the nightmare of fedayeen attacks, threats of destruction and the rest. We fought for a tremendous goal – peace. And if it were not for the Franco-British involvement, Israel would have achieved this goal.'[32]

Ben-Gurion's enthusiasm, verging on hubris, culminated in a letter to the soldiers of the 9th Division, in which he declared, 'The Third Kingdom of Israel has risen!'

'We were intoxicated with success,' Herzog commented, 'and determined to achieve victory before withdrawing.'[33] He was also moved by the historic dimension of Israel's reaction to the operation – at last, the Jewish people had achieved a victory after thousands of years of defeat and enslavement.

That elation was matched by the dismay and anxiety that struck Israel's leaders the following day, 8 November, one of the worst in the country's history. The international situation changed abruptly. Only days earlier the USSR had been pre-occupied with a popular anti-communist uprising in Hungary. But by 4 November it had crushed the revolt, and was free to tackle the Middle East. In the United States, Eisenhower had just won a second term by an impressive majority, and he too was now free to resolve the crisis. The UN General Assembly, led by the Afro-Asian bloc and

Dag Hammarskjold, applied massive pressure to Israel. The General Assembly adopted a resolution ordering Israel to withdraw from the Sinai Peninsula forthwith, and agreed to create a UN force to replace the foreign troops that had invaded Egypt.

The President of the USSR, Marshal Nikolai Bulganin, sent sharply worded, menacing letters to France, Britain and Israel. Those to France and Britain hinted at a possible world war, while the letter to the Prime Minister of Israel, dated 5 November, was offensive, contemptuous and questioned Israel's future existence. 'The government of Israel is playing in a criminal and irresponsible way with the fate of the world and the fate of its own people,' Bulganin warned. 'It is sowing such hatred for the State of Israel among the nations of the East as must inevitably make an impact on Israel's future, and casts doubt on its very survival as a state ... At this moment the Soviet government is taking steps to stop the war and restrain the aggressors.'

Ben-Gurion was distraught. 'The letter that Bulganin honoured me with,' he noted in his diary, 'if it did not bear his name, I might have thought it had been written by Hitler, and there is not much difference between those two hangmen. I am worried because Soviet weapons are pouring into Syria, and may be accompanied by "volunteers".'[34] He decided to send Golda Meir and Shimon Peres to Paris, to ask for French assistance. The French government did promise to support Israel with all they had, but warned against the tremendous might of the USSR, with its missiles and non-conventional weapons.

After delivering the threatening letter, the Soviet Ambassador was recalled to Moscow that same day. Worrying reports came from all over the world – five Soviet warships were seeking to pass through the Dardanelles on their way to the Mediterranean; six Soviet submarines and a team of frogmen had arrived in Alexandria; Soviet paratroops were on alert; NATO sources reported that Soviet squadrons had flown over Turkey en route to Syria; a British Canberra fighter plane had been shot down over Syria –

which intelligence sources interpreted as evidence that Soviet experts were already operating Syria's air defences.

'The Soviets have adopted a policy of outright war,' Herzog noted in his diary, describing the previous few days as 'a decisive turning-point.' He felt that the landing of Franco-British forces and the Soviet threats 'awakened a deep dread of a world war.' Twice he telephoned Eban in New York to ask him to declare once again before the UN General Assembly that Israel was keeping the ceasefire throughout the Sinai Peninsula.[35] The French and the British were forced to abandon their attack against Egypt and announce that they too accepted the ceasefire. But the crisis was not over. Israel was told to declare immediately that its forces would withdraw from the Sinai.

Early on 8 November Ben-Gurion received a strongly worded letter from President Eisenhower, the first since the start of the campaign. It was unprecedentedly harsh. 'My attention has been called,' Eisenhower wrote, 'to statements attributed to your government, that Israel does not intend to withdraw from Egyptian territory. I must tell you frankly, Mr Prime Minister, that the United States regards this information – if it is true – with grave concern. Any such decision by the government of Israel could undermine the urgent efforts made by the United Nations to restore the peace in the Middle East, and will cause Israel to be denounced as violating the principles and instructions of the UN ... I urge you to accept the resolutions of the UN General Assembly and announce the fact immediately. It would sadden all my countrymen if Israel's policy in a grave issue that concerns the entire world should in any way harm the friendly cooperation between our two countries.'

The US State Department officials who delivered the written missive to the Israeli representatives added that since Israel was endangering world peace, the United States might react with practical measures. Speaking to Israeli diplomat Reuven Shiloah, the Assistant Secretary of State Herbert Hoover listed the

In the Thick of War

American threats if Israel persisted in its refusal to withdraw: cessation of all American government and private aid to Israel – i.e., all the help Israel was getting from US foreign aid sources, as well as the income of the United Jewish Appeal and the Israel Bonds; the imposition of UN sanctions; and possible expulsion from the UN. According to one source, the Americans stated that they would not intervene to help Israel in the event of an attack by Soviet 'volunteers'. Dag Hammarskjold met Israeli representatives and expressed doubts about Israel's continued existence. His harsh criticism was backed by the Afro-Asian bloc, which was unanimous in condemning Israel.

Eban hastily telephoned Herzog to report the American threats. He also wired Ben-Gurion, 'The world is waiting very tensely for your reply to Eisenhower's letter. There are growing appeals from Jewish circles and others, urging you to retract Point Six in your speech yesterday [in which Ben-Gurion refused to allow an international force to enter the occupied territory]. The general consensus is that fateful issues are now in your hands.' Ben-Gurion noted nervously in his diary: 'Eban phoned, full of fears. His telegrams also spread terror and alarm. Hoover must have warned Shiloah that they will cut off all relations with us, stop all aid and perhaps expel us from the UN. Russia must have scared them. According to reports, weapons and "volunteers" are pouring into Syria.'[36]

Fear of a Soviet attack gripped the world. The most worrying report, which originated in Paris and was probably leaked by CIA sources, warned that the USSR might annihilate Israel in a massive attack within twenty-four hours.

Ben-Gurion was also frightened, but managed to conceal it. 'Today was a nightmare,' he wrote in his diary. 'Reports are coming in from Rome, Paris and Washington about a stream of Soviet planes and "volunteers" into Syria, about a promise to bomb Israel – airfields, cities, *et cetera*, if the Syrians and Jordanians should go to war against us ... These reports may be exaggerated, but Bulganin's letter to me ... and the Russian tanks rampaging in Hungary, show what these Communist Nazis are capable of.'[37]

Most of Israel's leaders were stunned by the global dimensions the crisis had assumed and by the tangible threat of a world war that had escalated from a local conflict with Egypt. They knew how to tackle Egypt and how to buy time in disagreement with the United States. But they did not know how to withstand the combined pressure of both super-powers, and the risk that the mighty USSR would carry out its threat to annihilate Israel. The French decision to obey the ceasefire and withdraw also hurt Israel. 'The abyss of the unknown has opened before Israel,' Herzog wrote, 'and her leaders have recoiled.'[38] It was a very difficult moment. Israel felt alone and isolated. Herzog saw his country as a pawn in an intense, international war of nerves. The UN Secretary General, the Americans and the Soviets were all applying massive pressure.

International pressure, the Soviet threats and above all the dreadful shadow of a world war, shook Ben-Gurion's resolve. His only hope was to explain personally the true situation to Eisenhower and obtain his understanding and support. When the American ultimatum was delivered in Jerusalem, Ben-Gurion immediately contacted Abba Eban and offered to go to Washington and meet the President. He wanted to seek Eisenhower's support for a proposed withdrawal in exchange for peace negotiations. But Eban replied that the atmosphere in Washington was hostile to Israel and a meeting with the President was out of the question. Ben-Gurion understood that he had no choice. 'He bowed his head bravely in the face of reality,' Yaacov Herzog recalled, 'and agreed to withdraw – without a peace agreement.'[39]

Ben-Gurion had an urgent talk with Golda Meir and summoned his associates to a meeting. Then he called in the leaders of the opposition, too, to inform them about the gravity of the situation. All the participants felt the burden of terrible isolation.

In the Thick of War

The President of Israel, Yitzhak Ben-Zvi, suddenly appeared in Ben-Gurion's office – an unprecedented event which made a powerful impression on all who were present.[40]

The Prime Minister's office buzzed with jumpy advisors and officials; there were grim, hasty consultations, tension and anxiety. The telephone did not stop ringing and telegrams from all over the world brought gloomy reports. In the afternoon Ben-Gurion received the official American and Soviet ultimatums, which he handed to Herzog to interpret. 'The messages from Eisenhower and Bulganin were filtered by Yaacov Herzog,' Yitzhak Navon recalled. 'He drafted the replies, analysed this report and that letter.'[41]

Herzog calmly evaluated the reports and the threats, and concluded that the world was not really on the threshold of war.[42] Nonetheless, in view of growing international pressure, Ben-Gurion called a cabinet meeting to decide if Israel should withdraw from the Sinai without a peace agreement. Instructed by Ben-Gurion, Herzog drafted replies to Bulganin and Eisenhower. The letter to the former was cold and proud and did not commit Israel to withdraw. 'The operation we launched at the end of October was required by self-defence, it was not dictated by foreign will, as you have been told. We have responded to the UN call for a ceasefire ... We are willing to enter at once into direct peace negotiations with Egypt for a durable peace and cooperation, without preconditions and under no compulsion ... I must express my astonishment and regret about the threat against Israel's security and existence contained in your letter. Our foreign policy is dictated by our own vital needs and our desire for peace, and no outside force dictates or will dictate it.'

'Ben-Gurion was frightened by the Russian threats, but decided to submit to the Americans,' wrote one of his associates. Indeed, in the letter to Eisenhower he expressed his willingness to withdraw, but did so together with a last minute desperate effort to obtain certain concessions for Israel. Having made the decision, he now tried to slow the process down. He realized that he had to announce it that very day, in order to defuse the explosive charge hanging over Israel and dispel the hysteria at the UN and in Washington. In his heart of hearts he did not give up the hope of annexing at least the Tiran Straits and perhaps the Gaza Strip too, but at this moment he wished above all to prevent the IDF withdrawing entirely empty-handed.

Yaacov Herzog came up with a solution. 'I recommended to Ben-Gurion that [the Cabinet's decision to withdraw] would include "coordination with the UN force".'[43] He hoped to obtain a UN commitment that as the IDF withdrew, it would be replaced with a UN force, rather than the Egyptian army, and an American promise to work towards a final Middle East peace agreement. Ben-Gurion accepted Herzog's advice and instructed him to carry out what seemed like an impossible assignment.

The cabinet meeting began at 5 pm. Herzog realized that many of the ministers clearly feared a possible world war.[44] Some five hours later the decision to withdraw was made. In the meantime, technicians from Kol Israel, Israel's national broadcasting service, had arrived to broadcast a live speech by Ben-Gurion. The address was repeatedly delayed from 8 pm to 9 pm and so on. The reason was simple: Ben-Gurion refused to withdraw without getting anything in return. He wanted to delay Israel's retreat as long as possible – first, so that the world's fear of impending war would subside; and second, to try and salvage some of the Sinai campaign's achievements. He wanted to make Israel's complete withdrawal conditional upon specific arrangements with a UN emergency force.

Ben-Gurion emerged from the cabinet meeting and told Herzog to telephone Eban to find out if the atmosphere in Washington and at the UN was receptive to the demand that UN emergency forces should enter the region. Just before 9 pm, with panic rising in the Prime Minister's office, Herzog picked up the telephone and calmly began to make the necessary inquiries abroad. He latched on to a sentence in an earlier telegram, in which Eban had proposed that Israel should announce its willingness to withdraw 'once satisfactory arrangements are made with the international force that would enter the Canal area.' Herzog asked Eban to find out if this was achievable. Eban needed time to answer the question. Ben-Gurion had, in effect, empowered Herzog in Tel Aviv and Eban in New York to negotiate with the US government and the UN leaders to obtain tangible results for Israel – or, at any rate, to gain time before the actual withdrawal, in which to campaign for some of Israel's objectives.

'The government had to decide,' Abba Eban related later, 'if the pressure was so bad, and the Soviet threat so serious, that we had no choice but to turn around and retreat without anything in return, without any effort to salvage something from the withdrawal. The question was expressed in two forms – one that said, Israel is withdrawing its forces from the Sinai and Gaza, period. If this wording had been accepted we would have withdrawn in mid-November, without a UN force entering the Gaza Strip to prevent infiltrations, and without the stationing of a UN force ... in Sharm al-Sheikh, making that isolated site the focus of a major naval and commercial interest.

'There was another form. We would announce that we were ready to evacuate the Sinai and Gaza once satisfactory arrangements were made for the stationing of a UN force. The government was agonizing about how to make the conditional proposal that could provoke a physical attack by the Soviet Union while we were without American backing. The debate went on and on. Yaacov had an idea how to rescue the government from this conundrum. He said, we are here, out of touch with the international bodies – let's ask our Ambassador in Washington to find out what would be the outcome of the saving formula, perhaps something can be salvaged after all. He dictated a telegram, and said there were two versions. Ben-Gurion is waiting for a message. It's up to you, use all kinds of contacts. I know what a responsibility it is.'[45]

The exchanges between Herzog and Eban proceeded by telephone. Eban said, 'Yaacov, this is all very well, but what if I choose the conditional version and the world's nations attack us, and the whole thing will be spoilt. You're telling me to consult – I begin by consulting with Yaacov Herzog. Then I go to Dulles . . . I want to know what you think.'

Yaacov replied, his heart in his mouth, 'I prefer the second version. It may be risky, but if it does succeed then our sacrifices have not been in vain and we may yet salvage something.'[46]

Herzog conducted the phone calls from a little alcove adjoining the Prime Minister's office. He spent hours in marathon conversations with his brother's brother-in-law (Abba Eban and Yaacov's older brother Chaim had married two sisters, Susie and Aura Ambache from a well-to-do Jewish family living in Cairo). Yaacov was 'a model of calm and self-control'.[47] Eban told him he would put the proposal to Dulles and see how the United States responded – which would take some time.

The cabinet ministers were pacing up and down, nervous and in some cases terrified, while Yaacov bent quietly over the telephone. He and Eban had a private code, in which each of the world leaders had a name taken from Jewish tradition. 'The brothers-in-law talked in a low voice about Pharaoh, Haman, Mordechai and Ahasuerus,' Navon recalled. 'Nobody understood what they were talking about – who was Haman, who was Ahasuerus . . . They talked in very strange Hebrew, and you'd have to know a lot of the Torah by heart to follow. Tell them "Rachel, your daughter . . ." – all kinds of verses and signs. Herzog sat there, whispering quietly with Eban, and nothing else interested him.'[48]

The cabinet ministers, particularly the moderates, were in shock. 'Withdraw, withdraw, withdraw!' Pinchas Sapir roared, thumping the table. Zalman Aranne chainsmoked and paced up and down. 'You people have an Israeli mentality,' he confessed. 'Me, I'm a diaspora Jew and I'm scared. You're forgetting the world! You've lost the Jewish sense of fear. It will be outright extermination!' They went to Herzog and told him to stop the negotiations. 'Stop it now, why are you arguing with them? – We've got to withdraw and be done with it!'[49]

But Yaacov was unshaken. 'Why talk to me?' he said to the two ministers. 'Talk to the Prime Minister.'[50] Yitzhak Navon was greatly impressed. 'I couldn't believe my eyes,' he recalled. 'There was Yaacov, a pale, skinny weakling, but wise – backed by Ben-Gurion – very quiet, perfectly calm, doing his work. Ben-Gurion said to him, I want to accomplish this and that, I want to get out but with a UN presence and unobstructed shipping. And Yaacov sat there, with his English accent, holding the receiver, mumbling with Eban, perhaps this or perhaps that, without recoiling or giving up.'[51]

The people of Israel had been told that the Prime Minister would address them by radio, but the negotiations in New York were prolonged, and Ben-Gurion did not want to announce the withdrawal before he had accomplished his objective. Herzog felt that Ben-Gurion was not frightened by the Russian threats. He did not want to withdraw unconditionally, and was determined not to return to the status quo ante.

Just before 9.30 pm Eban announced that a formula acceptable to the US government had been found: 'Israel will withdraw in coordination with the effective activity of the UN force.' This, Herzog believed, was the crucial wording. It obviated the need for an immediate withdrawal, since it would have to be coordinated with the introduction of the UN force. Israel obtained a hiatus that would allow it to put its case to the world. Herzog credited Eban with a decisive role in framing the 'conditional withdrawal', now tied to the creation of the UN force.[52] Navon attributed the achievement to Herzog – 'his patience, perseverance, cool head ... With another person, less patient, jumpier, I think we would have declared a withdrawal, and got nothing in return.'[53]

Ben-Gurion and Herzog immediately began to draft the letter to President Eisenhower. The key sentence they came up with stated: 'We shall willingly bring back our forces as soon as the appropriate arrangements regarding the arrival of an international force at the Suez Canal are concluded with the United Nations.' Ben-Gurion added, 'Neither I nor any other authorized spokesman of the Israeli government ever said that we intended to annex the Sinai desert.'

Now, at last, Ben-Gurion could address the nation. By then, normal radio programmes had ended for the night. People glued to their receivers heard an improvised broadcast of Israeli songs, punctuated with announcements that the Prime Minister's speech would be aired shortly. Finally, at about half past midnight, Ben-Gurion's voice came through. He announced that Israel had decided to withdraw from the Sinai, and added the agreed statement which enabled a delay. He also quoted his replies to President Eisenhower and Marshal Bulganin.

'We had set ourselves three major objectives in the Sinai campaign: one, the destruction of the forces which were constantly poised to defeat us; two, the liberation of the part of the homeland which had been seized by the invader; three, to secure the freedom of our shipping in the Eilat Straits and the Suez Canal. Though so far only the first and principal clause has been fully accomplished, we are confident that the other two objectives will also be attained.'

One of the purposes of the speech was to forestall the danger of Soviet squadrons attacking Israel. Immediately after Ben-Gurion's speech, Abba Eban and his aides contacted Dag Hammarskjold, and Arkady Sobolev of the Soviet UN delegation, and informed them that the IDF would withdraw from the Sinai peninsula. In his diary Ben-Gurion sought to minimize the Soviet threat: 'I asked my colleagues in the government not to panic for fear of the Russians. The world is not yet completely lawless.'[54]

Only later, with hindsight, were Herzog and a few like-minded colleagues proven right. They had assessed correctly that the entire Soviet threat against Israel was an act of intimidation, without any

In the Thick of War

operational basis. On 6 and 7 November the USSR carried out the most brilliant operation of psychological warfare since the Second World War. All the doomsday reports had been false – Soviet squadrons had not flown over Turkey and landed in Syria; Russian submarines had not surfaced in Alexandria; Syrians rather than Russians had shot down the British 'Canberra' plane over Syria, and all the stories about the imminent Soviet intervention, the stream of Russian 'volunteers', the threat of annihilating Israel in hours, had all been a sophisticated misinformation campaign. Nikita Khrushchev would later boast in his memoirs that he had disseminated false reports about the arrival of Soviet 'volunteers' in the Middle East. But in the bitter moments of 8 November, no one in Israel was willing to bet that the Soviets would not act, and many of Israel's leaders felt that an imminent threat of annihilation was hanging over the state.

The crisis revealed a new Yaacov Herzog to all who were present in the Prime Minister's office on that terrible day – a calm, cool-headed man determined to stay his course, impervious both to the threats of world leaders and to the doubts of fearful colleagues. Though the ground was shaking, the rabbi's son bent over his desk like a Talmudic scholar, and succeeded in his undertaking. And so Israel's awful day became Yaacov Herzog's great day.

The young diplomat's qualities would be demonstrated repeatedly in the months of wrangling that followed. When the military campaign was over he was not released from his post but remained at Ben-Gurion's side to assist in the international diplomatic campaign, notably in Washington and the UN General Assembly. He was given a special appointment by Walter Eytan, director-general of the Foreign Ministry, 'to attend to all issues that might arise in the UN General Assembly as a consequence of the Sinai campaign, particularly such as would demand ongoing consultation with the Prime Minister.'[55]

Several months later, when the subsequent international

struggle had ended, Ben-Gurion wrote to the Chief Rabbi, Yaacov's father. 'These past months,' he wrote, 'were indeed full of anxiety such as I had not known for years. But I have to say that one of the finest, wisest, most diligent and loyal members of the Foreign Ministry staff has been of great help, and I can hardly express all that I owe him for his help during these last critical months. The name of that official is Yaacov Herzog, and I can say without fear of exaggeration or flourish, happy is the woman who gave birth to him.'[56]

Ben-Gurion gave Yaacov a photograph of himself, inscribed, 'To Yaacov Herzog – *Zofnat Pa'aneach** of the State of Israel'.[57]

---

* Pharoah's name for Joseph in the Old Testament, describing an interpreter of codes and dreams. In Biblical lore Joseph represents the ultimate insightful, wise advisor.

2

Two Worlds

'From childhood, I was drawn to two worlds.'
Yaacov Herzog[1]

Throughout his life, Yaacov Herzog experienced dualities: the religious home into which he was born, and the secular environment in which he was brought up; the rabbinic calling he inherited, and the diplomatic world he chose; his formal English education and the rough Sabra ways of Israel; the Western culture he embodied and the Middle Eastern reality he encountered; the Jewish life he led, and the Gentile milieu of his diplomatic missions.

The duality began early, when he was a small boy in short trousers, school blazer, and the peaked cap and tie of Wesley College, the prestigious co-educational English school in Dublin. One photograph shows him grinning in this uniform, as he stands beside his brother Chaim. Yaacov was born in Dublin during the festival of Hanukkah, on 21 December 1921. Chaim, three years older, was born in Belfast, where the family had lived before moving to Dublin. The boys attended the same Methodist school where a fifth of the pupils were Jews. The most famous former pupil of Wesley College was George Bernard Shaw. The school was run by a Methodist minister, the teachers wore academic gowns, and prayers were held every morning. The Herzog brothers were known to be mischievous, and occasionally received the standard punishment of six strokes of the cane, on the bottom or on the palm of the hand.[2]

'At school, Yaacov's Jewish schoolmates called him Yankele, but the non-Jews called him Jackie,' said his classmate Solly Steinberg.[3] His schoolfellows remembered him as a good student with unusual ambitions. One day, when the pupils were asked about their aspirations, Yaacov surprised everyone by saying he wished to be a diplomat.[4] He excelled in the humanities, particularly history. He would later state that he never studied mathematics, as his friend Solly Steinberg helped him inordinately in this subject, and that he took no interest in science and chemistry lessons.[5]

This was his frame of mind when he joined the Junior League of Nations, and worked energetically to recruit more members. 'I'll try my best,' he wrote to his friend Charles, 'to explain not only why I joined the Junior League of Nations, but why it is so vital that all the nations of the world should wholeheartedly support this wonderful institution of world peace ... No other world organization is as democratic as this one. Its ideal is an inspiration to anyone who loves peace, irrespective of faith, race or religion. The situation in the world is very alarming these days and no one knows what the future holds. The protective walls of peace and democratic freedom are falling before evil influences ... Many of the leading states of Europe have succumbed to these terrible enemies of true peace and liberty. The only protective wall which has maintained its sublime ideal is the League of Nations.'[6]

But the schoolboy and future diplomat was also the son of the Chief Rabbi of Ireland, Rabbi Isaac Halevi Herzog, and a scion of dynasties of famous rabbis and scholars. 'I was familiar with the world of the Babylonian Talmud from childhood,' Herzog reminisced, 'but also intensely interested in international events.'[7] The young member of the Junior League of Nations, who signed his eloquent letters 'Jackie', was also an outstanding pupil of the Dublin Jewish community's Torah school. At the laying of the cornerstone for a new Torah school, the 11-year old boy delivered a speech he had written for the occasion. As his proud grandfather noted in the margin of the typed text, 'A copy of the speech made by my grandson Yankele ... composed by himself without the help of anybody else's ideas or wording.' Young Yankele, chosen to give thanks for the new school on behalf of the pupils, said as follows (in Hebrew): 'A great thing has happened on the 19th day of Kislev in the year 5693 [1933]. It is that a fine new Torah school is being built, which boys and girls can attend to learn the Law that the Lord Almighty gave Moses on Mount Sinai, to teach the Children of Israel to learn God's commandments. Every Torah school and every place where the Torah is taught, helps the people of the world, not only Jews. Who would have thought that a city as small as Dublin could give so much help to the mission of the people of Israel in the world. The mission is to learn and teach the Torah ... The spirit of the Torah is still in our heart. We can see for ourselves that when our Jewish ancestors scattered through all the countries of the world they had no other sign to show that they were Jews, except the Torah. If we study well in the beautiful new Torah school that is being built, the name of Dublin will spread among the world's Jews as a very important place of Torah study.'[8]

The two worlds coexisted in Yaacov's home. On the one hand, he came from a renowned rabbinic dynasty. His great-grandfather, the Hassidic rabbi Naphthali Hirsch Herzog, had been the rabbi of the town of Lomza in Poland, with a Jewish community of several thousand. His son, Yaacov's grandfather, Joel Leib Herzog, married Miriam Leiba Sarowitz, and fathered four children – the girls Esther and Elka and two boys. The elder son died young, and the younger, Isaac Halevi Herzog was Yaacov and Chaim's father. Rabbi Joel Leib Herzog was 'an impressive figure', as his grandson Chaim described: 'Short but sturdy, bearded, with a deep, hoarse, resonant voice ... He was a brilliant speaker, tough and determined, and his children obeyed him absolutely.'[9] Rabbi Joel Leib Herzog's Judaism was closely bound with Zionism. He joined the

Hovevai Zion [Lovers of Zion] movement, and was elected a delegate to the first Zionist Congress held in Basel in 1897, but could not attend because of his older son's illness.

He took comfort in his younger boy, who at the age of nine was exceptionally gifted. The proud father decided to devote all his efforts to educating the brilliant boy. This was not an easy matter in the town of Lomza, especially given the family's economic straits. They lived in an attic and suffered 'great hardships'.[10] The father was the boy's main, sometimes only, teacher.

Determined to start a new life, Rabbi Joel Leib Herzog sailed to the New World, and became the rabbi of the Jewish community of Worcester, Massachusetts. But he did not last long there; a man of principles and strong opinions, he did not get on with the moneyed leaders of the community. Six months later he returned to Europe and became a rabbi in Leeds, in northern England, where his family joined him. Just before the outbreak of the First World War, he was invited to serve as rabbi of the Orthodox Jewish community in Paris, and settled with his family in the Marais district.

Young Isaac was educated in England and France. He was gifted, curious and open-minded, and even in his youth showed the duality that would later characterize his younger son Yaacov. He studied Torah and Talmud and other religious texts, in an atmosphere laced with his father's Zionism. At the same time he was drawn to general subjects – 'from law, classical studies and Oriental languages, to mathematics and marine biology'.[11]

While in England, Isaac lived for a while with Rabbi Yaacov David Wilkowsky of Safed, one of the greatest Talmudic scholars of the time. Wilkowsky was impressed by his guest's extensive knowledge of the Talmud – at 16, the young Isaac knew the entire Talmud by heart. Wilkowsky, who ordained him as rabbi in 1908, stated that the young man, who accompanied him on his travels in England, was one of the leading Talmudic authorities in the world.

Isaac excelled not only in Talmud, but also in Oriental languages which he studied at the Sorbonne, and classics which he studied at the University of London. His first degree was in mathematics, and the second in Semitic languages. In 1914 he was awarded a doctoral degree for a dissertation on 'The Dyeing of Purple in Ancient Israel',[12] written on the use of the murex snail to extract purple and blue dyes for the robes of the High Priest at the Temple.[13]

In 1916, Isaac Halevi Herzog was appointed rabbi of the Jewish community of Belfast, Northern Ireland. 'Herzog was soon recognized as one of the great rabbinic scholars of his time, besides being a linguist and jurist, and at ease in mathematics and natural sciences. The charm of his personality, which combined ascetic unworldliness with conversational wit and diplomatic skills, made a great impression.'[14]

The young rabbi was devoted to his father's Zionist tradition, and was one of the founders of the religious-Zionist Mizrahi movement in England and Ireland. When war broke out in 1917, the shortage of foodstuffs gave rise to a rabbinic debate over the Passover holiday's dietary restrictions. Some felt that Ashkenazi Jews (of Eastern European origin) should be permitted to eat pulses and rice, as prevalent in the less restrictive Sephardi Jewish (of Middle Eastern origin) tradition. Rabbi Shmuel Isaac Hillman, the head of British Jewry's Beth Din (religious court), invited rabbis around the country – including the young Rabbi Herzog – to discuss the matter at his London home. Rabbi Hillman, an authoritative and respected man with a sense of humour, was the namesake of his ancestor, the rabbi of Metz, Alsace. Rabbi Hillman's family tree went back through Rabbi Katznelbogen of Hamburg to Rashi of Troyes and, it was said, all the way back to King David.[15] But this had nothing to do with the emotion that seized young Rabbi Herzog when Rabbi Hillman's beautiful, dark-eyed daughter, Sarah, entered the room, carrying a tray of tea for the guests. The emotion must have been mutual, because the young woman tripped and the tea tray flew straight at Herzog. They were married in August 1917 and a year later their elder son Chaim was born. In 1919 they moved to Dublin, where Rabbi Herzog served first as the rabbinic head of the city's Jewish community, and later as Chief Rabbi of the Irish Free State. Most of Ireland's Jews in those days came from Lithuania. Dublin's community numbered only 3,000 – 'a small community in a very devout Catholic country'.[16] The Herzogs' second son was named Yaacov David, after Rabbi Wilkowsky, who had ordained Isaac as rabbi.

Chaim and Yaacov grew up in a very unusual household. As the home of the Chief Rabbi, it was strictly observant in matters of religious law, but it was also progressive and open. The Herzog home was receptive to the surrounding, Gentile society and was well integrated into the broader community. 'My family was typical of those Jews who are torn between two distinct societies,' Chaim Herzog said.[17] 'My younger brother Yaacov and I had a very special relationship with our father. He was very strict with us in all matters of religious observance, but did so in a most positive way. He never tired of explaining the logic and qualities of the Jewish religion. He wanted us to be devoted to it from our own free will, not simply from obedience to his will.' The father would spend hours strolling with his two sons in the botanical and zoological gardens, and linked every plant and animal to events and places mentioned in the Bible.

Apart from his role as a rabbinic scholar and teacher to the Jews, the rabbi was also an Irish patriot. He was greatly respected by the Irish, for both his religious leadership and his political stand. Everyone knew that he was a staunch supporter of the Irish struggle for independence. He was a close friend of Eamon de Valera, who became the first Prime Minister of the Irish Free State.[18] Books about the Irish struggle mention Rabbi Herzog's relationship with its leading figures. 'After the establishment of the Irish Free State, when Eamon de Valera found himself in the opposition, he used to frequent our house,' Chaim Herzog recalled.[19] He would come in the company of a Jewish friend, Robert Briscoe, who was one of the leaders of the Irish Free State. Rabbi Herzog's and de Valera's friendship lasted many years. After the establishment of the State of Israel, the Irish leader was one of the first foreign statesmen to visit. They dined at Rabbi Herzog's house in Jerusalem, together with David Ben-Gurion and Robert Briscoe.[20]

Rabbi Herzog was also on friendly terms with the heads of the Christian churches in Ireland, especially the head of the Irish Catholic Church, Cardinal McRory. Once they were entertained at a formal dinner, and the rabbi did not eat anything. McRory, who was sitting beside him, teased him for not tasting the pork dish that was served, and Rabbi Herzog shot back: 'We'll discuss the matter at your wedding party ...'

But relations between Jews and Christians were not always witty. Chaim Herzog remembered 'hoodlums who often threw stones at us, believing there was no better way to settle the score with the Jews who had supposedly crucified Jesus'.[21] At Wesley College the Jewish pupils were sometime subjected to anti-Semitism – for example, the 'crude and offensive' attitude of the Gaelic teacher. 'The teachers treated the non-Christians like heathens,' wrote Avraham Avihai, 'which was hardly the way to win them over ... Yaacov was thirteen years old when he organized his Jewish classmates and marched them to the headmaster's office ... where they presented an ultimatum – if one more offensive remark was made, they would all walk out of the classroom.'[22]

At school, Yaacov also excelled at French and Latin. He showed the same talent in his studies at *cheder* (Jewish religious school) and in private lessons. Even as a child, he spoke English, Yiddish and Hebrew. He studied Talmud with his father and Rabbi Joseph Unterman[23], brother of a future Chief Rabbi of Israel.

Yaacov shone at an early age. His brother Chaim said in a radio interview, 'Yaacov was the youngest of the group ... he had a sharp mind and a comprehension of problems that seemed beyond his age ... So much so, that he was treated like an adult by the Jewish community. I remember that we used to go to the synagogue with our late father, and afterwards ... the Jews would talk about this and that, international politics, local politics, Zionism and what was happening in this country. And though Yaacov was still a boy, he took an active part in these discussions and certainly did not lag behind the grownups. And he was still pre-bar mitzvah.'[24]

Relations between the brothers were unusually affectionate and appreciative, and would remain so for the rest of their lives. Both of them engaged in sports, and little Jackie followed his brother in taking up boxing. They trained at the local 'Maccabi' club. This was not a common hobby for the sons of a rabbi, but according to Chaim, 'my father was secretly proud that we were following in the footsteps of great Jewish warriors of past times ... ' The Jewish community was thrilled to think about Jewish lads who 'were thumping Gentiles'.[25] Chaim became 'Maccabi' champion for his category, and even Yaacov, who was smaller and skinnier, won a medal for featherweight boxing. Years later he would quip that he had won not so much for his blows, as for his ability to avoid his opponent's fists.[26] Yaacov was a keen football player and was better than Chaim at cricket. They also played rugby, and in the summer swam or rode their bicycles around the countryside.

It was quite an adventure for the two boys to travel about on their own, on bicycles, in Ireland's green wilderness, and visit places with romantic names like Blackrock or Dun Laoghaire. Obtaining a bicycle was not equally easy for the two brothers. Chaim had to struggle long and hard with his anxious mother before he got one, whereas his younger brother, as he put it with a tinge of envy, 'never had such a problem. On his bar mitzvah he got his own bicycle, with Mother beaming at him proudly.'[27]

The brothers also visited their grandfathers in London and

Two Worlds

Paris. These were voyages of discovery – in London they stayed in the East End, an area full of Jews with a lively cultural life, a Yiddish newspaper and Yiddish theatre; on Saturdays Grandfather Shmuel would put on his Sabbath suit, don a top hat, and lead his grandsons to his own synagogue in Aldgate. In Paris, staying with Grandfather Joel at his apartment on the rue des Francs Bourgeois, in the heart of the Jewish Orthodox 'ghetto', life was stricter.

This did not prevent the lively Irish-born lads from indulging in pranks which did not suit the family of a revered rabbi. One day, from the balcony of their grandfather's apartment they threw gravel at the tables of the outdoor café below. One of the pebbles struck a man's head and he turned out to be a policeman. He rushed up to the apartment to seize the two rascals, who by then were trembling with fear. The rabbi had to placate the furious policeman with a few hundred francs before he dropped the case. Instead of punishing the two terrified boys, their father and grandfather took them for a pony-ride in the Bois de Boulogne.[28]

Chaim was the more mischievous of the two brothers, and whenever he was reprimanded, Yaacov would come to his older brother's defence. They always enjoyed summer holidays with their paternal grandmother in a Paris suburb. The home she rented had a private zoo, and the two boys spent hours observing the animals.

The brothers also had fun in Dublin. Together with a few Jewish friends they set up a secret gambling den in their friend Molly Grewson's (Goldwater) garage, where they played roulette with nuts for money.[29] But when not occupied in games, sports and hikes, Chaim and Yaacov were active in *habonim*, a Zionist youth movement. Yaacov attended *habonim* events diligently, and spent part of his summer holidays in the movement's seaside camps. He also participated in a Hebrew speakers' group that met on Saturday evenings, and called itself *Pirhai Yehudah* ('Flowers of Judah').[30] A friend, Louis Hyman wrote, 'I remember Yaacov as a small boy when he joined *habonim*, which I'd founded. I remember testing him in Jewish history and religion before admitting him ... Twenty-five years later, Yaacov remembered the questions I'd asked him. One of them was about the position of the Patriarch Abraham in Jewish history, and Yaacov spoke at length about Abraham's monotheism.'[31]

Yaacov frequently corresponded with his two grandfathers, in London and Paris, and sent them questions and arguments from his Talmud studies.[32] When his bar mitzvah drew near, his grandfather in Paris sent him *tefillin* (phylacteries) as a present. Yaacov wrote a reply in Hebrew, thanking his dear grandfather, the great rabbi, and his dear grandmother, and invited them to the bar mitzvah. 'There are still three months and five days left,' he wrote. 'I hope you will come to the bar mitzvah and see me put on *tefillin*.'[33]

But the grandfather did not live to see that day. Two months before the event, in the middle of the Succoth holiday, Chaim Herzog heard his father 'running to the telephone in his study. It was my aunt telephoning from Paris, to tell him to come at once. Their father, Rabbi Joel Herzog, had died.'[34]

And so, the only grandparent present at Yaacov's bar mitzvah was his grandmother. His maternal grandfather, Rabbi Shmuel Isaac Hillman, had moved to Palestine not long before, and sent him a congratulatory letter from Jerusalem. 'How great this grave and holy day,' he wrote, 'when you cross the threshold of the holy congregation, among the specially blessed, and how dear to us too as parents the moments of this revered and blessed day, to rejoice with you and your loving parents ... ' The grandfather wanted to mollify his grandson, who was disappointed that he had been present at Chaim's bar mitzvah and not his. 'Believe me, dear heart, we shall rejoice with you as we rejoiced in the delightful company at the bar mitzvah of your brother, Chaim, because on your head too we have always seen God's light, in your gifts and excellent qualities, and why should you be deprived? Yet what can we do? It is too difficult for us, we have travelled too far, and time which rules all has separated the kinsmen and does not let us rejoice with our child in the blessing of God Almighty.'

Yaacov should take comfort, the grandfather wrote, in the 'blessings sent to you and your parents and their congregation ... for they come from a holy place, the mountains of Zion.' Finally Rabbi Hillman blessed his grandson, 'Don your weapons, your shield and bow, which are your excellent talents ... Emerge from dewy childhood and, garbed as a man, come among your fellow Israelites, hold fast to the boughs of the tree of life, observe wholeheartedly the Torah and commandments and all that is holy in Israel, devote your ideas and imagination to the Law of Israel, the People of Israel and the Land of Israel, and then it shall be said of you, "Thy name shall be called no more Yaacov, but Israel", and "David behaved wisely in all his ways", and God will be with you all the days of your life ... '[35]

At his bar mitzvah Yaacov made two speeches, in Hebrew and in English. In his Hebrew speech, entitled *pilpul* (Talmudic argument), he discussed a forgotten episode from his father's childhood that he had found in his grandfather's book, *Imrei Yoel*. There, his proud grandfather quoted an original commentary on the miracle of Hanukah, originally proposed by his son Isaac (Yaacov's father). The choice was Yaacov's way of expressing admiration for his father.[36] His English speech was chiefly an expression of gratitude to his parents for their love and devotion, and the usual promises to be a loyal son to his people and faith. 'I am ready to join the ranks of my people to fight, not with the sword but with the spirit, as is written in my *haftarah* [the Bible passage read by the bar mitzvah boy]: "Not by might, nor by power, but by my spirit." I shall strive to work for my people, whose greatness I know, who have suffered and are still suffering in many countries from the hatred and evil of their enemies for no cause.'[37]

After his bar mitzvah Yaacov actively continued his studies. He kept sending Talmudic arguments and questions to his grandfather in Jerusalem, while his interest in the non-Jewish world deepened. His essays from that time abound with quotes from the Bible as well as from English poets, such as Coleridge.

At the age of 14 he won a competition organized by the Irish section of the League of Nations with an essay about the international organization.[38] At this time, he also began to correspond with the leader of the British Labour Party, Clement Attlee. 'In those days we did not have radio receivers,' wrote Yaacov's childhood friend, Hubert Wine, 'so we borrowed a crystal set and on this little gadget Yaacov heard that his hero, Clement Attlee, was about to speak, and he waited and waited till he heard his voice.'[39] Finally he dared write to Attlee, who was astonished to discover that the young man writing from Ireland was only 14.[40] He must have been impressed by the letters, because he wrote back and informed him about the forthcoming appearance of his political book.[41] 'Dear Major Attlee,' Yaacov wrote in a letter whose draft has survived, 'I am only 14 years old, but my ambition is politics. I have studied all the political parties and come to the conclusion that the solutions to the problems of the world can only come through social-democracy. It is encouraging to see that the British Labour Party is not extremist but moderate in its position, because history has shown that the extremes are only good for a while but do not last long ... Today there is a very distorted opinion of socialism in the world. Many regard socialism as a non-religious [i.e. anti-religious] party, and the socialists as anti-religious people who are determined to destroy everything that has to do with liberty or the sublime idea of peace.' But Jackie Herzog rejected these 'distorted opinions', being convinced that a socialist state would strive to achieve peace, social justice, freedom and equality. He congratulated Attlee in fulsome terms about the Labour Party's decision to boycott goods from Germany, and on its support for sanctions against totalitarian regimes. 'Believe me, sir,' he concluded, 'as I wrote in my previous letter, I long for the day when the Labour Party and you at its head will form the government; I am sure the day is not far off.'[42] When he visited London that year, Attlee invited him to the Houses of Parliament, an experience he found intensely exciting.[43]

In those days Herzog wrote a number of long essays which have been preserved, though it is not known if they were ever published. They are characterized by a colourful, often flowery, style and expressive ability, as well as by boyish enthusiasm, innocence and idealism. Though they deal with various subjects, they are all infused with intense pride in being a Jew, firm Zionist conviction, and a profound sense of belonging to the Jewish people and religion, which he regarded as inseparable.

An essay entitled 'A Jewish Boy Looking at the Jewish World' begins dramatically with the words, 'I awoke from a dreamless sleep. For the first 14 years of my existence I had been fast asleep, unaware how complex is the world in which I live, especially the world of my fellow Jews. Now that I have woken up, I discover at every step this Jewish world of celebration, pain, trials and hardship.' He went on to mourn the great injustice which had been done to the People of Israel through the ages, and reached the decisive conclusion – 'We must obtain a national home, and it must be in our ancient homeland, the Land of Israel.' Nevertheless, he stressed that once the Jews were in their own country, they must not turn their backs on their religion and tradition.[44]

The same idea appeared in another essay, 'The Zionist Congress', in which he described the structure of the Congress, implied his support for David Ben-Gurion and the Zionist Labour Party, and denounced 'with shock, revulsion and anxiety' the Revisionist Party's withdrawal from the Zionist body. He described in dramatic, high-flown terms the Zionist movement as the last hope of the Jewish people, which would lead them to the Land of Israel, and protested against the stormy dissension in its ranks. 'Jewry is caught in a ramshackle ship shaken and rocked by the waves of anti-Semitism and assimilation; its hull has been pierced and the water is rushing in, and the Jews of the world will have to struggle hard to save the ship from foundering ... The passengers, who entrusted the ship to the crew [the Zionist Congress], have discovered that the crew are quarrelling among themselves and endangering the ship in their folly.'[45]

Another essay, 'A Racial Difference', touches briefly on Germany's vicious treatment of the Jews, but deals chiefly with the persecution of black people by the white race. Yaacov angrily denounced the white man's hypocrisy and cruelty to the black race, which was still going on, and proposed steps to ameliorate the situation of black people in the world.[46] Yaacov also wrote about 'Social Justice from a Jewish-Religious Viewpoint',[47] and an essay about the international situation, particularly Britain's diplomatic efforts against Italy's war of conquest in Ethiopia.[48]

The ease with which he wrote may have prompted him to consider becoming a journalist, as well as a diplomat. That same year, he wrote to a school of journalism in London for information. He must have enclosed an essay or two, because the head of the school replied, 'Your writing is exceptionally good for a boy of fourteen ... but you need not start studying journalism for another two years.' He advised him to continue writing, and noted, 'You already have an unusual capacity for reasoning, for which I congratulate you.'[49]

Yaacov's aspirations for a future career in journalism or diplomacy did not prevent him from becoming his father's amanuensis from the age of fifteen. During Passover in 1937, Rabbi Herzog received a question from Rabbi Shlomo Sasson about Jewish dietary laws and the rabbit's apparent chewing of the cud. Yaacov replied: 'Since my father is barred from writing on account of the holiday, I write for him.'[50] He directed Rabbi Sasson to a source his father had referred to in connection with this question, and concluded with ample blessings: 'Let me use this opportunity to wish you and your family a happy and kosher holiday. And on this holiday of our liberation, may God heal the holy nation of all its afflictions within and without, and lead His people to their ancestral land in our lifetime. I pray to our Father in Heaven to come speedily to our aid, because our plight is unbearable, and restore the heart of His people to His holy Torah, and may we all see salvation before long. Amen. "And may our eyes behold God's merciful return to Zion".'[51]

Yaacov could not know that the death of his grandfather Joel would significantly change his entire family's life. His father had previously been invited variously to serve as rabbi of the Vienna congregation, as Chief Rabbi of France, and as president of Yeshiva University in New York. But he had turned them all down, 'because he did not want to move too far away from his father, who lived in Paris, or to be superior to him by becoming Chief Rabbi of France.'[52] Rabbi Joel's death closed a chapter in Isaac Halevi's life, and he began to think of accomplishing his Zionist dream by settling in the Land of Israel. In May 1935 he travelled to Palestine to bury his father's remains in Jerusalem, and while there submitted his candidacy for the post of Chief Rabbi of Tel Aviv. He did not get it, but a year later in December 1936 he was invited to serve as Chief Rabbi of the Jewish community in Mandatory Palestine (described by Jews as Eretz Israel or the Land of Israel), successor to the legendary Rabbi Kook.

Isaac Halevi and Sarah Herzog sailed from Marseilles to Alexandria, and proceeded to Haifa, where they were given an emotional and ceremonious reception. Ironically, this fulfilment of Rabbi Herzog's dream caused the family to separate temporarily. The rabbi and his wife settled in Jerusalem where their elder son Chaim had been studying at the Hebron Yeshiva since 1935, while young Yaacov remained in Dublin to complete his schooling and matriculation. He was fifteen when his parents left Ireland, and would only be reunited with them in 1939.[53]

Yaacov lived with a traditional Jewish family, the Wines, close friends of the Herzogs.[54] Their son Hubert was his good friend, and years later he recalled their pillow fights with nostalgia. But

Yaacov felt lonely. Unlike his older brother, who had begun to show signs of rebellion and independence, Yaacov was very close to his parents and needed their presence. 'It has been said,' wrote Yair Sheleg, 'that the period in which he was separated from his parents at the age of 16 caused him to be distant with people afterwards.'[55] Yaacov grew up to be a quiet young man, withdrawn, incapable of chitchat, reluctant to expose his inner self, and he always preferred intellectual company.

He exchanged weekly letters with his family. Some of his father's letters to him have been preserved, and they are full of love and warmth, especially those in which he congratulated his son on his success in examinations. 'May God bless you, my son!' he wrote on one such occasion. 'Go from triumph to triumph and may God be with you all your days!' He signed the letter, 'Your father who misses you.'[56] He also apologized for writing short letters. At this time Rabbi Herzog was setting up a rabbinical court of appeal, which took up much of his time. 'Work in the Beth Din is hard,' he informed Yaacov. 'It is not merely a rabbinical court but a higher court of appeal, and the work demands much thought and concentration. On top of all this, I'm continuing my literary work, the second volume of my book on Hebrew Law.'[57] (The book, which grew into five volumes, was published in England under the title *The Main Institutions of Jewish Law*.) This letter was signed, 'Your father who loves you dearly and hopes to see you soon.' In another letter he begged Yaacov to be 'very careful in the coming winter days, because of the cold in your country.'[58]

But the father's sincere longing for his beloved son concealed a deeper layer of emotion. By then, Rabbi Herzog had realized that his eldest son, Chaim, would most likely not succeed him in the rabbinic dynasty. Chaim disliked the closed Yeshiva atmosphere and found it oppressive. He discovered the company of non-observant youth, joined the Haganah (the Jewish community's mainstream military arm, not officially recognized by the Mandatory authorities), became a *Noter* (a member of the Haganah's civil guard), and was generally impatient with the atmosphere in his parents' home. 'The pressures that my parents were under,' he wrote frankly in later years, 'left them almost no time for their children. The confrontations caused by the new situation gave rise to a certain antagonism on my part. It became clear – at least to me – that I was not going to follow in my father's rabbinic footsteps.'[59] By 1938, Chaim had left the Yeshiva to study law in England. While Yaacov was still in Dublin, his parents apparently decided that their younger son would succeed his father and continue the rabbinic lineage of the Herzog and Hillman families. His father hinted as much in one of his letters. 'I hope that you devote many hours of your day to the Torah. As for plans for the future ... we have come to a decision, which will be given to you by your mother.' Further on he hinted at his intention: 'God willing, you have a brilliant future before you. Grow strong and firm, and be a great man in the Torah, faith and wisdom, because the nation of Israel needs great men, and the religious community, in this difficult and decisive hour, is suffering from a lack of truly great men ... '[60]

Yaacov's path was being charted by his parents, but he was in no hurry. He finished his schooling in Dublin, passed the British matriculation exams with flying colours, and moved to London. 'He left Dublin aged 15,' [actually 16] wrote his boyhood friend Hubert Wine. 'I felt I had lost a wonderful, faithful friend.'[61]

In London, Yaacov spent a year with relatives and completed the Intermediate BA at London University.[62] He also studied at the Etz Hayim Yeshiva in London. Finally in 1939 it was his turn to go to Palestine. Before leaving he met his brother Chaim, in what would be their last encounter before the war. The brothers spent a few days together, and Chaim wrote, 'The short time we spent together was full of affection, intimacy and hope. My brother was never really a young man – he was always mature and serious. In many ways Yaacov was more like my father than I was

– a rabbinic scholar and true intellectual. Yet he also had an instinctive understanding of political subtleties ...[63] When he arrived in Eretz Israel he became our father's helper and great advisor, in fact, his right-hand man.'[64]

The Land of Israel thrilled Yaacov and revived his spirits. 'My expectations are fulfilled,' he wrote to a close friend. 'What I had hoped for for many years has become reality. I was in Eretz Israel. Like many who have come to the country I felt elated when I saw our people's revival and the rebuilding of our ancient homeland.'[65]

3

War

Yaacov Herzog was 17 when he arrived in Palestine. While boys of his age were active in the scouts and enjoying Tarzan, he had matriculated, obtained a university degree and enjoyed a reputation in Jewish learning and world culture. He joined his parents in Jerusalem and became his father's right-hand man. As his secretary, advisor and speech-writer, he corresponded on his father's behalf with rabbis, laymen and the British authorities, and stood in for the Chief Rabbi with authority and wide knowledge, but also very modestly. He made no effort to attract attention and did not project self-importance. He admired his father wholeheartedly, and regarded working at his side as a mission of the highest order.[1]

He was deeply happy about living in Jerusalem. 'When ... I left my native country, Ireland, my objective was not Israel but Jerusalem. Without Jerusalem Israel is only, as the Arabs say, a collection of refugees, and its chronicles are merely journalistic-political chronicles, however interesting and brilliant. Jerusalem is what gives Israel dimension and perspective.'[2]

A few months after Yaacov's arrival, the Second World War broke out. His brother Chaim, who was studying in England, joined the British army, and served in England and later in Europe. Seven years would pass before he returned to Jerusalem, as a decorated major in the British Intelligence Service.

Yaacov himself joined the local Jewish volunteer forces when he was 18, but it seems that his soldiering never progressed beyond some basic training, and occasional parades.[3]

The war raging in Europe and threatening the Middle East greatly affected Chief Rabbi Herzog's workload. He was occupied with the needs of Allied Jewish soldiers stationed in Palestine, and those of Jewish volunteers from Palestine serving in Europe and North Africa. On his recommendation, the British authorities appointed Yaacov as liaison officer between the Chief Rabbinate in Mandatory Palestine and the Jewish Chaplain of the British armed forces in the Middle East.[4] The British addressed Yaacov as 'Reverend', and the Jews called him 'Rabbi Yaacov Herzog', though he would not be ordained until years later, in 1948.[5] Yaacov handled local rabbinic matters and religious problems encountered by Jewish soldiers, including matters of personal status such as divorce – and the provision of Bibles to the battle-fields. Sometimes he wore a British army uniform; at other times he was in mufti. Throughout this time he attended the Harry Fischel Talmud Institute in Jerusalem.

Despite his considerable responsibilities by his father's side, Yaacov embarked on an unusually ambitious project – an English translation and commentary of the Mishnah (the first compilation of Jewish oral law written in the post-Temple period). He began to work on it as soon as he arrived in Jerusalem, but the war intervened and prevented him from completing the translation. Nevertheless, during the war years, he finished translating the tractates *Berakhot*, *Pe'ah* and *Demai*, including the original commentary by Rabbi Ovadiah of Bartenura, as well as writing his own commentary.[6]

In September 1942, at the height of the war, Yaacov applied to the British authorities for an allowance of paper to print the book, but evidently failed to obtain it.[7] The translation was published in Jerusalem in 1945 and in New York in 1947. He had not yet been ordained as rabbi when it appeared to warm acclaim. A reviewer in an American Jewish newspaper in New York noted, 'Herzog's English translation and commentary will soon popularize the study of the Mishnah. The commentary is both profound and simple, and there is no need for additional explanations or a teacher's help. We hope every Jew in America will acquire this book.'[8]

The young scholar wrote in his Introduction, 'The Oral Law forms an integral part of every chapter in the age-old Jewish story. Its influence has been decisive in shaping the strivings and aspirations of the people for whom it has always symbolized the indestructibility of their religio-national mission and the guarantee of the inevitability of its ultimate fulfilment. The underlying inspiration of the Oral Law can be felt in every movement that has taken place on the scene of Jewish history. Israel has sensed it in the forces preserving the unity of its soul at all times, even during the physical dispersion of the nation. Without it, the Sinaitic message would be but a noble heritage from a distant past, a pale shadow on the human scene; with it, past, present and future merge into a timeless unity, and the eternal summons assumes an irresistible force in directing the destiny of men.'

The Introduction dealt with one other issue – Hebrew Law. 'The two qualities which impute to Jewish Law its specific character are religious faith and judicial reasoning. Both are indispensable to its legal operation, and both must be taken into account if its true nature is to be comprehended. Their mutual relationship is a matter for special study, but, as a general observation, it may be said that while their boundaries are clearly and unmistakably defined, they are constantly interacting. The normal principles of judicial reasoning enjoy a fullness of application in the Jewish legal system, but they are consistently applied against the background of the divine origin and purpose of the law. Jewish Law, eminently practical and alive to human needs, never fails to emphasize its religio-moral basis. A living and thriving system, endowed *ab initio* with an inherent elasticity which assures it perennial vitality, it is ever rooted in the scene of the revelation on Sinai of which it constitutes the deathless message, and whence it derives the title-deeds of its eternal and unchanging validity.

'It is this consciousness of divine origin which marks off Jewish Law so sharply from other legal systems. Its foundations are immutable for they are believed to be the expression of ineffable wisdom and to enshrine the absolute ethic. The legislature, the jurist and the judiciary have their functions to perform in the application and expansion of this system, but they must always build on the unshakeable foundation laid down in the original dispensation. The limits with which the legislative authority may operate are fixed by divine command.'[9]

Yaacov's work on the Mishnah remained unfinished. Events took over. Throughout the war, he was immersed in his father's relentless struggle to save as many of Europe's Jews as possible from Nazi extermination. Rabbi Herzog organized assemblies, prayers and fasts, fired off telegrams to world leaders such as his friend Eamon de Valera, Winston Churchill and others. In 1941 he travelled to England, the United States and South Africa on behalf of European Jewry. He persuaded the Soviet government to allow thousand of Yeshiva students from Poland and Lithuania to travel through the USSR to the Far East. In 1943 he went to Turkey, to persuade the government to give Jews entry and passage through her territory. Young Yaacov composed many of his father's speeches, letters and telegrams and accompanied him on some of his meetings. He met the Vatican representative Archbishop Roncalli in Ankara and was deeply moved by his determined efforts to save Jews.

'I believe,' he wrote later, 'that his intervention was especially critical in saving some ten thousand Jews of doubtful Turkish nationality who were living in France. Roncalli sent to the Balkans, via the diplomatic post of the Apostolic embassy in Ankara, vital material to save these people, and his secretaries personally helped people who were engaged in saving our brothers, in Budapest and other places.'[10]

When the Chief Rabbi visited Istanbul people saw that he was always accompanied by a young man who carried his briefcase and acted as his secretary. Before their meeting, Archbishop Roncalli wondered how he should address Rabbi Herzog – 'Your Highness? Your Grace?' He telephoned the Red Cross representative who had just met the Chief Rabbi and asked him. The man replied that he had also been puzzled about it, but he heard the Chief Rabbi's secretary saying to him, 'Abba, put on your coat, it's cold outside.' So that must be the way to address him, he said – unaware that the word meant 'Father'.[11]

Yaacov's diplomatic skills were central to his father's lengthy struggle for the Vatican's help in saving Jewish lives. In December 1942, Yaacov – writing either in his father's name or in his own capacity as the Chief Rabbi's private secretary – sent a number of urgent appeals to the Church's representatives in Jerusalem and Cairo. He reported that Jewish prisoners-of-war held in Italy were about to be sent to Poland, where they would certainly be put to death. Herzog asked that Pope Pius XII intervene against their deportation to Poland.[12] In January 1943 he again approached the Vatican representatives with a similar appeal on behalf of 500 Jews from Czechoslovakia and Poland who had found temporary refuge in Italy. This time the Pope replied, through his delegates in the Middle East, that 'the Holy See is doing all in its power everywhere to help the persecuted.'[13]

At first the Chief Rabbi was delighted with the Vatican's response and sent a warm letter of thanks. He quoted the response in his correspondence with Jewish and other leaders all over the world, but soon discovered that it was an empty promise. Nevertheless, he persevered throughout 1943 and 1944.[14] In May 1944 the Chief Rabbi again begged the Pope to intervene to stop the deportation of Hungary's Jews to Auschwitz. Yaacov did everything he could to get his father an audience with the Pope, but they had to be satisfied with a meeting with the Vatican Middle East representative, Monsignor Hughes, that took place in Cairo on 5 September 1944. Yaacov's role in these meetings is revealed by a remark made by the Chief Rabbi. The Pope's representative asked, 'Does Your Worship have any suggestions?' Rabbi Herzog replied, 'Permit me to ask my son if he has any suggestions.'[15]

Yaacov did, in fact have some. They spoke about possible Vatican protection for Jews in their hiding places. In a certain Catholic convent, German soldiers searching for Jews were stopped by the Mother Superior, who stated that the place was under the Pope's direct supervision. Yaacov enquired if such protection could be extended to Jews in all their hiding places and was especially interested in similar measures for concentration camps located in Hungary. Monsignor Hughes responded favourably, describing the suggestion as 'extremely important', and promised to forward it directly to Rome, with a recommendation for its implementation. The two Herzogs came away from the meeting greatly encouraged, and the Chief Rabbi sent a telegram to the Vatican, no doubt drafted by Yaacov: 'In these fateful moments the eyes of the People of Israel ... are upon the Pope. All our suggestions have been put to him ... We are absolutely certain that the Pope will not remain indifferent to the greatest tragedy in history. May God guide his moves ...'[16]

The gratitude was premature. Though Herzog's suggestion was transmitted to the Vatican, the Pope did nothing, as before.[17]

On 8 May 1945 the war in Europe ended, and the Nazi horrors were revealed. The Chief Rabbi and his young assistant set themselves a new objective – to save as many Jewish survivors as possible and bring them to the land of Israel or other friendly countries. Rabbi Herzog was anxious to restore the connection to Judaism of those cut off from it by the upheavals of war, and again asked to see the Pope. This time he received a positive response. The Chief Rabbi met Pius XII in the spring of 1946, when he stopped in Rome on his way to the displaced persons' (DP) camps and Jewish centres in Europe. Accompanied by Yaacov, Rabbi Herzog asked the Pope to ensure that the Jewish children who had hidden in monasteries during the war (at the initiative of the particular monasteries, rather than as Church policy) would be restored to the Jewish people. The answer was not favourable. The rabbi came out of the audience deeply upset. 'He [the Pope] doesn't want to let out the children they've caught.'[18]

Eliezer Aliner, a young officer attached by the *Va'ad Le'umi* (the national committee representing the Jewish community of Mandatory Palestine) to the UN Welfare and Employment Agency, was in the crowd which witnessed Rabbi Herzog emerging from the papal audience, saluted by the Vatican guard of honour, while his son Yaacov, in his officer's uniform, walked ahead, clearing a path for his father. When Yaacov saw Aliner, tall and impressive in his uniform, he said admiringly, 'You look like Joab son of Zeruya [King David's captain]!'[19]

Father and son's journey in 1946 through devastated Europe searching for remnants of perished Jewry was a frightful experience. Yaacov was visibly shaken by what he saw at the DP camps in Italy and Central Europe. 'Our journey through Europe lasted six months,' he wrote,[20] 'and we visited every city on the Continent. We saw such devastation as had never been seen in human history, and when we saw the heap of rubble that the Warsaw Ghetto had been reduced to, we felt as though history had shrunk and we were 2,000 years back, on the hills of Jerusalem when the flames engulfed the last walls of the Temple.

'What destruction, what solitude, what desolation! The sight alone could overturn the accepted scale of human values, and a man can only avoid plunging into the abyss of total despair by holding on to the eternal Rock in whose shadow we have made our journey through history.'

Yaacov went on to describe the purpose of the journey. 'Our main mission was to save Jewish children everywhere and the remnants of Poland's Jewry. We visited kings, prime ministers and military commanders all over the Continent. With God's help we had many successes, the most important of which was rescuing 1,000 children, obtaining thousands of French entry visas for

Polish Jews, and persuading the UN Agency for Welfare and Employment (thanks to Mr La Guardia, whom my father saw in Warsaw), to keep the perimeter of the American sector [in occupied Germany] open, and to house the refugees from Poland, thousands of whom had crossed the border.'

Fiorello La Guardia, later New York's legendary mayor, headed the UN welfare agency and was very helpful to Rabbi Herzog, as were many other leaders whom the Herzogs met. These included the Czech Prime Minister Klement Gottwald, the French Prime Minister Georges Bidault, the Italian Prime Minister Alcide de Gasperi, Belgium's Prime Minister Camille Huysmans, British and American generals, the Archbishop of Canterbury, and Britain's Prime Minister Clement Attlee. At this time the problem of Palestine was prominent on the world agenda, but when the British authorities tried to engage Rabbi Herzog in political discussions, he refused to be drawn in. In Ireland he met his old friends Briscoe and de Valera, and the Irish Prime Minister contributed 1,000 head of cattle, which provided one million cans of beef for the DP camps.

While in Poland, the rabbi and his son visited the tomb of the Rabbi of Kotzk. As they stood in the cemetery they were surrounded by a crowd of hostile Poles. Tension was high in Poland then, because 42 Jews had been murdered shortly before by Poles in the town of Kielce. (The previous year, just after their country's liberation from the Nazis, Poles had murdered 353 Jews.) The armed guards protecting the Jewish group drew their weapons, and the crowd dispersed.[21] Although the rabbi and his son were accompanied by 10 armed men, the government urged them to leave the country.[22]

In Prague, they met Alpen Reese, of the Council of Protestant Churches, who was working in Czechoslovakia for the UN welfare agency, and who arranged for Rabbi Herzog to meet Klement Gottwald. Reese revealed to Yaacov that he had been told by the British government 'to stop the flight [of Jews] at all costs.' But Yaacov persuaded him to continue helping Jews, which Reese did with loyalty and devotion.[23] Reese was deeply impressed by Yaacov's diplomatic work at his father's side, and by the rabbi's reliance on his son. He was also moved by Yaacov's modesty. 'He was a genius at avoiding the limelight,' he wrote years later to Pnina Herzog, Yaacov's wife. 'If ever a person was active behind the scenes, he was the one. I've often wondered how many of his countrymen know about his role in that exodus.'[24]

Determined to rescue as many Jewish children as possible, Reese was sometimes upset by Rabbi Herzog's strict adherence to the Sabbath law. 'I don't think the Jewish Sabbath is any more rigid than the nonconformist Welsh Sabbath of my youth,' he wrote. 'But it was frustrating when we managed, with great effort, to get a train for a Saturday [to transport Jewish children], and couldn't use it! It was always Yaacov who pacified me and made me understand that if these children were to return to – or even get to know – their fathers' religion, they had to begin at once.'[25]

The representative of the American Jewish Relief Committee in Europe[26] also admired Herzog. At the Committee's conference in Montreux, Switzerland, he wrote, 'Rabbi Yaacov showed his diplomatic skill and sincere feelings in dealing with the camp refugees ... His proposed plans of action were always adopted by all the representatives, most of whom were twice or three times his age.'[27]

During his journey through Europe at the side of his adored father, Yaacov relished the admiration and appreciation showered on the Chief Rabbi. 'Father's prestige has gone up tremendously, and he enjoys unprecedented respect and honour,' he wrote.[28] The letters he wrote to his brother at the time express his overwhelming feelings for his father. He never wearied of describing the Chief Rabbi's achievements and the praise lavished on him during the journey and following their return, his success in rescuing Holocaust survivors and – repeatedly – the Irish government's gift of one million cans of beef for the DP camps.[29] For himself, he felt that the journey had opened new vistas. The young man met heads of government and senior cabinet ministers, and enjoyed great diplomatic success. 'For me the journey was very valuable,' he wrote. His horizon had broadened considerably, 'without undermining my basic beliefs'.[30]

Rabbi Herzog was hopelessly impractical, and Yaacov was entrusted with planning the journey, arranging transportation, making appointments, as well as taking an active part in the meetings. He was very pleased with his newly-discovered organizational ability. 'The same special Providence which has guided [father's] path in life has been especially marked this past year, and it has given me great satisfaction that the planning and execution of this historical journey has been mine from start to finish.'[31]

This was the background of Yaacov's irate response to a letter in which Chaim had presumed to accuse his younger brother of 'insane extravagance' for taking his father all over England and Ireland in private planes and hired cars. Yaacov furiously attacked his brother in return, described his criticism as 'hysterical', and added, 'Since you have not seen fit to give me the basic right to explain, I shall treat your views with the same contempt. However, hoping that in future you will stop using me as an object for your neurotic outbursts, I would like to clarify some things.'[32] These were exceptionally harsh words from the usually mild and courteous Yaacov.

He proceeded to enumerate the objective reasons for every 'extravagant' move he and his father made, and explained why in some cases – in the absence of regular transport by land or air – they were obliged to hire a plane or car in order to reach their appointed meetings with British and Irish leaders on time.

The furious Yaacov also tried to figure out the identity of the anonymous sources who had whispered in his brother's ear that 'all London' was shocked by the extravagance of Chief Rabbi Herzog. 'It seems to me that you heard these stories ... from our aunt, embellished by our uncle's neurotic imagination, giving you the impression that "all London" (including, I suppose, Downing Street) were discussing them at present ... Our aunt is a noble soul, deserving of sympathy and respect, but she is shallow and limited, lacks judgment and is easily affected by outside influences.' She had addressed similar hints to Yaacov, but since 'I did not feel obliged to apologize for what was the right thing to do, and since she had no right to intervene in such matters, I kept my mouth shut.' (Yaacov was referring to David Hillman, his maternal uncle, and his wife Dr Annie Hillman.)

Then he turned on Chaim. 'It is time you shook off your childish habit of apologizing for yourself and your family to a ridiculous degree. I feel no compunction about the way I managed things on our journey ... When you've done something similar, then you'll have the right to criticize. Till then give me the benefit of the doubt and do not presume to criticize the conduct of others.'[33]

Yaacov's uncharacteristic sharpness revealed not just his great sensitivity, but also his considerable confidence and inner conviction.

Astonishingly, Chaim did not resent his younger brother's harsh attack, but accepted his explanations and said as much in a later letter. The argument did not diminish their affection, though it seems that as Yaacov matured, he sometimes assumed the role of elder brother. That is the impression left by their correspondence, for example, Yaacov devoted time and attention to Chaim's plans for his future after his discharge from the British army.

The Herzogs thought that Chaim should become Ireland's honorary consul in Jerusalem, and the Chief Rabbi and his younger son proposed this in their meetings with Ireland's leaders. Rabbi Herzog pulled all the strings he could, and Yaacov, by now an experienced diplomat, advised Chaim how to approach the right persons in Ireland and bring up the question in a discreet manner during his next visit,[34] mentioning the subject again in his following letter. But Yaacov knew that being an honorary consul was not a job, and encouraged his brother to become a lawyer. Chaim had already worked as a lawyer in London before he joined the army, and the idea of studying for the Palestine Bar Association did not appeal to him. But Yaacov explained, calmly and lucidly, that the examinations were not difficult, that he would have plenty of time to prepare, and 'personally, I can't see any other profession [for you] than the law, at which many of the lawyers here do very well.'[35]

When the Herzogs were in Prague, they received the disturbing news that the Mandatory government had sentenced two Jewish underground* fighters to death. They decided to go to Paris, where the British Foreign Secretary Ernest Bevin was at that time. The Chief Rabbi wanted to plead with him to commute the sentence, and time was of the essence. 'Rabbi Herzog persuaded the head of the Joint (the American Jewish Joint Distribution Committee, an international Jewish welfare agency) in Prague to provide funds for a special plane to take the two Herzogs to Paris. Rabbi Yaacov Herzog viewed the matter gravely and anxiously, as though the two men were members of his family ... He did not stop planning how to tackle the issue in the best way to obtain a pardon. Unfortunately, he did not succeed.'[36] (According to the Irgun operative, Nahum Snapiri, Yaacov told him that the flight to Paris was cancelled at the last moment, because of a false report that the two men had already been hanged. When they did get to Paris – after their trip to Poland – Bevin was no longer there,

---

* The Irgun Zvai Leumi, known by its Hebrew acronym Etzel, and the Stern Gang, also known by its Hebrew acronym Lehi, were dissident Jewish underground organizations fighting the British. The Irgun and Stern Gang were more aggressive than the Haganah, reflecting different political streams in the Zionist movement. The Haganah was affiliated with the moderate Mapai faction, led by Ben-Gurion, whilst the Irgun and Stern Gang were affiliated with the Revisionist faction led by Menachem Begin.

and Rabbi Herzog delivered the plea for pardon to the British Embassy in Paris.)[37]

Indeed, the turbulent war years had also thrust Yaacov and his father into the sometimes clandestine world of the struggle for Jewish independence. In the 1940s, the Irgun and the Stern Gang stepped up their armed struggle and terror attacks against the British and the Arabs, and the British authorities responded with a heavy hand. A number of Jews were arrested and charged with terrorism, and the British courts were harsh in their sentences – long prison terms, deportations and hanging. The two organizations and the families of the condemned men appealed to the Chief Rabbi and his son and begged them to help. Afterwards Yaacov Herzog kept a note that they had received, written in capital letters and full of spelling mistakes: 'God willing. Great Rabbi, for God's sake beg the commander of the British army in the country to spare the life of the young man Matityahu Shmulevich, who was today sentenced to death. He has no friends but yourself. Save a Jewish soul.' The note was unsigned.[38]

Although he favoured the Haganah, and later joined its ranks, Yaacov worked hard to save the condemned men, and the prisoners and deportees from the other underground organizations. He wrote letters on his father's behalf to the British High Commissioner, pleading for the prisoners. One surviving letter mentions the illness of a woman prisoner held in Bethlehem prison – who was the wife of the Stern Gang's leader, Natan Friedman-Yellin.[39] In later years Menachem Begin remembered the Chief Rabbi's efforts – through his son Yaacov – to save the life of Dov Gruner, who was condemned to death and hanged, as well as Yaacov's mediation between his father and the Irgun.[40] Yaacov also accompanied his father to a very unpleasant meeting with the High Commissioner, whom the Chief Rabbi tried in vain to persuade to commute the death sentences of other condemned men.[41] They also visited deportees in Kenya and Eritrea after their conviction for bombing a wing of Jerusalem's King David Hotel.

Among them were Yitzhak Shamir, a future Prime Minister of Israel, Meir Shamgar, a future President of Israel's Supreme Court, and Shmuel Tamir, a future Minister of Justice.

A strange incident marked that trip. In Cairo, a British sergeant responsible for the allocation of seats in Royal Air Force planes asked Yaacov which regiment his father belonged to. Without batting an eye, Yaacov replied, 'He serves in the Army of the Lord.' The sergeant, not over-endowed with imagination, wrote it down. Then he asked, 'What rank?' and Yaacov replied, 'Field Marshal.' And which regiment did he himself belong to? Yaacov replied he too was serving in the Army of the Lord. Rank? 'Colonel,' Yaacov answered, as most appropriate for a Field Marshal's aide. All this was duly noted for the official record.[42]

Once the aircraft had taken off, the forms were examined by the sergeant's superior officer, who must have been embarrassed by his subordinate's obtuseness but amused by Yaacov's sense of humour. He radioed the plane, 'I hope the Army of the Lord is flying safely . . .'[43]

The visit to the detention camps presented Yaacov with a moral dilemma. Before and after the journey, the Chief Rabbi and Yaacov secretly met Menachem Begin, who at the time was wanted by the British police. 'Yaacov was very young, in his twenties,' Menachem Begin recalled. 'One day . . . he accompanied his great father to a secret meeting with me in Tel Aviv . . . The Chief Rabbi was very agitated, and Yaacov took an active part in his discussion with some of the Irgun commanders.'[44] The Herzogs discussed their visit to the deportees, but refused to take any messages from Begin to his comrades in exile, because they had promised the British authorities that they would not carry messages to or from the deportees. Yaacov had struggled with himself about giving his word to the British, but in the end had agreed, realizing that otherwise they might not be allowed to make the journey.

When they returned from Africa, Yaacov asked to meet Chaim

Landau, then a member of the Irgun high command. He told Landau that although he had brought a letter from the senior Irgun commander, Yaacov Meridor, containing a code for correspondence between the leaders of the deportees and their commander at home, he could not hand it over because he had given his word to the British authorities. Landau tried to persuade him, but Yaacov would not budge. Landau saw that he would not break his word, however badly it made him feel – he was an honest man and bound by his word of honour.

'I understood the man. He was a man of integrity. Integrity was probably his main characteristic.'[45] He realized that Yaacov wanted above all to avoid the shedding of Jewish blood. 'I revealed to him,' said Landau, 'that the deportees had made up their minds to escape, no matter what. But it was up to us to make it possible, and what is more, to prevent mishaps which might be not only very serious, but tragic. I tried to convince him that it was a matter of life and death, and that he was holding the key.'[46] Yaacov was persuaded and handed over the code. 'The escape was planned and, as we know, it succeeded; the deportees reached Paris, led by Meridor.'[47]

Landau went on: 'I revealed to Yaacov one of our most highly confidential plans, and I had no doubt whatever that he would keep the secret. Though he was a Haganah man, he was given one of our most secret operational plans, unhesitatingly, in all confidence.'[48]

Yaacov's code-name in the Irgun was 'the little one', and his liaison with the group was their point man in Jerusalem, Nahum Snapiri. He often came to the Chief Rabbi's house and was briefed by Yaacov about his father's activities.[49] Yaacov would receive him 'warmly' and convey the requests of the Irgun 'faithfully' to the Chief Rabbi.[50] 'My brother took care of the secret arrangements between my father and the command of the various underground groups,' Chaim Herzog recalled,[51] 'and the role suited Yaacov to perfection. The mutual confidence between him and my father was rock solid, and he was also naturally endowed with the finest diplomatic skills. He was respected by all who dealt with him – representatives of the Mandatory government and Jewish underground leaders alike. He also developed close working relations with the leadership of the Yishuv (the Jewish community in Palestine), including David Ben-Gurion and Golda Meir.[52]

At a later stage, amid the upheavals of the War of Independence, the 'Altalena' affair* and the assassination of Count Bernadotte,† several clashes between the authorities of the newly established State of Israel and the dissident underground groups might easily have deteriorated into civil war. Yaacov played a crucial role in mediating between the different factions and organizations. 'I was aware of Yaacov's special role in Jerusalem,' Menachem Begin recalled, 'in preventing civil war, in always striving to obtain an agreement between the Haganah and the Irgun ... His was a very significant function. Both sides had complete confidence in him ... He not only contributed a great deal towards reaching an agreement, he also kept it going during the difficult months of the siege of Jerusalem and the struggle of the Haganah, the Irgun and the Stern Gang to save the city.'[53] According to Golda Meir, Yaacov and his father also helped to resolve confrontation between the Haganah and the Irgun in Tel Aviv. 'Those were very difficult days of internal dissension,' Golda recalled. 'I'll never forget one of the worst incidents, when it seemed that in the following few

---

* The *Altalena* was a ship loaded with Irgun fighters and military equipment that arrived in Israel on 20 June 1948, after an agreement had already been reached on the absorption of the Irgun into the Israel Defence Forces – the new State's army – and the cessation of independent arms purchases by the Irgun. When efforts to unload the weapons peacefully failed, Ben-Gurion ordered their seizure by force. Sixteen Irgun fighters and three IDF soldiers were killed in the incident.

† In September 1948, members of the Stern Gang assassinated UN peace mediator Count Folke Bernadotte to protest his diplomatic efforts to modify the UN partition plan for Palestine. Rather than two states, Bernadotte had proposed a union of Arabs and Jews in a small Jewish entity and an expanded Transjordan, and Transjordanian control of Jerusalem. The Israeli government rejected the Bernadotte plan.

hours something very bad was likely to happen [between the Haganah and the Irgun], and it was necessary to influence people in Tel Aviv. On the Friday morning, at five o'clock, the Rabbi and Yaacov left Jerusalem and came to my place in Tel Aviv, and also called on people who could influence things.'[54] Yaacov and his father helped to prevent the further deterioration of relations between the organizations. Moshe Sharett would say to a friend, 'You should know that that young man prevented fraternal bloodshed.'[55] Yaacov himself noted in an abridged curriculum vitae: '1946-1948 – liaison between the President of the National Committee and the Irgun.'[56]

Indeed, Yaacov's code name of 'the little one' in his contact with Snapiri and his colleagues could not have been more misleading. During the Second World War and Israel's War of Independence, he developed a solid outlook on life and displayed natural leadership qualities. His interlocutors all noted the maturity and wisdom he radiated. 'I read your letters with pleasure and appreciation,' wrote Rabbi Louis Rabinowitz, senior Jewish chaplain of the British Eighth Army, who had become his friend.[57] 'I'm amazed and delighted by your command of English, and the depth of your thinking.' Rabinowitz described his friend Yaacov's style of writing as 'full of Victorian sentimentality, quite inappropriate in a lad who has just emerged from his teen years'.

Chaim Herzog, who had not seen his brother during the war years, met him again in the autumn of 1945. He saw a slender young man with an open, smiling bespectacled face. 'I liked and admired the man who had grown up from the boy I'd known,' he noted.[58] Yaacov's maturity and intelligence were evident in letters he wrote to Chaim in 1946, in which he analysed his behaviour and even advised him about his future. These letters read rather like those of an older brother to a younger sibling. Chaim had recently fallen in love with Aura Ambache, who came from an established Jewish family in Cairo. The dashing British officer had personally conveyed greetings from Abba Eban and his wife Susie (née Ambache, Aura's older sister) to the Ambache family, and had been captivated by Aura's beauty and intelligence. That summer, on holiday in Switzerland, Aura accepted Chaim's proposal of marriage. The Chief Rabbi's family was not pleased with Chaim's independent choice. The assertive Sarah Herzog had another, more religiously observant candidate in mind for her first-born. Yaacov became his brother's ally and arranged to meet Aura in Cairo. He found her very impressive, but urged Chaim not to act in haste. 'There have been many family discussions about your private matter,' he wrote and presented their parents' wish that Chaim postpone his proposal until they could discuss the matter with him in person. Aura was visiting Jerusalem at the time, and Yaacov undertook to introduce her personally to the family during the Succoth holiday.[59]

One of Yaacov's letters contains a detailed description of his meetings with Aura: 'In our first conversation [Aura] was very frank and asked me how to conduct herself [with the family]. I gave her [the advice she asked for], with the proviso that since I was still inexperienced in personal relations, she should not ... make any move without prior consultation with you. She agreed ... '[60]

The two met several more times – at Aura's request, as Yaacov made clear. She was taking a course for future Israeli diplomats in Jerusalem. 'She's lonely,' Yaacov wrote to his brother, 'and counting the days till you arrive ... I find her charming as always, intelligent without being too clever, down-to-earth yet idealistic, and she has a thorough understanding of human nature, which has not distorted her natural simplicity and kindness. She has ... a most charming personality, combining the basic truth and characteristic feelings of the East with the rhythm and equilibrium of Western culture. She will be a worthy companion to you. It's your decision. Mother, with her usual conservatism, is quite reserved, but I sense that she is not unaware of Aura's good qualities. Since the matter will only be decided after your arrival,

I'm not pressuring Father or Mother to express their final opinion right now ... What amazed me most about Aura was her profound understanding of your personality. As for her religious tendencies, I've already told you that under the right influence her qualities of "a virtuous woman" [will be revealed] ... .'[61]

Aura was genuinely impressed by the Herzog family – the realism, practicality and forcefulness of the Chief Rabbi's wife, and the Rabbi's warm heart that overflowed with kindness and generosity. This often landed Rabbi Herzog in trouble because his financial naiveté led him to donate generously to all who asked. But above all she felt 'that this was a family with a royal quality. They never felt inferior to any Gentile.'[62]

Yaacov and Aura walked the streets of Jerusalem for hours. 'He loved the city and walking with him was an experience.' When her son Michael (Mike) was growing up, Aura asked Yaacov to show him Jerusalem as he had shown her.[63] Yaacov and his young nephew developed a close attachment on these Jerusalem walks, and years later, Yaacov did the same with Chaim's younger son, Isaac (known by his nickname Bougie, he is now a Labour Member of the Knesset). Once, in one of their earlier meetings, Aura said to Yaacov, 'I spoke with Goushie.' Yaacov jumped, utterly surprised. 'Goushie' was his private nickname for Chaim while Chaim called him 'Ye'. Finding that Aura even knew Chaim's intimate nickname, he 'realized that the matter was serious'.[64]

These were difficult times for Chaim Herzog. After a successful career in the British army, where he had attained the rank of Major, he was uncertain about his future as a civilian. He was a personality in his own right, knew his own mind and had been responsible for soldiers under his command. But his parents were cool towards his marriage to Aura, and he deliberated about his future place of residence. He had spent the previous seven years in England, and had postponed his return to Palestine, partly due to religious differences with his parents. Some of Chaim's letters to

Yaacov hinted at his desire to distance himself from Jerusalem. 'What are your plans?' Yaacov wanted to know. 'Evidently you're indecisive, if you've made me your confidant.'[65] He urged Chaim to return to Palestine to meet their parents – if only briefly. 'I still think, as I've always thought, that deep down you're with us in your views and religious feelings, but that childhood distortion in this matter has left you with painful impressions in everything that has to do with the home, and the religious atmosphere is a vital part of it ... In any event, the idea that because of your opinions you won't be able to live in the same country as your parents is, if I may say so, quite ridiculous ... The main thing is that you should be here and we'll have an opportunity to discuss it frankly.' Yaacov described his elder brother's notion of living far from home as 'childish illusions'. He eloquently lectured his brother about the need to reappraise his plans. He asked him if he was willing to throw away the golden chance that life in Eretz Israel could offer him. '[Several] lawyers have talked to me repeatedly about your chances of success working in Eretz Israel. And while Jews all over the world, even in England and America, regard Zion as the source of their hopes, is it not ridiculous to forgo a career here for a reason that is not really important? Think carefully – I think that the path you're contemplating is worse than hasty, and will cause you to regret it to the end of your life. After all, here there is more stability and continuity for our people than anywhere else.' Yaacov made a number of suggestions to Chaim – to come over for a month, return to London for six to eight months, sit for the Bar examination in Jerusalem the following year, then undertake the management of an international fund in Cairo. He concluded the letter with renewed pressure on his brother to come to Eretz Israel, as his duty to his parents.[66]

It is not known if Yaacov's letters were decisive in persuading Chaim to abandon his plans of building his future overseas. The fact is that he returned, married Aura with his parents' blessing, and integrated successfully into the Zionist civilian and military framework prior to and after the establishment of the State of Israel.*

'After our marriage Yaacov would come to us at eleven-thirty at night, and I'd put on a dressing-gown and give him supper,' Aura recalled. 'He was wonderful company. Though he was the man of ideas, as opposed to Vivian (Chaim's name in the British Army) who was a man of action, he had a wonderful sense of humour, he always had a twinkle of joy and humour in his eyes. There was something very charismatic about him. He liked people, liked to be in company, and created a pleasant atmosphere around him. I'd knitted Vivian a nice green pullover and Yaacov immediately said, "What about me?" So I knitted one for him too. He accepted it gladly, and lost it the next day. As I said, he was great company...'

Aura noted that the brothers did not waste time in small talk, but focused on things that mattered. 'Between them there was love and envy, as between brothers everywhere.' The brothers enjoyed spending whole evenings together, talking. 'They got tremendous pleasure from it,' Aura says. 'They'd say, "It's our night!"'[67]

Nevertheless while Chaim was considering his future, towards the end of the war and after, the differences between the brothers became more apparent. It seemed that whatever drove Chaim away from home, attracted Yaacov. Chaim rebelled against his religious upbringing, while to Yaacov religion was a fascinating world. Chaim did whatever he could to leave home, while Yaacov stayed under his parents' roof. Chaim remained the rebel, impulsive and more daring than his brother. Yaacov was more thoughtful and deliberate, older than his years, and the good son, who lived harmoniously with his parents.

The profound attachment to his father would leave a deep imprint on Yaacov Herzog and affect his entire life. The image of his father was never far from his thoughts. He once told a close

* In interviews with family members, they questioned the seriousness of Chaim's intentions to remain abroad.

friend, 'Every time I feel weighed down by worry about the future of Israel, I try to visualize the image of my late father, and try to make my faith reflect his.'[68]

Yaacov was indeed his father's successor – and his pride.

4

The Secret Agent

Malka Ben-Zvi, a beautiful, blue-eyed young woman, was a student of history and psychology at the Hebrew University in Jerusalem. In her free time she worked as a proof-reader in her father's printing shop on Yannai Street in Jerusalem. There she met a young observant man, well-dressed and wearing a hat – 'very different' – who came to proof-read his translation of the Mishnah. Working on the proofs he gave the impression of being a 'pedant and a perfectionist'. When they began to talk, Malka discovered that Yaacov was 'very shy' but steady and serious, and came to respect and appreciate him. 'If I hadn't come to know him, I might have thought he was a bit ridiculous – an old young man,' she said. But she did get to know him. 'He was handsome, clear-skinned, pale, with a marvellous forehead. And the wisest of men.'[1]

Yaacov felt awkward in her presence. They did not really have any common interests, did not read the same books or live in the same social milieu. In those days Yaacov did not go to the cinema, though he knew what films were showing in town and could name the best ones. They talked about politics and relations between the Jewish community and the British authorities.

In 1946 Malka married Alex Keynan a government employee, and Chief Rabbi Herzog officiated at their wedding. The fact that she was married made her relations with Yaacov 'much easier'.[2] He liked to visit them after the Sabbath for tea and biscuits they bought specially in a kosher pastry-shop on King George Street and kept in a separate box.

'He was a unique character,' says Alex Keynan. 'A man from an extraordinary world. There was something aristocratic about him, in appearance and behaviour. He never lost his temper or got carried away, but could be cynical and sharp-tongued. He didn't like a lot of people, but he liked being with us and our closest friends, and we all realized that he was much more learned than any of us, even where general knowledge was concerned.' The Keynans and their friends regarded Yaacov as 'amazingly intelligent', with 'wordly understanding', and felt that it was an experience to talk to him on 'any subject'. He confided in them that he had met a young woman in London, named Pnina, with whom he had fallen in love at first sight.

One day Malka told Yaacov that she was 'an activist', hinting that she was in the Haganah. Naturally, he, as the son of the Chief Rabbi, was not actively involved in any underground organization, but mentioned that he was in touch with a senior British official by the name of Sherringham, whose first name remains unknown to this day. They met often, Yaacov said, and discussed current issues. Malka thought that this could be an important source of information for the Haganah, and told her superior officer, David Shaltiel, head of Haganah Intelligence in Jerusalem, about it. Should she invite Yaacov to join the Haganah, she asked. 'Do what you think right,' Shaltiel replied. 'If you succeed I'll pinch your cheek, and if not, I won't.'

Malka waited for Yaacov to come to the printing shop, and informed him 'very cautiously that I was active in the Haganah, and suggested that he might use his talks with Sherringham to obtain information we could use. He said it was possible and that he was willing.'[3] Boris Guriel, who headed the political section of Haganah Intelligence, tells it differently. He maintains that Malka Ben-Zvi approached him, not David Shaltiel, and that it was he who met Yaacov Herzog on behalf of the intelligence section. 'One day in June 1947 I heard that Rabbi Herzog's younger son wished to see me. His name was already known, because of his work to save and rehabilitate the Jewish survivors in Europe. I was also keen to meet him, though I didn't think that such a brilliant man, the son and assistant of the Chief Rabbi, would join an underground operation which was not always perfectly pure, from the standpoint of absolute morality.'[4]

At first, Guriel says, he was a little sceptical, 'because too many intellectuals hung around the intelligence section, and were not particularly useful. Yaacov also seemed to him as 'very young'.[5] But his doubts vanished at their first meeting. 'I was struck not only by his realistic attitude towards our actions, but chiefly by the wealth of ideas Yaacov had for developing the political concepts needed in the process of obtaining information.'[6]

At their first meeting, Guriel recalled, Yaacov Herzog argued that it was essential to penetrate the nerve centre of British power in the Middle East, located in Cairo. He offered to go there, and Guriel obtained Shaltiel's authorization for him to do so. Yaacov returned after ten days, with important information about British plans in the region. The information was passed to Ben-Gurion, who was greatly impressed, and asked Guriel to bring Yaacov Herzog to see him. 'The results of this mission are described in Ben-Gurion's diaries, and they helped determine the future offensive policy of the Zionist organizations, in the latter half of 1947 and the first half of 1948.'[7]

This is a curious story. There is no confirmation of the information Yaacov Herzog supposedly brought back from Cairo. He himself never mentioned it, and Malka Ben-Zvi never heard about it – she thought it was Vivian (Chaim) who had gone to Cairo, rather than Yaacov.[8] Certainly no documentary evidence has been found of the sequence of events described by Boris Guriel.

By contrast, Yaacov Herzog's principal and undoubted contribution was 'Operation Sherringham'. Sherringham was a senior figure in the Mandatory government, assistant-secretary of the Political Department. Yaacov concentrated on him and used their friendly relations to turn him into an unwitting source of information for the Haganah. One of Yaacov's reports for the intelligence section describes the Englishman's personality in detail. Sherringham grew up on a remote farm in Northern Ireland, and his only friend before university was the vicar who taught him. He read Semitic Studies at Dublin and Oxford, graduating with honours, and apparently also studied in Nazi Germany. He became a minister of the Church of England, later developed religious doubts, left the church and volunteered to serve in Palestine. Arriving there in 1940, he improved his command of Hebrew and Arabic, and rose through the ranks of the colonial hierarchy until he became head of the Arabic Department and advisor to the chief of staff of the High Commission. He married a Christian Egyptian woman.

'His knowledge of Jewish subjects,' wrote Yaacov, 'such as Talmud, Jewish history, philosophy, is greater than that of any non-Jew, and even in England there are few comparable or superior to him.' He had worked for years on early post-Talmudic manuscripts and translated large excerpts from the Toseftah (an early commentary on the Mishnah), which he intended to submit as his doctoral thesis at Oxford. 'He has at home a large collection of complex Talmudic studies, and other Jewish books. Before the uprising he used to take part in Jewish gatherings and meetings.'[9]

It seems that their common background – Ireland – and their love for the Talmud brought the two together. According to some sources, Herzog was Sherringham's mentor on the subjects of the Talmud and Mishnah. They became friends, and used to meet in cafés in various parts of Jerusalem, and at least once at Sherringham's home.

'Operation Sherringham' was conducted entirely by Yaacov and Malka. Yaacov's cover name was 'Harno'. Malka was Yaacov's liaison with the intelligence section, and he did not meet other members of the Haganah command. Before a meeting with Sherringham, Yaacov would discuss with Malka the kind of questions he should put to the Englishman, or hear the instructions she had been given by her superiors. 'He was so wise, he knew how to phrase the questions in such a way that Sherringham may not have suspected anything, and always answered all our questions.' Some of Malka's questions were quite specific. At one point, Ben-Gurion requested information about the Arab armies and their plans of attack.[10]

After seeing Sherringham, Yaacov would meet Malka at her flat on Shlomo Molcho Street, or at Yaacov's parents. They would sit in his modest, book-filled room, and the rabbi's wife would serve them tea and refreshments. Yaacov would dictate the conversation, which he remembered in great detail, and Malka took it all down by hand, sometimes for hours on end. The reports were typed and passed to Boris Guriel, Malka's immediate superior, and from him to David Shaltiel, Reuven Shiloah, Israel Galili, Moshe Sharett and other members of the leadership, who studied them avidly. 'We heard that Sharett did not think highly of the material,' Malka recalled. 'He didn't think the British would leave.'[11]

Yaacov was open about Sherringham. He told Malka that the man was 'anti-Zionist and anti-Semitic', and enjoyed provoking Yaacov by saying that the Jews did not stand a chance of winning. Their close friendship did not blunt Yaacov's critical ability. A report he wrote for the intelligence section provided a gripping psychological portrait of Sherringham.

'His brilliant brain is stamped with a "split personality" in the worst sense. Since he never lived among people in his youth, he has not developed social awareness or loyalty, and since he has never known real happiness, his soul is profoundly corroded by endless frustration, which resounds in a vacuum of disdain and hatred. Subconsciously he feels that he does not belong to humanity, and there is no truly valid relationship in his life. Outwardly, he projects an image of sociability, but his inward personality, involuted and lonely, finds artificial solace only in observing the paradox of negation and destruction. Feverishly, he seeks an outlet for his tortured imagination, and having found it, nothing can stop his efforts to endow his destructive tendencies with a realistic appearance. Once launched on his offensive speeches he totally ignores his situation and surroundings. When the verbal outburst runs out, he returns at once to the dignified reserve of an experienced colonial official. The secret of success with him lies in gaining his confidence and steering the conversation for a while to marginal subjects, until his impulse to dominate takes charge.

'Though he was a student in Nazi Germany, he doesn't quite fit the usual definition of an anti-Semite ... Intellectually, he admires the Jewish spirit and appreciates its contribution to human civilization. He seeks to reconcile his wish to see the end of Zionism with his advocacy of continuing Judaism in the diaspora. He's not thoroughly loyal to England, and is capable of supporting the Arabs' demands even if they clash with his country's interests.

'In the past few months I have repeatedly recommended that [his] information be given the greatest consideration, and events have shown that my reading [of him] has been correct. His prognoses have been realized beyond all expectation ... At times it looks as though the Foreign Office bases its assessments on [his] analyses. I have known him for several years and in the course of academic discussions have succeeded in forming the closest connection with him that is possible for a Jew. I should point out that he believes I support the political outlook of Brith Shalom*.'[12]

Consciously or not, Herzog operated like an experienced master spy. He knew his source well, understood his personality and motives, and succeeded in forming a close relationship with him. Knowing Sherringham's weaknesses enabled Herzog to manipulate him very skilfully, so that the Englishman's 'outbursts' provided important information, without his being pumped. He

---

* Also known as the Magnes Group, a Zionist organization founded in 1925, associated with Judah Magnes, Martin Buber and Gershom Scholem. Brith Shalom acknowledged that the Land of Israel belonged to two peoples, a position not adopted by mainstream Zionist organizations.

willingly provided Yaacov with information till his last day in the country.

The information and opinions voiced by Sherringham probably reflected to a large extent those that prevailed in the High Commissioner's residence. It was information straight from the inner sanctum. Yaacov had definitely succeeded in handling the most senior source available to the Haganah in that critical year, 1947–8. The Chief Rabbi's son, an inexperienced amateur, proved as skilful and able as the most senior members of the organization's intelligence section.

However, with hindsight, it is clear that Sherringham did not really supply Yaacov, and through him the leadership of the Haganah and the Jewish Agency, with truly significant information. Yaacov's reports marked 'Top Secret – Read & Destroy!' were reverently passed on to his superiors, but an analysis of Sherringham's responses and assessments of the situation in the Middle East and the prospects in Palestine in the following days and months reveals that the bulk of his information was unfounded and useless.

Sherringham was a great admirer of the Arabs, and contemptuous of Jewish leaders. A report of one of his earliest meetings with Yaacov Herzog is dated 25 November 1947 – four days before the UN General Assembly passed the resolution on the partition of Palestine. The conversation took place at Sherringham's house, in the presence of his wife and a few friends.[13] Sherringham declared that, in the event of partition, 'His Highness the Mufti', Haj Amin al-Husseini, would be president of the Arab state. He dismissed talk about Arab armies planning to invade Palestine/Eretz Israel, arguing that '[King] Abdullah [of Transjordan] would not allow the Saudis to pass through his country, Iraq would only contribute money, and Egypt was not interested at all . . . Above all, the Arabs of Palestine don't want war.' He also told Herzog frankly that he did not believe in the possibility of a Jewish state. 'There are two possibilities – one, that you will have external problems, in which case the Haganah will join the dissidents [the Irgun and Lehi], and they will all go to hell together. The second possibility is that you'll have a civil war and finish each other off. So you don't stand a chance.'[14]

Two days later, Sherringham reversed his opinion and spoke about the bellicose intentions of Syria and Egypt, and the 'rivalry' over Palestine that might arise between them and other Arab states. In brief – war with the Arab countries was possible.[15] The day after the UN partition resolution he quibbled, 'This morning we analysed the UN resolution. Legally speaking, no decision has been taken to divide Palestine ... All the UN has done is recommend partition ... We'll see what the Security Council will do next week.'[16]

When they met two months later, Sherringham poked fun at two Haganah intelligence agents, Chaim Sacharov and Chaim Herzog (it is unclear whether he suspected Chaim's relationship with 'Harno') who were feeding the British misinformation about the Arabs, which he described as 'childish rumours and amateur speculation'. He also maintained that they (the Haganah intelligence officers) were 'utterly confused, mix up the names of villages, places and leaders,' and are quite incapable of understanding the real situation on the ground.[17]

Herzog mentioned the explosion in the offices of the daily newspaper *Palestine Post* in Jerusalem on 2 February 1948, which had been carried out by deserters from the British police and armed forces. He noted that British officers must have been involved. Sherringham retorted furiously that the Jews had in fact been responsible. It is thought, he said, 'that it was a Haganah vehicle packed with explosives ... There are some question marks about the whole affair ... First, grenades went off inside the building at the same time. Where did they come from? Second, how come the entire staff were outside when the bomb went off?'

Later, Sherringham maintained that the Palestinian Arabs were pulling themselves together and would fight hard if necessary.

'The [leaders of the] Jewish Agency have suddenly woken up from their dream, but they're still issuing ridiculous statements. Ben-Gurion said that he can hold the whole of Palestine, including the Arab parts. What's wrong with him? Sharett has more sense, he'll never say such things. As I told you a dozen times in the past nine months, the problem is that the Jewish Agency refuses to see the situation as it is. You laughed ... You've all become complacent under the leadership of the [Jewish] Agency. I think you have been so complacent, you haven't prepared properly [for war]. You'll soon see that the Arabs are quite serious. Then we'll see how serious the Agency's preparations have been.'

'Is it not possible that Britain will change her policy and adopt a positive attitude towards us? [Dr Chaim] Weizmann* thinks there's a chance this will happen,' argued Herzog.

'Weizmann is clever,' said Sherringham, 'but deep down he doesn't believe in partitioning the country.'

'You're talking nonsense,' Herzog snapped, momentarily losing his self-control.

'No,' Sherringham persisted. 'In his heart he doesn't believe in partition, or he wouldn't speak as he does.'[18]

He also dismissed Herzog's argument that the Palestinian Arabs were doing little to prepare for war. 'They're preparing in secret on a large scale. The Samaria triangle [a dense cluster of Arab villages] is under actual Arab military rule. Over there their units are organized in a military way, at least as well trained as the Haganah, and well disciplined. They are under strict instruction to keep their movements completely secret.' He revealed that sometime earlier the first Arab force had crossed the Jordan (this was the 'Army of Liberation', commanded by Fawzi al-Qawuqji, a leader of the Palestinian Arab Revolt of 1936), and now a second force had come over. 'The Arabs are preparing for a long war. They can afford it – they have vast lands behind them and can continue to pour in troops and armaments.'

* Later, first President of the State of Israel.

'If they are defeated in one decisive battle, that will be the end of it,' Herzog ventured to say.

Sherringham dismissed this out of hand. 'The delusion of the [leaders of the] Jewish Agency is that if they hold out for some time, the Arabs will be willing to come to an agreement. Hitler had a good many victories before his defeat in Russia – because Russia could afford to retreat. That's my opinion . . .'

They met again four days later, and Sherringham informed his young friend that while 'Abd al-Khader al-Husseini [the Mufti's nephew] is a very poor officer, Fawzi al-Qawuqji is a first-rate guerrilla general, and a very dangerous enemy.'[19]

'Would he be considered good in a European army?' asked Herzog.

'His expertise is guerrilla warfare. In that he's regarded as first-class, and will be similarly regarded in any army.'

'The Arabs don't have any first-class generals,' Herzog argued.

'Nor do the Jews. Both sides are amateurs, and as such they will wear each other out.'

Herzog asked Sherringham if the British authorities could not expel the 1,400 irregular Arab troops gathered around Nablus. Sherringham replied that there was no point, because others would come in their place. Anyhow, he added, 2,000 more had already crossed the Jordan. 'We've received a report that the first force brought heavy artillery. It's known that they have a large number of mortars. People who have seen the Arab Liberation Army say it's a very fine force, well disciplined and with excellent commanders.'

'The numbers are not very terrifying,' said Herzog.

But Sherringham was not about to be deflected from his pro-Arab position. 'That's just the nucleus of the force,' he said. 'Large numbers of volunteers are being mobilized now, and others will come across the Jordan.'

'How will they be supplied?'

'They've brought their own food,' Sherringham retorted, but

did not explain how an entire army could bring its own food supplies for months of prolonged fighting.

'I should think the Haganah will be able to block a force that size,' Herzog said.

'They'll soon be equal to the Palmah [the Haganah's commando force],' Sherringham continued. 'Their ultimate purpose is to create two parallel armies of 15,000 each, apart from their guerrilla forces.' He added that the Arabs would attack in the Galilee, the Negev and Jerusalem. The 'Muslim Brothers' of Egypt were about to attack in the Negev – they had already reached the area, he stated.

The item about the Muslim Brotherhood was one of the few real facts provided by Sherringham. He was also correct in his assessment that King Abdullah of Transjordan would be unable to sign a separate peace treaty with Israel.

But these few facts were overwhelmed by the flood of nonsense spouted by Sherringham to Herzog – for example, the likelihood of Arab military units being incorporated in the international force the UN would post in Jerusalem. If the UN did not include Arab units in this force, the Arabs would fight against the UN and leave it, along with most Asian states, including Turkey, Iran, Pakistan, India, and so on. He also discussed the international arena – 'You must understand,' he said to Herzog, 'that the objective factors militating against [the establishment of] a Jewish state are so powerful, that whoever tries to tackle the problem, no matter how well-intentioned, would have to withdraw his support from it.'

The only hope Sherringham could see on the Jewish side was the Brith Shalom group. 'The Magnes group is not as small as you think. But they're afraid of the Jewish Agency. If you believe Ben-Gurion, you'll have to fight.'

'Ben-Gurion said this week,' Herzog noted, 'that the Jews will carry the war beyond the boundaries of this country.'

'Yes, I read his speech. But he's a megalomaniac: nobody takes him seriously any more. Not even Sharett and Kaplan [of the Jewish Agency], who are serious men, talk as he does.'

Sherringham estimated that the war would last about two years. Some information about the strength of the Haganah must have reached him, because on this occasion he admitted to Herzog that if the Haganah built up a very large military force, it might achieve some 'brilliant victories', and may even 'repulse the Arabs quite significantly', but the Arabs will always regroup, because like the Russians, they had vast territories, and 'can afford to suffer temporary defeat, whereas the Jews do not'.

Herzog tried repeatedly to get Sherringham to talk about Jerusalem. Again and again he received extreme and biased replies. A few weeks before 'Operation Nachshon', in which thousands of fighters broke the siege of Jerusalem, Herzog told Sherringham, 'The Haganah can send 5,000 men from Tel Aviv and reopen the road.'[20]

'Again, your childish military calculations!' Sherringham said scornfully. '4,000 may reach Jerusalem, but the road will not be reopened. To assure a permanent safe passage, thousands of Haganah men would have to patrol the road and the surrounding hills. Where will you get them?' Sherringham predicted that the Haganah and Irgun forces in the Old City would be cut off and destroyed. 'You don't stand a chance. That's what will happen in other parts of Jerusalem, too. I can't understand how the Haganah believes it can hold on to Jewish Jerusalem. Their policy looks suicidal to me ... When we leave, how can the Haganah take our place? The possibility doesn't exist.'

Sherringham practically justified the Arab attacks on Jewish convoys to Mount Scopus and Hadassah Hospital.* He argued that the hospital was serving as a base from which Jews set out to kill Arab women and children. He found reasons to justify every

---

* The Hebrew University and Hadassah Hospital, both located on Mount Scopus, in Jerusalem, were surrounded by Arab villages and cut off from their supply routes.

attack by Arabs on Jews. When Herzog mentioned the Arab attack on the oil refineries, Sherringham replied, 'The Haganah does the same thing every week or two. The Haganah [fighters] ... are no better than the terrorists. They're murderers of women and children. We can prove it.'

Herzog returned to the subject of Jerusalem. 'What if the siege of Jerusalem becomes unbearable – what should the Jews do?'

'No one in Palestine can save you. You'd have to fly to Cairo and seek terms of surrender for the city from the Mufti.'

'What will he demand?'

'Recognition of Jerusalem as the capital of the Arab state. He's the only one capable of making peace with you.'

'And what if the Jewish defence forces refuse?'

'The Jewish peace camp will either have to suppress them, or accept the total annihilation [of the Jews].'

Finally Herzog asked Sherringham, 'What would you do if you were a Jew?'

'Go abroad. It's my advice to you as a friend.'[21]

Two weeks later Sherringham declared, '[Jewish] Jerusalem is doomed.'[22]

Sherringham's extreme bias distorted his assessments of other fronts, making his opinions equally worthless.

'It seems that there has been a turning-point favouring the [Jewish] Agency,' Herzog said on another occasion.[23] They were talking about the battle at Tirat Zvi, in February 1948, in which Qawuqji's forces were defeated and suffered hundreds of casualties.

'Our information says the turning-point is in the opposite direction,' Sherringham retorted.

'... A few more defeats like Tirat Zvi, and the Arabs will surrender,' Herzog said.

'Nonsense. They learned tactics in that attack.' Sherringham explained that the Arabs had stopped their assault when a British officer on the spot told them that 'he had seen a white flag being prepared under the roof of the watchtower of Tirat Zvi'.

'You're joking!' Herzog snapped.

'Word of honour – that's the report we got ... The Arab detachment was part of the Liberation Army, but it was very foolish of them to launch their first battle in Tirat Zvi.'

'Do the Arabs believe the casualty figures published in their newspapers?'

'Yes.'

'The Haganah broadcasts in Arabic deny them.'

'If the Haganah radio says one thing and Damascus radio says another – whom do you think the Arabs will believe?'

Sherringham's stories sometimes recalled those of Baron Munchhausen. He claimed that: the Mufti, who had been Hitler's faithful ally during the war, had changed his position and was now a friend of the British; Turkish officers had already arrived in Palestine and were training the 'Liberation Army' in the Nablus area; Pakistan was getting ready to send volunteers and armed forces; large quantities of arms, vehicles and aircraft were on their way to reinforce the Arabs; no state would recognize the government of the Jewish state, its ships would not be protected by law and would be attacked and sunk by the Arab forces; and that Harry Truman would not be re-elected President of the United States because of his Middle East policy. Sherringham repeatedly tried to scare the wits out of his Jewish friend.

On 22 April 1948, after the Haganah had scored a number of victories, the two met again. Sherringham was clearly embarrassed because his predictions had been disproved. He conceded that 'the Arabs [referring to the Palestinian Arabs and Qawuqji's forces] had not proved themselves as expected', but because they were weak, there was a greater likelihood that other Arab armies would join the war. He repeated his prediction that after a year or two of fighting, 'you will be defeated, like Napoleon and Hitler in Russia'. He also assured Herzog that Moshe Sneh (a former head of the Haganah and a political maverick, with Zionist right-wing inclinations at the time), would try to carry out a putsch and seize power in the Jewish state ('there were many such types in Germany before Hitler'), and announced, 'I've no doubt that there will be a civil war in Jewish Palestine.'[24]

In the final analysis, the most significant piece of information that Sherringham passed to Herzog, was that the British had really resolved to leave Palestine on the date set by the UN. It may also have been thanks to Sherringham that Yaacov Herzog learned that the British authorities, as he reported to his superiors, would quit Jerusalem not on 15 May 1948, as expected, but a day earlier.[25] This was crucial to the Haganah who were able to move in and occupy all the government premises in Jerusalem as soon as the British evacuated them.

Although in practical terms there was little value in the information Herzog obtained, his work in the underground strengthened his position among the Yishuv leadership and opened new horizons for him. After all, the Chief Rabbi's son had snared a senior British source, analysed his character shrewdly and handled him adroitly. Yaacov was attracted to such secretive work, which entailed personal danger, forethought, conspiratorial skills, psychological understanding and a battle of wits. His discovery of this talent for intelligence work would later bear important fruit for the State of Israel.

Alex Keynan was transferred to Haganah headquarters while Operation Sherringham was at its peak, and he and Malka had to leave Jerusalem. The night before they left Yaacov came to say goodbye. Malka asked him anxiously, 'What's going to happen?'

Yaacov replied, 'There will be a miracle.'

When they met again after the War of Independence, Yaacov said to them, 'There was a miracle.'[26]

5

Redeeming Lands in Jerusalem

On the 13th day of Nissan, in the year 5708, according to the Hebrew calendar, or 22 April 1948 in the Gregorian calendar, as battles raged all over the country and around Jerusalem, Rabbi Isser Zalman Melzer sat at his desk with a sheet of paper bearing his name and title.

Rabbi Melzer, a renowned rabbinic figure and head of the famous Etz Hayim Yeshiva in Jerusalem, wrote, 'I hereby speak the praise and glory of the dear rabbi, the worthy, brilliant, scholarly, fine and cultivated Rabbi Yaacov Herzog, long may he live, the son of my friend the great master of Torah, our teacher Rabbi Yitzhak Isaac Halevi Herzog, long and good may his days be, amen, whom I know to be excellently gifted. We regularly study in company every week, and I enjoy his excellent comments as we study; therefore I raise my hand to ordain him in the ordination of Sages, to teach his teaching and judge his judgements in accordance with the Law and the Torah . . . '

The wording was unusual, as rabbis were usually ordained with the words 'to teach his teaching', whereas Rabbi Melzer added the rare appreciative note, 'judge his judgements'. He also added a sentence embodying the hopes that many, including himself, placed in the young rabbi: 'He will yet rise higher and higher to be a great master of Torah in Israel and conduct God's congregation to the founts of Torah and faith . . . '[1]

Thus Yaacov Herzog was formally ordained as a rabbi, to his parents' great pride and joy. It was another stage in the fulfilment of his destiny, as he had been chosen to continue the glorious heritage of both parents' dynasties, and be a great scholar and rabbinic authority. It seemed like a natural and inevitable development, since he was already known as a genius. Rabbi Melzer himself, who so admired his brilliant student, would record Yaacov's original commentary in the margins of his Talmud, noting, 'Thus said to me R.Y.D.' (Rabbi Yaacov David).[2] Yaacov's future path seemed clear and promising.

He was ordained in the midst of the war of 1948, while preoccupied with 'Operation Sherringham' and writing reports about the attitudes of the world powers to the Israeli-Palestinian conflict. The timing of his ordination symbolized the dual nature of his personality; his profound involvement in religious study which never faltered even in those stormy days, and his intensive, secretive work in both the political and intelligence fields.

Although he had been addressed as 'rabbi' for a long time, due to his scholarly qualities and the major role he played at his father's side, it was only now that he became officially and legally a rabbi. For a while he used the title 'Rav' (rabbi in Hebrew) in his official correspondence, especially after the establishment of the State and his appointment to a senior position in the Ministry of Religious Affairs. In the following few years he signed his letters, Rabbi Yaacov Herzog, but later dropped the title and never used it again. His ordination was expected to be the start of a rabbinic career as his father's successor – but this was not to be.

'It was not easy for Yaacov to depart from the precinct of the Torah,' said Abba Eban years later, 'and launch himself into the challenges and tests of the political struggle. The Holocaust and the danger which threatened the Jewish community in Eretz Israel compelled him to forego the rabbinic, scholarly side of his personality and devote himself to every stage of the struggle.'[3]

While Yaacov did not take part in any of the IDF's actual battles during the War of Independence, the political analyses he submitted to Colonel Binyamin Gibli in Jerusalem were recognized as military service during the siege of the city.⁴ The IDF regarded him as having been on active duty for seven months.⁵ For a while longer he continued to work at the Fischel Institute which had published his Mishnah translation.⁶ In July 1948 he was appointed head of the department of Christian Communities in the newly-created Ministry of Religious Affairs, headed by Rabbi Yehuda Leib Fishman-Maimon.

In retrospect, it could be argued that Yaacov had made the wrong choice. His exceptional talents and the experience of the previous year had made him a perfect candidate for Israel's intelligence community, which was where his brother Vivian (Chaim) found himself. He might also have joined the team that set up and established Israel's Foreign Ministry, headed by Moshe Shertok (Sharett), who had known and respected him for years. The Ministry of Religious Affairs looked like a dead end, and was already seen as tainted with religious politicking. Yaacov seemed over-qualified for his post and some claim that he disliked working there.⁷

However, these impressions were misleading. His new post enabled Yaacov to deal with matters of decisive importance to the State, and it is doubtful if anyone else could have done so as effectively. There is no doubt that Yaacov regarded the work as extremely important, and that he performed it brilliantly. This unique post called for diplomatic skills, extensive knowledge of the political world and its historical hinterland, familiarity with Christianity's various churches and movements, and a high degree of personal credibility. In all probability he opted for this post because it combined his two principal interests – religion and diplomacy.

Senior officials in the Ministry of Religious Affairs appreciated the importance of the department, in that it held 'a potential of influence and action that goes beyond the narrow administrative work, e.g., ... supervision of religious courts, houses of worship and education, holy places and the religious interests of all

Christian communities.' They focused mainly on the department's 'field of political work', which called for close coordination with, and direction from, the Foreign Ministry.[8]

The Ministry's director-general, D. Weiss, set a number of objectives for the department: to foster good relations with Christian communities in Israel in order to strengthen the country's international standing; to build bridges with various church authorities throughout the world which might help the Foreign Ministry after independence; to protect the interests of Jewish communities abroad by creating a good rapport with various churches; to build links with Christian churches in neighbouring countries through their clergy in Israel; to establish a system of observers (later to be attachés) in principal Christian centres such as Rome, Moscow, Buenos Aires, London and Washington.[9]

Weiss presented to Moshe Sharett, the Foreign Minister, his ambitious plan for the new department headed by Rabbi Yaacov Herzog. He proposed that the department cooperate with the Foreign Ministry, since Herzog had 'for several years been in contact, on behalf of the Chief Rabbinate, with representatives of the churches in the East and in Europe, on missions saving Jews, and other national causes'.

Sharett fully endorsed the proposal and thought so highly of it, that he designated the director-general of the Foreign Ministry to be his liaison with Yaacov Herzog's department.[10]

Yaacov Herzog's work was, indeed, largely diplomatic. He met heads of the churches in Jerusalem, Jaffa and the Galilee, and visited the heads of the various communities and the abbots of the monasteries. He also held discussions with ambassadors and consuls-general of governments which had a special interest in the Catholic and Orthodox churches in Israel – in particular Italy, Spain, France, Greece and the United States. The symbolism of his role as a religious Jew, rabbi and son of a rabbi, representing the Jewish state to the Christian world, and to the Vatican in particular, did not escape Yaacov. The leading authorities of the Christian world, which had for centuries despised and humiliated Jews, now had to negotiate with a young rabbi about matters close to their hearts – the status of Christianity and its representatives in the Holy Land, and the future of the holy city of Jerusalem.

'In the process,' recalled the former Minister of Religious Affairs, Zerach Warhaftig,[11] 'it became clear that a religious Jew could deal with [the Christian representatives] far better than anyone else. Firstly, [because] he is not intimidated ... Here was a young man, imbued with Jewish and general culture, fluent in several languages, face to face with the leaders of the Christian world, who found a way to communicate with them. He surprised them with his high level of culture, and could discuss spiritual and religious matters with them on a level that appealed to them ... There was a Jewish distinctiveness about him. He had self-respect as well as respect for the other religions ... Thus he helped create Jewish-Christian dialogue on a basis of equality and mutual respect. Indeed, that is the way a Jewish state can communicate with the Christian world.'

Yaacov had to devote much of his time to an unpleasant problem that arose during the War of Independence – namely, the desecration of churches and monasteries by IDF soldiers, the looting of their properties, and offensive misuse of their premises.[12] Such abuse had occurred in many places throughout the war, and fed hostile anti-Israel propaganda by Catholic forces in Europe and the United States, encouraged by the Arab states. Herzog threw himself into the fray, dealt with each case separately, met representatives of the affected churches, ensured the return of stolen properties, placated offended clergy, and obtained compensation and financial aid to restore damaged buildings. He maintained direct contact with IDF officers, and demanded repeatedly that they supervise and protect Christian religious premises. He initiated the posting of special liaison officers in the army units that controlled monasteries and churches; drafted precise and reliable responses to hostile statements; and manoeuvred between protecting the interests of the Russian Orthodox Church in Israel and fending off accusations by certain American circles which claimed that he was helping the USSR in the Cold War. He also encouraged visits by leading churchmen from abroad, to see for themselves that the state of the holy places was far better than the image depicted by hostile propaganda.

Herzog gradually succeeded in assuaging the Churches' anxieties until the issue faded from the headlines. He obtained letters from senior figures in different churches congratulating Israel on her efforts to repair damages and maintain good relations with the foreign religious institutions in her territory.[13] He also received foreign correspondents, dealt skilfully with their questions, and convinced them of Israel's goodwill and liberal policies.[14] He developed especially good relations with representatives of foreign churches in Jerusalem. His wartime experience and past contacts with church figures, particularly with the Vatican, were of great help. But the churchmen were also greatly impressed by him. 'He had a profound appreciation of the Greek spirit,' recalled the Greek Orthodox Patriarch Benedictus of Jerusalem. 'He admired Aristotle and Thucydides. He frequently found points in common between the Greek and the Jewish nations, both of whom had given the world the light of civilization, yet suffered greatly throughout their histories ... He treated our Patriarchate with interest and respect, and always spoke lovingly and admiringly about the Greek Orthodox church in Jerusalem.'[15]

Yaacov also urged the government to permit the return of Archbishop Hakim, the head of the Maronite Christian community, who had been deported in the early days of the war after he provoked public anger in Israel with his hostile remarks against the Jewish state.[16] The initiative to permit the Archbishop's return came from the Minister of Police, Bekhor Shalom Shitreet, considered an expert on Arab affairs. Hakim was allowed to return and carried out his duties successfully. He even appeared beside Herzog at a press conference with foreign correspondents, to dispel rumours of anti-Israel propaganda. The journalists reported on Hakim's return and his freedom of movement and expression as proof of the Israeli government's openness and respect for human rights.[17] In later years Herzog would benefit from Hakim's help in his secret initiatives (see chapter 12).

This was the first time that Yaacov worked with a large number of people, in daily contact with dozens of Jews and Christians, government officials and ministers, diplomats and military brass. He made a strong and favourable impression on his colleagues. 'He was the youngest of all of us,' recalled his colleague Yaacov Yehoshua, 'which is why we liked him and boasted about him. We admired his vast knowledge and broad education. He couldn't stand pointless arguments ... Sometimes we saw him in his office, alone, smoking, deep in thought. When he joined the group travelling from IDF headquarters, in Tel Aviv, to Jerusalem along the 'Burma Road',* which took hours, he would sit in a corner of the car, poring over a Mishnah text.[18]

'... The old Minister [of Religious Affairs], Y. L. Maimon, used to consult him not only about non-Jews, but also about Jewish affairs ... He was the Minister's favourite as well as his advisor.'[19]

Yaacov also advised many other government officials and public figures, who always sought his opinion on various matters. His warmth, openness and humanity made those who talked to him feel a sense of closeness and elation. Later they would eagerly repeat what Yaacov had said.

According to Yaacov Yehoshua, Herzog was not 'an office type', and differed from his colleagues. When asked for his opinion, he would shut himself in his office to think. Only rarely did they see him writing; he usually dictated his letters and memoranda to a secretary, in excellent Hebrew but with an English accent. 'I rarely saw him smile. He was always serious

---

* A secondary route to Jerusalem to by-pass the besieged main road.

and thoughtful, and when he presented his argument he spoke warmly and cordially. Sometimes he snapped, but he quickly came around.'[20] Although a man of religion, dealing daily with religious matters, his moderation and tolerance deeply impressed foreign visitors. An American journalist in Israel once invited him to lunch at his house, where his wife served pork. 'Yaacov saw the food, politely declined the dish offered him, and withdrew with me to another room. I cracked a joke about the pork, and Yaacov responded in a similar vein.'[21] The Patriarch Benedictus was also impressed by Yaacov's quiet, understated observance. 'He was strictly observant,' Benedictus wrote. 'He never drank anything without covering his head.'[22]

Israel's relations with the Vatican were one of Yaacov's main responsibilities in his new post. The Catholic Church refused to recognize the State of Israel as long as the problem of Jerusalem was not settled to its satisfaction – namely, by its internationalization, with a central role for the Vatican. The US Ambassador to Israel, James McDonald, stopped in Rome en route to Israel and tried to persuade the Pope to receive Chaim Weizmann, Israel's President. 'Not only did the Pope refuse to see Dr Weizmann,' McDonald told Yaacov Herzog, 'he criticized the US government which had seen fit to recognize Israel while continuing to withhold diplomatic recognition from the Vatican ... The Pope said repeatedly that regardless of Israel's constitutional, spiritual and political structure, recognizing it would mean [the Vatican's] acquiescence in the independence of Israel in the Holy Land.'[23]

In the autumn of 1948 Yaacov and his advisor, Dr Chaim Vardi, travelled secretly to Rome, to meet the Pope's Foreign Secretary and personal advisor.[24] The meetings were extraordinary: for the first time in its history, the Vatican had to negotiate its status in the Holy Land with Orthodox Jews who were ruling the country. 'I entered the office of the Vatican's Minister of the Interior,' Herzog recalled a few years later. 'He said, "Gentlemen, I hear you arrived from Palestine three days ago." We said, "We came from Israel three days ago." The words stuck in our throat. We were left speechless when we realized what we had just said – that after two thousand years we were the first to enter this global fortress and say, Gentlemen, something has happened in history, there has been a change, we come from Israel.'²⁵ Yaacov Herzog, aged only 27, was seized with a sense of history when he came to negotiate with the Vatican on behalf of the State of Israel. When he met the Vatican's Foreign Minister, he said, 'Don't see me as a young man – I carry thousands of years of Jewish suffering on my shoulders.'²⁶

The question of Jerusalem, which both the UN and the Vatican wanted to place under international rule, was the main topic of the meetings. The two sides did not reach an agreement, but the Vatican did soften its position. This led to a significant improvement in the relations between the Vatican and Israel. The senior churchmen promised Herzog that the Holy See would be neutral in the Jewish-Arab conflict.²⁷

'He returned from Rome full of optimism,' recalled Boris Guriel, now of the Foreign Ministry. '[He said that] this whole project of internationalizing Jerusalem, which the United Nations was about to adopt, would never be implemented ... I immediately wired this to Sharett in Lake Success [the seat of the UN at the time], and his response was very sceptical.' But Herzog stood his ground. He quoted the prophet Isaiah: '[All ye of far countries ...] Take counsel together and it shall come to nought.' Guriel kept exchanging telegrams with Sharett, until the latter responded impatiently, 'Stop your Talmudic hair-splitting!' ²⁸

As it turned out, Herzog was right. Sharett was impressed by his intelligence and achievements, and praised his visit to the Vatican. He wired Walter Eytan, director-general of the Foreign Ministry, 'I'm impressed with Herzog's report. Believe he has shown gravity, dignity and diplomatic ability. Did good work on the ground ... Important that Foreign Ministry regard the mission as its own and follow it up ... '²⁹ (This telegram contradicts the historians who argue that Herzog had been sent to Rome by Moshe Sharett. In fact, Sharett and the Foreign Ministry adopted Herzog's mission after it had succeeded.) Sharett instructed the director-general of the Foreign Ministry to give Herzog and his advisor Vardi all the necessary assistance.

On the same trip Herzog had also stopped in Paris to meet Archbishop Roncalli, now papal nuncio, whom he had met in Turkey during the war. Roncalli was known for his efforts to save Jews from the Nazis, but he was not typical of the Church of Rome, and his war-time activities were the exception. On his visit to the Vatican Herzog got the impression that 'Roncalli has little influence in the [Vatican] Foreign Ministry.'[30]

But five years later Roncalli's influence increased dramatically. As Pope John XXIII, he changed the Vatican's rigid attitude towards the State of Israel. Moshe Sharett at the Knesset Foreign Affairs and Security Committee, lavished praise on Yaacov Herzog. 'I must note the considerable progress in our relations with the Vatican's representatives in Israel,' he said, 'and with the heads of the Catholic Church, and with the Greek and Maronite churches which adhere to Rome ... Much of the achievement in this area is due to Yaacov Herzog, one of the most important people at the Ministry of Religious Affairs, who combines a diligent mind with the gift of diplomacy – a precious asset for the State and its diplomatic activity on this front.'[31]

His work at the Ministry of Religious Affairs revealed yet another dimension of Yaacov Herzog – not just the wise young scholar, whose intellect embraced different worlds, but also an efficient and thorough manager who successfully steered his department. His diplomatic qualities and personal charm suffused with wisdom, the ability to communicate and sense of humour, all added up to an irresistible charismatic personality. 'It did not take much imagination,' wrote Avraham Avihai, 'to see the bright youthful face, the friendly blue-grey eyes, the high forehead, which hid – and at times revealed – a computer-like brain, taking part in endless discussions in church offices and corridors, explaining, complimenting, persuading, debating, and always with humour, always with enthusiasm rooted in faith. It seemed he was always on the way to or from a meeting, but always calm and fully absorbed in the issue at hand, as though nothing else mattered.'[32]

But there was another matter which Yaacov valued even more than relations with the Christian communities, and to which he devoted no less time and effort – that of Jerusalem.

'Yaacov was perhaps the greatest redeemer of land Jerusalem has ever known,' Teddy Kollek said years later,[33] disclosing a hidden aspect of Yaacov Herzog's work for the city he loved. In 1949–50 Yaacov Herzog quietly negotiated the purchase of extensive plots of land in West Jerusalem from the foreign churches that owned them. Many of these plots were 'what is called in legal terms "dead spaces", belonging to churches which did not need them and had no use for them.'[34] He manoeuvred skilfully, shrewdly and sometimes cynically among the different sects and religious institutions. The main transactions were with the heads of the Greek Orthodox Church, with whom he cleverly cultivated good relations. He acceded to their financial demands and assisted them in matters concerning their church properties, and was regarded by them as a good friend. 'We knew Yaacov,' Patriarch Benedictus wrote to Pnina Herzog, 'when ... we negotiated the lease of the lands of the Monastery of the Holy Cross and western Nikiphoria to the Jewish National Fund*. We deeply respected Yaacov as an intellectual and jurist, rabbi and diplomat, a man who stood for international understanding and world peace ... He was scrupulously honest, an excellent negotiator and a very good friend.'[35] Yaacov Yehoshua witnessed some of the land transactions. 'Once when the treasurer of the [Greek Orthodox] Patriarchate, Benedictus [later the Patriarch] was about to come to

---

* The Zionist organization responsible for land acquisition and development.

Redeeming Lands in Jerusalem

the Ministry of Religious Affairs, [Yaacov Herzog] asked me not to go home for lunch, as he was expecting an important visitor and would need me.'[36] Benedictus spoke some Arabic and Herzog needed Yehoshua as an interpreter. But this was an excuse. The negotiations were at a very sensitive stage, and 'I suppose he needed time to think while negotiating, which is why he asked me to translate what he said.'[37] Herzog also invited the head of the Greek Orthodox Church in Athens, Patriarch Timotheos, to come to Israel, and obtained a positive response to his request to purchase land.[38]

Herzog gradually negotiated the acquisition of large tracts of land from the churches, including the area of Givat Ram, later the site of the new Hebrew University campus, the Israel Museum and government ministries. An important stage in the secret negotiations with the Greek Orthodox Church was concluded successfully on 15 November 1951;[39] three days later he began negotiating the purchase of additional properties.[40]

Initially, the agreement with the Greeks was for annual leases. In addition, Yaacov Herzog purchased land and buildings from the Lutheran church in Jerusalem.[41] But he had to fight the state authorities, especially the Ministry of Finance, to obtain funds for these purchases. This was Israel's most difficult period economically, and the poverty-stricken state was hard pressed to finance Herzog's ambitious plans. But he did not weary of appealing to the Ministry of Finance, and warned the Minister, Eliezer Kaplan, that Israel might miss an historic opportunity.

A few months later, negotiations with the Greeks moved into the decisive stage of converting the leases into a kind of outright purchase. Herzog sent a top secret letter to the Minister of Finance: 'One of the principal elements in our international struggle against the UN decision to internationalize Jerusalem,' he wrote, '... is the secret understanding between us and the Greek Patriarchate.' Under the agreement Herzog had made with the Greek Church, the Patriarch informed the UN of his 'satisfaction with the existing state of affairs in Jerusalem'. In return, Israel undertook to protect the Greek Orthodox community in Jerusalem, to free its properties from the supervision by the Custodian of Absentee-owned Properties, and to pay a monthly fee of 1,500 lira in foreign currency, remitted to the Old City.

The Greeks subsequently agreed to lease the State of Israel extensive land in Jerusalem for 100 years for an annual fee. It now became possible, Yaacov Herzog wrote, to convert the annual payment of 170,000 lira to a one-time payment, which would not only eliminate the monthly payments but would also strengthen the Greek Orthodox Church and help it in its fight against the dangerous infiltration of communists into its ranks. This would be Israel's contribution to the Cold War efforts of the United States. 'In spite of the difficulties the State has in obtaining hard currency,' he concluded, 'it seems the historic opportunity opening before us must not be missed. There is no telling if after a while, even a short time, the situation in the Old City will allow the Greeks to make us the offer they are making now.'[42]

Herzog's efforts eventually succeeded and in 1952 he completed the largest land purchase in Jerusalem.[43] 'What is so interesting,' said the journalist Moshe Zack, 'is that this man, who was primarily an intellectual, was able to conduct such practical and complex negotiations. In effect, it was he who ensured that the centre of Jerusalem would be in Jewish possession.'[44] There are estimates that during that period Yaacov Herzog acquired about one-sixth of the area of Jerusalem for the State.[45]

Herzog's practical endeavours on behalf of the city, together with his profound awareness of its spiritual value, were typical of his distinctive perception of the city. 'Jerusalem is Jerusalem,' he said. 'The only city in the world, the only place that connotes at the same time earthly as well as sublime concepts, beyond time.'[46]

Apart from the secret manoeuvring for land in Jerusalem, Yaacov Herzog was also engaged in the public and fateful struggle over

Redeeming Lands in Jerusalem

the city's future status. In the ongoing debate about it at the UN, many states, Christian and others, urged the implementation of the 'Jerusalem clause' in the 1947 Partition Resolution – namely, internationalization. The plan's most ardent supporter was the Church of Rome, which hoped to play an active role in the governance of the internationalized city. Its position was supported by Catholic states, and those with a substantial Catholic minority, while other countries were motivated by political considerations.

Yaacov was convinced that internationalizing Jerusalem would be a disaster, and should be prevented at all cost. He discussed this with Ben-Gurion and found himself in complete agreement with the Prime Minister. He often told his friends about Ben-Gurion's meeting with the Vatican's representative, the American Monsignor McMahon, in his room at the Eden Hotel in Jerusalem. The Monsignor spoke at length about the Vatican's position on Jerusalem.

'I don't understand you,' said Ben-Gurion. McMahon repeated his speech all over again.

'I do not understand you,' Ben-Gurion said again.

McMahon lost patience. 'The Prime Minister does not understand English?' he asked.

Ben-Gurion replied, 'I don't understand you. After all, we, the Jewish people, were in Jerusalem long before your Church came into being. In fact, it was born 2,000 years ago in Jerusalem, among the Jewish people, fairly late in our history. Now the Christian world expects us to agree to turn the city, which we have sanctified as our eternal spiritual inspiration, into a Christian city?'[47] Ehud Avriel remembered the 'pride and joy' with which Yaacov Herzog repeated Ben-Gurion's words. 'Yaacov was wholeheartedly in accord with this attitude, which he saw as proof that Ben-Gurion was a "completely liberated Jew". Obviously, he was implying that he regarded himself as an equally liberated Jew.'[48]

It was only natural that Yaacov Herzog would be the one to report to President Weizmann on these developments. Yaacov observed the old and ailing Weizmann with admiration mingled with sadness. 'When [the President] spoke about Jerusalem,' he noted, 'its place in Jewish and world history and its resurrection as the capital of renewed Israel, it seemed to be the focus of his deepest thoughts about his personal history and his role in re-uniting his people in their ancient homeland. When he spoke in his quiet office, or during his afternoon stroll in the spacious gardens surrounding his residence, he continued to address the world. At the same time, he was absorbed in inward contemplation, trying to define the nature and motive of the issue for which he had campaigned for decades.

'In those days Dr Weizmann walked slowly, his speech sometimes slurred, his eyesight failing. Nevertheless, his physical frailty did not dim his forceful personality, his natural dignity, his firmness and nobility of soul.'[49]

Yaacov was fighting for Jerusalem on all fronts, and his work was highly appreciated. When the UN adopted the resolution to internationalize the city, Boris Guriel, the Foreign Ministry official who had received Yaacov's first report about his mission to the Vatican, called him and asked in Yiddish, '*Vos tut men?*' – Now what do we do?

'Herzog said, "Very simple, we go to Ben-Gurion and try to persuade him to move the government to Jerusalem." I [Guriel] replied, "I'm not going to Ben-Gurion." It seemed so absurd, so illogical, after that decision at the UN! That morning all the papers here and abroad came out with headlines: "Jerusalem internationalized!" "The United Nations have decided!" "We are finished with Jerusalem!" "Jerusalem not ours!"

'He [Herzog] went to Ben-Gurion. I didn't go. I didn't have the guts, I didn't dare. I was afraid Ben-Gurion would throw me out, and say, Get out of here! What are these fantasies? To tell the truth, I was afraid. But Herzog went.'[50]

That week Ben-Gurion moved the seat of the Israeli government to Jerusalem. 'It was Ben-Gurion's personal decision,' Guriel stated, 'to respond in this way to the UN resolution on Jerusalem. But I think that Yaacov had a considerable share in that decision.'[51]

In October 1949, Yaacov was appointed advisor on religious affairs to Moshe Sharret, the Foreign Minister.[52] In June 1951, he was appointed the Minister's special advisor on Jerusalem.[53] In March 1952, at the initiative of the Foreign Ministry, Herzog was put in charge of a special department for Jerusalem affairs in the Ministry of Religious Affairs, established to implement the government's policy on the city.[54] In this role, he was attached to the committees preparing Israel's position for the UN debates, contributing his authoritative knowledge and diplomatic skill. He often took part in high-level meetings at the Foreign Ministry, where Moshe Sharett made use of his counsel and assistance, and had him write speeches and letters for him. Thus Herzog became one of the Foreign Ministry's senior officials, a kind of 'adopted son', though formally not a member of its staff. Sharett kept in close touch with him. 'Please come at once to New York!' he wired Herzog in November 1949, when Jerusalem's internationalization was due to be debated.[55] In fact, Yaacov was attached to Israel's UN delegation, after he had paid another secret visit to Athens and the Vatican, and later, in 1950, was among those responsible for Israel's international information campaign regarding Jerusalem. He also published a booklet entitled 'Jerusalem, a Living City', presenting the Jewish people's stand on the Holy City.

Before the UN debate, Yaacov held lengthy meetings with the leaders of the various Christian communities in Israel and persuaded the Eastern churches to support Israel at the UN. At a certain stage he drove a wedge between the Greek Orthodox church and the Vatican, by describing to the Greeks how the Church of Rome would dominate Jerusalem if the UN decided on internationalization. He gave the Eastern churches various benefits, freed the properties of the Armenian and Greek Orthodox churches from the supervision by the Custodian of Absentee-owned Properties, and allowed them to transfer funds to the Old

City and abroad,[56] in return for their support on Jerusalem.[57] 'In this way,' he wrote to the Foreign Minister, 'it may be possible to rally the support of the Greeks and Copts as well [as the Armenians] for the UN General Assembly [debate].'[58] His efforts brought positive results, and the heads of the Coptic, Armenian and Greek Orthodox churches wrote to the UN Secretary General, backing Israel's objection to the internationalization of Jerusalem.[59] He held up approval of the Armenians' financial transactions for a few months, as a subtle warning that these could be stopped if the Armenians failed to keep their promise to support Israel's position.[60] In fact, the Armenians kept their promise and abandoned the 'two-faced' attitude they had maintained till 1950. 'It seems that the shrewdest oriental merchants,' Herzog noted cynically, 'have concluded that Israel has returned to Jerusalem for good.'[61]

Yaacov 'detested' the activities of Christian missionaries in Israel, but avoided taking strong measures against them as long as the UN debate continued. It was important to him that Israel project an image of openness and complete religious tolerance.[62] 'Our hands are tied to some extent,' he admitted frankly, 'because of the struggle for international recognition of Jerusalem as the capital of Israel.'[63] But he jealously defended the honour of the Jewish state. In his letters to heads of churches he always used the Hebrew date, followed by the Gregorian date in brackets.[64] Years later, when negotiating with the Vatican about the status of the holy places following the 1967 Six Day War (Herzog was then director-general of the Prime Minister's office), he refused to use the title 'Sacra Congregatione' preferred by the Vatican's Foreign Ministry. He explained that there was no Hebrew equivalent for 'sacred congregation', since only Jewish institutions could be sacred and he insisted on removing the adjective 'sacred' from the Vatican's definition. The crisis escalated, and the historic, first joint statement to be issued by the Foreign Ministries of both Israel and the Vatican was almost aborted. Finally, the Vatican

Redeeming Lands in Jerusalem

acceded to Herzog's demand, and Monsignor Felici, the representative of the Church's Foreign Ministry, agreed to have his office demoted to a mere 'congregation'.[65]

When Herzog visited Rome some time later, he found that the senior Vatican leadership still showed him great respect. Out of appreciation for his 'intelligence, charm and sense of humour', and for the easier relations Herzog had established between the Church and Israel, the Vatican's Foreign Minister, Monsignor Casaroli, accepted an invitation for coffee at the Israeli Embassy. The meeting went very well, and at the end Yaacov smilingly expressed his appreciation. 'I'm glad I drank only my favourite drink, tea. After all, tea is a much more Jewish drink than coffee, which is, after all, the Romans' favourite drink.'[66]

From the moment he entered the Foreign Ministry, Yaacov was completely at home in the world of diplomacy. In discussions and conversations, and in his letters to Israel's representatives abroad, he drew on his vast knowledge of customs and protocol, and showed a fine understanding of the minds and motives of foreign leaders. Even when writing to people senior in age and status, his telegrams were quietly authoritative. He issued directives, analysed and criticized reports from the world's capitals, encouraged or discouraged ambassadors' proposed initiatives — all not as a 30-year old, but as a veteran diplomat.

Yet the smiling, courteous external persona hid a strong, stubborn character. Yaacov was capable of fighting implacably for objectives he believed important. Thus, when he thought it necessary to dispatch staff to South America to promote Israel's position on Jerusalem, he brought it up repeatedly before the heads of the Foreign Ministry. Moshe Sharett objected and Yaacov appeared to submit;[67] but in the end the delegation was sent and Herzog won. Likewise, when outsiders, no matter how senior, tried to question the right of the Jewish people to the country and Jerusalem, he stood up to them. At the Maronite Archbishop

Hakim's house in Haifa he clashed sharply with the Vatican's representative, Monsignor McMahon. Herzog demolished McMahon's arguments against Israel one by one, until even Hakim rebutted some of the accusations made by the visitor. When the argument about Jerusalem grew heated, McMahon spoke angrily about 'Zionist agents' who had sabotaged the implementation of the 1947 and 1949 UN resolutions to internationalize Jerusalem, about the pressure that Israeli 'agents' had applied to America's UN delegation, and about how 'Zionist propagandists' had misled Catholic representatives. He even threatened to rally the support of 30 million American Catholics to pressure the US government.[68] But Herzog held his ground, and re-affirmed strongly Israel's right to Jerusalem and the impracticality of the proposed internationalization.

'By now [McMahon's] face was very red, his gaze wandering and violent, his fists clenched,' Herzog wrote. 'Toohey [a representative of the US Embassy, who was present] was leaning forward and clasping his knees, and Hakim's face was ashen. I was also quite agitated, and said to [McMahon], that being familiar with history, he must be aware of our suffering through the ages. We paid for our admission to the family of nations with blood and tears. The State of Israel represents the consolation of Providence to our tormented people. Why could he not leave us in peace?'[69]

Deeply moved, Moshe Sharett wrote Yaacov a personal letter. 'I was intensely absorbed by your report on the conversation with McMahon. I had not read such an instructive document for a long time. I congratulate you on your powerful debating points, and on the thoughtful presentation of your report ... Please send a copy of the report to the Prime Minister and make sure he reads it.'[70]

Throughout 1951–3 Herzog was occupied with the Foreign Ministry's move to Jerusalem and the world's reaction to it. Israel was especially worried that the Vatican would mount a diplomatic and propaganda campaign against the move, and no one was better qualified than Yaacov Herzog to deal with it.[71] After his

Redeeming Lands in Jerusalem

appointment as advisor at the Foreign Ministry, he left the Christian communities department at the Ministry of Religious Affairs, though he continued to serve as advisor on Jerusalem. Yaacov took with him the political aspects of his work with the Christian churches, especially the Vatican, to his new post, leaving behind a less interesting department at the Ministry of Religious Affairs.

The two government ministries agreed that in future the department of Christian communities would not deal with external relations and general issues, but would concentrate on 'the on-going practical problems of the Christian communities in Israel'.[72] Nevertheless, Herzog's spirit continued to hover over the department, and he dealt personally with every significant problem, such as attacks on churches, the State's attitude towards the missionaries, and particularly sensitive issues, such as the dislocation of the Christian Arab communities of Bir'am and Ikrit, two villages on Israel's northern border.

While holding both posts, of advisor on Jerusalem at the Foreign Ministry as well as at the Ministry of Religious Affairs, Herzog sometimes got his two hats confused. On one occasion, the director-general of the Foreign Ministry had to issue a statement that an official letter Herzog had written to the Cabinet Secretary did not reflect the Foreign Ministry's position on the subject. Yaacov sent a letter of apology, admitting that he had in fact written the unapproved letter from his position at the Ministry of Religious Affairs.[73]

Yet Yaacov Herzog was neither a politician nor a leader of men. From the start, the personality that emerged was that of a senior official who carried out policy, rather than a policy-maker. His primary concern was to present Israel's case to the outside world, whether in contacts with foreign governments or via the press. He concentrated far more on explaining Israel's policies and positions than on attempts to form them. For all his extraordinary abilities, he faithfully served senior officials and cabinet ministers who were less intelligent than he was.

Yaacov was also a man of extraordinary integrity, which manifested itself in everything he did. In recognition of his work to purchase land in Jerusalem, 'The Society for Religious Initiatives' invited him to join its management. Despite the approval of the Minister of Religious Affairs, Yaacov declined it firmly. One of the Society's functions was to distribute ten percent of its income to religious institutions. 'I think it would be inappropriate,' he wrote to the Deputy Minister of Religious Affairs, 'in view of my work in government.'[74] He never tried to get his way in an aggressive manner, never elbowed anyone aside, nor was he consumed with ambition to rise through the government hierarchy. Indeed, he did not need to be, given his meteoric rise in the Foreign Ministry.

'It has become necessary,' the director-general of the Foreign Ministry, Walter Eytan, informed his staff and Israel's delegations abroad, 'for the Ministry to coordinate information and policy on general defence issues – such as Israel's links to the Mediterranean region as a whole, the Balkans, the Balkan *Entente*, the American plans for this region, including Pakistan and Persia.' The job was given 'temporarily' to Yaacov Herzog.[75] It seemed like an odd appointment – what did the advisor on Jerusalem have to do with the Balkan *Entente*? What did the holy places have to do with American plans for Pakistan? The common denominator was Yaacov himself, whose versatile abilities made him a suitable candidate for a post so different from his earlier responsibilities. Indeed, soon after his appointment, he began to bombard his superiors with detailed reports on the situation in the Balkans, the plans for greater military power, and the elements of the Balkan *Entente*.[76] He adapted to his new post very rapidly and before long was attached to the Foreign Ministry's team dealing with Palestinian refugees, and even coordinated its operation.[77]

Yaacov's weakness was his wordiness. His memoranda and letters were often much too long. His writing style, too, was flowery, sometimes excessively so. Years later, when he held senior positions in the government, he would produce in a matter of days journals and reports of hundreds of pages, with the fullest descriptions of all he had seen and heard. His long letters did not always receive appropriate replies. Thus, in August 1953 he wrote a long letter to the director-general of the Ministry of Finance, Pinchas Sapir, asking for $20,000 and 10,000 Israeli liras for the public information campaign on Jerusalem. He couched his request in a detailed, expansive and eloquent political presentation to stress the importance of the campaign, and backed it with precise calculations. Sapir responded curtly: 'Having investigated the matter, I have found that, unfortunately, we cannot exceed the Foreign Ministry's budget for the matter in question.'[78]

His excessive eloquence notwithstanding, Herzog's performance in his new assignments was very impressive. Yet despite his success and achievements, his new appointment came as a surprise. Walter Eytan announced, without any preliminaries, that beginning on 4 April 1954, Yaacov Herzog would be acting head of the United States section at the Foreign Ministry.[79] The appointment of an external person to head the most important department in the Ministry was quite extraordinary, and demonstrated the high standing in which Herzog was held by Moshe Sharret and his senior officials. They felt confident entrusting him with Israel's complex relationship with the United States. Several months later, when the appointment became permanent, Yaacov left the Ministry of Religious Affairs for good and settled in his new office. But he never neglected his first love, Jerusalem, and even as head of the United States section, he continued to concern himself with the issue, and sometimes signed his letters, 'Advisor on Jerusalem'.

An important change had also taken place in Yaacov Herzog's personal life. In January 1954 he wrote to a good friend who was serving abroad, 'How are you and yours? ... Since we last met I have been married, fulfilling the proverb, "Whoso findeth a wife, findeth a good thing," and there is a delightful addition, one year old, in our home.'[80]

6

At First Sight

Pnina Shachor was 12 years old when enemy planes bombed Tel Aviv. It was the first attack of the Second World War on the city and her anxious parents sent their daughter to stay with relatives in Jerusalem. One Saturday she visited her aunt and went for a walk with her and her little cousin. When they returned home they were unable to open the door – the key had jammed in the lock. The three stood in the street feeling helpless, when they saw a young man wearing a grey suit, hat and tie. 'It's Yankele,' said the aunt. 'I know him. He's the Chief Rabbi's son.' She asked him to help and, smiling, he agreed, climbed over the balcony and opened the front door from inside.[1] He stayed a while, and when Pnina had to return to her other relatives' house they all hastened to accompany her. Yaacov looked at her and said teasingly, 'You're as idle as a rabbi.' Taken aback, and probably hurt, Pnina described the occasion in a letter to her mother. 'Is that a way for a Chief Rabbi's son to talk?' She gave so many details that the mother understood only too well – her daughter had fallen in love. 'Put him out of your mind,' she scolded, 'and come back. The school year is about to start.'

So it did, and was followed by the war years. In 1946, Pnina graduated from secondary school and went to Manchester in England, to study to be a pharmacist. Both her parents, Zalman and Frieda Shachor, were dispensing chemists. The family was observant, but liberal and open-minded. Zalman was a descendant of the renowned Rabbi Naftali Zvi Yehuda Beilin (known as the

Neziv), head of the Volozhin Yeshiva, and Frieda was the daughter of a Hassidic rabbi. Zalman owned a pharmacy in Jaffa, and was well liked by the Arabs, who called him 'Hakim' (physician) – though the good relations, as Pnina put it, 'did not prevent them from setting fire to his pharmacy during the 1936 riots.'[2] Frieda ran a pharmacy of her own on Nahmani Street. They gave their three children, Pnina, David and Eliezer, an enlightened, progressive religious upbringing. The children all attended religious school, and Pnina studied at Talpiot school in Tel Aviv. She dressed modestly but attended gym classes in shorts, and played tennis. On Saturday mornings, she and her brothers were taught the weekly Bible portion by their father, who was a great scholar and a natural teacher. But during the lesson Pnina's girl friends would stand outside whistling to her, urging her to join them for a walk along the beach.

Zalman was politically active, as chairman of the religious-Zionist movement, Mizrachi, in Tel Aviv, and the two boys were members of the Haganah. Eliezer was killed in the War of Independence, aged 17.

Pnina was not in Israel during the War of Independence. She spent three years studying in England, like her mother before her. By then, the child who had been attracted to Yaacov had grown into a beautiful young woman. One day in late 1946, she travelled from Manchester to London to hear a lecture by her relative, Rabbi Berlin [Bar-Ilan]. There she ran into a young woman named Ayalah, whom she had met on the ship to England. They went for a walk in Hyde Park, and Pnina heard that Chief Rabbi Herzog had just returned from his rescue mission in Eastern Europe. They stopped in front of the Dorchester Hotel where he was staying with his son, and Ayalah said to Pnina, 'I'd like to go inside, because I'm crazy about Yaacov Herzog.'[3] At that very moment Yaacov came out and invited the two young women to join him inside. He was struck by Pnina, but gave no hint of it.[4] Once more their ways parted, and four years passed before they met again. In 1950, when Pnina was back in Israel, she met Yaacov at the house of relatives in Tel Aviv.

This time he saw her home, and she was greatly impressed by him – 'A rare inner beauty, a combination of intelligence and humour, kindness and humanity.'[5] They began to meet in Tel Aviv and Jerusalem. 'He didn't dance, and there weren't so many cafés, so we went to concerts and the theatre.' This went on for two years. Yaacov would come to the pharmacy in Tel Aviv, and wait patiently until Pnina had finished work and changed out of her white coat. 'When the relationship with Pnina began,' Aura Herzog recalled, 'he used to bring her to our house in Jaffa. Then we saw a lot of them.'[6] Yaacov even took Pnina to his meetings with the heads of the Greek Orthodox Church when he was negotiating the Jerusalem land deals. Pnina would sit at the side, at some distance from the negotiators. '[Pnina] could see us but did not hear our discussions,' recalled Patriarch Benedictus years later.[7] Yaacov was entranced by Pnina and felt a great urge to tell his friends about her. At this time he became friends with Yitzhak Navon*, then secretary to Moshe Sharett, who regarded him as 'a charming person, noble-minded and wise'.

One day Yaacov said to Yitzhak, 'A miracle has happened.'

Yitzhak did not ask what it was.

'A great miracle,' Yaacov stated.

When he had said it for the third time, Yitzhak asked, 'What miracle?'

Then Yaacov told him about Pnina.[8]

Yaacov and Pnina met more and more frequently, until finally 'in 1952 we decided that was it'[9] and the two swore to each other that henceforth 'we are one'.[10] They were married on 14 February 1952, in the presence of both political and religious leaders of Israel with the Chief Rabbi, Yaacov's father, performing the marriage ceremony.

---

* Navon became President of Israel 1978–83.

At First Sight

Pnina Herzog was the ideal wife for Yaacov. Of broad outlook, she impressed everyone who met her. 'A rare combination of charm and intelligence!' enthused James McDonald, the US Ambassador to Israel who became a family friend, when he first met her.[11] She was a personality in her own right, and in later years would hold central positions in both national and international organizations. Yaacov adored her. The young couple settled on Ramban Street in Jerusalem, and Pnina resumed her work as a pharmacist. She believed that 'a woman should be able to stand on her own feet at any moment'.[12]

Yaacov and Pnina were also in complete harmony on the subject of religion. Though religious and observant, they both disliked zealotry, fanaticism and superfluous customs. Even as a very young man, when he was working at the Foreign Ministry and then in the Prime Minister's office, Yaacov did not wear a skullcap, except when saying blessings or praying. As a diplomat abroad, he would eat vegetarian food in non-kosher restaurants. He was open-minded and tolerant, both with regard to other movements in Judaism and to other religions. Pnina was very much like him. 'My father and mother loved Jewish values,' she reminisced many years later, 'and observed the commandments joyfully. I don't know where this custom of separating men and women at weddings has come from. At my wedding to the son of the Chief Rabbi, men and women sat together. And who, outside the ultra-Orthodox quarters, has heard that it is necessary to wear stockings and long sleeves in the hot Israeli summer? My mother, who was the daughter of a Hassidic rabbi and married the offspring of a famous Mitnagdic rabbi, never wore a wig or any other head covering. And as a girl at the beginning of the century, in her father's house, she played tennis and hockey.'[13]

Marriage at the age of 30 opened a new chapter in Yaacov's life, not only because he became a family man. Though a senior official in the Foreign and Religious Affairs Ministries, he had lived with his parents until then. This could have delayed the growth of his independent personality. He was subject to his parents' great, perhaps excessive, influence. They still regarded him as their gifted young son and continued to hope that he would follow in his father's footsteps. His mother, an intelligent woman of strong character, dearly wished that her son would become a great rabbi, while father and son were linked by mutual regard and admiration.

Leaving home meant that Yaacov, for the first time, was distanced from his parents' constant influence. Though he visited them often for family meals and various social occasions, he was now head of his own household, creating his own family framework.

Yaacov and Pnina's daughter, Shira, was born a year after they married. James McDonald congratulated the young parents by sending a letter to their newborn daughter. 'Dear Shira,' he wrote, 'you are truly a clever and lucky young lady to have chosen such wonderful parents ... Tell your father not to work too hard. He need not seek to be a great Talmudic scholar, a learned jurist and a skilled diplomat all at the same time. Each of these occupations would be sufficient for most people.'[14]

Most people, but not Yaacov Herzog. At that time, in addition to all his other occupations, he graduated from the Faculty of Law at the Hebrew University in Jerusalem and did his articles in the legal department of the Foreign Ministry. The President, the Prime Minister and senior figures in the Foreign Ministry recommended that the Attorney General reduce the period of his articles, in view of the important posts he held.[15] Their requests were granted, and before long Yaacov Herzog also became a lawyer.

He emerged from relative anonymity into the position of head of the United States section in the Foreign Ministry during a time of uncertainty and unease in Israel. Only a few months earlier, in December 1953, Ben-Gurion had left the premiership and moved south to the Negev, to live in Kibbutz Sdeh Boker. Mapai, the ruling party, chose Moshe Sharett to succeed him as Prime Minister, over Ben-Gurion's objections. Ben-Gurion was an 'activist' and tough on matters of security and in Israel's relations with the Arab countries, and he considered Sharett to be too soft and conciliatory.

When Sharett became Prime Minister, he retained the Foreign portfolio, and initiated a few moderate moves in foreign policy, which proved unsuccessful. From the start, he was assailed by the younger Ben-Gurionists who supported the 'Old Man', to whom they owed their careers. Among them were the Chief of Staff Moshe Dayan, the director of the Ministry of Defence Shimon Peres, Nehemiah Argov, Teddy Kollek and Ehud Avriel. Sharett was also opposed by the new Minister of Defence, Pinchas Lavon, a brilliant but cynical and arrogant person. Although aggressive in matters of defence, Lavon himself clashed with the young Ben-Gurionists as well as with Sharett. His manner, language and open contempt for Sharett caused the Prime Minister and the Mapai leadership endless difficulties.

1954 saw numerous provocations against Israel by its neighbours, chiefly Egypt. Infiltrators frequently slipped across the border to carry out robberies, gather intelligence and commit sabotage. The worst case was the ambush of a bus on its way from Eilat when 11 passengers were killed. Israel was forced to show restraint, but nonetheless retaliated with a number of limited actions.

The crisis which most stirred the Israeli public that year came to be known as the 'Lavon Affair'. A network of Israeli agents in Egypt, made up of idealistic young Jews, had carried out acts of sabotage against British and American institutions in Cairo and Alexandria, in order to undermine the confidence of these powers in the stability of the Egyptian regime. At this time the British government, headed by Winston Churchill, was planning to evacuate its military bases in the Suez Canal Zone and withdraw its last military units from Egypt; the Israeli covert operation was intended to make London reconsider or even abandon this plan.

The operation was naive, foolish and dangerous. It was based on a total incomprehension of the international situation, and recklessly risked innocent young lives in what amounted to a useless and hopeless act of provocation. After a few amateurish and ineffectual acts of sabotage, the Egyptian authorities captured the entire network, put all those involved on trial and gave them harsh sentences. Some were condemned to die by hanging, others to spend many years in an Egyptian prison. Israel reacted with outrage. In public, Israel's leaders utterly denied the charges and described the case as a latter-day 'blood libel'. In private, however, the question was asked who had given the order to carry out this irresponsible operation. Colonel Binyamin Gibli, the head of Military Intelligence, and the Minister of Defence, Pinchas Lavon, traded accusations. Eventually, a secret investigation by an internal court of inquiry led to Lavon's resignation.

Subsequently, David Ben-Gurion, leader of the activist wing of the ruling party, returned from his Negev retreat and replaced Lavon as Minister of Defence in Sharett's government. A few weeks later, on 28 February 1955, Ben-Gurion gave an order to carry out a military strike against the Egyptian army in the Gaza Strip. The idea was to punish Egypt for the actions of infiltrators who had murdered an innocent cyclist, stolen documents from a government institute and carried out other acts of sabotage. Command of the operation, dubbed 'Black Arrow', was entrusted to a young paratroop officer, Major Ariel ('Arik') Sharon. The operation entailed an attack by 149 paratroopers on an Egyptian base near Gaza. However, the action was expanded further than its projected scope, and cost the lives of 38 Egyptian soldiers and eight Israelis. This caused a dramatic escalation of the Israeli-Egyptian conflict and started a grim cycle of retaliation and counter-retaliation.

Israel was condemned by governments all over the world, including the United States. The US Secretary of State, John Foster Dulles, reacted furiously.[16] The heads of the Foreign Ministry were in a quandary, and responded defensively and apologetically. Yaacov Herzog was a confirmed believer in preserving the friendship of the United States. A few weeks earlier he had been horrified by a conversation he had held with the Chief of Staff Moshe Dayan, in which the latter described an 'activist' defence plan which would no doubt have led to 'a head-on collision with the United States'.[17] Herzog had responded by saying that 'if it is not a matter of survival ... it is out of the question.'[18]

At the same time, seeing the barrage of American condemnations of the Gaza operation, Herzog adopted a different, cynical and sophisticated position. 'We must make the most of the Gaza operation's positive effect,' he wrote to his colleagues, 'namely, the lesson that while we have the strength, we can cause upheavals in neighbouring countries, thereby confounding US plans. That is what the Secretary [of State] is warning us against, so it's good to let him know that there is no telling what we'll do if our existence is threatened.'[19] A few days later he added, 'In the long run, the incident will help to show the Secretary [of State] the urgent need to consult with us. The two considerations which might impel him to do positive things for us are Jewish public opinion in the United States, and anxiety about the results of our desperation.'[20] This certainly was not the attitude of the heads of the Foreign Ministry.

The Gaza operation also caused a serious rift in Israel's leadership, notably an increasingly bitter confrontation between David Ben-Gurion and Moshe Sharett, who was horrified by the results of the operation. Ben-Gurion attacked Sharett's policy of moderation, which received a bad blow when Israel was barred from taking part in the Bandung Conference of non-aligned nations, in July 1955. Sharett had made Bandung a cornerstone of his policy, believing that Israel's friends in the Third World would lead to better understanding with the Arab countries. This hope was dashed, and Bandung actually saw the emergence of the Egyptian President, Gamal Abd al-Nasser, as one of the foremost leaders of the Third World. Sharett and Ben-Gurion were unaware that another, dangerous development had taken place at the conference

– Nasser had used it to form contacts with leaders of the Eastern Bloc, and had asked for Soviet weapons. Moscow acceded to his request, and in September 1955 the world heard about what was then a huge arms deal between Egypt and the Soviet Union, by way of Czechoslovakia (see chapter 1).

Israel regarded the Czech arms deal as a death sentence. The immense quantities of arms that began to flow into Egypt shattered the already uneven balance of power that had existed in the Middle East since 1950. Moshe Sharett went on a desperate mission to Paris and Geneva, where the Foreign Ministers of the 'Big Four' – the USSR, the US, Britain and France – were meeting, and asked them to provide Israel with arms to confront the new danger, but he encountered only avoidance and evasions.

By this time Sharett was no longer Prime Minister. General elections had taken place in the summer of 1955, and Mapai chose Ben-Gurion to lead it. Once more the veteran leader became Prime Minister and Defence Minister. Yet, despite their profound differences of opinion, Ben-Gurion made it a condition of his return that Moshe Sharett should be Foreign Minister.

In view of the growing threat from Egypt, Israel followed a two-pronged policy: firstly, to try to obtain American support to guarantee Israel's existence; secondly, to try to obtain arms to strengthen the IDF and restore the balance of weapons in the Middle East. Another idea, which at this time Ben-Gurion still kept to himself, was to launch a military campaign that would restore Israel's power of deterrence.

Since the autumn of 1954, secret talks had been held between Israel and the United States concerning a possible defence pact between the two countries; in effect, Israel wanted the United States to guarantee her borders. At that time, the United States was building up a system of military alliances to surround the USSR. Washington created the 'Baghdad Pact', based on cooperation between Iraq and Turkey, with British participation, and planned to supply Pact member states with masses of armaments. The Pact

Above   Jerusalem, 1947—a family photograph. Left to right Chief Rabbi Herzog, Chaim, Sarah Herzog, Yaacov.

Below   Yaacov, as a young man, studying with his father.

Above
14 February 1952 — Pnina and Yaacov at their wedding.

Below 1957—at home:
From left
Shira and Eliezra.

Above   The Herzog brothers
Left 1960—Yaacov and Chaim.
Right The two brothers in school uniform Dublin in the late 1920s.

Below   1969—Speaking at Manchester United Jewish Appeal event.

Above Yaacov with Rabbi Yaacov Weinberg, Montreux, Switzerland.

Below The rescue mission, 1946. Left to right Rabbi Wolgelernter, Rabbi Botschko, Rabbi Zev Gold, Rabbi Moshkovsky, Rabbi Herzog, Moshe Chaim Shapira, Yaacov Herzog, Yehuda Elinson.

Above   At the Ben-Gurion — Adenauer meeting, New York.

Below   Yaacov carrying his newborn son, Yitzhak, at the circumcision ceremony.
        Left to right   Foreign Minister Abba Eban, Interior Minister Moshe Chaim Shapira,
        Rabbi Zevin, Chief Rabbi Nissim, Prime Minister Levi Eshkol, President Zalman Shazar.

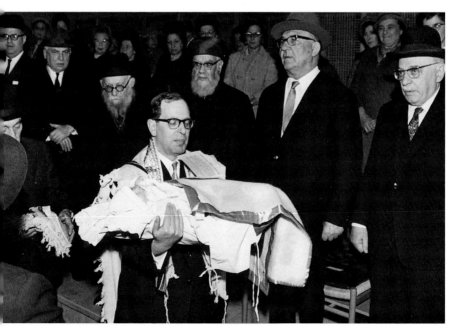

In the service of four prime ministers.

Above Meeting with United Nations Secretary General Dag Hammarskjold. Left to right Golda Meir, Prime Minister David Ben-Gurion, Yaacov Herzog, Arthur Lurie, Shabtai Rosen, Pinchas Rosen.

Below With Moshe Sharett and the Greek delegate to the UN.

Above Cabinet meeting led by Levi Eshkol. Left to right Joseph Burg, Israel Galili, Levi Eshkol, Yaacov Herzog, Gen. (res.), Efraim Ben-Arzi, Abba Eban.

Below Cabinet meeting led by Golda Meir. Left to right Golda Meir, Yaacov Herzog, Yigal Allon, Pinchas Sapir.

Above   Above Washington, D.C., July 1958—with Ghanaian Prime Minister, Kwame Nkrumah.

Below   Washington, D.C.—Left to right Hubert Humphrey, Pnina Herzog, Yaacov Herzog, Irish Ambassador to the U.S., John Hern.

was signed on 24 February 1955, much to the annoyance of Egypt, Iraq's main rival for the leadership of the Arab world. In fact, this Pact was the chief reason why Egypt sought to acquire weapons from the Eastern Bloc, though later Nasser would claim that it had been Israel's Gaza operation of 28 February that had compelled him to search for new sources of arms.

The Unites States had intended to placate Egypt with declarations of friendship and some supplies of arms, but this approach was, of course, abandoned once Egypt made her arms deal with the USSR. Now the US sought to calm Israel's anxieties with vague promises of weapons, but chiefly with discussions about American guarantees of Israel's existence, or a mutual defence alliance.[21]

There was not the faintest chance of such an alliance being made, but from his position at the Foreign Ministry, Yaacov Herzog worked hard to make the Americans fulfil their hints and promises. At the same time, he warned his colleagues that the request for American guarantees would never be approved by the US Congress, and recommended instead that Israel demand that the United States apply the same policy towards Israel and the Arabs alike. 'A US guarantee of Israel's existing borders,' he wrote, 'in the absence of a prior agreement with the Arabs, would mean, in effect, imposing peace upon the Arabs, and I doubt that we can expect such a move from the present administration, or its approval by the Senate.'[22] Herzog suggested a simpler and more reasonable demand − instead of guaranteeing her borders, something the US had never done for any country, Israel should ask the United States to make the same commitment she had made to certain Arab states − such as with Iraq in the framework of the Baghdad Pact − namely, a military defence agreement and the supply of American arms. This, he thought, would present the Americans with a solution that maintained a balance between the Arabs and Israel, without obliging them to make a one-sided and extraordinary gesture towards Israel − the likelihood of which was negligible. 'Israel should demand an agreement of military assistance, followed by a security agreement,' was how Herzog spelled it out to Sharett. 'In this way we would be demanding for ourselves, on the basis of equality and non-discrimination, what has already been granted to Iraq, and might be granted to other Arab states.'[23] But his advice was not taken and the idea of an American guarantee was, predictably, dropped.

John Foster Dulles began to speak about an American plan for solving the Middle East problem. His ideas did not preclude, among other measures, adjusting Israel's borders in favour of the Arabs. Nor did Dulles express any reservations about the statement made by the British Prime Minister, Anthony Eden, in his Guildhall speech in late 1955, in which he called for Israel to make territorial concessions. The moderate Moshe Sharett was obliged to declare in the Knesset that such territorial concessions were out of the question.

While pursuing these efforts to achieve an alliance with the US, Yaacov Herzog was also busy with a number of other issues. During that period his understanding with Moshe Sharett reached its highest level, though it never took the form of personal friendship – for Yaacov, Sharett always remained 'Mr Sharett', or 'Foreign Minister'.

'Yaacov's personal views,' said Eli Eyal, a friend, 'were closer to the Weizmann-Sharett school of political caution than to Ben-Gurion's activism. But he was a civil servant through and through – not a trail-blazer or initiator of new political concepts, but their gifted interpreter. As such, he faithfully fulfilled his post under every Prime Minister or Foreign Minister he served.'[24]

Sharett grew increasingly dependent on Yaacov's advice. When Israel's Ambassador to the US, Abba Eban, asked for Yaacov to be appointed minister to Washington to serve at his side, Moshe Sharett was horrified. 'It is inconceivable,' he wired back, 'that we would send Yaacov. Without him the Ministry would not be able to withstand the American front for a single day.'[25]

At First Sight

Yaacov, in fact, was active in all sectors of the 'American front'. On top of his various tasks, he also conducted an extensive and exhausting campaign that lasted many months – the struggle for Israel's water sources. In 1953, the UN Armistice Commission decreed that Israel must halt the irrigation project she had constructed in the north using the water of the Jordan River. President Eisenhower tried to calm the situation by creating a system of regional cooperation. He dispatched Dr Eric Johnston as his special ambassador, to develop a project for the division of the Jordan water between Israel and the Arab countries which bordered on the river or its tributaries. Johnston hoped that an agreement on water would lead to wider negotiations between Israel and her neighbours – to the problem of refugees, the territorial claims of both sides and eventually to a peace settlement.

Johnston visited the capitals of the states in question four times between 1953 and 1955. The negotiations were exhausting, prolonged and punctuated with crises and disappointments. The Arabs refused to meet the Israelis, even at the professional experts' level, and all the proposals and counter-proposals were transmitted through Johnston. Yaacov Herzog was the main Israeli representative in the process, alongside water experts and other senior officials. A researcher examining Herzog's bulging files from 1954–5 might think that this was the only issue on his mind. At times the negotiations were promoted to a higher level, and Moshe Sharett and his aides spent days and nights with Yaacov Herzog, discussing strategy, arguing about how many cubic metres of water could be added or subtracted here and there, analysing the water reserves, the irrigation projects and the volume of the Sea of Galilee and the Huleh Lake. When a compromise was finally reached, the Arab states refuse to approve it. Israel and Jordan solved the problem by drawing from the river as much water as each was allocated in the project, though it was never ratified. Some years later Herzog wrote to Johnston: 'The people of the Middle East owe you a great debt of gratitude for your impressive initiative and persistence in trying to bring them to agree a regional water project. Though the project did not achieve political resolution, the technical agreement you managed to bring about has been a landmark in the history of the Middle East.'[26] One positive outcome of the negotiations was that Johnston was enchanted by Yaacov Herzog's personality, and remained his good friend for many years.

Following Ben-Gurion's appointment as Minister of Defence, his relations with Sharett deteriorated, and the two men clashed repeatedly on foreign policy and defence issues. In March 1955, after several acts of sabotage and murders committed by fedayeen from across the Egyptian border, Ben-Gurion proposed to the Cabinet 'to expel the Egyptians from the Gaza Strip'. Sharett prevented the proposal from being adopted. The two also clashed about the policy of retaliation. These confrontations increased after Ben-Gurion resumed the premiership. In December 1955, Ben-Gurion suggested to the Cabinet that a military operation be launched to break through the Tiran Straits, which Nasser had blocked to Israeli shipping. But a group of Cabinet ministers, led by Moshe Sharett, defeated Ben-Gurion's suggestion.

On 11 December 1955, following a Syrian attack on Israeli fishermen in the Sea of Galilee, Ben-Gurion ordered a retaliatory attack against the Syrian positions dominating the lake. The world reacted angrily, and the United States condemned the action in strong terms.[27] Later Moshe Sharett claimed that it was on account of this action that the US withheld weapons from Israel.[28]

This was not, in fact, the case. But Sharett went so far as to whisper in the ears of the Americans that he had not known about the planned operation. This was, indeed, true because he had been out of the country when it took place, and Ben-Gurion had not informed him of his intentions. But his relations with Ben-Gurion were an internal, confidential matter which should not have been revealed to the Americans. In doing what he did, Sharett failed in his responsibility as a senior member of the cabinet, merely to please the Americans. To do this, he even made use of Herzog, who faithfully carried out the mission. 'I have consulted with the Minister,' Herzog wrote to Abba Eban, 'and he thought that I ought to inform the [US] Ambassador in strict secrecy that Sharett had not known of the incident. I said this last week to both the Ambassador and White [the minister at the US embassy], in the clear understanding that it would be kept completely secret. The minister himself, speaking with [Ambassador] Lawson last Friday, repeated it, noting that Sharett had been abroad at the time, and the Acting Foreign Minister [i.e., Ben-Gurion himself] was in place.' Herzog added in the margin, 'I must ask you to destroy this letter after you've read it, and confirm to me in writing that you have done so.'[29]

At the end of January 1956, President Eisenhower sent his personal friend, Robert Anderson, an aide to the US Defence Secretary, on a confidential mission as an intermediary. Anderson (later to be appointed Treasury Secretary) flew to Israel, met Ben-Gurion and Sharett, then flew back and forth several times to Egypt, to meet President Nasser. The meetings were held in the strictest secrecy, both in Jerusalem and in Cairo. Nasser assured Anderson that even his bodyguards were not aware of their meetings. Ben-Gurion decided to assign the handling of Anderson's mission to two individuals he trusted completely – the director of the Prime Minister's office, Teddy Kollek, and Yaacov Herzog. The two men were close friends, and actually lived in the same apartment block on Ramban Street in Jerusalem.

In the course of his mission, Anderson met Kollek and Herzog many times. They supplied him with background information and current political reports, and accompanied him on his meetings with the Prime Minister and the Foreign Minister. Herzog's role in the secret negotiations indicated the complete trust that both Ben-Gurion and Sharett placed in him. 'Only five people in Israel knew about Anderson's mission,' wrote the journalist Moshe

Zack, 'Ben-Gurion, Sharett, Teddy Kollek, Isser Harel and Yaacov Herzog. Yaacov wrote the minutes of the talks, calling Anderson "Jonathan", so that even the secretary who typed them would not know his identity.'[30]

The Israeli leaders were willing to do anything to achieve a direct dialogue with Egypt so as to dispel the tension and bring about peace between the two states. But it soon became clear that Nasser was not interested in peace, nor even in pacifying their shared border. In his final meeting with Ben-Gurion in Jerusalem, Anderson admitted that he had failed in his mission.

On 3 April 1956, Ben-Gurion received the final response from the United States to Israel's request for arms – the answer was no. This was a heavy blow to Israel, as a supply of arms at this difficult time might have created an equilibrium and prevented a flare-up in the Middle East. Washington's refusal drove Israel to plan a pre-emptive war against Egypt before it assimilated the new arms supplied by the USSR.

Deliverance came from France. In contrast to the Americans, France's military establishment had developed close relations with its Israeli counterpart. Since November 1954, France had been embroiled in a bloody conflict in Algeria, where the National Liberation Front (the FLN) had rebelled against its rule. President Nasser provided the rebels with aid, money, arms and training, and France was inclined to favour Israel, hoping that by combining their efforts they might defeat the Egyptian leader and thereby put down the Algerian revolt. Shimon Peres, the Ministry of Defence's young director, built up a close understanding with Maurice Bourgès-Maunoury, France's Minister of Defence, and his immediate aides and senior staff in French military headquarters. These relations circumvented the Foreign Ministries of both Israel and France, and increased the tension between Moshe Sharett and David Ben-Gurion. In the spring of 1956, Shimon Peres succeeded in obtaining a sufficient quantity of modern weaponry from France to balance the Czech-Egyptian arms deal –

At First Sight

Mystère-4 fighter planes, AMX-30 tanks, recoilless cannons, anti-tank missiles, and other weapons.

Ben-Gurion expostulated that Dulles' reply to Israel's request for defensive arms was 'infamous', and called an urgent meeting. Foreign Minister Sharett, Chief of Staff Moshe Dayan, Shimon Peres and Yaacov Herzog all took part. Ben-Gurion was furious and seemed to despair of the United States, while Sharett argued that 'the absolute meaning of Dulles' answer was not yet clear, since the American responses were inconsistent'.[31]

Once again, the differences between Ben-Gurion and Sharett came into the open – the former resolved to abandon the 'Anglo-Saxon orientation' and turn to France, Sharett continued to 'disparage France'.[32] According to Yaacov Tzur, Israel's Ambassador to France at that time, Sharett was also influenced by a senior Foreign Ministry official, Gideon Rafael, who incited him against the first aircraft deal with France (when Israel purchased 'Ouragan' fighter-planes). 'The French want to sell us that old rubbish,' he had said, 'in return for our dollars.'[33]

Now a sharp dispute broke out between Sharett and Ben-Gurion about who was responsible for obtaining the French weaponry – the Foreign Ministry or the Ministry of Defence. Sharett did not know that the arms were given to Israel as part of an unwritten understanding between the Defence Ministries of the two countries to create a joint front against Nasser.

Herzog was in an awkward position. He was close to Ben-Gurion and enjoyed his trust, but he did not hesitate to act for Sharett in matters that were in dispute between the two men. He had already revealed to the Americans that Sharett had not known about the Sea of Galilee action, and had helped Sharett frustrate Ben-Gurion's plan to attack the Gaza Strip. When the proposal was being debated in the government, Sharett sent Herzog to the representative of the National-Religious Party in the cabinet, the Minister of Religious Affairs, Moshe Chaim Shapira, with whom he was on good personal terms. 'Last night Yaacov Herzog invested an educational effort in Moshe Shapira,' Moshe Sharett noted with satisfaction in his diary on the day the cabinet voted on the issue. 'He stayed with him till one o'clock in the morning, and the result was plain to see. The Minister of Religious Affairs suggested postponing the vote for a fortnight, and when pressured to explain why, he muttered that we should first investigate the state of our relations with the United States, for which I ought to fly over there and talk with Dulles.'[34] Ultimately, as we have seen, Ben-Gurion's suggestion was defeated. Yet defeating it was not Herzog's job. He was not a political man and did not have to take part in the discussions and decisions at the political level.

Herzog also sometimes passed on to Sharett secret information he had heard in the course of his close dealings with Ben-Gurion's office. Thus, for example, he told Sharett in November 1955, 'in the strictest confidence', that the Chief of Staff had presented the Minister of Defence with a plan for breaking the Egyptian blockade of the Tiran Straits.[35] Similarly, after the Sea of Galilee action, he revealed to Sharett, again in confidence, that Ben-Gurion had expanded the planned operation a day before it took place – in contrast to the information he had given his Foreign Minister.[36] Similarly, in the spring of 1956, Herzog accompanied Gideon Rafael to Ben-Gurion, on behalf of Moshe Sharett, to persuade him to abort a retaliatory attack which he had already ordered.[37] Perhaps he acted this way because of his close relations with Sharett, which were much stronger than the standard relations between a Minister and one of his officials. He was devoted to Moshe Sharett and 'loved him dearly'.[38] But his actions also reflected a quality which characterized Herzog throughout his career – loyalty to his superior, as a civil servant in the British tradition. He did not wish – nor perhaps could – separate his official position from any unusual undertaking on behalf of his superior.

This was exemplified in the consultation Sharett held at his house after the 1955 elections, when matters were coming to a head and he was considering resigning as Foreign Minister. Present

At First Sight

were some of his closest associates, as well as his wife Zippora, and the minutes show that much time was devoted to what Herzog said about Ben-Gurion. These were harsh words. Sharett opened the discussion with sharp criticism of Ben-Gurion's attitude towards him, then gave the floor to his guests. The minutes show that Arthur Lurie made a brief and non-committal statement, and advised Sharett to take a holiday. Herzog, on the other hand, spoke very sharply about Ben-Gurion, making it plain that he was fully supportive of Sharett and his political viewpoint.

'YDH [Herzog] said: "This is Ben-Gurion's emotional season. He can't be judged by the usual standard. He's frustrated because he went to Sdeh Boker to be a prophet, and failed. He's riding on the hills of history, which are very steep. Ben-Gurion doesn't have a clear political outlook, it isn't possible to determine at this time how it will be possible to act in certain circumstances. There is the essential Ben-Gurion, who is rational, and there is the Ben-Gurion of emotions, and this is the season of emotions ... Already in Sdeh Boker I sensed his frustration. A month and a half ago at B.G.'s house I sensed his disillusion with all his dreams of literature and knowledge, that's why he's full of emotion and groping to find his way. That explains the aggressiveness. He has no friends, except his disciple Nehemiah. There's no telling what he'll do when he becomes Prime Minister ... If it were a question of a minor change of policy [in the event that Sharett resigns], it might be possible to give a chance to a different policy, but here – when will Sharett come back and why would he come back? What will happen in the meantime? Moreover, if [Sharett] resigns, B.G. will feel obliged to prove that his policy is successful, and who knows how far he'll go, while Sharett remains on the outside, consumed by remorse ... Once [Sharett] resigns, Herut and Ahdut Ha'avodah* will declare that their policy has won. Ben-Gurion's

---

* Herut was Menachem Begin's Revisionist Party – precursor to the present-day Likud Party. Ahdut Ha'avodah was the activist wing of Mapai – precursor to the present-day Labour Party.

[policy] is not [Menachem] Begin's policy. Begin has a policy (possibly a mad one), but B.G. doesn't, so clearly it will lead nowhere ... B.G. seeks to do great things – perhaps if we find great things for him, such as immigration from Russia, or if he convened a conference of US Jews it would give him satisfaction and a mission in life.'[39]

In June 1956, as the alliance with France grew firmer and Ben-Gurion began to lead the country towards a war with Egypt, he resolved to get rid of Sharett. The crisis between the two leaders was causing an upheaval in the Labour Party. It was not merely a personal conflict, but a clash between opposing political philosophies, whose followers would in future be dubbed doves and hawks.

On 2 June, at the height of the crisis, Yitzhak Navon telephoned the influential Finance Minister Pinchas Sapir, to tell him that 'if Sharett does not resign by five o'clock today, Ben-Gurion will quit the government and return to Sdeh Boker'.[40] Sapir asked the minister Zalman Aranne to accompany him, and they went to see Sharett. They found him giving an interview to the American journalist Joseph Alsop with Yaacov Herzog beside him.

Seeing Sapir and Aranne, Sharett understood that this was 'the end'. He cried out, in Herzog's presence, 'I know why you've come – to slaughter me! I agree!'[41]

To replace Sharett, Ben-Gurion appointed Golda Meir, whose 'activist' views were much more congenial to him.

Herzog was shocked and upset. He made a last-minute effort to prevent Sharett's dismissal, going so far as to propose a revolt. He suggested to Sharett that 'the senior officials in the Foreign Ministry who worked closely with him ... It might be the right thing for them to offer their resignation with his.' Sharett objected, saying – rightly – that such a move would undermine Israel's civil service.[42] According to Golda Meir's biographer, Dr Meron Medzini, Gideon Rafael and Arthur Lurie wanted to take part in the collective resignation that Sharett rejected out of hand.[43]

But Herzog did not give up. He asked to see David Ben-Gurion (according to him, with Sharett's permission), to plead that Sharett be retained as Foreign Minister. 'I clearly remember the conversation with Ben-Gurion,' he recalled. 'He was thoughtful, praised Sharett very highly, his talents and integrity, but said he had one good reason for replacing him, but ... he could not reveal it. I was puzzled, but did not insist.'[44]

Ben-Gurion gave Herzog the reason six months later, after the Suez war. One night, quite late, he asked Herzog if he knew the journalist Randolph Churchill, Winston Churchill's son. 'No,' Herzog replied.

Ben-Gurion told Herzog that Churchill had come to interview him for the London press. 'He's quite bold,' he added.

'How?'

'He was here today and asked me why I'd sacked Sharett.'

'What did you tell him?' Herzog asked.

'[I said that] in times of peace Moshe Sharett was, in my opinion, the best Foreign Secretary in the world, because of his international ways and his intellectual stature. But he was not a wartime Foreign Minister.'[45]

Despite all this, once Golda Meir was appointed Foreign Minister, Herzog hastened to call on her and promise her his support and that of other senior members of the Ministry. 'I remember that one morning he came with Arthur Lurie to see me,' Golda Meir recalled, 'to say that I should go ahead, that I would find comradeship and cooperation, and so it was. I remember that morning very well – it greatly eased my entrance into the Foreign Ministry.'[46]

But a person who knew Golda Meir well recorded the events quite differently. Rather than remembering Herzog and Lurie's words of encouragement, she remembered their intention of resigning in solidarity with Sharett to protest against her appointment in his place. 'Golda did not forgive [those who wanted to resign with Sharett – i.e. Herzog, Rafael and Lurie] that move,' wrote Medzini, 'and found ways to hurt them subsequently. They are civil servants, she said, and had no business mixing personal sentiments like loyalty to a previous minister with their work. But it was an empty threat on their part. She would not have been especially sorry if they had actually resigned.'[47]

It was years before Herzog was able to analyse coolly Sharett's failings. 'In fact,' he said, 'he quit the government against the background of his disappointed hope of reaching a peace settlement with the Arabs ... Sharett symbolized a primary Zionist assumption, from the early days of Zionism, namely, that the Arab objection [to the existence of the State of Israel] was in some way not essential, not rooted, but stemmed from external factors, from all kinds of side issues, but for some reason the early Zionists did not understand the root source of Arab hatred. Possibly there was a kind of fairly understandable psychological incomprehension. Sharett assumed that the Arab world was willing to be in touch with us and achieve peace.

'Even in the years 1946–8 he persuaded world leaders that if only we stand up to the Arabs' first military challenge, they would accept the inevitable, understand the situation and join in a system of regional cooperation ... Perhaps he also believed, with the rise of Nasser, that Nasser's socialist trend would ... anyway lead to peace.

'... Yet not only were his hopes dashed, and his belief that it was somehow possible to break out of the cycle of hate ... disappointed, but he himself, his political career as Foreign Minister ... was ended because these hopes were frustrated, meaning that his way and Ben-Gurion's were totally divergent.'[48]

In the meantime there were dramatic developments in the international arena. Strengthened by the tremendous support he enjoyed in the Third World, as well as by the Soviet arms supply, President Nasser was encouraging subversive movements in the region's Arab states, with the intention of becoming a pan-Arab and pan-Muslim leader. His moves angered the United States, which already regarded him as a threat to pro-Western regimes in the Arab world. Early in July 1956, John Foster Dulles announced that the United States had decided not to finance the construction of the Aswan Dam, which was the cornerstone of Egypt's development projects. Egypt was bitterly disappointed.

But Nasser's reaction stunned the world. A few weeks later, on 26 July 1956, he made a speech in Alexandria in which he announced the nationalization of the Suez Canal. He told the cheering crowd of thousands that income from the Canal would finance construction of the dam. It was a slap in the face to the West, above all to Britain and France, who had economic and military interests in the Canal. The leaders of these two countries, accompanied by senior military and security personnel, met directly after the act of nationalization to discuss their course of action. They agreed that only force would stop Nasser. In an underground bunker in London generals pored over maps of the region and began to plan the conquest of the Canal.

This was the first step towards the Suez war.

The Sinai operation began on 29 October 1956 – and Yaacov Herzog was summoned by Ben-Gurion. The days he spent at the Prime Minister's side catapulted him to Israel's political summit.

7

Acting Foreign Minister

Throughout the Sinai war, Ben-Gurion and Yaacov Herzog were inseparable. As the Prime Minister's senior political advisor, he spent much of the day and part of the night with him. When Ben-Gurion went to bed, Herzog would go to his office and spend long hours sending instructions to Israel's missions overseas, or telephoning her delegates in the world's capitals. Sometimes he returned to Ben-Gurion's house later in the night, to bring him an important telegram or message from a foreign government. As one of the few individuals permitted to wake the Prime Minister, he had an arrangement with Paula Ben-Gurion, whereby he would tap on her bedroom window and she would open the door to him.

Together with everyone else in Israel, Herzog was caught up in the maelstrom that lasted until the night of 8 November 1956, when Ben-Gurion announced that Israel would withdraw from the Sinai Peninsula. But Herzog discovered that as far as he was concerned, the crisis was not yet over, and it would be a long time before he could return to his office in the Foreign Ministry. The real political battle was only just beginning, more exhausting and nerve-racking than before, and he had to remain at Ben-Gurion's side. As he put it, the foreign policy effort now had a new objective, namely, to advance from the reality of armistice, which meant 'nightmares ... raids, threats of annihilation – to peace. We felt very strongly that before retreating, we had to achieve peace.'[1]

But the hope of reaching a peace agreement with Egypt soon evaporated. Although Ben-Gurion declared that the armistice was dead and buried and proposed peace talks with Egypt, no one was listening, neither in Egypt nor in the international arena. The UN Secretary General, Dag Hammarskjold, made no bones about his intention of getting Israel out of Sinai as soon as possible. Ben-Gurion had to redefine the goals of the struggle. Five days after his sombre speech, which informed the nation and the world of Israel's imminent retreat from Sinai, he formulated a new policy – delay.

'It is now our political necessity to put off completing the withdrawal as long as possible,' Ben-Gurion told the IDF's top commanders at a meeting on 13 November. He needed the interval for two reasons, one of which he had stated in the retreat speech: 'The delay is essential, so that the world can review things calmly, without hysteria, without panic, but with a clear understanding of the situation.' Ben-Gurion estimated that when things grew calmer, and the fear of a Soviet attack in the Middle East subsided, the international community as well as the UN would adopt a more balanced and considered attitude towards Israel. The United States, too, might change her position, if Israel used the delay to explain her own position in Washington.[2]

His other reason for putting off the withdrawal was to use it as a bargaining chip, to obtain concrete results in exchange for returning the conquered territory. And there was a third, hidden, purpose, which he revealed only to his close aides – he was still hoping that Israel would not be compelled to give up all the captured territory. 'Though it's far from certain,' he said to Moshe Dayan, 'I think we may not have to withdraw from the Straits of Eilat and from Gaza.' Once fear of a third world war abated, he thought the world would accept Israel's retention of the Tiran Straits and the Gaza Strip.

Naturally, Israel's procrastination drew sharp criticism from other countries, as well as from moderate circles within Israel. It also reintroduced the risk of Soviet intervention. Ben-Gurion was aware of the danger and feared it. As he said a few months later,

'The [Soviet] threats may have been false and unreal – but the fear was real.'

On the night of 15 November, at eleven o'clock, Yaacov Herzog brought Ben-Gurion a new letter from Bulganin [President of the Soviet Union]. 'This has as much truth, integrity and humanity as the first letter,' Ben-Gurion fumed. Bulganin repeated his harsh accusations against Israel, and again dropped broad hints that Israel might be destroyed. 'Israel's present policy of inciting hatred for the Arabs and oppressing them, is a danger to overall peace and may lead to Israel's annihilation ... The government of the USSR [considers it] imperative to take steps to prevent possible new provocations by Israel against neighbouring countries, and to ensure a calm and stable peace in the Middle East.' The letter was backed by rumours of Russian squadrons flying over Turkey en route to Syria. The Israeli cabinet was again filled with foreboding, and Golda Meir even proposed complaining to the UN Security Council about Bulganin's threats. Ben-Gurion's reply to Bulganin, with its clear imprint of Yaacov Herzog's wording, protested that 'certain expressions in your letter regarding Israel may not be interpreted by the Arab rulers as encouraging peace in our region.' Ben-Gurion also rejected Bulganin's demand that Israel pay Egypt compensation, and reiterated that 'Israel is ready to settle her dispute with Egypt by peaceful means, as stipulated in the UN Charter.' Only in early December did fears of intervention by Soviet forces, disguised as 'volunteers', evaporate, when Moscow issued a formal statement that 'Soviet volunteers would not be sent to Egypt, in view of the evacuation of British, French and Israeli forces from Egyptian territory.'

Thus ended the risk of Soviet intervention in the conflict, but not, as Ben-Gurion had hoped, international pressure on Israel. Dag Hammarskjold did not let up, and repeatedly summoned the UN General Assembly. On six separate occasions it demanded that Israel withdraw from Sinai and threatened sanctions if she continued to hold on to the conquered territories.

Acting Foreign Minister

In his journal, Ben-Gurion vented his fury on Dag Hammarskjold, whom he described as an anti-Semite and a confirmed enemy. But Ben-Gurion had to contend with another, far stronger and more dangerous, opponent – President Eisenhower, who took a harsh, uncompromising line with Israel and even supported the threat of sanctions.

On 15 November, Israel announced that she was beginning to withdraw, but only on 3 December did the IDF retreat some 50 kms from the Suez Canal. After France and Britain informed the United Nations that they would evacuate all their forces from the Canal Zone by 18 December, the pressure on Israel intensified, and Ben-Gurion undertook to retreat at the rate of 25 kms a week. Visibly reluctant, and amid sharp clashes with the UN Secretary General and the US President, Israel retreated bit by bit, and in mid-January halted at what looked like her 'red line' – the border of Mandatory Palestine (which had included the Gaza Strip), and Sharm al-Sheikh, which dominates the Tiran Straits. Ben-Gurion also took steps that revealed his unspoken wishes – he approved Moshe Dayan's proposal to settle IDF Pioneer Corps outposts in Sharm al-Sheikh and along the Tiran Straits, and imposed Israeli law on the inhabitants of the Gaza Strip.

The confrontation with the United States intensified throughout November and December. A new war of words began, with numerous messages exchanged between Ben-Gurion, Eisenhower and Dulles, with official statements, instructions to Israel's information officers, guidelines for Abba Eban's speeches at the UN General Assembly, and scores of telegrams, letters and directives. All these flowed from the desk of Yaacov Herzog, who enjoyed Ben-Gurion's unqualified confidence, and he conducted the political campaign authoritatively and coolly. Herzog had become the manager of Israel's foreign policy. In his telegrams, which usually noted that they expressed Ben-Gurion's orders, he issued instructions and directives to Israel's foreign policy-making aides, headed by Foreign Secretary Golda Meir and Ambassador to the US Abba

Eban.[3] Herzog also sometimes sent Eban and others general assessments and 'reflections' on the steps to be taken, without specifying if these were Ben-Gurion's or his own, and Israel's representatives accepted them unreservedly.[4]

Herzog also maintained close ties with the world press, held frequent meetings with foreign ambassadors, and built up a special relationship with the American Ambassador, Edward Lawson, who was pivotal to the most important decisions in the crisis.

During those dramatic days, Yaacov Herzog revealed yet another side of his persona – more mature and self-confident, with clear notions of what should be done. While during the Sinai operation itself he had acted as Ben-Gurion's advisor and aide, now he did not hesitate to express and defend his own opinion at the highest level of discussions which determined Israel's position. His view often prevailed, because Ben-Gurion took his advice, the cabinet confirmed Ben-Gurion's proposals, and Herzog would promptly implement the decisions he had initiated. Thus he became one of the driving forces behind the State in those frenetic days. As Dr Meron Medzini put it, 'During the Sinai campaign and after, Herzog reached the peak of his political influence. Show me another country in which the head of the US section at the Foreign Ministry determines the country's foreign policy. At that time he had the maximum influence over Ben-Gurion. As political advisor at Ben-Gurion's side, he was unique. Nobody questioned his material when he phrased his telegrams and suggestions. He was a fount of wisdom.'[5]

Herzog's new standing was frequently manifested, as for example in the consultation at the Prime Minister's house on 3 January 1957, when Ben-Gurion and the Chief of Staff discussed the next stage of the withdrawal, and Herzog took the lead. Dayan was scheduled to meet the chief of the UN Observers, General E. L. M. ('Tommy') Burns, to inform him of the next stage of Israel's withdrawal. Dayan brought a map showing the new line of deployment that cut across the Sinai. It began in the north, 25 kms east of El-Arish, and ended at the southern rim of the Peninsula, except for the area around Sharm al-Sheikh. Dayan wanted to propose this line to Burns as an 'additional line of withdrawal' for the second week in January.

'There is no need for you to announce a further withdrawal at this meeting,' Herzog said. He explained that the main effort must be to gain time. He reminded the others that Israel had undertaken that by the end of the first week of January there would be no more Israeli forces west of El-Arish, and that General Burns had pointed out that A-Tur was west of El-Arish. 'All you have to do,' Herzog said to Dayan, 'is announce the evacuation of A-Tur and every other place that lies west of El-Arish along a straight line to the southern shore.' In this way, he explained, we will have kept our word that by 7 January there will be no Israeli forces west of El-Arish.[6] His suggestion was accepted.

Herzog went on to explain that this would gain Israel another fortnight before the 'crisis in the General Assembly', during which Israel would explain her position to several governments, above all to the United States. 'I hope,' he added, 'that the next meeting with the [UN] Secretary General will not take place before 8 January, so that we can announce further withdrawal only on 10 January. After the next withdrawal we'll have leeway before the final withdrawal, which will take time.'

Ben-Gurion laughed. 'The Secretary General will probably jump on us on 6 or 7 January,' he said.

After this meeting, Herzog went to Jerusalem and wired the decision to the Israeli UN delegation. 'If Burns should ask about the next stage, Dayan will reply that he has received no instructions ... If you are asked what Dayan is going to say to Burns [tomorrow], say that you still have no information, because otherwise they might pressure you to agree to a further withdrawal.'[7]

The next day Nehemiah Argov telephoned Herzog to tell him that the Dayan-Burns meeting had followed 'the agreed lines', and the conclusion was exactly as Herzog had predicted.[8]

Herzog clearly directed much of the political campaign. Ben-Gurion relied on him and Dayan acquiesced, though not wholeheartedly. Dayan was bitter because Ben-Gurion no longer consulted him, but 'conducts the policy with Abba Eban and Yaacov Herzog'.[9] But Herzog was the ideal man for the post – an experienced diplomat, a man of strong nerve, who knew exactly how far it was possible to push things without risking sanctions. Herzog did not hesitate to argue with whoever disagreed with him. In a telegram about guidelines that he sent Abba Eban in December, he rejected, politely but firmly, the latter's advice regarding their policy towards Dag Hammarskjold, and the status of the international force being created by the UN. Eban recommended a more conciliatory attitude towards the United Nations.

'I have never hidden my true opinion, no matter who is listening,' Herzog wrote to Eban. He explained lucidly why Israel should not submit to the UN Secretary General's pressure, and why she had to stand resolute on two issues – one, firm guarantees of freedom of navigation; two, the kind of UN force to be stationed in Egypt. He ended with an appeal to Eban – 'I beg you in all friendship and respect to remember that freedom of navigation in the Red Sea can free us and give Israel an international position, both political and economic, and in the long run completely change our situation. I'm sure you agree with me that where such a fateful issue is concerned, we must search our hearts most thoroughly and be willing to struggle to the utmost of our ability.'[10] The following day he received a telegram from Golda Meir: 'My thinking is similar to yours.'[11]

But the dispute with Eban did not end there. After a tense meeting with Hammarskjold on 5 January, Eban sent a telegram recommending, in effect, Israel's surrender on the political front. 'The time-gaining stage is over,' he stated. 'It's becoming increasingly clear that our continuing retention of territory in the Sinai Desert is weakening rather than strengthening our position in the crucial struggle for freedom of navigation in the Red Sea and for

Acting Foreign Minister

Gaza ... If we come to the General Assembly while holding on to Sinai territories other than Sharm al-Sheikh, it will be difficult to win any support on the issue of free navigation. All of us [in Israel's delegations in New York and Washington] believe that an unequivocal statement about the complete evacuation of Sinai is needed to win any support in the world for our cause ... We must inform Hammarskjold of our readiness to complete the withdrawal from Egypt's territory, except for Sharm al-Sheikh, by 18 January ... A new proposal for a staged withdrawal will not gain us time, but rather hasten the confrontation.' Eban also recommended inviting Hammarskjold to Israel, to explain Israel's position to him.

Following Eban's telegram, Ben-Gurion held a consultation with Levi Eshkol the Finance Minster, Moshe Dayan, Walter Eytan and Yaacov Herzog. Dayan was opposed to withdrawing beyond the Abu Aweigila line; Eytan argued in favour of retreating to the international border. Herzog recommended inviting Golda Meir and Abba Eban to take part in the decisive discussion about Israel's future moves. 'I have to speak quite frankly,' he opened his rebuttal of Eban's suggestion. 'Our UN delegation is not in accord with our thinking, and you do not send soldiers to carry out a mission when their commander insists that it is impossible. In such a case you either replace the unit or call in the commander and persuade him.' Herzog noted that while he disagreed with Eban, he had the highest respect for him, and 'there is no limit to the debt we all owe him for his tremendous stand in this campaign'.

Herzog's recommendations were the opposite of Eban's. 'Right now we can avoid making another statement to the UN Secretary General about the withdrawal, by telling him that the Foreign Minister and Eban are returning home immediately for consultation, and on Friday we'll inform him about a 25 kms withdrawal within seven days, and thus gain another four days before the crisis.' Herzog clung to his essential idea that the main objective at that moment was to gain time, if only a few days, because Israel's information campaign was beginning to bear fruit in various capitals, and in the US Congress. He also maintained that after 20 January 1957, the American President would begin to receive representations from American political bodies who would apply pressure in support of Israel. He added that it was also important to give the Minister of Trade and Industry, Pinchas Sapir, who had just left for the US, enough time to obtain a loan from the Bank of America, and to transfer all the funds of the United Jewish Appeal and Israel Bonds out of the US, 'against the possibility of their being frozen as part of US sanctions'.

Ben-Gurion followed with a passionate speech on the need to stand firm in Sharm al-Sheikh and Gaza. 'A nation that isn't willing to make sacrifices does not deserve achievements,' he declared, and spoke about the supreme value of the political test 'to toughen the nation'.

Herzog interrupted. 'I agree in principle about standing firm,' he said, 'but the campaign is not something to rejoice about, and we must first explore all political avenues.'

Ben-Gurion accepted Herzog's suggestion to summon the Foreign Minister and Abba Eban for consultation, and said that the UN Secretary General should be informed about a further withdrawal of 25 kms. Herzog again interrupted him, noting that Hammarskjold was insisting on Israel's evacuation of the Sinai, but regarded the question of Gaza and the freedom of navigation as 'residual matters'. 'Our delegation should ask what he means by that.'

Ben-Gurion said he did not agree that they should ask Hammarskjold about it.

But Herzog insisted, and finally Ben-Gurion said, 'Wire them in your own name.'

'How?' asked Herzog. 'Every comment I make is approved by you.'

But Ben-Gurion did not budge.

Herzog drafted a telegram to Golda Meir and Eban, in which he asked them to return to Israel for consultation, informed them

Acting Foreign Minister

in Ben-Gurion's name about an additional 25 kms withdrawal, and told them to ask the UN Secretary General what he meant by 'residual matters' with regard to Sharm al-Sheikh and Gaza. He noted that 'the Prime Minister maintains that the negotiations with the UN Secretary General must not continue, but allow me to suggest that you inquire about Hammarskjold's meaning'. When he brought the written telegram to Ben-Gurion for approval, the Prime Minister's face betrayed his reservations about that passage, but he approved the telegram and Herzog got his wish.[12]

Now the United States began to carry out her threat of sanctions – she broke off bilateral talks about a loan, a grant and food surplus to Israel. On 19 January, the UN General Assembly passed its fifth resolution demanding Israel's complete withdrawal, by 74 votes against the two of France and Israel. Yet it was precisely in these difficult moments that Israel's information campaign was beginning to produce results. Several countries in Western Europe and South America began to acknowledge the justice of Israel's claims. The General Assembly's resolution in January, too, was more moderate than previous ones, and did not include harsh warnings against Israel.

Not so President Eisenhower, who actually hardened his stance and decided to intervene in person. On 3 February, the US Ambassador Edward Lawson brought Ben-Gurion a new letter, with wording that exacerbated the relations between the US President and Israel's Prime Minister. 'It is my firm hope that the withdrawal [from Gaza and the Straits] will be accomplished without further delay,' Eisenhower wrote. 'Continuing to ignore the law of nations, as expressed in the UN resolutions, will almost certainly lead to further measures by the UN, which could seriously damage relations between Israel and members of the UN, including the United States.' Ben-Gurion, who was ill in bed again, exploded with rage. 'Yaacov!' he shouted, 'write and tell him to fire guided missiles at us. He has atomic missiles – why not fire them at us? Let them carry out their sanctions!'[13]

Ben-Gurion recommended that his cabinet reject Eisenhower's demand. Then, having moderated his initial response, with Herzog's help, he formulated its final wording. He reiterated Israel's willingness to evacuate Sharm al-Sheikh if guaranteed freedom of navigation, and to withdraw the IDF from the Gaza Strip. But he insisted on leaving an Israeli civil administration, including police, in the Strip, in coordination with the UN. Ben-Gurion vented his injured feelings and sense of frustration in an emotional appeal to the American President: 'Are we not entitled by the UN Charter to security and freedom from attack like any other nation? I ask you, Mr President, with respect – why has nothing tangible been done so far by the government of the United States and the other governments that supported the United States' proposals to provide us with such security? Do Israel's inhabitants not have the right to be secure from murder by gangs of terrorists organized by Egypt, which is a member of the UN? Do Israeli vessels have no right to sail in international waters, like the vessels of other nations?

'Your letter hints at possible "measures" that may be taken by the UN against Israel for failing to carry out in full the General Assembly's resolution. Such "measures" have never been applied to Egypt, which violated for years the resolutions of the Security Council and articles of the UN Charter, and remains in violation to this day ... Is it conceivable that the United States, the land of freedom, equality and human rights, would support such discrimination, and that UN "measures" will force us to go back to a situation in which we are prey to murder and quarantine?

'... It is inconceivable that now, when we have recovered our independence in our ancient homeland, we shall submit to discrimination. Our people will never accept this, however great the sacrifice we have to make.'

American pressure and a sense of isolation at the UN led many of Herzog's associates at the Foreign Ministry to favour a conciliatory position and seek a way out of the crisis in which Israel would actually be compelled to forego her demands. Even Yaacov Herzog's good friend, Gideon Rafael, who was with the UN delegation, sent him a private, confidential letter strongly opposing Israel's official position. He expressed doubts about Israel's struggle with enemies and friends alike, and the efficacy of defying the sanctions that might be imposed on her.[14] But Herzog remained resolute, alongside Ben-Gurion.

The political situation changed unexpectedly a few days after Rafael's letter. On 11 February there was a surprising turning-point in the crisis, when Herzog received a telegram from Abba Eban, that 'the issue of sanctions is collapsing under pressure from the Senate and the press'. It was the first in a series of excited telegrams from Eban, one of which reported his talk with Secretary of State John Foster Dulles and an *aide-mémoire* he had received from him. The new optimism was at least partly justified, as the US Administration admitted for the first time that Israel's claims had some validity. Dulles' *aide-mémoire* stated: 'The United States believes that the Gulf of Eilat is an international waterway, and that no nation has the right forcibly to bar free and innocent passage in the bay and through the Straits leading to it ... The United States is willing to implement, with regard to vessels flying the American flag, the right of free and innocent passage, and to join others in securing a general recognition of this right.'

This declaration was a highly significant victory for Israel: at long last, the United States acknowledged Israel's right to demand free passage through the Red Sea Straits. Herzog now replied, with unusual brevity, to Gideon Rafael's pessimistic letter: 'Allow me only to remind you that in a debate that took place about two months ago I argued that if we succeeded in arousing public opinion in the US and elsewhere, the test would be if the US joined the Arabs in the matter of sanctions.'[15] And indeed, the US backed out of the call for sanctions.

But the US did not change its stance on the withdrawal itself. Dulles reiterated: 'Clearly, Israel's right to enjoy free and innocent passage will depend on her prompt withdrawal, in accordance with UN resolutions.' Similarly with regard to the Gaza Strip: 'Israel's withdrawal ... must take place immediately and unconditionally, leaving the future of the Gaza Strip to the efforts and good offices of the United Nations.'

The *aide-mémoire* infuriated Ben-Gurion. Though he admitted in a telegram he wrote with Yaacov Herzog that 'the *aide-mémoire* shows a will to find a positive solution,' he added, 'but the proposed solution is not positive, and we cannot accept it. Israeli navigation is not guaranteed, and we cannot in any circumstances return to the armistice agreement, which means Egyptian rule in Gaza ... We cannot move from this position, even if they impose sanctions on us.' A special cabinet meeting convened on 14 February and affirmed Ben-Gurion's position.

Though it did not reject Dulles' *aide-mémoire*, Israel's reiteration of her other demands was viewed by Washington as a negative response and angered the US Administration. Dulles refused to modify his position and demanded immediate withdrawal. Eisenhower said to his aides that he was tired of Security Council resolutions which only censured Israel, and wanted a resolution that would impose sanctions.

The UN General Assembly was again summoned to a special session, probably to decide on sanctions on Israel.

At the last moment Ben-Gurion sent a message to Dulles: 'At the eleventh hour, to avoid a fateful misunderstanding between our two nations, I appeal to you personally to postpone the discussions in the General Assembly for a little while, and to arrange for a commission consisting of representatives of various disinterested states to come without delay to Israel ... Withdrawal in the present circumstances could be disastrous for us. If the United Nations, supported by the United States, seeks to compel us to do so by means of sanctions, it would be an historical injustice, and a possibly fateful blow would be struck against the moral foundation of the international organization.'

Acting Foreign Minister

Eisenhower could not contain his fury with Israel, especially since he found that there was mounting opposition to sanctions in the House of Representatives and the Senate. He summoned 26 Congressional leaders to the White House and tried to persuade them to support his position on Israel, but they refused. The press and Jewish organizations also expressed growing opposition to the President's stand. It seemed that Eban and Herzog's moves were bearing fruit – the atmosphere in Washington was changing; public opinion and the political establishment moderated their criticism of Israel and showed greater understanding of her motives. Eisenhower sent another letter to Ben-Gurion on 20 February. Herzog took it to Ben-Gurion's house after midnight and read it to him. 'I shall greatly regret,' the President wrote, 'the need for the United States to adopt a position in the UN, and for the UN itself to adopt measures, that might have far-reaching consequences on Israel's [foreign] relations throughout the world.'

Ben-Gurion grew very worried. He got out of bed and put on a dressing-gown. 'He paced up and down for a long time, deep in thought,' Yaacov Herzog recalled.[16]

That night Ben-Gurion poured out his heart to Herzog, and told him about his meeting with Eisenhower in 1945, when the latter was still in uniform as supreme commander of the Allied forces in Europe. They had met in Frankfurt, and Ben-Gurion was impressed by the General's humanity. He wondered how such a man could fail to understand Israel's position. He said that he deplored America's political stance, which stemmed from foreign policy considerations, but was more offended by Eisenhower's moral criticism of Israel. He was convinced, he said to Herzog, that in the same situation Eisenhower and Dulles would have acted exactly as he had. He also compared Israel's present predicament to the age-old isolation of the Jewish people among the nations.

'We mustn't forget,' Herzog replied, 'that in these circumstances Israel could find herself in a much worse predicament.'[17]

Apparently Ben-Gurion was willing to take responsibility for possibly aggravating the situation and having sanctions imposed on Israel. Herzog had already witnessed an exchange between the Prime Minister and the Minister of Finance, Levi Eshkol, on 7 January, in which Ben-Gurion asked Eshkol how long Israel could withstand economic sanctions. Eshkol left and returned a few hours later armed with facts and figures. Ben-Gurion told Herzog that according to Eshkol, Israel had sufficient reserves for three months, which could be extended by means of rationing.[18] The information bolstered Ben-Gurion in his position; moreover, he argued, the imminent test would be very important on the home front.[19] He instructed Eban to continue fighting for the freedom of navigation in the Straits and although Ben-Gurion also insisted that the Gaza Strip was not to be returned to Egypt, Herzog sensed that he was in two minds about it. On the one hand, he did not want the Strip to return to Egyptian control, but on the other, he did not care to annexe Gaza with its hundreds of thousands of refugees. Herzog thought it significant that not once in those four months of political struggle did Ben-Gurion visit Gaza.[20]

President Eisenhower saw that opposition in Congress was growing. Republican Senator William Knowland and Democratic Senator Lyndon Johnson (the future President) refused to support his hard line on Israel. The irate President decided to address the American people over the heads of Congress and his speech to the nation was even harsher than his letter to Ben-Gurion: 'If we agree that an armed attack can achieve the attacker's purpose, it would mean that we have turned back the clock of international order ... I believe that for the sake of peace, the UN has no alternative but to put pressure on Israel to obey the resolutions on withdrawal ... Should a nation that attacks and conquers foreign territory and is denounced by the UN be allowed to attach conditions to its actual retreat? The UN must not be allowed to fail!'

The decisive confrontation between Israel and the United States was due to take place on 26 February, the day of the

Acting Foreign Minister

General Assembly session. 'Tonight the General Assembly opens,' Ben-Gurion wrote in his journal. 'I'm afraid that by the end of the week we will have faced a decision on sanctions. Hammarskjold is seeing to it.'

But a dramatic development occurred at the last moment.

'We hear from New York about a surprising proposal by Pineau [the French Foreign Minister],' Ben-Gurion wrote in his journal on 27 February. 'But we have not yet seen the text.'

A few hours, later Eban telegraphed the French Minister's proposal – Israel would declare its complete withdrawal from Gaza, based on the 'assumption' that UN forces would take responsibility for the military and civil administration of the Strip, and would remain there until the achievement of a peace settlement. In the event that Egypt broke the arrangement, Israel would retain the right to self-defence. The United States and other countries would declare their confirmation of Israel's 'assumptions' in the General Assembly, thereby providing an international basis for Israel's position.

What Eban did not, and could not, know was that the 'French proposal' had actually been instigated by John Foster Dulles, who had skilfully manoeuvred the French Prime Minister and Foreign Minister to his purpose – that France, as Israel's closest ally, would be the one to make the proposal, which Israel would be unable to reject.[21] Herzog received the reports of the Israeli representatives in Washington and New York who had seen the text, and was impressed by the fact that it had indeed been presented as a proposal, and that France had made no attempt to pressure Israel to accept it.[22] Ben-Gurion read the telegram and said to Herzog, 'This is the end of the campaign.' He summoned an urgent cabinet meeting for that evening, and at two o'clock the following morning the government approved the French proposal.

Immediately after the meeting, Ben-Gurion and Herzog wrote a telegram with detailed instructions to Eban. For his part, Eban, with Dulles, drew up a careful timetable of the next steps to be taken – Foreign Minister Golda Meir would make a statement at the UN in keeping with the French proposal; she would be followed by the US representative, Henry Cabot Lodge, who would state his government's positive view of Israel's statement and the 'assumptions' it contained. Then a number of maritime nations would state their support for freedom of navigation in the Straits. Ben-Gurion informed Dayan about the agreed scenario, but Dayan, a confirmed sceptic and realist, was unconvinced and opposed the plan.

Dayan was right. The United States did not deliver her part in the agreement.

On Friday, 1 March 1957, a special cabinet meeting held at the Prime Minister's house confirmed the text of the statement that Golda Meir would make at the UN. Herzog telephoned her in New York to inform her of the confirmation. That evening Israel received a bitter blow in the General Assembly. After Golda Meir delivered the agreed statement about Israel's 'assumptions', the US ambassador, Henry Cabot Lodge, came to the podium. The Israeli delegates were stunned to hear him making a speech that was plainly at variance with what had been agreed in the preliminary talks between Israel and the US. Cabot Lodge described Israel's positions as 'not unreasonable', but proceeded to restate the former position of the US Administration, and did not repeat the wording that had been agreed in advance. Golda Meir was deeply frustrated, and felt that the United States had deceived Israel. 'There was nothing I could do,' she said later. 'I just sat there biting my lip.' Golda had no doubt that the Egyptians would now return to the Gaza Strip and that Israel would, in effect, withdraw unconditionally, without any guarantees that Gaza would not revert to being a launch-pad for terrorism and infiltration.

Ben-Gurion heard Cabot Lodge's speech on the radio and was profoundly upset. At first he wanted to call off the withdrawal, and prepared a speech to that effect to broadcast on national radio. He sent one of his bodyguards to fetch Herzog from synagogue and bring him to his house. Herzog had already heard what had happened at the UN. 'On Saturday I went to synagogue at 9 am,' he noted in his diary. 'Approached by Jews who had listened to the radio and were angry about Cabot Lodge's speech. I was puzzled.'[23] When the Prime Minister's bodyguard came up to him, Herzog took off his talith and hurried to Ben-Gurion's house. He found him in pyjamas and dressing-gown, 'altogether shocked.' Ben-Gurion told Herzog to telephone Eban, instruct him to consult the Foreign Minister and then seek an urgent meeting with Dulles to discuss Cabot Lodge's statement. Herzog telephoned at once and woke Eban – it was 3 am in New York. Ben-Gurion stood beside Herzog during this conversation and told him word for word what to say.[24] Later he described to Herzog his meeting the previous evening with the top commanders of the IDF. He had summoned them to his house after he had made the decision to withdraw from the Tiran Straits and Gaza, to explain his reasons and listen to their reactions. He told Herzog that, despite the atmosphere of mutual understanding, the meeting had upset him deeply.

After a messenger had delivered the text of Cabot Lodge's speech, Herzog analysed it. 'Lodge was all right on the issue of Sharm al-Sheikh,' he said, 'but there are serious complications on Gaza.'[25] He pointed to the paragraphs that he considered dangerous. Suddenly Ben-Gurion said to him, 'Close your eyes!'

'What?' Herzog wondered.

'Close your eyes!' Ben-Gurion repeated.

Herzog did as he was told, and when he opened his eyes he saw that Ben-Gurion had marked the worrying passages in Cabot Lodge's speech with a pen. As it was the Sabbath, he had told Herzog to close his eyes, 'because he didn't want me to see him writing.'[26]

The furious Ben-Gurion 'roared with growing frenzy' that he wanted to broadcast a speech to the nation, attacking what Cabot Lodge had said in the General Assembly. 'He yelled so loudly that he felt obliged to apologize,' Herzog noted.[27] Responding calmly and quietly, Herzog persuaded him to give up the idea, and got him to discuss possible responses in a restrained, matter-of-fact way. Then they agreed on a number of diplomatic steps to be taken in Washington, and on an official statement to be issued by the Foreign Ministry in Jerusalem.

That wintry Saturday, after talking to Herzog, Ben-Gurion summoned the cabinet to a special session – the first time since the establishment of the State that the cabinet met on the Sabbath. The ministers were gloomy. The meeting resolved to instruct Eban to demand from Dulles a clear statement that Gaza would not be returned to Egypt. Dusk had fallen as the ministers left, and after ten minutes Ben-Gurion looked out of the window and said to Herzog, 'The day is over, you can write the instructions.' Though in the midst of a grave political upheaval, Ben-Gurion showed consideration for Herzog's religious principles and took pains not to lead him to break them. For his part, Herzog not only respected, but felt great affection and concern for Ben-Gurion. Later that night, when he returned to the Prime Minister's house to report on his talks and exchange of telegrams with Eban, 'he was sleeping so soundly that I spared him and didn't rouse him'.[28]

He was back at Ben-Gurion's house the next morning. That morning Ben-Gurion and Herzog realized that Israel's attempts to extract a firm commitment from the United States, along the lines of Dulles' promises to Eban, were doomed to failure. Ben-Gurion had to be content with the letter from President Eisenhower that Herzog brought him. 'I believe that Israel will have no reason to regret having acted in accordance with the strong sentiment of the entire world community,' Eisenhower wrote. He referred to the 'hopes and expectations' expressed in Golda Meir's speech at the General Assembly, 'and others' speeches,' and concluded: 'I am of the opinion that there is a basis for the hopes and expectations of all, and I want you to know that the United States ... will endeavour to ensure that these hopes have not been in vain.'

Ben-Gurion realized that he was cornered. That morning, before the weekly cabinet meeting, he talked briefly with Herzog and the Minister of Justice, Pinchas Rosen. 'I shall tell my son and grandson,' he said glumly, 'that they had better skin carcasses in the market rather than become prime ministers of Israel.' To which Herzog responded, 'Today even the carcass skinner is worried.' Ben-Gurion muttered, 'But he's not responsible for the decisions.'[29]

Herzog left and went to his office. Later, when he returned to the Prime Minister, he heard that the government had indeed decided to withdraw from Sharm al-Sheikh and Gaza. Thus ended the political campaign.

Israel withdrew from the Gaza Strip and UN forces took her place. A few days later, the Egyptian military administration returned to the Strip, arousing great anger in Israel. Ben-Gurion decided not to respond with a military operation. 'I am not inclined to act in Gaza,' he said to Moshe Dayan. Herzog had the impression that he took this position because he feared that a fight over the status of the Gaza Strip might jeopardise Israel's principal achievement – the freedom of navigation in the Gulf of Eilat.

Indeed, it was better this way, because the Egyptian presence was quite limited, and Nasser made a secret agreement with the US State Department and the UN Secretary General, Dag Hammarskjold, to desist from launching attacks on Israel from the Strip.

The Sinai/Suez campaign did not bring about the downfall of President Nasser, nor was he deposed, as Ben-Gurion had hoped – on the contrary, he became one of the most admired leaders of the Third World. Nevertheless, Israel's military victory bore some worthwhile fruit. Ben-Gurion achieved much less than he had wished, but much more than he had hoped.

Firstly, and importantly, the campaign gave Israel ten years' peace. One by one, the borders became quiet. The fedayeen did not return to Gaza, and infiltration from the Strip ceased – disproving Nasser's claims before the Sinai campaign that Egypt was unable to prevent the incursions. Israel enjoyed *de facto* peace on her borders, with only rare incidents, until the Six Day War. This was due to the new military balance in the Middle East. The Sinai campaign had revealed that the gap between Israel and her neighbours had grown since the War of Independence, and it was doubtful if the Arabs could overpower her in the foreseeable future.

A second positive outcome was the development and prosperity of the port of Eilat, and the laying of the pipeline to the Mediterranean. But the greatest – if unintentional – achievement for Israel was the stationing of UN forces in the Straits and in Gaza, which was a vindication, by the international community, of Israel's motives for going to war against Egypt. The UN Secretary General, and several member states, demanded that UN forces be stationed inside Israel as well. But Israel rejected this demand and the international community showed understanding. Although President Eisenhower warned in a speech that 'the aggressor must not be rewarded,' the blue helmets of the UN troops were in fact Israel's reward. From the standpoint of international law, Israel had been the aggressor in the Sinai war, yet the UN forces were stationed in the country which had been the victim, rather than in the 'aggressor's'. The UN forces were there to constrain the attacked country, not Israel, which had attacked it. They were there to compel Egypt, the victim of aggression, to permit free passage to the attacker's navigation and to keep the peace on the attacker's border.

The dark predictions that Israel would become 'painfully isolated' as a result of the Sinai campaign were confounded – in fact, there followed a period of unprecedented political success. The IDF was respected and admired all over the world. Many states in the Third World – in Africa, Asia and Latin America – established diplomatic ties with Israel, sent delegations and requested technical assistance in developing their economies and armies. In the decade

1957–67 Israel's relations with countries of the Third World reached their zenith – a direct outcome of its victory in the Sinai campaign.

Israel's relations with the West also improved markedly. France provided Israel with know-how and equipment to build a nuclear reactor in the Negev and to develop missiles. She also supplied Israel with up-to-date weapons. In the meantime, Israel's relations with the United States also grew closer, and in a matter of years she became America's closest ally in the Middle East.

Yaacov Herzog drew several lessons from the military campaign and its international consequences. In his view, the Sinai campaign produced four important achievements: the crushing of Egypt's war machine; the long-term effect on inter-Arab relations, as other Arab states lost their fear of Nasser's giant stature; the securing of freedom of navigation in the Straits, enabling Israel to build up a presence in Africa; and the establishment of Israel as a permanent factor in the Middle East.[30] He concluded that in the Sinai campaign 'Israel exploited her political opportunities to the full, and acted correctly, stage after stage.'[31] He saw only one error in Israel's political assessment; namely, that she had failed to foresee the intensity of the international reaction to the operation carried out in cooperation with Britain and France. Nevertheless, he maintained that in the long run the results vindicated the action. The military operation had gone well, and the withdrawal was also carried out intelligently and courageously, based on political realism that correctly estimated Israel's limitations. The decisive achievement was the freedom of navigation – had this not been won, Israel would have been prepared to face severe economic sanctions.

Herzog greatly appreciated the contribution of Jewish organizations in the United States, who had fought against the imposition of economic sanctions – but though he regarded their action as significant, he did not think it decisive. He explained the distinction in typical Ben-Gurion terminology: 'We had in our hands a more powerful weapon – we were in the Sinai, and no one could have driven us out of there except by force.'[32]

Ten years after the Sinai operation, in 1966, Herzog was asked to reassess its consequences. His response was frank and realistic: 'Despite the great significance of promises made by friends and other outside factors, in the final analysis, the value of such promises depends on Israel's own strength.

'... [On the international front] information proved most efficient in creating sympathy for Israel's problems in public opinion in the world ... International relations are in constant flux. It pays to take a deep breath. What seems blocked today may open up tomorrow. Israeli-Arab relations are interlinked with two other circles of tension in the region – inter-Arab and inter-bloc relations.' Herzog estimated that a joint American-Soviet stand could promote a peace settlement in the region.

'... Though we are still far from peace,' he added, 'in the long term the Sinai campaign brought it closer.' But his principal conclusion placed the turbulent campaign of 1956–7 in the broad perspective of Jewish history: 'Today, as 3,000 years ago, "Israel is a people that dwells alone."'[33]

8

Birds Over the Cedars of Lebanon

'I had confidence in Yaacov Herzog's management in Washington ... ' Abba Eban wrote. 'Herzog's life is a unique drama in the story of our foreign service. The son of the Chief Rabbi, Rabbi Isaac Halevi Herzog, Yaacov was brought up in scholarly isolation and reverence, close to his father's spiritual world, while creating a distinctive inner world of his own. His quick mind moved restlessly from scholarship to politics. He was an original figure, orthodox without being pious, intellectually ambitious, yet curiously reluctant to assume any central responsibility. He always worked in somebody else's shadow – first Ben-Gurion, then Golda Meir, then Eshkol and Golda again. He served us all with skill and dignity, with un-Israeli courtesy. When he came to me in Washington I had the feeling that I was advancing his release from his parents' custody, which though doubtless warm, was restricting. He brought to diplomacy a sense of encompassing history with sophisticated imagination. He had no time or thought for anything that was not directly connected to the interests of the Jewish people.

'Everything about him was quick, sudden; his style, his speech, even his physical manners. He would come in and talk to me at length and in detail, and then, before I had time to look up, he had already risen and was hastening from the room. He radiated a sense of constant haste, as though aware that fate was after him.'[1]

This is how Eban saw the new minister at the Israeli Embassy in Washington, who arrived in the United States in September 1957.

Yaacov Herzog

After his brilliant work at Ben-Gurion's side during the Sinai campaign and the subsequent political struggle, Golda Meir, in consultation with Ben-Gurion, decided to appoint Herzog minister at the Israeli Embassy in the American capital. It was a very important post, particularly as the Ambassador, Abba Eban, was also Israel's Ambassador to the United Nations, and divided his time between Washington and New York.

Washington was always the front line of Israeli diplomacy, and it became even more important after the Sinai campaign and its repercussions on Israel's relations with the US. On the one hand, there was heightened tension between the two countries, because of America's perception that France, Britain and Israel had deceived her by going to war behind her back. On the other hand, the understanding that had developed in the turbulent days following the Sinai campaign was expected to provide the basis for a new relationship between Israel and the US.

Yaacov's departure was accompanied by warm good wishes from the entire Prime Minister's office, since he was known as 'Ben-Gurion's man'.[2] He had become, in a short space of time, a close friend of Shimon Peres, Nehemiah Argov, Yitzhak Navon, Teddy Kollek and Ben-Gurion's faithful aide and advisor Chaim Israeli.

Before Herzog left for the US, Ben-Gurion gave him a personal letter to his good friend, General Walter Bedell Smith, formerly one of the heads of America's intelligence community, who was then recovering from an operation. 'Dear General,' Ben-Gurion wrote, 'Yaacov Herzog, the son of our Chief Rabbi, now posted to our embassy in Washington ... is one of the most able and gifted young men, and as loyal as he is gifted. I shall be glad if you would – hoping you are fully recovered – give him an opportunity to meet you. One of his great qualities is complete discretion, he is familiar not only with the situation in Israel but in the entire Middle East, and you can at all times ask him for information, and rely entirely on his confidentiality.'[3]

Birds Over the Cedars of Lebanon

After the two met in Washington, Bedell Smith wrote to Ben-Gurion: 'Mr Herzog gave me your letter ... and we had a most interesting and informative conversation. I got the impression that he's highly intelligent, extremely knowledgeable and a fascinating personality ... I promise to provide him with any assistance and advice he may require.'[4]

Ben-Gurion's letter was not merely an appeal for assistance from an old friend – it was also a message to all who met and worked with Yaacov Herzog in Washington that the new minister was especially close to him, and was his man in the American capital. This status pleased Yaacov, who asked Yitzhak Navon to inform him from time to time about 'the direction of the PM's thinking in matters of foreign policy'.[5] He also sent Ben-Gurion situation assessments through Chaim Israeli.[6] With the latter he corresponded almost weekly, and most of his long, detailed letters, filled with information and analysis, were probably intended for the Prime Minister's eyes as well.

The Washington appointment was Yaacov Herzog's first diplomatic posting. Though he and Pnina were already accustomed to travel, the family's sea voyage was an unusually long one for them, and the opening of a new chapter in their life. When they arrived in New York, the two small girls were ill with influenza – which promptly also felled both their mother and nanny. The elder daughter, Shira, who was born in 1953, now had a sister, Eliezra, born in 1955 and named after Pnina's brother Eliezer, who was killed in the War of Independence.

The great experience on this voyage, which brought tears to Yaacov's eyes, was 'seeing Jews from all walks of life in the US, standing tremulous with awe in the ship's synagogue, as an American naval officer read a prayer for the welfare of Israel'.[7] The family settled happily in the handsome Myrtle Street residence of Israel's minister to Washington. Yaacov threw himself wholeheartedly into his new position. Within a fortnight he met the entire diplomatic staff, dozens of diplomats and American

Administration officials, and the staff at Israel's Consulate General in New York, and even managed to dispatch 31 letters of farewell, thanks and good wishes to people back in Israel. 'But you need not fear that I'll compete with you in burdening the courier,' he assured Walter Eytan, director-general of the Ministry, who was amazed by the volume of Herzog's correspondence.[8]

He began to make his way among members of Congress and senior officials in Washington. His excellent English with its lilting Irish accent delighted his listeners. He was a fascinating conversationalist, with wide knowledge of history and literature. Herzog did not wear a skullcap, but he emphasized his Jewishness, and his profound belief in Jewish tradition and religion. This combination of a skilled diplomat, a wise man, a product of English culture, a man of the world, yet a representative of the Jewish state, and himself an observant Jew – all added up to a unique figure never seen before in Washington.

Yaacov reported home about meetings and lunches with senior figures. The director-general of the Foreign Ministry in Jerusalem wondered how a religious Jew like Herzog could dine in Washington's non-kosher restaurants. Herzog replied, 'As for your question about the meals – there's no problem. The great restaurants here are full of all kinds of food, various salmons and other kosher fish, salads and fruit, which can satisfy a person all his life without touching meat. In fact, most of the people I eat with choose the same dishes as I, since the midday meal here is what they call a business lunch. If you should come here, I'll prove to you that keeping kosher not only does not affect your health, but actually keeps you slim.'[9]

'We faced a very difficult assignment,' said Abba Eban, 'to repair Israel's relations with the US after the great difficulty we had been in [following the Sinai war]. There was a crisis of confidence. It was the nadir of Israel-US relations, which is why we really had a sense of destiny when we undertook to rehabilitate relations with the US. When Yaacov came to Washington it was in fact his first sortie from the home atmosphere. The wide world was strange to him and I was amazed by his ability to adapt to the ways of the world. Without foregoing his distinct appearance, his religious observance, his way of life, he was soon at home in this complex world, the world of international relations.'[10]

This somewhat patronizing description was not quite accurate, of course. Yaacov had been travelling and meeting world leaders from an early age. He had often visited the United States, too, in connection with his senior position in the Foreign Ministry, and was familiar with the international scene. He was not, as Eban's statement implied, a country boy who had come to Washington's marble halls straight from the fields. But Eban went on, 'He had a special gift for winning people's confidence. Yet he was not unworldly, and I was especially struck by his ability to conduct complicated and exhausting negotiations on material issues, and to see how well-versed he was in every aspect, and how he communicated his expertise to others. In a matter of months he became a unique spectacle, a distinctive institution in Washington life.'[11]

Yaacov laid down some basic rules for his work in Washington. 'I'm getting to know my colleagues,' he wrote to a close friend shortly after arrival, 'and the large staff, which in Washington and New York comes close to 200 people ... The first thing I learned is that a man can spend several years meeting dozens of people a day, and be doing nothing. This means that the first precept is to avoid diversions and digressions from the essential aims and the vital ways of achieving them.'[12] He wrote in a similar vein to the director-general of the Foreign Ministry: 'The range is so immense, that if you do not concentrate on the essential aims and pick and choose your contacts and associations ... you are liable to diversify, disperse and wear yourself out, without achieving anything. That is why I'm determined to study and learn, to stay in Washington as much as possible.'[13]

Herzog made up his mind to ignore the immaterial and concentrate on what mattered; to form contacts with the really important people, those who determined American policy in the Middle East and made the day-to-day decisions concerning Israel and her neighbours. His intelligence and charm opened doors to him, even to people thought to be anti-Semitic and enemies of Israel. One of these was Under-Secretary of State Loy Henderson, a very influential person in the State Department, though ostensibly in charge of administration. Reaching him was not easy, but at their first meeting Herzog broke the ice. Henderson told him that during the Second World War President Roosevelt had ordered him to help rescue hundreds of Yeshiva students from Lithuania, who were transferred to Shanghai. He asked Herzog what distinguished the Lithuanian Yeshivas, and in what way they differed from those in Poland. Yaacov promptly launched into a lecture on 'Lithuania's Jewry and its tradition, the Gaon of Vilna's system of plain interpretation, Hassidism, and so on'.[14] Henderson was fascinated and wished to hear more, and Yaacov spoke about Talmudic thought, Maimonides, exegesis, the Babylonian scholars, and the Second Temple period. The conversation flowed, but Herzog feared that it would continue to revolve around antiquity, which was not the purpose of his visit to Henderson. 'Then I suggested that we move on to more immediate matters, concerning the Middle East and the Third Temple.'[15] So they moved on to discuss current issues, but when Henderson saw that Herzog was hurrying to another meeting, he invited him to return the following day. They had a frank, gripping exchange, in which Henderson talked freely about US policy in the Middle East, though he insisted that he was only an administrator. At some point he let slip that he had to go over the statement of the US Ambassador to the UN, concerning a Syrian complaint against Israel. Herzog noted wryly, 'I suppose that too was an administrative matter!'[16] These early exchanges led to a friendly relationship, numerous meetings and lunches, at which Henderson analysed frankly his country's Middle East policy. Herzog evidently captivated Henderson, even though he was known to be anti-Israeli. Two and a half years later, when Herzog was about to leave Washington, it was Henderson who invited him, with a large number of senior diplomats, to Blair House – the White House's official guest-house – for a strictly kosher farewell dinner.

Yaacov also became friendly with Robert Murphy, another Under-Secretary of State. They met often, and Yaacov even visited Murphy at his house, and heard him speak dolefully about his wife's serious illness.[17] He also found common ground with Agriculture Secretary Ezra Benson, whose help was needed when Israel sought to obtain American food surplus worth 35 million dollars. Herzog discreetly arranged for articles in support of Benson to appear in numerous American Jewish newspapers, in English and Yiddish. 'I arranged it through a certain person in New York,' Herzog reported to Jerusalem, 'a most reliable man, who promised that no one would know about my part in the matter.'[18] Herzog also answered Benson's questions on biblical subjects. A devout Mormon who was familiar with the Scriptures, Benson thought that the biblical 'river of Egypt' was the Nile, but the scholarly Herzog told him it was the stream of El Arish in the Sinai. The two men held a learned debate on the matter.

'Yaacov's distinctiveness aroused curiosity,' one of his colleagues recalled, 'and gave rise to talks and discussions quite unlike those of other Israeli diplomats. He was a man of his time, not of today. Today no American cabinet minister would argue with an Israeli diplomat about the location of the "river of Egypt", or biblical commentaries. Nowadays people in politics are made of different stuff ... Yaacov did not have a great philosophy about which river the Land of Israel, or the State of Israel, should reach, but if Ezra Benson believed that the "river of Egypt" was the Nile, Yaacov was able to convince him that it was the stream of El-Arish.'[19] Golda Meir noted, 'Herzog turned the Bible almost into a political document, on which he based many of his arguments.'[20]

As his influence spread, Herzog's analyses about the situation in the Middle East and the rest of the world came to be highly regarded. 'When I visited the United States I saw that this was not simply a political connection,' Golda Meir added.[21] 'It was a deep and friendly connection with these people, an attitude of complete confidence in what Yaacov said, and respect for his knowledge and his Jewish stand ... I saw them listening to him like pupils to their rabbi, being taught the Torah by him.'

It got to the point that a senior official named Berry in the State Department asked Herzog for his help in formulating a position on Middle Eastern issues. Herzog presented him with private memoranda, offering his own recommendations about the policy the United States should adopt in the region – without clearing them with his superiors in the Foreign Ministry. When this became known in Jerusalem he was severely reprimanded by the Ministry's upper echelons. His colleague, Michael Comay, sent him a 'personal and confidential' letter – in English, so that the Ministry's secretaries would not leak its substance: 'I have a serious complaint, shared by Walter [Eytan], about the memoranda you gave Berry, with your personal recommendations to the Americans regarding their policy in the present situation ... Although you did emphasize to Berry that your memoranda express only your own personal views, any serious person in the State Department would assume that you had been given the green light to put these ideas to a foreign government ... It would be extremely awkward if we have to tell the State Department ... that your comments were not approved, and do not reflect the ideas of your government. I must, therefore, demand that you desist from this habit.'[22] It was no use Herzog explaining that his memoranda were private, 'off the record, and would not, heaven forbid, be filed in the archive of the State Department's Middle East section.'[23]

'Yaacov had relations with Senators, [members of] Congress,' Golda Meir recalled, '... he had a close relationship with the then-Secretary of States Dulles, and I think Herzog contributed a lot to educating Dulles.'[24]

Birds Over the Cedars of Lebanon

According to Golda Meir, the education of Dulles began when Eban and Herzog visited him on his 70th birthday. 'I congratulated him on the day,' Eban recalled, 'and he expressed, as well as thanks and appreciation, also some reservation. "How can you congratulate me," he said, "when according to the Book of Psalms this is the end, and whatever comes after is superfluity which you can't count on. It's really a very gloomy prospect."'[25] Dulles went on to say that he regularly read the Book of Psalms, but did not quite understand the verse, 'The days of our years are threescore years and ten; and if by reason of strength they be fourscore years, yet is their strength labour and sorrow; for it is soon cut off, and we fly away' (Psalms 90:10). He also referred to Robert Browning's famous poem, 'Rabbi Ben Ezra', which describes old age as a time of spiritual uplift.[26] The three met again after some time, at a formal dinner at Abba Eban's house, and Dulles repeated his question. Yaacov replied: 'As far as I remember, some commentators explain the verse in terms of spirituality, rather than physical ability.' Dulles was interested in these commentaries and asked Herzog to send them to him in writing.[27]

'Yaacov explained to him,' Eban continued, '... that the traditional interpretation of that verse in Psalms is that it is a hopeful time, as "by reason of strength" [*gevuroth* in Hebrew] one reaches [the age of 80], ten years after the landmark of 70. Dulles asked how can one ascribe "strength" to the age which is generally marked by frailty. Yaacov said ... that he would write and show him that the Hebrew term *gevuroth*, according to Sages and especially the tractate *Pirkai Avot*, is a concept of spiritual vigour that one attains, a special capacity for observing the experiences of the world and creation.'[28]

Herzog returned to his office and wrote Dulles a letter.[29] 'The Hebrew term *gevuroth* is generally interpreted in the physical sense. An alternative interpretation, however, assigns it, and with it the background for that biblical verse, to the spiritual sphere. According to Rabbi Shimon ben Zemach Duran (1361–1444), who belonged to the Sephardi school of commentators, the meaning is that a stable moral balance takes a person to age 80. Rabbi Menahem Meiri (1244–1306), of the French school of commentators, notes that from the age of 80 on, a person is sure to develop deeper spiritual awareness. Both commentators state that the verse makes it clear that in the seventh decade of life and thereafter, a man reaches the full awareness of the eternal moral values of human destiny, in contrast to the transience of impulses and material desires. The seventh decade is, therefore, a time of maturing awareness, whose impact one begins to perceive as the eighth decade of life begins.' Herzog added that this was also the commentary in *Pirkai Avot*, chapter 5, verse 24. He included biblical quotations, and also referred to Robert Browning's poem that Dulles had quoted to him. 'The opening lines of the famous poem, "Rabbi Ben Ezra", by Robert Browning, were probably inspired by the same idea of the greater understanding that grows with age:

"Grow old along with me,
The best is yet to be ..."

'To conclude,' Herzog added, '... in view of the fateful crisis in which human destiny finds itself nowadays, international diplomacy is a ceaseless test of understanding and spiritual evaluation.'[30]

Dulles was impressed by the memorandum and wrote Herzog a personal letter, thanking him for 'the thorough research you have made about the Psalms text ... I found the commentary very interesting and have been impressed by your knowledge of these subjects.'[31] Herzog reported the exchange, entitled 'A Psalms verse', to the Foreign Ministry.[32] Eban noted that 'from that time on, Yaacov became very close to Dulles, beyond what might be expected of their different ranks, not to mention the difference in the sizes of the countries we and Dulles represented. It was one of a thousand instances of his ability to rise above the usual stuff that occupies political figures, and thus gave a distinctive quality to his presence and his representation of the Jewish cause.'[33]

Unfortunately, Dulles had little time to enjoy the pleasures of old age and the 'reason of strength'. He died a year later.

Yaacov won a distinctive position in Washington, one that was especially apt in those days. His friend, the journalist Ari Rath, noted that 'after the establishment of the State we tried to depict Israel as being not merely a political but a spiritual entity – the prophets' visions fulfilled. And Yaacov was an exceptional spokesman for that concept. Today it would not have happened.'[34]

Herzog settled smoothly and comfortably in the United States. As always, he was extremely busy, but strongly taken with his work. He undertook to reorganize the consulate in New York. 'For the first time in my life I have to administer a fairly large organization,' he wrote to Walter Eytan.[35] 'Only now have I realized that it is a science.' He established close, cordial relations with the leaders of the Jewish community, which would later serve him when he needed to mobilize them to pressure the US Administration.

Addressing American-Jewish audiences, Herzog revealed himself a born speaker and lecturer – gripping and charismatic, he fascinated them with his talk about the continuity of the Jewish people and the unbroken link between the distant biblical past and present-day Israel. As Louise Cohen, a mutual friend of Herzog and Yitzhak Navon, wrote to the latter from Chicago, 'I had the privilege to discover another facet ... of this man's marvellous personality – his ability as a speaker. He hadn't made public speeches in the US section [in the Foreign Ministry], and certainly not in the Prime Minister's office. I realize that he'd avoided the task till now, but pressure grew, and the speech he made here and which I heard, was the eighth in a series. It goes without saying that the analysis he presented to the audience and the general explanation of the situation was the clearest and most gratifying possible. But this was after all Yaacov Herzog, from whom you expect only the best. His voice was carried very well by the microphone, and as I peeped at the audience, now and then I saw that they were sitting open mouthed and wide eyed, drinking in every word.

'I'm sure, Yitzhak,' she went on, 'that you love this dear man as I do.' After conversing with Herzog in company with some friends, she returned home deeply moved. 'When I got back in the small hours, I felt joy mixed with pride and gratification, that fortune has provided me with the great honour and privilege to work alongside this man, to know him, and to take in his personality ... Few people in the world can influence one so much.'[36]

Public speaking and appearances were an added burden, on top of Herzog's hard work in Washington. Pnina was also required to take part in various social and diplomatic events. The two went out often, to diplomatic parties, sometimes to a concert or a film. Yaacov liked historical war films, and Pnina would 'shut her eyes' until the battle scenes were over.[37] When the diplomatic gatherings ended, Pnina would return home and Yaacov would go back to the embassy and report to Jerusalem about his conversations with various diplomats. The pressure was such that he put off many plans for other things. 'When time allows,' he would say to Pnina. But he greatly enjoyed his stay in the US capital. 'Myrtle Street is as peaceful and remote as ever,' he wrote to his predecessor in the post, Reuven Shiloah. 'The external appearance of the house is attractive and soothing, and the interior is bright, now it has been painted. If it weren't for the pressure of work and the worrying circumstances, one could enjoy Washington's charms and stateliness.'[38]

Nevertheless, he was often very homesick. 'Though the work here is fascinating ... still now and then longings creep in. At first the novelty was so powerful and gripping that I didn't notice them, but nowadays they don't pass unnoticed. On Friday night a couple of weeks ago when I was saying kiddush [the blessing over the wine] and reached the word *shamayim* [heavens], my little two-year-old daughter [Eliezra] raised her hands and cried out,

"Let's bring down a plane from heaven and go to *Eretz Israel*." '[39]

Recent events in Israel had upset Herzog terribly. A mentally-unbalanced man, Moshe Duek, threw a bomb from the visitors' gallery in the Knesset into the hall below, injuring Ben-Gurion and some cabinet ministers; Ben-Gurion was taken to hospital. His military secretary, Nehemiah Argov, a close friend of Herzog's, was upset that he had not been at Ben-Gurion's side to protect him physically. Driving back from Jerusalem, where he had visited the wounded Prime Minister, he hit a cyclist. The man was badly injured, and Argov thought he had been killed. He went home, wrote a farewell note to his friends, and shot himself.

Yaacov was badly shaken. One of the first letters he had written to Israel immediately after arriving in Washington had been to Nehemiah Argov, in which he shared his concerns and the problems of being a foreign diplomat in the US capital. 'If for years I wanted to have a heart-to-heart talk with you but never had a chance,' he had written, 'all the more so now, when I'm groping my way in the wilderness of nations and countless questions come to mind, but I can't pop over to Nehemiah to consult him.'[40]

That consultation would now never take place, and Yaacov was devastated. 'I imagine the shock that the tragedy of Nehemiah has caused you,' he wrote to Shimon Peres, one of Argov's colleagues who found his dead body. 'If I, being far away, can't get over it, how much worse it must be for you, who were close and saw the terrible sight.'[41] In a letter to Yitzhak Navon he wrote, 'When I think of Jerusalem the image of Nehemiah in the PM's office appears before me, with all his overflowing vitality, gaiety and his deep and loyal friendliness.'[42]

Crises and trials followed one after the other on the international level. Herzog worked hard to obtain a large loan from the United States, and succeeded. Early in 1958 some worrying unions formed in the Middle East – between Egypt and Syria, who created the United Arab Republic, and between Iraq and Jordan. Soviet influence increased and appeared most threatening following the worst crisis – in July 1958, General Abd al-Karim al-Qassem seized power in Iraq in a bloody coup, in which the King and other members of the royal family, as well as Prime Minister Nuri Said, were assassinated.

The crisis aroused profound anxiety in Washington, which feared that the entire system of alliances the United States had created to contain the USSR would collapse, as would the pro-Western regimes in the Middle East, notably King Hussein's Hashemite Kingdom of Jordan.

Britain launched an airlift to carry troops and matériel to Jordan's capital Amman, to protect the King whose life and regime were in danger. But the airlift would have to pass over Israel, and the US government undertook to mediate between London and Jerusalem.

Negotiations were held in Washington, with Herzog playing a central part. Yitzhak Navon, then Ben-Gurion's secretary, recalled a conversation between the Prime Minister and Herzog, conducted in their own original code. 'The birds will fly past the cedars [of Lebanon] to the lands of Reuven and Gad.'[43] In actual fact, this was a telephone conversation between Navon, Herzog and Reuven Shiloah, on the subject of birds (i.e., aircraft). The text of that conversation, which has been preserved in one of the state archives, reads like a brain-teaser. Herzog: 'The sons of Korah [i.e., supporters of Gamal Abd al-Nasser] are among the half-tribe of Reuven and the tribe of Manasseh, and it is feared that things will begin to happen, and the birds [aircraft] want to get through to deter them. They will pass between Tuviah [referring to Tuviah Arazi, who had in the past been active in Lebanon] and later between Aram and us, high up. What is more, it's as if we know nothing, and could say it happened to Tuviah and the neighbour Aram.'

Shiloah was less poetical: 'Let their air man [the air-force attaché] get in touch directly with Fatti [Yehoshafat Harkabi, chief of Military Intelligence].'

Birds Over the Cedars of Lebanon

Herzog persisted: 'A. I'll say they should pass between Tuviah and Aram and us. B. We know nothing. C. They won't tell the infant [Hussein] that we know. They shouldn't know over there... Have you received what I sent you [the telegram]?'

Shiloah: 'No, I'm waiting for it.'

Herzog: 'It has to do with the birds to the land of Gad, Reuven and the half-tribe of Manasseh. It has to do with a demonstration. Very high up and near the cedars. There and back. You know where the cedars are. It's where Tuviah used to be, they pass near Tuviah. It's because of serious worries in Gad and Reuben... Korah and his company there at Reuben's and Gad's, they'll see the birds and behave themselves, and of course the birds will return to their nests. [Meaning, that after the show of strength the planes will return to their bases outside the Middle East, and the balance of powers in the region would not be upset.] Are you in touch with silver hair [Ben-Gurion]?'

Shiloah: 'Yes, yes.'

Herzog: 'Tell him immediately and also the lady [Golda Meir], and reply within an hour... The birds are ready and it's urgent.'[44]

Herzog obviously enjoyed the game of coded telephone calls, as he had in his historic exchange with Eban on 8 November 1956. He relished secret work and the operations of the secret services, as revealed in the Sherringham affair, the Sinai war and in the 'flight of the birds'. Adhering strictly to confidentiality and the need to prevent leaks, and acutely conscious that beleaguered Israel needed a cloak of secrecy and unusual means of implementing its policies, Herzog built up a close relationship with the 'services'. More than once he reported directly to Ben-Gurion via Mossad agents in Washington.[45] Before long, the skills he acquired, and his thorough knowledge of the intelligence world, would have a significant bearing on events.

Except for a short interruption in the 'flight of the birds', which was due to Soviet pressure and caused John Foster Dulles to explode with anger against Eban and Herzog,[46] the operation was entirely successful. The Jordanian elements supportive of Gamal Abd al-Nasser began to move to topple King Hussein, but British paratroops airlifted to Amman suppressed the threat to the Hashemite regime, and the situation gradually stabilized. However, this did not prevent Nasser's influence from spreading throughout the Middle East, leading to the fall of pro-Western regimes and the rise of extreme radical forces.

At the same time, Ben-Gurion secretly prepared the groundwork for a daring political-military project. He sent emissaries to the non-Arab states around the Middle East – Ethiopia, Sudan, Iran and Turkey. He himself went to Turkey and met her Prime Minister and Foreign Minister, and later went to Iran and met the Iranian leadership. Together with these governments, Ben-Gurion formed a secret alliance, dubbed 'the periphery pact', whose purpose was to block Nasser's expansionism and, together with the West, to check Soviet infiltration into the region. When the elements of the pact were in place, Ben-Gurion wrote to President Eisenhower and John Foster Dulles, asking the West to help set it up. Herzog was deeply involved in confidential talks in Washington regarding this pact. He also frequently met the leaders of Iran and Turkey who visited the US capital.[47] The project was successful, as the United States welcomed the formation of a peripheral cordon around the Middle East and was willing to support it with money and intelligence. The importance of this pact marked the gradual improvement of Israel's position in Western capitals, and especially in Washington.

Herzog certainly played a part in improving Israel's relations with the US, but instead of a reward, he received a slap in the face. In late 1958 Abba Eban returned to Israel to run on the ruling Mapai party list in the national elections. His obvious successor was Herzog, who was instead made chargé d'affaires pending the appointment of a permanent ambassador. Herzog would dearly have liked to become the Ambassador, as Ben-Gurion recommended to Golda Meir.[48] But the Foreign Minister did not want a person who was 'Ben-Gurion's man', rather than hers, to hold the most important position in Israel's foreign service. 'Some diplomats maintained regular contacts with the Prime Minister,' explained the historian Dr Medzini, 'and did not always trouble to inform the Foreign Minister. One of these was Yaacov Herzog.'[49]

Golda Meir rejected Herzog's candidacy on the formal ground that it was not customary to promote an incumbent minister to the ambassadorship in the same country. This was true, but of course had she wanted to appoint Herzog, she could have made an exception. Herzog had already created a precedent when he was appointed head of the US section in the Foreign Ministry by a highly unusual procedure, because the then-Foreign Minister had wanted him in the post.

This time Ben-Gurion did not fight for the appointment. The good-natured Herzog, not being a politician and unaccustomed to elbowing his way, or to applying pressure and using contacts, did nothing to advance his cause. 'Yaacov should have been Ambassador to Washington,' said his brother, President Chaim Herzog, 'but Golda prevented the appointment, probably for reasons of party politics [Herzog was not a member of the ruling Mapai party].'[50] In the end she appointed Abraham Harman, a lacklustre person, as Ambassador in Washington. The author considers this a grave mistake, as there was no comparison between Yaacov Herzog, with his brilliant reputation among both Gentiles and Jews in the United States, and Abraham Harman.

As expected, Yaacov hid his disappointment, and put himself at the disposal of the new Ambassador with characteristic loyalty. In the months before Harman arrived in Washington to present his credentials, Herzog reported to him meticulously and extensively about events there, and also informed his interlocutors in the American Administration about Harman's imminent arrival and spoke very favourably about him.

Herzog's next target was to prepare for Ben-Gurion's visit to the United States.

On Saturday, 9 January 1960, after the Sabbath had ended, Yaacov Herzog went to Ben-Gurion's house in Jerusalem. Herzog was on home leave, and had been asked by Ben-Gurion to give him a preparatory course on all matters American. Herzog had already given the Prime Minister such a course the previous year, but 'the Old Man', who continued to think very highly of him, asked for additional information. At their previous session, the week before, Yaacov had covered two subjects – 'America and Israel', and 'America and Israel among the nations' – but the 'seminar' was cut short by the Bible study group that met in Ben-Gurion's house.[51] This particular evening the topic was to be, 'America and Israel in the Middle East'.[52]

When Herzog finished speaking, Ben-Gurion surprised him with a new question. 'I told Yaacov in brief about my concern about [Israel's] security. The burden is increasing, and we need momentum in the United States, Germany and France at a high level to help us ease this security burden, which will only grow heavier.'[53]

'The Big Four' – leaders of the US, USSR, France and Britain – were scheduled to meet in the spring of that year and Ben-Gurion, wanting to reach an agreement before the summit, planned a quick trip to Europe and the US. He hoped to gain help for Israel in the form of arms, in recognition of Israel's assistance to Western interests in Asia and Africa.[54] 'It is essential to have a talk with Eisenhower before the summit,' he said to Herzog, 'and if it is arranged, it should be allocated at least two or three hours ... It is [also] necessary to discuss these matters with de Gaulle and Adenauer, and perhaps Macmillan. We need at least 150 million dollars for armaments in the next three years, and some of the weapons may be available for free, particularly American armour kept in France.'[55]

Birds Over the Cedars of Lebanon

Ben-Gurion was disclosing his deepest anxieties, which were publicly unknown. Some people thought he was planning his overseas journey simply as a 'victory parade'. In the most recent general elections, in November 1959, Ben-Gurion had led his Mapai party to the greatest electoral victory of his career. Israel's military situation had been strengthened after the Sinai campaign, as was its international standing. It had achieved a significant position in Africa and Asia and became a symbol of a young nation making its way despite tremendous challenges.

Israel's position was also stronger in Europe. France supplied almost all of the IDF's needs in matériel, and the top echelon of the Ministry of Defence had built up a confidential relationship with West Germany. Even Britain was becoming friendlier towards Israel, and relations with the United States had improved in the previous two years. The stormy summer of 1958 had impelled the US to take some dramatically different steps with regard to Israel. She had supported Israel's actions in Asia and Africa and the formation of the 'periphery pact'; and had supplied Israel with 1,000 recoilless cannons – the first 'firearms' ever sold by the US to Israel. She had also approved some important grants, which Herzog had been instrumental in achieving, and had informed Israel discreetly that she would subsidize her purchase of Centurion tanks from Britain. This was financed with a 10 million dollar grant from the 'Development Credit Fund' that Dulles had promised Golda Meir in October 1958.

Yet despite all these achievements, Ben-Gurion did not feel triumphant, but rather increasingly worried. He complained about America's 'indifferent' policy in the Middle East, her obtuse attitude towards Israel and unfriendly moves in the United Nations. Surprisingly, John Foster Dulles, yesterday's tough opponent, seemed to be changing his attitude towards Israel and becoming convinced of her value to the West. But in 1959 Dulles fell ill with cancer and had to retire, aware that his end was near. Ben-Gurion was convinced that if he could meet the American

President he could persuade him to support Israel. However, Eisenhower did not care to invite him and ignored his hints that he was willing to come to Washington. A senior American official on a visit to Israel asked the Prime Minister, 'Why don't you come to the United States?' to which Ben-Gurion replied glumly, 'I am not wanted, and I don't like to go to places where I am not wanted.'

In fact, given the nebulous character of US–Israeli relations at that time, it was unthinkable that Israel's Prime Minister would be extended a formal invitation. Yaacov Herzog maintained that, 'if it is not possible to enter by the front door, one must go in through the window'. Arrangements were quietly made for Brandeis University (which was Jewish) in Boston to invite Ben-Gurion to receive an honorary doctorate. This made it a private visit, as the Foreign Ministry made amply clear – most of the telegrams exchanged between Herzog and the Ministry spoke of 'Ben-Gurion's vacation' ...

Nevertheless, it was obvious to the organizers that once Ben-Gurion was in the US, and asked to meet the heads of the Administration, the US government would be unable to refuse. When the Foreign Ministry approached the State Department, it was told that President Eisenhower would be willing to receive Ben-Gurion in Washington for a talk.

Ben-Gurion arrived in the US in March 1960. He held some important meetings in Boston and New York, and in Washington he met President Eisenhower and Vice-President Richard Nixon. Yaacov Herzog had cultivated good relations with Nixon, regarding him as a sure presidential candidate. He knew that Nixon's relations with the Jewish community were problematic, and had heard that the Vice-President had complained that no matter what he did for the Jews, he would get nothing in return. Herzog therefore launched a similar operation to the one he had organized for Ezra Benson. Very quietly he persuaded the editors of the leading Jewish newspapers to ask for a frank and wide-ranging meeting with Nixon.[56] The manoeuvre paid off, and Nixon gave Ben-Gurion a warm, friendly welcome.

Herzog's special contribution to Ben-Gurion's visit to Washington was a series of informal meetings with all the people who mattered in the capital. On the Friday Ben-Gurion left his hotel and came to stay with Yaacov and Pnina, leaving their house after the Sabbath. Throughout that day, at agreed intervals, leading US Senators came to meet Ben-Gurion, among them potential Democratic presidential candidates – Stuart Symington, Hubert Humphrey, Lyndon B. Johnson and John F. Kennedy. At the time Herzog did not particularly appreciate Kennedy – his first impression was that 'the man is very superficial and unfamiliar with the details about the region'. At the same time, however, he thought Kennedy had 'a good chance of being the Democratic presidential candidate in 1960'.[57] Ben-Gurion was not greatly impressed by him either. 'He looked to me like a twenty-five year old boy,' he recalled. 'I did not take him seriously at first.'[58]

The most important and impressive event of Ben-Gurion's visit was his meeting with the West German Chancellor, Konrad Adenauer. This took place at the Waldorf Astoria Hotel in New York, and was rightly dubbed an historic meeting by journalists and commentators, as it symbolized the new relationship between the Jewish state and the 'new Germany' born after the war. At the meeting, Adenauer promised his country's firm support for Israel, and undertook to give Israel a loan of half a billion dollars to develop her industry and agriculture.

At the centre of the small group of Ben-Gurion's close associates, who dealt with the delicate aspects of the negotiations and the wording of official statements, was the familiar figure of Yaacov Herzog. He played a crucial role in preparing the official statements of both sides, was a gracious and courteous negotiator, but remained adamant where Israel's interests were concerned, and his wording was usually adopted.[59]

When Ben-Gurion returned to Israel, Herzog could rightly

claim a major share in the success of the visit.

At the end of March 1960, a few days after Ben-Gurion returned to Israel, the Foreign Minister informed Herzog that she was appointing him Israel's Ambassador to Canada.

It was an important post, even if not the one he had sought. The person best suited to represent Israel in Washington was sent to a neighbouring country, a large and important state, but lower on Israel's order of political priorities. Yaacov did not express any bitterness or dismay. On the contrary, he thanked Golda Meir effusively for the appointment. 'Dear Mrs Meir,' he wrote, 'I wish to express my profound gratitude for the confidence you have shown in me by appointing me Israel's representative in Canada. I know how highly you regard this place from both the international and the Jewish standpoint, and I promise to do my very best to improve Israel's international standing in Canada and to deepen the relations of Canadian Jewry with Israel.'[60]

9

The Challenge

That snowy morning in January 1961, hundreds of students thronged Hillel House at McGill University in Montreal, Canada. The entrance lobby and the staircase leading to the first floor were crowded. The auditorium was packed and loudspeakers were placed throughout the building to transmit the sounds to all those who failed to get into the hall.[1] The audience was made up of students, local Jews, representatives of the press and even some diplomats, including someone from the consulate of the United Arab Republic. At noon exactly a public debate was about to begin between Israel's Ambassador to Canada, Yaacov Herzog, and the British historian, Professor Arnold Toynbee.

The debate caused unprecedented excitement among the Jews of Canada – as well as in Israel – even before the first word was spoken. Toynbee was a world-famous historian, an Oxford graduate who had served in the Foreign Office and been a member of the British delegation to the Paris Peace Conference in 1919, and had opposed the Balfour Declaration. Between 1934 and 1961 he devoted himself to research and writing, and published many books, of which the best known was his 12 volume *A Study of History*. He claimed to have deciphered the underlying significance of the historical movements of nations and human communities and of all history. Historians, according to Toynbee, ought to concentrate not on nations, countries and states, but on cultures.[2] He isolated 21 civilizations, among them 'backward', 'failed', and 'fossilized' civilizations. The last category included the

Zoroastrian Parsee community in India and the Jews. Later he developed his theory and took it further, arguing that the final goal of various civilizations was the birth of transcendental religions, and he foresaw a future universal religion which would combine the tenets of Christianity, Islam, Hinduism and Buddhism.

Toynbee's theories were controversial; not only his doctrine, but also his methodology and conclusions were widely criticized. But he was a gifted writer and charismatic speaker, and after retiring from academia he continued to draw large audiences to his lectures all over the world. He opposed Zionism and the State of Israel, and argued that in 1948 the Jews had treated the Palestinians the same way the Nazis had treated them.[3] Many regarded him as not only anti-Zionist, but anti-Semitic.

In January 1961 Toynbee came to McGill University to give a series of lectures known as the Beatty Lectures. These drew vast audiences – some 4,000 people at every lecture – as well as extensive press coverage. When he addressed the Jewish students at Hillel House, he was asked if he continued to view the Jews as 'historic fossil', and whether he still maintained that the Israelis treated the Arabs as the Nazis had treated the Jews. Toynbee confirmed that he did, and proceeded to explain why he thought so.[4]

Israel's enemies were, of course, delighted. The Cairo daily *Al Goumhouriyeh* described Toynbee as 'the voice of justice ... The voice of history, science and philosophy ... The brave voice ... that refuted the Zionists' pretexts and demolished every Jewish historical argument ... The greatest scientific and historical voice that supports Arab nationalism.'[5] Herzog was immediately informed about Toynbee's Canadian lecture – the *New York Times* correspondent in Montreal telephoned him and asked for his response to Toynbee's arguments.[6] He also heard that Canada's Prime Minister John Diefenbaker had quoted the visiting historian at a formal dinner.

Herzog was appalled. 'A foreign ambassador,' he said to a friend,[7] 'cannot remain in a country in which such things have

The Challenge

been said about his people. An ambassador cannot remain in a country in which his nation's honour is violated not only from a political standpoint, but from the standpoint of its moral and historical character. If he keeps silent and stays on, it's as if he concurred with the shedding of his people's blood.'

He had never before felt such anger and indignation. To his amazement, he discovered that many of Canada's élite read Toynbee's books and were familiar with his views about the Jewish people and the State of Israel. He found out that Toynbee had never been 'publicly challenged' about his accusations.[8] 'I felt at once that Toynbee's statements would receive considerable coverage in the press, on radio and television, and that a man of such standing could not be simply repudiated. I felt that the only way to try and puncture the bubble was to challenge him to an open debate.'[9] He published a communiqué saying 'Professor Toynbee's statement has nothing to do with morality or the facts ... Truth does not tolerate distortion at the hands of anyone, no matter how exalted ... In view of the gravity of Professor Toynbee's declaration, I challenge him to debate me openly in a public venue of his choice.'[10] Without consulting anyone, Herzog sent Toynbee a telegram to this effect. 'I was stunned to hear the declaration you made yesterday ... about Israel and the Israeli–Arab war of 1948. In view of the extreme gravity of your arguments, I would like to invite you to hold an open debate with me in any public forum you care to choose.'[11]

To his friend Chaim Israeli he wrote, 'For the past five years this man has been maligning the Jewish people and the State of Israel ... I decided on the spur of the moment to challenge him to a public debate, as I saw no other way to balance the impact, all the more as I couldn't stand the situation in which I have to read and listen to his slander without trying to debate him before public opinion. I was well aware of the risks, and some people here have questioned the wisdom of the debate. But in such a situation you have to trust your intuition, which is what I've done.'[12]

A few days later, speaking to another friend of his, Herzog said that he knew the 'pragmatists' in the Foreign Ministry would 'turn up their noses' and the chief of protocol 'may reprimand' him. He was aware that 'it did not quite tally with the customary conduct of a foreign diplomat in a host country'. But he felt very strongly that history, too, had a protocol, and that Jewish history was 'a very ruthless recorder'. And Jewish historic protocol stated, 'My traducer shall not go unanswered!'

Nevertheless, the justification was born after the act. Herzog's challenge to Toynbee was a spontaneous reaction straight from the heart. At that moment he was not a civil servant and government official, but an untitled spokesman of the Jewish people fighting for its honour, which was why he did not seek permission. 'His very leap into the debate,' wrote Yeshayahu Avrekh (a columnist in the Hebrew daily *Davar*, writing under the pseudonym Yotam or Yoav) years later, 'was a visceral need to defend the honour of Israel, an agitated moral sortie that left no room for a discussion of protocol.'[13]

Toynbee accepted Herzog's challenge to hold a debate, and suggested 31 January 1961.[14] Hearing this, Rabbi Shmuel Kass, director of Hillel House on the McGill University campus, invited Toynbee and Herzog to hold their debate at his venue. This made sense because that was where Toynbee had made his original statements. The two disputants accepted the offer, and agreed to meet on that day at twelve noon.

News about the forthcoming debate caused a huge outcry in the Jewish community in Canada. Many of its leaders responded with typical diaspora timidity – do not provoke the Gentiles, keep your head down and wait for the storm to blow over. They feared a public confrontation which would bring the 'Jewish Question' to the surface and provoke anti-Semitic reactions. They were conscious of the parallel between the proposed encounter and the famous medieval disputations between rabbis and priests. Regardless of outcome, those encounters often ended with the Jewish

The Challenge

spokesman being put to death. The anxious leaders feared that Herzog would be defeated, but if the unlikely happened and he did win, it might still rebound on the Jews. As Avraham Avihai wrote, 'Subconscious memories and conscious fears from the days of medieval disputations all came to the fore.'[15]

Those who reacted with hostility and anxiety to Herzog's idea offered feeble arguments, such as that Toynbee was old and himself 'fossilized', and that no one took him seriously. His statements, they said, had no social or public value. But these were hollow assertions – Toynbee was a much admired figure, and his ideas reverberated widely. In fact, in the eyes of various political and public figures he remained for years afterwards one of the world's great historians.[16]

Moreover, many of the Jewish leaders in Canada had not yet come to know the new Israeli Ambassador. Herzog had only been in Ottawa six months, and though he soon won general respect, he was still an enigma to the local community. His initiative was extraordinary and aroused deep anxieties.

Irwin Cotler, who would later become a renowned academic and jurist, was then a 20-year-old student, and vice-president of the Hillel Association. 'Local Jews, including some of the old-guard leadership,' he recalled years later, 'pressured us to cancel the debate. Many telephoned us. "What do we need this for?" some of them asked. Others got mad at us: "Who gave you permission to hold this debate?" "We should keep a low profile and let the wave roll over." We replied, "What do you mean, who gave us permission? We don't need your permission."'[17]

The Jewish leaders went so far as to form a delegation and to call on Ambassador Herzog at home, to dissuade him from the risky adventure. 'I'll never forget the evening when that delegation came to our house,' Pnina Herzog recalled. 'There were eight or nine Jewish leaders, including Professor Maxwell Cohen, dean of the Law Faculty at McGill University, the chairman of the Zionist Federation in Canada, and other well-known leaders.

They came to dissuade Yaacov to withdraw from the debate with Toynbee.'[18]

Herzog refused. It was he who had asked for the debate, he told his visitors, and he could hardly withdraw his challenge. But if Professor Toynbee were to publicly retract his statements about 'fossils', and the comparison between Israelis and the Nazis, the object of the debate would be invalidated and then he would withdraw. The delegation seized on this idea and asked for an urgent meeting with Toynbee. But the professor refused to retract his statements, and the delegation returned to Herzog's house, to try again to dissuade him. 'What if you should fail in the debate?' they kept asking anxiously. 'Yaacov was a young man,' Pnina Herzog went on, 'and they were afraid he would be unable to stand up to Toynbee.' Herzog rejected their arguments unequivocally.[19]

A few of Herzog's Foreign Ministry colleagues were also displeased with his initiative. 'Jerusalem was ominously silent,' wrote Avraham Avihai. 'Herzog's superiors maintained radio silence, suggesting profound apprehension.'[20] Arieh Levavi, deputy director of the Foreign Ministry, wrote: 'I don't know if such a "duel" between an ambassador and a professor is customary (though of course it's always possible to innovate if necessary).'[21] He admitted that 'Toynbee is ... a charlatan, trying to hoodwink the public with empty generalizations ... His attitude to facts is the very opposite of an honest scientific approach ... He makes a mockery of both facts and reason. And above all, he is consumed with hatred of Zion, which in my opinion – despite his pious disclaimers – are only another manifestation of anti-Semitism.' Nevertheless, Levavi did not even wish Herzog success in the debate which was to take place two days later.

Another Foreign Ministry colleague, serving as a diplomat in America, probably spoke for many: 'The debate with Toynbee – I opposed it. What good could it do? Already then I regarded Toynbee as merely another historian ... Who was Toynbee? An

The Challenge

associate professor from Oxford with a discarded theory ... I did not regard him as a higher power, and he was also anti-Israeli. I didn't think that this debate could be won by anyone ... It was also peculiar – since when does an ambassador debate with a scholar? So what if he's an intellectual ambassador, so what? What for? What is this – the Middle Ages, when people debated against the Christians? Maybe it was appropriate in the thirties. With such people you don't argue, you let time take care of it.'[22]

Years later, Golda Meir admitted, 'At first I was a little anxious, because I knew that there was no limit to that man's hatred ... In the beginning I worried for two reasons: firstly, I didn't think that man [Toynbee] ... could be influenced by anything. And then I wasn't sure it was a dignified thing for an Israeli representative, Israel's Ambassador, to argue in public with such a person.'[23] But Herzog paid no heed to the voices or the silence, and was consumed with the mission he had undertaken. There were less than three days from the moment he received Toynbee's reply till the debate itself, and he threw himself wholly into the preparation. He shut himself in his study, heaped his desk with Toynbee's writings, as well as books and documents about the history of Israel, the War of Independence, the problem of the Palestinian refugees, the UN resolutions ...

The girls were warned not to disturb their father, and they would remember the tense atmosphere in the house, their father smoking non-stop in his room, and the prohibition even to knock on his door.[24] He read everything he could lay his hands on about Toynbee. He researched Toynbee's career in the British Foreign Office and his opposition to the Balfour Declaration, and found out that during the 1930s he had belonged to an upper-class British group that favoured appeasing the Nazis – as indeed had the Prime Minister, Neville Chamberlain – and that he regarded Nazi Germany as the Western bastion against the USSR.[25]

Herzog suspected Toynbee of 'Christian anti-Semitism'.[26] He also discovered that many historians were sharply critical of

Toynbee, and that 'his scientific weakness is well known among the experts'. Nevertheless, 'he enjoys a high position in public opinion, having achieved it through a keen sense of public relations.'[27] He wrote to Chaim Israeli: 'I have had some difficult days ... I have spent three days and nights reading his books and things written against him ... His position is so high, that people are aware of his slanders, but not about the responses to them.'[28] He filled whole pages with his spidery handwriting, noted quotes, facts and figures, outlined points and highlights for his side of the debate. He formulated his opening and headings for different parts of the debate, and prepared relevant excerpts from Toynbee's statements. It seemed as though he had hardly slept or eaten during those days, regarding the imminent debate as not merely a scholarly dispute but a fateful contest for the honour of Israel.

The day of the debate, as Yaacov and Pnina Herzog prepared to set out for Montreal, a telegram arrived from the President of Israel, Yitzhak Ben-Zvi: 'Good luck!'[29]

On 31 January, at exactly 12 noon, Yaacov and Pnina entered the crowded auditorium and made their way to the stage. An Orthodox Jew seized Yaacov's hand: 'We're praying for your success!'[30] A tense silence fell in the hall. Herzog and Toynbee shook hands and exchanged a little polite small talk. Their wives sat side by side in the front row, and the debate began.

Toynbee was a tall man with thinning grey hair, and – in the words of one of the spectators – 'looked like an aristocratic academic of international renown, nearing the end of his career, with a slightly diffident manner of speech which he used to sharpen the edge of his arguments ... Herzog was not much larger physically, but was about half Toynbee's age, a vital, tense, sharp man, whose voice reverberated with history and passion.'[31]

'First let me clarify that I am here in my personal, and not in my official, capacity. Indeed, over the past 48 hours, since Professor Toynbee agreed to this debate, I have done very little in the nature of my official capacity and have been more or less traversing

The Challenge

beyond space and time a few thousand years of history, back and forth, trying to disentangle civilizations – and fossils.

'In this hall last week an analogy was made, a comparison was drawn and a word was evoked – a word also enshrining a concept, the word "morality" ... Before this body last week Professor Toynbee ... compared from a moral standpoint the attitude of Israel to the Arabs in 1947 and 1948 with the Nazi slaughter of six million Jews. ... I must first say that the Professor clarified that he was not comparing the two events statistically, but he insisted ... that the moral comparison is valid. Secondly, he is quoted as having said that the Jews had no historical right to Israel.

'As far as one aspect of this analogy [is concerned] – the Nuremberg International Court made a finding that in the summer of 1941 plans were made for the final solution of the Jewish question in Europe. This final solution, as we all know, embraced in fact the putting to death, in circumstances of unprecedented cruelty, of six million of our people, including over a million children. It is a crime which human imagination still finds difficulty in grasping, and, in the biblical phrase, "The earth cannot cover the blood in which it is soaked." There was here cold-blooded planning, there was government responsibility, there was execution to the magnitude of six million ... Professor Toynbee himself has denounced this crime in incisive terms. Indeed, till the end of days mankind will brood on the significance of this spectre, unprecedented, of man's inhumanity to man. As for my people, our mourning is endless. It is a mourning to eternity.

'Let us take the other side of the analogy. In 1947 over two-thirds of the members of the United Nations took a decision on partition [of Palestine] with separate Jewish and Arab states. The Arab representatives on the spot announced they would resist, and within days an armed attack began against the Jewish community in Palestine. Writing on that period, the then-UN Secretary General, Trygve Lie ... says: "From the first week of December

1947, disorder in Palestine had began to mount. The Arabs repeatedly asserted they would resist partition by force. They seemed to be determined to drive that point home by assaults upon the Jewish community in Palestine." On 21 January 1948, the British representative at the United Nations, Sir Alexander Cadogan, told the Security Council: "For the Arabs in Palestine the killing now transcends all other considerations." On 16 February 1948 the United Nations Palestine Commission reported to the Security Council that, "Powerful Arab interests, both inside and outside Palestine, are defying the Resolution of the General Assembly, and are engaged in a deliberate effort to alter by force the settlement envisaged therein." Again, in April 1948, the Commission referred to "continued threats and acts of violence".

'With the expiry of the British Mandate on 15 May [1948], the Arab armies invaded ... the Secretary-General of the Arab League, Azzam Pasha, speaking in Cairo, ... said, "The world would now see a war of extermination and momentous massacre which will be spoken of like the Mongolian massacres and the Crusades." It was a war of heavy suffering on both sides, casualties both military and civilian. Through this war large numbers of Arabs in Palestine were uprooted. At the same time, through this war large Jewish communities throughout the Middle East were uprooted. ... Large numbers of Arabs left the country in order to come back in the wake of the victorious forces. No international authority has defined responsibility for the Arab refugee problem. It is our contention ... that the refugee problem was the result of the war proclaimed by the Arabs and the result of an appeal [to the Palestinian Arabs] by their leaders to leave in order to return. As an Arab newspaper in Jordan put it, "They told us to get out so that we could get in. We got out; they did not get in."

'But let us look at the results of the analogy in terms of morality, Professor. Of the Arab population, there are now 200,000 in Israel, enjoying equality and every right, side by side with their Jewish fellow-citizens. I represent these Arab citizens just as I represent

The Challenge

Jewish citizens, because they are all Israeli citizens. In the refugee camps, it is true, there are large numbers of Arab refugees. At the same time a quite considerable part of them have been absorbed into the economy of the neighbouring countries. ... In any event, there is a difference even between a parasitic existence and between total extinction. They continue to suffer because the Arab governments, who originated this suffering, refuse to relieve it by cooperating in the settlement of the Arab refugee problem ...

'Professor, there is a relationship between the two events to which you referred. In both cases, the Jewish people was assaulted. In one case, a third of our people was destroyed; in the other, we resisted, in self-defence, and under a merciful Providence, we succeeded.

'The second point of the relationship is that, through the experience of this Holocaust in Europe, our will strengthened that we would do everything in our capacity that never again should such a tragedy befall our people. But how can the two events – the destruction of a third of our people and the Arab refugee problem, created through a war started by the Arabs themselves ... be mentioned in the same breath? Should we pass an amendment to Article 51 of the Charter of the United Nations on the right of self-defence, an amendment which says that if you are attacked you may resist, but remember, no matter what you suffer in the process, if the man attacking you suffers, you will be condemned by history ... as having been affected by Nazi influences? You speak, Professor, with respect of Gandhi and of his concepts, you link him across the span of history to Rabbi Yohanan ben Zakkai, one of our great masters of the law at the time of the destruction of the Second Temple. But I would say this: that as far as I have read, Gandhi, while opposing activist self-defence, never denounced those who pursued it. What should we have done? Allowed the Nazi experience to be repeated? ...

Now, the criterion of moral defensibility, I submit in all respect, Sir, in this case it is vague and indiscriminate ... Ernest Renan has spoken of "*La vérité est dans les nuances.*" But here you do not even have the nuances. You have two entirely different contexts of right and wrong.' ...

Toynbee began, 'Boxers shake hands before they fight,' he said. 'Perhaps that is rather a good example for ambassadors and professors. I am afraid that we shan't give such an entertaining performance as boxers might do, but still, this is a very important and serious occasion ... The first [question] is this question of the parallel that I drew in a book that I published in 1954, between what the Nazis did to the European Jews and what the Israelis did to the Palestinian Arabs which was brought up in one of the questions that were put to me at the meeting the other day in Hillel House, and I answered, yes, I had written that, ... in the terms that I stated in print ... I still held to it.

'Now, the Ambassador has really anticipated one point in telling you, very kindly, that ... I was not making a numerical comparison – because obviously there is no numerical comparison between figures that run into millions and figures that run into three, or at most, four figures. The second set of figures I am talking about is the massacres of Arab civilians behind the lines during the war between the Arab states and the Israeli forces in 1948. Every increase in numbers produces an increase in suffering, but it's impossible to be wicked or criminal more than 100 per cent. Let me put the point bluntly: if I murder one man that makes me a murderer. I don't have to reach the thousand mark or the million mark to be a murderer ...

'I wonder if there are any Egyptians in the room? I know there are a number of Egyptians in Montreal. Is there any Egyptian present? Perhaps not. Let me suppose that some of the Egyptians of Montreal were here at this moment and would say to me, "How do you, being an Englishman, defend the slaughter in the fall of 1956 of civilian inhabitants of ... Port Said by bombardment from the air, which ran into four figures?" ... Now, supposing I were to answer, "Why, that's not murder. We only killed people

The Challenge

up to four figures. To be a murderer you must reach the million mark. Those Germans over there, they reached it, they murdered several million people. They are murderers, but we, the British, we are not murderers." What would you think of that answer? What would Egypt say, what would the world say? ...

'Now we come to this point of morality. And I utterly agree with the Ambassador that this is the essential point and the point which concerns the future as well as the past. Now I have mentioned a case which is painful for me to mention – this British case of 1956 to show that I can look at the things that my own country has done, as well as what other people have done. But I do think that if there is any point in what I have said about the numbers, that in point of morality some of those massacres by Israeli armed forces in Palestine do compare in, so to speak, moral quality with what the Germans did. What we hate in what the Germans did was that it was planned beforehand, carried out cold-bloodedly with tremendous cruelty and with a purpose.

Now I am afraid ... that all those points apply to the massacres which, in numbers, don't compare, but I think in quality do compare, with what the Nazis did, and that were done at any rate by certain Israeli armed forces – the Stern gang, for instance, and the Irgun. I don't know how far the Haganah was also implicated. I have heard it stated, and I have never heard it denied, that after at least one of those massacres – that of the civilian population of all sexes and ages at Deir Yassin to the west of Jerusalem – the Israeli armed forces went round in cars with loudspeakers, speaking in Arabic, and said: "We have done this to the people of this place. If you don't want that to happen to you, get out." Now every civilian population that is in a war zone or is in danger of death very wisely does get out.

'Happily, after Hitler came to power in Germany, a minority, unfortunately only a minority, of the Jews in Germany did manage, with difficulty often, to leave Germany in time. Now the Germans couldn't take their lives any longer, but they could, and did, take and seize and hold their property. No one thinks that the European Jews who got out of Germany at that time forfeited their legal right to their property as a result of having managed, by prudence and foresight, to save their lives and their families' lives by getting out in time.

Let me take another case. In 1940, when the Germans invaded France, several million French people from northern France fled from northern France to the south for the same reason that the Arab population of the war zone in Palestine in 1948 fled from Palestine. No one, I think, would dream of saying that by flying, as all civilian populations do try to fly from a war zone, those French people forfeited their title to their land and property, ... in northern France. And if the Germans were to put in a claim today: "As we invaded the country, and these French people were ill-advised enough to run away, we have a legal title to this property, and it is really rather a shame and illegal that we don't possess it now," that would seem pretty fantastic.

But, as you will realize, the position in Israel today is that by far the larger part, I suppose, of the land in Israel is legally still the property of that civilian Arab population of Palestine which fled from Palestine during the war between the Arab states ... and the Israelis. The property that does rightfully belong to the Israelis is the property that they bought during the 30 years of the Mandate and long before that – I think, if I am right, the first agricultural Jewish settlements in Palestine go back to the 1880s – the Rothschild settlements. Now, they paid a very handsome price ... for that land, and that land is obviously – not only legally, but morally and fairly – their property. But it is, if I am right in my figures, a smallish proportion of the total land in the area now held by Israel; by far the larger proportion – ... the houses, removable property, the fruit trees and so on – is still the rightful property of the Palestinian refugees who are now living outside their homes, though often within sight of them, ... under conditions of misery and, at present, of hopelessness.

The Challenge

'Let me now make a general point, which concerns not Arab human nature or Jewish human nature but, I am afraid, human nature of all of us. As I say "of all of us", let me begin again with my own country. I think it is one of the nastiest sides of our wretched human nature that we are very much tempted, whenever wrong or injustice or suffering is inflicted on us – "tempted" is perhaps too conscious a word, because this is partly a kind of subconscious psychological reaction – but, whatever the reason, we often do the same thing to other people that are weaker than ourselves. Let me illustrate again by an example from the recent history of my own country. In the Second World War the civilian population in my country, Britain, was severely bombed. What did we do within 11 years of that ...? In 1956 we bombed, in an aggressive attack on Egypt, without declaration of war, and, condemned by the world for having done it, ... the civilian population, of particularly Port Said, to some extent of Cairo, I think, as well, and slaughtered certainly more than 1,000 innocent people, probably rather more than were slaughtered in those massacres by the Israeli armed forces in '48 ...

'Now this is a tragedy of human nature. What is the real tragedy is that people who have suffered a thing and had experience of it should inflict that suffering on other people ... But of course the British people just during one war they suffered this bombardment, just for a few years; the Jewish people have suffered murder, robbery, expulsion from their homes, not just for a year or two but for centuries running into ... 2,500 years. ... The more experience one has of what this means, I would say, the more it is morally incumbent upon one not to do the same thing again. The temptation to work it off – one is exasperated – is no doubt greater, but the moral duty to resist that temptation is at its maximum ...

'I have been surprised at the vehemence of the reaction to it in the Jewish community. I have wondered myself why ... if it is felt to be rather a preposterous suggestion, as you obviously feel it to be, you haven't said: "Here is a silly man, saying a silly thing. Why bother about it? It's so silly, to leave it alone." But the reaction to it has not been like that. It has been, as we know, very vigorous. I think here I am going to say rather a controversial thing: that any psychologist would tell you the reason. I would say that, rather inadvertently, in this comparison I have drawn, I have given the Jewish people a piece of what psychologists call "shock treatment". I have said aloud in startling words, I think something that your consciences – each of you who belong to the Jewish community of the world – are whispering inside each of you.

Now, let my voice fade out ... and listen to another voice which I will quote. "I am certain that the world will judge the Jewish State by what it will do with the Arabs." ... They are the words of a man famous in all your minds – Chaim Weizmann, whom I had the honour to know when I was a young man ... They were spoken, I believe, or written, in 1949, after the war between the Arab states and Israel, when Dr Weizmann was the first President of Israel. But I would ask you, let my voice fade out, let even Dr Weizmann's voice fade out, and listen to your own inner voice ... Because, after all, who ... was the first to wake up the human conscience? I would say it was the Prophets of Israel and Judah. I do not believe that any person of Jewish religion can ever escape from his own conscience. What is more, I don't believe any Jew ever wishes to escape from his own conscience, and I believe it has been the glory of the Jews since the time of the Prophets, and perhaps before: that in all controversial questions between Jews, or between Jews and the rest of the world, there have always been Jews who have had the spiritual insight and the moral courage to stand up and criticize their people. We shouldn't know what the criticisms of the Jews in the eighth and seventh centuries BC were if we hadn't got the writings of Jewish critics who had criticized them. And so I would leave you with your own consciences and with the existence of these Arab refugees – who now number 900,000, because many children have been born in exile. So, as I say, I leave it to you to

The Challenge

think over in your own consciences what is to be done about this situation ...

'I had the good fortune that my own family was not murdered, that my property or their property has not been robbed, that I have not been driven out of my country, so I don't know these experiences at first-hand. Just the strange inequality of human fortune. But in England, since the time that Hitler came to power, I have seen and met and talked to and sympathized with many European Jewish refugees. And since 1948 I have been in the places where the Arab refugees are now, and I have visited and talked to them, just as in the same way I talked to the European Jewish refugees, so I do know at second-hand what being a refugee is. Now many of you, Canadians of Jewish religion, have, I believe, come from Central and Eastern Europe rather recently, so that in your family tradition, in the time of your parents and even your grandparents, you have living family memories of this thing being done to your families, so you do know more vividly than I do what it means. So, as I say, I leave it to you to think over in your own conscience what is to be done about this situation, because we've opened a problem but we have not yet solved it.'

The audience in the hall listened attentively to the debaters' opening statements. Now the time had come for the shorter, brisker exchange between them that would determine the outcome of the debate.

10

The Duel

Herzog then summed up Toynbee's opening statement: '... There are three broad points. In the first place I understand that you agree that the Arab armies assaulted Israel when it came to life; in other words, what Israel was doing, she was doing as self-defence.'

To which Toynbee replied: '... Of course, the cry for independence was from the Arab point of view a provocation.'

Herzog remained calm: 'This provocation,' he replied, 'was the basis of a United Nations decision and every United Nations record attests to that ... On 15 July 1948, the Arab position having reached what it did in terms of a threat to the peace, the Security Council considered the situation in the category of a threat to peace, and said they might have to apply article 39, in terms of what's to be done in this situation. But you will admit, Professor Toynbee, that it is a fact that the Arabs attacked us.'

Toynbee did not respond, and Herzog went on: '... You argue that ... our people committed two grave atrocities: one, the Deir Yassin incident, and the other, driving out the Arabs and turning them into refugees. ... Very central to your thesis is that the Nazi impact of the persecution on the Jewish people brought them to commit such atrocities, and you have mentioned the British action in bombing civilians in Port Said in 1956. Now, Professor, in volume IV, page 128F, of your *Study of History* you say: "In the history of man's attempt at civilization hitherto there has never been any society whose progress and civilization has gone so far that in times of revolution or war its members could be relied upon not to commit atrocities." And you quote here the behaviour of the German Army in Belgium in 1914, the British Black and Tans in Ireland in 1920, the French Army in Syria, the German National Socialist Storm Troops (born in 1933 before World War Two) and the Italian Black Shirts. Am I correct, Sir, in assuming that you feel that this is the record throughout history? Now you said that because of the bombing of Britain by the Germans a certain state of mind, some impact, some scar, had developed in the British consciousness that reflected itself in the bombing of Port Said. (The Black and Tans were well over 13 years before Hitler came to power.) ... Would you agree with me that all these instances have an element of cruelty ... whether it be the bombing of Berlin in World War Two, whether it be the Black and Tans earlier, whether it be Hiroshima, whether it even be the treatment of the early American Indians? Right through this you feel that there is a sense of atrocity. Now how do you relate all this to Nazism?

'Secondly,' he went on, 'you agree that there were also Arab massacres of Jewish civilians ... long before Deir Yassin ... Were these also in the category of Nazi atrocities? And if so why don't you say both sides did this in such a category? Why do you choose us? Why do you single us out? Why don't you write that Britain and almost every country in the world falls under that definition?' ...

Herzog went on to list the Arab massacres of Jews in oil refineries, the Yehiam convoy, the blowing up of Ben Yehuda Street in Jerusalem with 50 killed and 70 wounded, and quoted the underground organizations' claim that the tragedy in Deir Yassin had occurred in the course of battle. He also stressed that the Jewish Agency sent King Abdullah of Jordan a letter 'condemning the action in most vigorous terms'. ... 'We heard no such expressions of regret for Arab massacres, although they were undertaken within the category of armed offensive against us. So to sum up, Sir, I would ask you: do you agree that there is a line linking every act of atrocity committed by soldiers in various countries down the ages? If so, would you agree that this odium of a Nazi impact would be attached to all such nations, not only to Israel, including to the Arabs for what they did to us. Particularly since they attacked us while we were operating in self-defence?'

Toynbee replied: 'Well, I suppose the Arabs could match atrocities. ... You could cite many more instances of massacres of Jews and they could give many more massacres of Arabs by Jews.'

But Herzog drove the point home: 'At the end of the first week after the 29 November Resolution, 105 Jews were killed and many more injured. In one week, right after the Resolution in November 1947.'

Toynbee repeated, 'There were things on both sides ... Indians call karma, [a] chain of moral evil ... there is something in human nature that makes us pass on to other people the evil that has been done to us ... we have to break this chain.'

Toynbee went on to say that the Jewish people throughout the world, including the Israelis, 'were horrified by the massacre done by the Israeli armed forces, and the Israelis are a rather small minority of people in the Jewish world, and I am sure that the majority of Jews in the world, as far as they knew about this, were also horrified and felt it as their responsibility: one has a slight responsibility for one's co-religionists ... I would make the point that all Israel has implicated itself, so to speak, in the results of that flight, or partial expulsion, and to a small extent in the massacre of the Palestinian Arabs because it has taken and held the land and the property which is legally and rightly still that of the Arabs. Now, to put it bluntly, this is robbery ... I have been in the refugee camps in the Gaza Strip and I have heard the songs that the children sing in their schools. If you wanted to see what it was like to be a Jew say 13 or 14 years after Nebuchadnezzar exiled the Jews, go to the Gaza Strip and study the spirit and state of mind of the Arabs there. They are saying just the same things that the Jews

The Duel

felt then and have continued to feel later: that this was their country and they meant to return.'

But Herzog refused to be diverted from the subject: 'You will pardon me if I come back to the original issue. ... The original issue was a question of comparison: what we did morally compared to what the Nazis did to us. Now I think it has been established that there was a war of aggression against us ... From what I understand from the quotation I gave and from what you have now elaborated, would you agree, Professor, that this stigma of moral comparison applies not only to our people but to those Arabs who were responsible for massacres ...? To most of the nations of the world who at any time had their soldiers in war, even in self-defence, have been guilty of atrocity.' ...

Toynbee: 'I agree that most societies have committed atrocities, but I do not think that condones atrocities.'

Herzog: 'You do agree that this comparison can be applied on the universal level to any country at war whose soldiers have committed atrocities against civilians?'

Toynbee: 'Yes, atrocities are atrocities and murder is murder, whoever commits it.'

Herzog: 'And would that also apply to Arab atrocities against Jewish civilian population, and the Black and Tans?'

Toynbee: 'Of course.'

Herzog: 'By the United States? Or the Indians? There is a whole realm; it is limitless. In other words, you were saying, if I now understand it, that, within the general category of denouncing violence or atrocities by military against civilians, Israel, in your opinion, was not separate from the rest of mankind but was guilty in the same way?'

Toynbee: 'Of course, I don't think that Israelis are different from mankind. I am not an anti-Semite ... It is curious of me to defend the Germans and the Nazis of all people, because my country suffered in two wars of aggression by the Germans, but they too, are human and what the Nazis did is not peculiar ...

Unhappily [it] is something that is in all human nature and we have to break it ... I have brought up the case of the Israelis in this connection ... [because] I was writing about the Palestine question and about the question between Jews and Gentiles in the world.'

Herzog did not ease up: 'But this would apply to any other nation too.'

Toynbee agreed: 'As the Ambassador has quoted, there are cases in my book where I brought up examples from the British and the French.'

Having led Toynbee to the admission that Israel was not different from other nations in the world, and that the 'Nazi' label he had applied to them applied to much of humanity, Herzog proceeded to attack the comparison with the Nazis.

Herzog: 'In analysing atrocities in history there are gradations. I feel the Nazi onslaught, what they did, is something quite specific ... Can it be compared to any other atrocity in human history? ... Take the people in Israel who went through the hell which were the Nazi death camps in Europe ... On coming out of those death camps they tried to get to Israel – Palestine at that time – and many of them on ships were held up by the British Navy, and arrested or sent over to Cyprus and put into camps ... Now you would be surprised, Professor, if you speak to these remnants today. Although they felt at the time that the British attitude was one of cruelty, and certainly political blindness, they did not equate it with the Nazis. These same people who went through the Nazi experience, the Holocaust, who escaped from it, their soul was not so shattered as to equate further evil as being on a Nazi level. And it is these same people you say were so influenced by the Nazis that they did similar things to the Arabs' ...

Toynbee: 'I said that Israelis are not different from other human beings. Yes.'

Herzog summed up the discussion with this point: 'In other words, the Nazi pall lies across the world, before the Nazis came, this business of atrocities and cruelty, and after they have gone.'

The Duel

Herzog now addressed the question of Arab lands. '... Any study of the British Mandatory Land Register would show that 70% of the land which is now Israel was government-owned: it belonged to the government of the Mandate and formerly to the Ottomans. ... As for the private property which was taken through the war – we have promised and are ready to give full compensation. This has been promised time and again at the United Nations, and in this respect I can speak officially, although here I'm in a personal capacity.'

Herzog reverted to the question of the historical connection to which Toynbee referred. 'You are quoted as having said that the Jewish people have no historical right to Israel. May I say some facts in this respect? Number one, the continuity of Jewish residence in the Land of Israel never ceased at any time in history, and I can quote you records on that century after century. Secondly, the return to Israel has been central in our religious faith – in our prayers, in our festivals and in every aspect of our national aspirations. Thirdly, the international community has recognized the validity of that right: the Balfour Declaration, the League of Nations, the United Nations. Fourthly, even the Arabs in the beginning did. There is a message from Emir Feisal to Dr Weizmann. He headed the Arab delegation to the Peace Conference in Versailles, and there was an agreement between them, and another letter on that agreement in which Emir Feisal writes that he "welcomes the Jews home".'

To which Toynbee responded: 'Yes, I was there.' The audience laughed.

Herzog went on to argue that the Jewish right to the land did not 'become obsolescent in AD 132 [the final collapse of Judea under the Romans] ... Some of our greatest religious thought and works have been produced there: the Mishnah, the Jerusalem Talmud, the Midrash, the Targum, the Assora, right down to the Shulhan Arukh, which is the basic code of Jewish law. All produced century after century in continuous residence there, and time and again our people hoped to achieve independence ... You speak of the first settlement being in 1881. I can show you documents of Jewish settlement and towns in Palestine of those days from the tenth century.'

Toynbee: 'Safad in the sixteenth century, is that the case?'

Herzog: 'Even earlier – Saadiah Gaon, Benjamin of Tudela in the twelfth century; Maimonides, Judah Halevi twelfth century; Nahmanides early thirteenth century – continuous residence. Rabbi Estori Ha-Parhi, author of *Kaftor va-Perrah*, continuous residence all the time, and the whole motive of our life was linked up with that. We feel that the present revival of the Third Commonwealth of Israel is a vindication of immortal prophecy. That has been our course down the ages. We have traversed the Valley of Death, and now, under graceful Providence, we have come to the uplands of fulfilment. That is how we see our history. You feel that we are a fossil that went off somewhere and sort of fell into the skating rink, in Montreal terms, ... We didn't. We remained vital and alive and creative. And may I, Sir, at this stage express some surprise that in your book you don't refer at all to that line of Jewish creativity – and by the way Einstein also belongs to that collective fossil category.'

'The Ambassador raised two questions,' said Toynbee. 'One was the question about the Jewish claim or title to Palestine, and the other was about the word "fossil" that I have used, not only about the Jews but about quite a number of different people, for instance the Parsees and various Christian sects, and to some extent the Greeks.'

But Herzog rejected these definitions: 'You do differentiate between fossilism – I've been reading your books – and archaism. The Parsees and we are in the fossil category, [while] as archaic you have there the Greeks, the Turks, the Norwegians and the Irish.'

But Toynbee avoided the main contention of the debate – namely, the Jews being a 'fossil' people, and concentrated on the 'injustice' the Jews had done to the Arabs following the Balfour Declaration. ' ... What is remarkable about the Jews was, I suppose, mainly the Jewish community, which exists today, as the Ambassador says, and the fact that they did not lose the memory of their homeland. In this they were exceptional among the people who were uprooted and deported by the Assyrians and Babylonians all that time ago in the eighth, seventh and sixth centuries BC ... whereas the Jews have kept their identity. And they have kept it by the memory of Palestine ... The Palestinian Arab refugees ... are in just this state of mind in which the Jews were immediately after the exile by Nebuchadnezzar ... I am extremely critical myself of the Balfour Declaration ... It was a short document. ... I can't remember the exact words, there are two sentences really ... the first is that Britain undertakes to uphold and support a Jewish national home in Palestine; the second clause provided that nothing is done to harm the interests of the existing inhabitants of the country, which at the time of the declarations made in 1917 were more than 90% Arabs of course. I blame the Balfour Declaration because the word "home" was vague. But it was made very clear (as I know directly from seeing the documents at the time, as a young temporary official in the British Foreign Office) ... and accepted by Dr Weizmann at the time that "home" did not mean "state", because if home meant state then the first clause of the Balfour Declaration would have been incompatible with the second clause ... '

Proceeding in his steady way, Herzog was not finished with the 'fossil' issue: ' ... In your study you say "the Jews live on, the same peculiar people, long after the Phoenicians and Philistines lost their identity like all the nations. The ancient Syriac neighbours of Israel had fallen into the melting-pot ... while Israel has proved impervious to this alchemy performed by history in the crucible of universal states and universal churches and wanderings of the nations." An extremely eloquent description, if I may say so, of Jewish survival ... We are the only people today in the Middle

East speaking the same language, practising the same religious faith, living in the same category of aspiration and spiritual continuity as our forefathers thousands of years ago and those who were exiled from there. There is nobody else from AD 132 in that category in terms of continuity.'

Toynbee, for his part, returned to the injustice done to the Arabs: 'By 1917, more than 90% of the population of Palestine were not Jews. That is the work of history *de facto* . . .'

Herzog: '. . . You have recognized, Professor, that there was a continuous Jewish residence in the Land of Israel, and the return became the goal of national life down the ages. It is also a fact that the Arabs never had Palestine as a separate political entity . . . after World War I . . . the international consciousness recognized that the Arab peoples deserve nationhood and deserve independence; deserve to achieve independence . . . and eight Arab states came into being, covering an area close to two million square miles. . . . Within that category of the Middle East, it was recognized that the Jewish people, having longed and lived for its return, should establish itself once again in the independence and freedom in the Land of Israel'.

Herzog challenged Toynbee's interpretation of the Balfour Declaration: 'Now you have an interpretation, Sir, of the Balfour Declaration, based on your association and work at the time with the British Government. But surely you will acknowledge, that Lord Balfour himself, Lloyd George the Prime Minister of the Government, [and] Winston Churchill, surely they should know what was meant by the Balfour Declaration, and they have clearly stated so down the years . . . Those responsible for the Balfour Declaration have clearly defined its purpose. There is talk there of religious and civil rights of other inhabitants, and on that there has never been any question . . .'

Toynbee remained firm: '. . . The fact that those eight Arab countries are happily independent does not affect the fate of the Arabs who lived in what is now Israel . . . On the Balfour Declaration I must say explicitly that I know that it was clearly understood at the time that the national home was not intended to be a Jewish national state, and this was clearly stated to the Zionist Organization by the British Government at the time that the Balfour Declaration was issued . . . '

Herzog: ' . . . I've read the interpretations given by those responsible for the Declaration, and the consensus of world opinion at the time . . . You will agree that the United Nations took a decision in November 1947 that there was to be a Jewish State in Palestine.'

Toynbee: 'They took a decision later that the Arab refugees were to be repatriated to Israel.'

Herzog: ' . . . No, they did not take a decision that the Arab refugees have to be repatriated to Israel. . . . The General Assembly of the United Nations in 1948 established a Palestine Conciliation Commission to deal with the whole complex of problems which had arisen between Israel and the Arab states . . . The Commission was supposed to study the possibilities either of repatriation or resettlement or of compensation, but all this as part of a general context of a peace settlement. The Resolution talks of the return of refugees as soon as practicable, and it also talks of those refugees who wish to live in peace. This Resolution has been dead now since 1948. It has been dead because the Arabs have never announced that they will live in peace with Israel . . . The Arab refugee problem, Professor, is one of a whole complex of refugee problems. I believe that since 1940 some 35 million people have been uprooted across the world: Korea, Vietnam, Germany, Finland. Nearly all of these problems either have been solved or are approaching a solution. In no case has a solution been through repatriation, but rather through absorption. Now what have we said? We have said we are prepared to pay full compensation; we have said that we are prepared to consider a limited repatriation within the framework of the reunion of families. But the problem will never move unless the Arab governments are prepared to cooperate in alleviating the suffering of the refugees ... There is no economic difficulty. Money is being voted by the United Nations, there is a promise from the United States government for an international loan. There is no social problem because they are living among their people ... The problem will never move until the Arab governments are prepared to cooperate in a humanitarian solution. I notice, Professor, that you yourself have criticized the Arab governments ... you have said very rightly, in talking of suffering, referring back to the first part of our conversation, why don't they take them out of this parasitic existence? Why don't they set them up in farms, villages and homes? Why keep them there as a political weapon? You who scan history over thousands of years, do you know of any other case, any precedent of holding hundreds of thousands of people as political hostages in camps – parasitic, no future ... so they can be ready as a political pawn for some ultimate programme to exterminate Israel, God forbid. Is that moral? Is that an approach? Have you read the Secretary General of the United Nations' report of last year? He views the solution in terms of economic integration into the area. Of course we will play our part in it.' Herzog noted that there were 200,000 Arabs living in peace in Israel '... But you want us to take back people who have been nurtured on hate for 13 years ... vengeance and destruction, and if we take them back ... they can rip us apart ... '

Herzog compared two refugee problems born from the 1948 conflict: some 550,000 Arabs on the one hand, and some 400,000 Jews and 70,000 Arabs, on the other. 'We have settled the second problem. We have absorbed over 400,000 Jews from Arab countries ... [and] we have settled 70,000 Arab refugees in the country ... Only last month, Professor Toynbee, a representative of the Arab refugees appeared at the United Nations. What did he speak about? The destruction of Israel, the extermination of Israel. He was probably told to do so by certain governments in the Middle East. He said so. So you tell us now in 1948 they talked of coming back in peace. Now to take them back after 13 years, and he says he wants to destroy you. Why not ... Please commit suicide so at least the Arab armies won't have to overwhelm you from without. That, Sir, I think, in the scan of history, you will find no nation has been prepared to do, and since you said earlier that in certain respects we belong to a whole category of nations in our behaviour, in this respect, too, we will not commit suicide.'

Toynbee riposted by saying: 'I think there are two points ... one is repatriation and the other is using refugees as pawns. I think there is an inconsistency in the Israeli stand. Your claim for Jews' repatriation into Palestine ... though since as long ago as AD 135, there has been no solid Jewish population in Palestine, though I agree ... that there have always been Jews in Palestine ... as a small minority. And since 64 or 63 BC there hasn't been a Jewish state in Palestine. Your claim for repatriation not in the terms of the Balfour Declaration, a Jewish national home, but not a state, but in the extreme form of a state, but at the same time you deny to the Arabs who were forced out of Palestine ... as recently as 1948 the very thing you claim as the central claim of the Jewish people ... I think some pretty telling comparisons could be made between their use of Jewish refugees as pawns and the Arab government's use of Arab refugees as pawns. I think ... both the Israelis and Zionists and the Arab states have been guilty of this, really disgusting thing to do ... As you can see I am not partial ... to Nazis ... but I have pointed out that the West German Government since the war ... received ... nine million refugees ... from East Germany and their territories, which were formerly Germany before the war and are now part of Poland and the Soviet Union ... The West Germans ... have taken the humane and sensible line of absorbing the refugees without renouncing claims to these refugees' homes and territory, into her life and into her industry, and one of the reasons why Western Germany is prosperous and powerful now is that she has given these refugees a chance of ... happiness ... '

This was an unfortunate example, as Toynbee was ignoring – innocently or wilfully – the fact that the refugees who were absorbed in West Germany were German, not a different and hostile nation. He went further, and accused the Zionist Federation and the State of Israel of using the Jewish refugees as a means of applying pressure. He also argued that those Jewish refugees from World War II would have been better off had they been directed to North America or Australia, but the Israeli government and the Zionist Federation had used them as pawns, just as the Arab refugees were now being used.

Herzog: '... I must – and this I do on the basis of personal knowledge – I must reject emphatically any suggestion that they were used as political pawns. The fact is that tens of thousands came to other countries: the United States, Canada, across the world. Those who came to Israel came because they sought independence and freedom and they sought restoration, and they felt they could only overcome the experience of what had happened to them at the hands of the Nazis ... with their own people.'

Now Herzog sought to draw the debate back to its main issue: 'I suggest that, as time is running short, we go on to the famous fossil thing, as I am sure the audience would like to hear about it ... As you have said, Professor, the title "fossil" has almost entered the international vocabulary since you used it in the context you did and as I understand from reading your works in the past few days – and nights, I might add. There are fossils and also peoples in the archaic sense. ... We seem to be in both. We are both fossils with the Parsees of India and when it comes to archaism, we have a link with the Norwegians, the Greeks, the Turks and the Irish. Well ... at least in the archaic angle I have associations from childhood with Ireland, but as far as the Parsees are concerned I am afraid I have no acquaintance.'

Toynbee: 'They are a very interesting people.'

Herzog: 'I am not an historian, but your thesis has been challenged by historians of great eminence and writers. There is

The Duel

quite a vocabulary of reply to, they call it in various terms, the "Toynbee Thesis" or the "Toynbee Heresy".'

Toynbee: 'Don't I know it! Aubrey Eban calls it the "Toynbee Heresy".'

Herzog replied by elaborating his religious-spiritual view of the persistence of the Jewish people: '... I could sum it up in a verse from the Psalms: it is "I shall not die but I shall live!" A fossil does not die, but he also does not live. Here we part ways. And as we live, and through our survival down the ages we see the hand of Providence, we have the sense of survival under Providence and we move ahead as we pray for spiritual fulfilment. Here lies the basic difference between us. You say to us: "You did not die (why is not clear), but you did not live. No continuity in terms of creative life and thought. You sort of slipped out of the stream of civilization to some remote island and got stuck there. Now and then your voice is heard as it shrieks at the passing ships." We say: "No, we have been in the stream. We have been in the stream in a distinctive sense: in our survival, in our prayers and in our hope, in our attachment to our land and in our belief in the fulfilment of immortal prophecy ..." As a modern Israeli representing my country and one who has seen the country come to life and independence, from the academic historical analysis point of view ... is there no significance in the following facts which cannot be denied: "Number One: of all the ancient peoples of the Middle East, we are the only one living in continuity today in the Middle East, speaking the same language, practising the same religious faith."

Toynbee interjected: 'With the Parsees.'

Herzog continued: '... Secondly, that after this passage through the Valley of Death down the ages ... we have come to life in our time. We have come to life without rancour, despite all that has passed between us and our Arab neighbours ... There is no rancour, there is no hatred. There is grief, but there is a hope for peace ... Nor is there rancour to nations across the world ...

'Thirdly: after these thousands of years we have assembled our people from 70 lands ... Has that link got no vitality? Was that a fossil? Is that how a fossil reacts? ... Finally, the question of democracy. After all this experience we are the only viable democracy in terms of the Israel–Arab complex in the area. ... The fact is that today many new nations from Africa and Asia turn to us for guidance and cooperation, and they find in our experiment and in our enterprises, they find something which draws them. There's a link. So we do have a message for the world and not, Sir, as you suggested, that our message ceased some time 2,300 years ago ... We believe in all humility and thanks to a grateful Providence that it has a relevance to the broad experience of mankind today. I would ask you, Sir, in all respect, whether you don't think all these elements have any basis on which you could possibly reconsider your concept of us as a fossil, non-creative, which suddenly fell out – neither died nor lived these past 2,000 years?'

'... I have never used [the word fossil] of the Jewish people alone,' Toynbee replied. 'I have always used it of a whole class of peoples ... I have tried to map out a kind of picture of civilizations, and I found there were several civilizations or series of civilizations, some of which died out perhaps several thousand years ago; others are alive today. But I did find that of the civilizations that died out quite a long time ago, certain exceptional communities: the Jews, the Parsees, one branch of the Buddhists and certain rather obscure Christian sects ... had become extinct, not in the sense of human beings, but had become absorbed into other civilizations, races, peoples and so on ... What I wanted to express in the word fossil was that these exceptional communities had survived from a previous age, just as fossils are a surviving record of forms of life that existed in a preceding age, and that they have survived by encasing themselves for many centuries on end ... They have encased themselves in a very rigid religious organization, particularly in the keeping of a very minute system of laws ... also in

The Duel

social customs ... All our labels are more or less imperfect ... I said could we take some word for a living creature ... in South Africa they found an antediluvian fish called the coelacanths – I could substitute the word coelacanth for fossil – would that be any more attractive to people I have labelled fossils? I thought probably it wouldn't and, after all, the coelacanth is a very archaic form of life and the present-day Jews are not archaic and are in the full stream of life ... Under the shock of the Roman wars I do think that the Jewish communities withdrew into a kind of shell, they gave up writing and speaking Greek and went back to Hebrew, or rather Aramaic, and for many centuries they remained encased partly by their own will, partly by the bad treatment they received from Christians, especially the Western Christians. It is only since the Napoleonic times, you might say, except in some very early enlightened countries like Holland and Tuscany ... in the sixteenth and seventeenth centuries, that the doors were opened to the Jews and they were brought back into the full stream of life ... The Jews in present times have, of course, become part of the general stream of life and have played this enormous part in it.'

This was, in effect, a refutation of Toynbee's essential argument, and Herzog seized on it at once. 'Defossilized, Sir?'

Toynbee was disconcerted: 'Israel can defossilize, just as you can defrost a car.'

Herzog commented: 'That's very interesting.'

Toynbee: 'I have not found another word to express what I mean ... Find me a better name and I will use it. That is all I can say really. It is not meant as an insult ...'

Herzog relished his triumph: '... What I am very happy about, is that you have agreed today that the fossil has become defossilized, and the problem is not so much now finding an alternative term for the fossil ... but to find a term for a new creature which has been defossilized.'

Toynbee: 'Remember, I said with some reservations. I am afraid that there are reservations on the Jewish side, as well as on the Gentile side, and these are serious, and we have to remember them.'

Herzog: 'Do you accept that these considerations of vitality I mentioned earlier related to Israel's return and restoration? Have they anything to do with the defossilization? Are they signs for you, historically speaking, of vitality?'

Toynbee: '... The Gentile Westerners invented nationalism, which I strongly dislike, and that the Jews caught this disease from the Western Gentiles, which is very unfortunate.'

Herzog agreed: 'Well, it has been a long, long, long disease with us and many physicians have tried to cure us down the ages, but we have refused to be cured. ... I know that you are opposed to the modern state. ... There are many people also in Israel who think that we must move to much more world cooperation without giving up independence. That is a different matter ...'

Toynbee: 'But I have never denied that the Jews have always been alive. ... I have criticized some forms of vitality that Israel has taken, but I never denied their vitality ... If you went to southern and eastern Asia, the perspective changes, and the Parsees, who have also been defossilized just about contemporarily with the Jews as a result of the modernization of India, will play an important part in history, which may surprise you, because India is going to play an important part, and they are to India what the Jews are to the Western World.'

Having disproved Toynbee's two principal arguments, and having obtained his interlocutor's semi-explicit admission to that effect, Herzog concluded by inviting the Professor to come to Israel and 'weigh up the process of defossilization ... and see this vitality ...'

Toynbee thanked him, adding 'vitality is not enough, let us come back to morality ...'

Herzog concluded the debate: 'On the morality issue you yourself have agreed that we are like other peoples, and that again can be looked into when you visit Israel.'

The Duel

The audience applauded vigorously. Herzog was clearly the victor in the joust, and Pnina Herzog overheard Mrs Toynbee, who was sitting nearby, saying to her husband, 'I told you not to take part in this debate!'[1]

Sitting beside the debaters was Irwin Cotler, then vice-president of Hillel. He was amazed by Herzog's method. 'He asked Toynbee question after question and led him the way a skilled advocate leads a witness to contradict himself ... [Herzog] had a historian's knowledge ... and no Jewish complexes. He didn't have to please the "goy" – what mattered to him was the historic truth ... Toynbee felt that Herzog had won the debate. He retracted his statements, began to stammer, seeming humiliated, like a boxer who's been knocked out. ... Anyone who witnessed the debate could only have wondered, "Is this Toynbee the historian?"'[2] He seemed confused and awkward. The longer it went on, the smaller Toynbee became in stature and the more Herzog grew.

'If the Jewish students had felt humiliated by Toynbee's lecture, now they felt pride and self-respect as Jews. What Herzog did had psychological no less than intellectual impact. The students came away feeling that Herzog had vindicated Judaism and Israel, and that the truth had finally emerged.'[3]

All who witnessed the debate were convinced that Herzog's triumph was clear and unequivocal. 'Toynbee did not emerge with his laurels intact,' wrote the *Maariv* correspondent who had been in the hall.[4] Even Herzog allowed himself to depart from his accustomed modesty, and wrote, 'If I had known in advance that [Toynbee] would be so weak, I wouldn't have burned the midnight oil in the three days between his agreeing to the debate and when it took place.'[5]

Herzog explained Toynbee's defeat by saying that he had not understood the proverb of the Sages, 'Seize too much – seize nothing.' 'Having resolved to outdo all his colleagues and become the number one expert and authority on the course of history to the present time, he had to devise rules and laws, and in his analyses he needed to adapt the facts to those laws — just like those preachers who have to distort the facts which contradict their principal beliefs.'[6]

The debate was broadcast, entirely or in part, by many radio stations in Canada and the northern United States, and that evening it was also broadcast in Israel. Many people listened to it attentively, although it was a time of exceptional political upheaval in Israel — the 'Lavon affair' was in full spate, and on the day of the debate Ben-Gurion resigned from the premiership. Nevertheless, as *The Jerusalem Post* reported, 'the broadcast became one of the most intensely discussed events of the week, in spite of its length and the late hour. There is no doubt that Mr Herzog's determined and fervent attack stood in marked contrast to Professor Toynbee's hesitant responses. But at the end of the debate one could still wonder if any debate could persuade Dr Toynbee that he had been mistaken in his approaches and insults against the Jewish people. He may declare that he is not anti-Semitic', added the correspondent ironically, 'but he obviously does not like the Jewish people, except some who are his best friends.'[7]

Most of those who heard the debate, including Christians, found Herzog's arguments persuasive, and sent letters of support to the Embassy. The day after the debate, leading articles in the Canadian daily press also expressed support for Herzog's position. Most of them objected to the comparisons drawn by Toynbee between the Nazi acts and attacks on Arab civilians by Israeli soldiers during the 1948 war. The Embassy in Ottawa was flooded with letters of congratulation, most notably from Yitzhak Ben-Zvi, Israel's President, who wrote, 'I was glad to hear that you invited Professor Toynbee to a public debate,' he wrote. '... Toynbee is well-known in the world, which is why we have to be aware that his anti-Semitic views are listened to by the Jewish and non-Jewish intelligentsia. You followed the counsel of the wisest of men, "Answer a fool according to his folly," for which I congratulate you.'[8] The President's wife, Rachel Yanait Ben-Zvi, also wrote to him: 'We trusted you, Yaacov, to let him have it ... Toynbee attacks us with nonsense, with foul words, slander and calumny, which were left almost unanswered. So bless you, Yaacov, for challenging him to a public debate, and defeating him.' She described Toynbee as 'a latter-day oppressor'.[9]

Abba Eban, who was then Minister of Education and Culture, also congratulated Herzog in warm words: 'I listened attentively to the broadcast,' he wrote, 'and felt very proud. My heartfelt congratulations on your courageous stand in defence of the nation's honour.'[10] Prominent Jewish figures in North America, Supreme Court judges, Members of Knesset, journalists and colleagues sent Herzog enthusiastic congratulations. Ben-Gurion followed closely the broadcast debate, Golda Meir overcame her reservations and sent Herzog a telegram of congratulations: 'Well done!'[11] Chaim Israeli wrote a letter which showed he was deeply moved: 'Paula [Ben-Gurion] listened to the broadcast to the end and then telephoned your mother to congratulate her. I heard her saying so much in your praise! I can't deny I enjoyed it.'[12]

Rabbi Yehuda Halevy Hirschhorn of Montreal put it in historical perspective: 'I had thought that the age of great debates between the sages of Israel and their priests, before popes and monarchs, had passed from the world, but evidently it still lives in a different form ... Your sagacity and intelligence *vis-à-vis* the nations of the world did not abandon you in that hour of needing to know how to respond, when you depended on the mercy of heaven, and thanks be to God that we came out of it safely.'[13]

But not all the reactions were so favourable. Some of the newspapers reported the dialogue without a comment. The headline in the *New York Times* stated, inaccurately, that 'The Historian and Israel's Ambassador to Canada Agreed: Murder is Murder, Whether Committed by Nazis or Jews'.[14] Herzog had to admit that 'the press did not reflect the debate correctly, which is understandable given its scope and the inability of the correspondents to encompass it in their stories.'[15] Certain Jewish leaders who had objected to the debate in advance, continued to argue that it had only provided Toynbee with another platform to disseminate his ideas.[16] Opinions were divided among Israeli diplomats. Michael Arnon, Israel's minister at the Embassy in Washington, congratulated Herzog for 'giving Toynbee hell', but remained convinced that the debate 'gave Toynbee's views the kind of publicity he might not have obtained otherwise'.[17] Other Israeli diplomats criticized Herzog in petty-sounding letters and comments.[18] A Foreign Ministry official who signed himself I. S. Israeli wrote a letter to the weekly *Panim el Panim* (*Face to Face*), saying 'Mr Yaacov Herzog made a great mistake holding a public debate with Professor Toynbee ... Herzog "summoned the bear from the forest" and indirectly gave tremendous publicity to Toynbee's ideas – more's the pity.'[19]

But Herzog's friend, the journalist Amos Elon, wrote to him from Washington: 'Those people who think you shouldn't have debated, they're precisely the ones who are more interested in scoring points and in public relations than in the truth, and you needn't pay them any attention.'[20] Others persisted in arguing that Toynbee remained unconvinced and did not admit his mistakes. This was a curious argument – after all, the debate was not a duel which only ends with one of the participants bleeding to death. From the outset it was clear that Toynbee would not retract all he had written and uttered for decades. Before the start of the debate he had said to Herzog, 'You realize that I must defend what I have written in my books.'[21] Even his willingness to change his mind and definitions was more than anyone could have anticipated before the debate. Herzog quite rightly wrote to a friend, 'I was surprised that so many in Israel thought that I'd set out to convince Toynbee. That was not my intention, and if I have done something out of the ordinary, it was because of my estimation of the grave harm caused by his original arrogant statement ... Some slogans carry a poison that penetrates the common man's mind, and I felt I had to challenge this man who enjoys such an exalted status in Canada. My way of speaking and general approach were aimed mainly at the hundreds of thousands of listeners all over Canada ...' Herzog added that from the reactions and opinions of the experts, he could conclude that Toynbee's 'semi-prophetic halo was somewhat dented, and that was the main thing'.[22]

Herzog wrote to his friend Chaim Israeli: 'I think that the poison of his calumnies – that is, in his vile selective comparison between us and the Nazis – was eliminated, as in the course of the debate he included almost all of humanity, and not only Israel, in his wicked definition.'[23]

Following the debate Toynbee did not change his position – he could hardly do so – but he mildly moderated his attacks on Israel and acknowledged the monstrosity of the Nazi crimes. Nevertheless, Herzog realized that Toynbee had not changed, 'Since the debate in Montreal he no longer feels comfortable with the comparison [between Israel and the Nazis] ... and turns defensive when questioned about it ... The substance remains as toxic as before, but in a different guise.'[24]

Herzog, then, had no illusions about Toynbee's hostility and hatred, yet he continued to correspond with him in the years that followed, and Toynbee sent a letter of condolence to Pnina Herzog on Yaacov's death. Herzog and his family enjoyed telling people and the media about the ongoing relations between them. In this Herzog was misguided – whether by excessive politeness or a futile hope of persuading Toynbee to become more sympathetic to Israel. If Toynbee was a confirmed anti-Semite and anti-Zionist, there was no need for Herzog to conduct a pleasant, courteous correspondence with him. With the passing of time, when important and dramatic events were forgotten, the memory of the Herzog–Toynbee debate remained vivid. The arguments of those who objected to it and their protests against Herzog faded from memory. The media, the academic world and modern historians remember and respect Herzog's memory because of his debate with Toynbee, and his triumph in it has been seen as a moral and historical victory for Judaism and Zionism.

A few days after the debate the Israeli author and publicist Yeshayahu Avrekh came to Ottawa, and spent a whole night with Yaacov and Pnina talking about the debate with Toynbee. He described it, years later in 1974, as 'a surrealist scene: in snowy Ottawa, capital of Catholic Canada, at the house of a traditional Jewish scholar, who was also an ambassador of independent Israel – an eccentric Jewish discourse took place about the Jewish people, its tortuous history and enigmatic future – far into the night'.[25]

'He was an exemplary Jew of our time,' Avrekh wrote. 'A harmonious, wondrous blend of nobility, worldly culture and Jewish wisdom, the wisdom and humility of the ages. Unfortunately, 25 years of Israeli education – or lack thereof – have distanced this figure from Israel's horizons ... It is certain that the figure of such a Jew – drawing on the sources of his people, proud of his Jewish heritage, wholehearted in his belief in his people's just cause and its eternal values – such a figure has not been envisioned by Israel's educators. If it were, perhaps many of the doubts plaguing young Israelis would not have become so depressingly dominant.' These words could have been written today.

The passing years have not erased the memory of the debate between the young, proud, wise Israeli and the elderly English historian, who was scarcely able to conceal his animosity towards Jews and Israel. Decades after Yaacov Herzog's death, his name remains associated with the debate, which grows in significance over time. But Yaacov Herzog could not have known, ironically, that that day in the depths of the Canadian winter, in a crowded auditorium in snowy Montreal, before a captivated young audience, would be his finest hour.

11

The Absent Father

The debate with Toynbee was the only independent political act Yaacov Herzog ever undertook without consideration for, or consultation with, his official superiors. It was the most significant event of his term in Canada, yet did not overshadow his diplomatic activities in the slightest. He developed excellent relations with Canada's leaders, and came to be on friendly terms with Prime Minister John Diefenbaker, who later said, 'My door was always open to him.'[1]

Diefenbaker was especially impressed by Herzog during the visit of the US President John F. Kennedy to Canada. While shaking hands with guests, Kennedy spotted Yaacov Herzog, gave him a hug and moved aside with him. Everyone was struck by the unusually friendly encounter. Diefenbaker came over to see what was holding up the reception line, and found that the other guests were waiting for Kennedy to finish speaking to the Israeli Ambassador. 'We have common ancestors,' Kennedy said to Diefenbaker. 'I didn't know you had Jewish blood,' replied the astonished Prime Minister. Kennedy laughed, 'I was referring to our Irish origins.'[2]

The special relationship with Diefenbaker would prove very useful to Israel. Late in 1960, an American U2 spy-plane photographed a huge structure under construction in Israel's southern desert, near the town of Dimona. US intelligence analysed the pictures and concluded that Israel was secretly building a large nuclear reactor. The story was leaked to the press and gave rise to prominent headlines around the world. The United States accused Israel of planning to develop nuclear weapons. John Kennedy, who had been sworn in as American President in January 1961, began to apply massive pressure to Israel to stop her nuclear programme. He demanded that American experts visit the installation in Dimona and report on it. Prime Minister Ben-Gurion decided that he needed to return to the United States to meet the President. The humiliating search for a pretext began once again.

And again, it was Yaacov Herzog who came up with the answer. He turned to Canada's Prime Minister, who said at once that he would be happy to invite Ben-Gurion to pay an official visit to Canada. Ben-Gurion could then stop in the United States to meet President Kennedy.

Ben-Gurion duly arrived in Canada in May 1961. Yaacov Herzog accompanied him during the five days of his visit, then flew with him to New York, where Ben-Gurion met President Kennedy at the Waldorf Astoria Hotel. Kennedy reassured Ben-Gurion that the two experts he had sent to the nuclear facility in Dimona had confirmed that it was designed for peaceful purposes, and not to build a nuclear bomb. Ben-Gurion was relieved to hear this, but disappointed to discover that Kennedy meant to demand Israeli concessions in the matter of the Palestinian refugees as a condition for the purchase of 'Hawk' ground-to-air missiles.

Finally Kennedy and Ben-Gurion were left on their own. Kennedy said, 'I know I was elected thanks to the Jewish vote. What do you think I should do?'

Ben-Gurion was taken aback – the question seemed to invite an informal deal. 'Do whatever is best for the free world,' he replied. Afterwards Ben-Gurion told his companions that Kennedy struck him as a 'politician' – a pejorative term in his vocabulary.

Yaacov Herzog returned to Ottawa, but continued to travel frequently to New York to help the UN delegation, and to lecture widely in Canada and the United States. In the Canadian capital he formed, as always, close relations with many diplomats

The Absent Father

and members of the local administration. 'He would meet foreign ambassadors and diplomats,' said Deborah Bregman, his secretary during his Ottawa posting, 'and speak with them about any number of subjects, not simply Israel or matters that concerned us, but world problems and global vision. It was amazing, his ability to speak with any person about any subject at all.'[3] The Canadian Foreign Minister, Paul Martin, who became his friend, thought that 'he was a man who understood the world – its complexity, its machinery, its merits and defects – yet despite this, in some way, he was not quite a part of it ... He was indeed a son of Israel, but he was more than that; he was a citizen of the world, and his overall view was greatly influenced by his religious background.'[4]

Herzog's letters back to the Foreign Ministry reflected the great importance he ascribed to Canada and her place in the world. He worked hard and drove his staff hard, and they responded willingly, with undisguised admiration. 'He worked all day and all night,' said Deborah Bregman. 'On Friday till the last possible moment, and on Saturday night as soon as the third star showed, we knew it was time to return to work.' He was always asking his staff to postpone their vacations for the sake of work. 'Whenever I wanted to take leave, I felt as though I was abandoning the State.'[5]

Yet despite his hard work, Herzog managed, during his stay in Canada, to complete his higher studies. In 1962 he received with commendation the 'Degré d'Études Supérieurs' in Law, under the supervision of the University of Paris and its Bar Association. The following year he obtained a doctorate in law from the University of Ottawa. His doctoral dissertation was on 'The Development of the United Nations' Concept of Human Rights'.

Here again the multi-faceted personality of this man, who had just turned 40, manifested itself. He was capable of existing in two parallel spheres, without his tremendous obligations in one detracting from his dedication to the other. His diplomatic reports were masterly, and his superiors described them as the best ever sent by an ambassador. They were detailed and lengthy – sometimes too lengthy – and written in precise, often rather florid, language. They reveal Yaacov's innate modesty, in that they were never self-congratulatory, or sought to impress his superiors with his success. He maintained his confidential connections with Israel's intelligence community, and exchanged almost weekly letters with Chaim Israeli, thereby maintaining his direct link to the Prime Minister's office.

Yaacov soon acquired a large following of admirers, but only a handful of individuals – intellectuals, philosophers, experts in international relations and religious scholars – could be described as his personal friends. He remained very close to his brother Chaim and his family. He continued to have boundless admiration for his father, despite the fact that the Chief Rabbi was sometimes criticized for his naivety and impracticality, as well as for his political views.

Yaacov was in Washington when his father passed away, in 1959. Some time later, at a memorial gathering held at the Chief Rabbinate in Jerusalem, he eulogized his father. 'It is not for me, as his son, to laud my father of blessed memory, for his scholarship and wisdom, his piety, lifelong experience and breadth of thought ... With the passing of time, as the first shock of his departure grows fainter, the appreciation of his role in his time, and his future impact, grows stronger. Not only was his personality marked by wholeness – it encompassed the spirit of his age.

'... My father of blessed memory was of whole mind – his personality was characterized by unity, bonding and spiritual brotherhood ... He was the last spokesman of the calamity that befell the House of Israel, and the first spokesman of the consolation that heralds deliverance ... I recall how shocked, horrified and devastated he was when he met the remaining survivors of Europe's hellfire after the war ... But if his body was devastated, his soul remained whole. He did not doubt for a moment that the rivers of blood and sorrow were the paths of deliverance, it being

The Absent Father

the age of the start of redemption, that the Holocaust would not reach Zion and that the third kingdom would rise and persist for ever.

'He, the last of the calamity, recalled the first of the calamity, Rabbi Yohanan ben Zakkai, who on his deathbed, nearly two thousand years ago, instructed his disciples to prepare a seat for King Hezekiah of Judah, as a symbol of the faith that Israel's fallen kingdom would rise again ... He saw and sensed that without the rise of Israel the ember might, God forbid, be extinguished – he saw the link and the bridge between destruction and redemption – an understanding and a faith whose significance and truth became clear to the entire nation. The period left its stamp on him and he upon it, until he became a part of it. And as it contained the accumulated experiences of the people of Israel through the ages, so his faith linked past and present, present and future.'[6]

Was Yaacov aware that in speaking about his father he was in effect speaking about himself? He himself was profoundly committed to the idea of Jewish continuity, the link between the people and the land, the rise of Israel as the response to the exile and the calamities it had inflicted upon the Jewish people. The idea of Jewish continuity suffused his world. In an interview with Eli Eyal on IDF Radio he talked about 'the Jew's timeless identity' through the ages. 'The greatest men of our past generations – Rabbi Akiva, Rabbi Yohanan ben Zakkai, Bar Kokhba – if they were to rise from their graves it would be as if they had never been gone. We would talk to them about all that has happened since their time, as though the Jewish experience has remained unchanged to this day.

'To an English child, the Duke of Wellington and Lord Nelson are historical figures, not living images in their inner mind. The same with Napoleon to a French child ... I think that ethnically Chinese continuity is stronger than ours – today's Chinese person is probably more like his ancestor of 3,000 years ago, than today's Jew is like his ancestor 3,000 years ago ... But ... supposing

Confucius were to rise from his grave in Peking [*sic*], would today's Chinese people feel an instinctive identification with him, as though he had never died? ... In today's Peking he would be like Plato or Aristotle in today's Greece – an exalted historical figure, but not necessarily part of the day-to-day consciousness of his people. Whereas I'm sure that if Rabbi Akiva were to rise today, the Jews would talk to him and question him about his attitude towards Bar Kokhba's war against the Romans, his personal feelings about Bar Kokhba, how he saw the destruction of the Temple ... They would talk to him about the nature of the Jewish people, its dialogue with God and with the nations of the world, the historical experience, continuity and the future – as though he had never been away.'[7]

This was a central idea in Yaacov's world view. It appears in most of the speeches, articles and interviews in which he spoke about the Jewish people. But other than this, he did not usually come up with new ideas. Mostly he confined himself to information and to defending the ideas of his superiors. Sometimes he had to devote all his energies to justifying and praising individuals who were his intellectual inferiors. A person as wise and as gifted as he would surely have been able to formulate an original worldview and to present Israel with important ideas in the areas of his expertise. But he did not do so.

Abba Eban said that Herzog 'submerged himself in the people at whose side he worked, without ostentation or self-importance, never seeking honours, but drawing satisfaction from the success of the person he supported ... He had a great respect for people who were willing to bear the heavy burden of power. More than once he wondered if he should not enter a new and independent field of endeavour, in which he would not only support others, but stand in his own right. He spoke to me about it several times. In this he was thwarted by one of his own best qualities – by his dislike of discord, his boundless tolerance for people who ... opposed [his views], his ability to examine every issue from all

The Absent Father

sides, his constant endeavour to reach the common and unifying denominator, and his inability to regard any Jew as an opponent. This was the source – as he admitted to me – of his unwillingness to expose himself ... amid flying arrows of criticism, and people stoning each other in rage ... He used to quote the Sages, who said, "Meanness, the evil impulse and misanthropy, these drive a man out of this life".'[8]

Years later, his daughter Shira wondered if her father's avoidance of assuming leadership and his tendency to serve others stemmed from the fact that in his youth he had acted as his own father's assistant, doing everything in the service of Rabbi Herzog, and not leaving his parents' home until he was 30, when his personality had fully matured.[9]

The Canadian Foreign Minister said, 'Some people make their work in the service of prime ministers into a vocation ... Yaacov Herzog served as bureau chief of several Israeli premiers ... When my wife and I visited Ben-Gurion in his kibbutz in 1958, he told us how essential Yaacov had been to him. In fact, Yaacov was Ben-Gurion's closest advisor during the Suez campaign.'[10]

'Yaacov was quick and nimble,' Abba Eban said, 'in his speech, his movements, his actions, his thinking, in his moving from subject to subject – as if he were in a hurry and what he failed to complete today might never be completed.'[11] It was this very quality that sparked the friendship and warm affection between Yaacov and President Zalman Shazar. The two met on a train from London to Southampton, where they were to board a ship for the United States. It was the year of mourning for Yaacov's father. 'On the way he told me,' Shazar recalled, 'that we would arrive at sundown, and he would gather a minyan [ten men, a Jewish prayer quorum] for the evening prayer, when he could say Kaddish [the prayer for the dead]. He impressed me doubly then – first by his organizational abilities that made use of every moment to get to the place on time, find a quiet nook for the prayer and the quorum for holding it; but I was even more struck by his sudden calm when the minyan was ready and he started praying. His nervous quickness vanished, and when he reached the blessings, he sang each one in his pleasant voice, clearly enunciating every word, as though time did not press and as if he were taking part in a normal evening service in a synagogue. He finished in time, dressed with his usual speed, and drew me along, so that we reached the gangway before the ship moved away ... That evening prayer revealed the quality of the man to me, and it was the start of our friendship.'[12]

In America, Yaacov Herzog gradually became Israel's 'national spokesman' – the one who was able to present the State's official positions in the most eloquent, intelligent and charismatic way. His audiences were enchanted by his rhetorical skill, his brilliant fluency, his Jewish and world culture, and the historical, cultural and religious tapestry he unfolded before them. And the themes of Jewish continuity and the eternal link between the people and their ancient land resonated through his speeches.

He was a man who carried out policies, not one who shaped them. On the historical night of 8 November 1956, when Israel was struggling to retain some of the achievements of the Sinai campaign, it was he who found the way to do it. When it was necessary to obtain a loan from the United States, he knew which levers to pull to bring it off, against all odds. When it was important to get Ben-Gurion to Washington and New York, again it was he who found the way to do it. Likewise, when a new political formula was needed to allow for Israel's new special relationship with Germany, it was he who devised it, and then defended it with all his might.

Later, when it became imperative to explain the Six Day War to the world, it was once again Yaacov Herzog who did so – persuasively, intelligently, charismatically.

He did all this in the service of others – Moshe Sharett, David Ben-Gurion, Golda Meir, Abba Eban ... Curiously, he seemed to

The Absent Father

avoid offering new and different ideas, though no doubt his fertile mind could have produced them.

Yaacov also had a wonderful way of reconciling his passionate and scholarly religious belief with the tolerance of a man of the world. He never tried to force his ways on others, neither the ultra-Orthodox nor the moderates, the secular nor the observant. He could have used his moderation as a bridge between the religious and secular camps, but he did not do so.

He was a devoted family man, yet did not spend much time with his family. His work came first while, at home, life revolved around him. When still a child, his elder daughter Shira swore that she would 'marry a man who could take his children to buy shoes' – that is, a man who spends time with his family.[13] In Canada he used to take her with him to synagogue on the Sabbath, and as they walked they had long conversations. But it seems Yaacov was somewhat reserved, and his daughter preferred the later hours, when her father would leave her with friends with whom she spent the rest of the Sabbath. 'I loved him dearly,' Shira said, 'but he was an absent father.'[14]

For Pnina, Yaacov and his work were the heart of the family and she was utterly devoted to him. She ran the day-to-day life of the family – shopping, keeping the accounts and making all necessary arrangements – because Yaacov's diplomatic realism and pragmatism were not obvious in his private life. In this he resembled his father, and like his father he needed a strong, intelligent woman at his side, a role that Pnina filled to perfection.

The Herzogs returned to Israel in the summer of 1963, when Yaacov was appointed deputy director-general of the Foreign Ministry. He said goodbye to all his friends and acquaintances, including the Canadian Foreign Minister, Paul Martin. Years later, Martin recalled an amusing incident from Herzog's last days in Ottawa, an episode that reveals Yaacov's utter dedication to his work, even in unusual circumstances.

A few days after their official parting, Martin recalled, Yaacov discovered that he needed to see him once more on an urgent matter. 'I was just about to leave my office for my usual midday swim, and said to Yaacov, "Well, if you want to see me, my dear friend, you'll have to join me in Brighton Beach, on the Rideau Canal, in the heart of Ottawa." He sounded surprised, but agreed. I went to my swimming place, and who should appear on the lawn of Brighton Beach, if not the Israeli Ambassador, dressed in swimming-trunks which had obviously just been bought, his very white skin standing out, showing that his exposure to the summer sun had not so far been excessive. Did he know how to swim, I wondered? He must, or he wouldn't come here, all set to plunge into the Rideau, if he couldn't swim. "Come, Yaacov," I said, "we can talk about anything you like while splashing about in this refreshing stream." He did this without hesitation, but to my astonishment, as soon as he plunged into the water he disappeared and then rose again, spluttering and gulping. In reality, he could not swim [here the typed text shows a handwritten addition, perhaps Martin's: "as well as I"], and did not take into account that the water was so deep. With a little help I led him to a shallower spot. Clearly he was determined, despite all dangers and difficulties, to hold that conversation with me. I've often laughed at that incident.'[15]

12

Dr Davis and Mr Charles

It was close to midnight on 23 September 1963, when an urgent and confidential message reached Yaacov Herzog at home in Jerusalem. Herzog at once telephoned the director-general of the Foreign Ministry, Dr Chaim Yahil, and they agreed that Yaacov would fly to London the following morning. At dawn Herzog held a quick consultation with Yahil, Arieh Levavi, Yael Vered and other senior officials in the Ministry, then left for the airport.[1]

When he landed in London, Herzog was met by the Israeli Ambassador to Britain, Ephraim [Effi] Evron, and diplomat Arthur Lurie. From the airport Evron telephoned a London number and was told to carry on as planned. Evron and Herzog – who was travelling under the name of Dr Davis – drove into central London and found themselves stuck in a traffic jam which almost caused them to miss their appointment. Dr Emmanuel Herbert, a Jewish physician, greeted them at his consulting rooms and told them that 'Charles' had already arrived and that he was alone. Hearing this, Evron went into a side room,[2] and Dr Herbert led Herzog into an inner room. The waiting man stood up and extended his hand to Herzog.

Herzog bowed and shook the man's hand. It was King Hussein of Jordan.[3]

'Thank you for flying here especially to meet me,' King Hussein said. It was the first time the Hashemite King had met a representative of the State of Israel and Herzog was thrilled by this privilege. The last meetings at this level had taken place towards the end of the War of Independence between Golda Meir and other Israeli representatives and the late King Abdullah, Hussein's grandfather. But Abdullah was assassinated in the Old City of Jerusalem for trying to make peace with Israel, and in the 12 years since then there had only been a few meetings between Israelis and senior Jordanians.

Coincidentally, Yaacov's brother Chaim Herzog had met a senior Jordanian representative three years earlier. As an IDF general and chief of Military Intelligence, he had met a special envoy of the King at a time when Jordan and Syria were at loggerheads and Hussein was massing his forces near the Syrian border. King Hussein then sent a senior officer from the Jordanian headquarters, Emile Jami'an, to ask Israel not to take military advantage of the thinning of Jordanian forces on the Israeli border. Ben-Gurion instructed Chaim Herzog to assure Jami'an that 'the existence of an independent Jordan ruled by Hussein is in Israel's interest, and it would be advisable for the Jordanian leadership to adopt a similar approach to Israel's existence'. To which Jami'an replied, speaking of the tension between his country and Syria, 'The statement about the mutual interest in the existence of Israel and Jordan coincides with Jordan's current understanding ... The army is standing firm and Syria will be unable to resist it. But we are not always able to overcome subversion, and would be very glad if Israel could help us in this matter.'[4]

The Israelis were very pleased with the informal cooperation thus established with Jordan, but the contacts never went beyond some low-level meetings. The exception was the Queen Mother, Zain, Hussein's mother, through whom messages were passed from Israel to the King, via the Israeli Embassy and the royal family's Jewish doctor.

At the end of August 1963, two Israelis were killed in a violent incident on the Jordanian border, and the Israeli government wished to send a message to King Hussein. The intermediary, Dr Emmanuel Herbert, asked the Queen Mother to tell him when he could pass on the message from Israel, but to his astonishment she replied, 'Why meet with me? His Majesty is in London and is willing to meet an authorized representative of Israel's Prime Minister.'[5]

Highly excited, Dr Herbert hastened to pass on the message to Israel's Ambassador, who reported to the Prime Minister Levi Eshkol and the Foreign Minister Golda Meir. (Ben-Gurion had resigned in May that year, and Eshkol succeeded him as Prime Minister and Minister of Defence.) The two decided to send Yaacov Herzog to meet the King.

Herzog had returned from Canada two months earlier and in August took up his new post as deputy director-general of the Foreign Ministry. He was now responsible for a number of departments, including the United Nations, the Middle East, Culture and Information, Church affairs and Research and Special Operations.[6] Yaacov was chosen for the post because of his particular abilities – his impressive personality, diplomatic skill, broad culture, excellent English, discretion and his international acumen. The latter was especially significant as the Middle East was experiencing great crises and upheavals at the time, most of them caused by Egypt's Gamal Abd al-Nasser's expansionism. Egypt did not stop striving for regional hegemony, and became embroiled in the civil war in Yemen, where she was helping the anti-monarchist forces with troops and weapons to overthrow the Imam. Syria was ruled by the quasi-socialist Baath party, which was unable to maintain a stable government. She had broken away from the United Arab Republic (the union with Egypt, which lasted from 1958 to 1961), and was moving closer to the revolutionary regime in Iraq. The two were apparently hoping to destroy the Jordanian monarchy, or at least wrench the West Bank from its rule and hand it over to the Palestinians. King Hussein was feeling isolated, struggling against Nasserist subversion and the plotting of neighbours to the north and south. The only state that had an interest in Jordan's territorial integrity, and had informed the United States about it, was Israel.[7]

Now, in the consulting room of a Jewish doctor in London, Yaacov Herzog stood before King Hussein and studied him with interest. A short, sturdy man, radiating warmth and energy, the King could not disguise his nervousness.[8] The two men sat side by side, and Dr Herbert remained in the room, as Hussein indicated that he did not object to his presence.

Herzog began by saying he was privileged to be the special envoy of Israel's Prime Minister and Foreign Minister, and the bringer of their good wishes and regard for the King of Jordan. They and the people of Israel felt sympathy and admiration for his statesmanship, leadership and personal courage. 'While the public aspect of the relations between our countries is tainted with the wounds of history, the conscious mind of Israel is deeply aware of the intertwined destiny linking our two nations, as expressed in their struggle for survival, and which we hope and pray will find new expression in increasing cooperation, leading to peace. We are convinced that the cooperation between your people and ours holds the key to stability and progress throughout the Middle East.'[9]

The King listened in silence, with smiles and signs of nervousness passing over his face. He offered Herzog a cigarette and lit it with his lighter.

Herzog briefly surveyed the situation in the Middle East, starting with the confrontation between the USSR and the West. Then he analysed inter-Arab relations. In his view, there were then three flashpoints – the break between Egypt, Syria and Iraq; the civil war in the Yemen; and the conflict between the government in Baghdad and Iraq's Kurdish minority. Then he spoke about the four ideological currents in the Arab world – Nasser's personality cult, the Baath's progressive but unstable regime, the Saudi monarchy's philosophy, and the ideology represented by King Hussein, which stood for gradual economic development and social reform. By combining past and present, said Herzog, this method could secure real progress in Jordan and serve as a constructive model for other states in the region.

Smiling, Hussein replied that he had been trying to construct a Jordanian nation, but it was not easy. In addition, he was always subject to the pressures of hostile elements who were trying to undermine his leadership and position, and sharpen the divisions in his country. 'I don't want war, because I realize that war would not solve anything.'

Herzog noticed that the King was picking his words carefully. 'All I ask,' he was saying, 'is a better life for my people.' He was optimistic, saying that he thought Jordan would reach economic stability by 1970, but the immediate future was likely to be very difficult. He knew that his people would have to accept the existence of Israel as a fact. 'In the past I was very extremist, but you must understand that my family experienced a tragedy. I hope a solution can be found and I am willing to work to achieve it.'

Hussein spoke frankly about his problems in the Middle East. His troubles were due more to his friends than to his enemies, he stated bitterly. The Americans were supporting Nasser at the highest level and without reservations, he noted more than once in the course of the conversation. He also complained that the Americans were supportive of the Syrian Baath, although it was an unstable and destructive force that would introduce communism into the region. The Americans were taking Jordan for granted. He had resolved to broaden his foreign relations and had opened diplomatic relations with the USSR and had visited France. Some members of the US Congress spoke very sharply against Jordan's new relations with the USSR. He personally had nothing against Nasser, he stressed, except that the Egyptian President did not tolerate an alliance of equals, and Hussein had to treat him very cautiously and avoid provoking him. As for the Baath, it was playing a risky game. The movement called for a union between Syria and Iraq, and he feared that the scheme included swallowing up Jordan. Herzog stated that Israel was much impressed by the economic progress and political stability in Jordan. He added that neither the Baath nor Nasser were actually trying to topple King Hussein, for fear that the other would benefit from the outcome.

Hussein laughed. 'That's very true,' he said. 'I enjoy the information that each of their underground movements delivers about the other's activities.'

Herzog proceeded to analyse Jordan's internal situation, and very cautiously advised the King how to handle the Baath and Nasser and their followers. He spoke about Nasser's embroilment in Yemen. The King smiled and nodded. They discussed recent border incidents in Jerusalem, each arguing that the other side had opened fire first. But Herzog did not pursue the argument, and accepted the King's assurance that he was taking all necessary steps to avoid further incidents.

As they spoke Herzog observed his interlocutor. 'I was struck by a strong contrast in his appearance – immaturity alongside leadership, light-mindedness beside nobility, an inclination to escape from reality together with responsibility. It seems that an almost crushing burden of high-risk leadership fell on this young man before he was ready for it. Looking at him closely, I recalled a description of George Bernard Shaw attributed to Chesterton – "I saw in him two souls, which sometimes moved so close together that I held my breath."' Later Herzog added, '[During the meeting] "Charles" seemed anxious and uncertain, and only rarely did his eyes reveal those glints of steel and determination that have ensured his survival. While waiting for me in the surgery he was so tense that the doctor became worried. During the meeting he was continually aware of the risk he was running.'[10] Herzog had the impression that King Hussein was 'a driven man, fearful for his safety,' who needed Israel's continuing interest in his survival.[11]

Having discussed the problems of the Middle East as a whole, the two moved on to more practical matters. 'Since a final settlement will take a long time,' said Herzog, 'it is our historical duty to develop in a discreet way areas of cooperation that would lead to the final settlement'.[12] The King agreed with this statement, and Herzog put the following propositions to him: in the matter of security – the creation of a mechanism for continuous exchange of intelligence; in the field of international relations – tightening the connections between Jordan, Turkey, Iran (and secretly Israel) to form a bloc representing itself to the United States as a barrier to Nasser's subversion in the region; intense Israeli campaigning in the US to improve Jordan's position in America and depict her in a favourable light in the US media; in the economic sphere – greater cooperation in utilizing the waters of the Jordan River, as well as Israeli efforts in the US to help Jordan obtain foreign aid and investments, both private and governmental. Hussein responded warmly, agreeing to all these proposals. On the other hand, Herzog's proposals regarding the Palestinian refugees led to no practical decisions, and the King was also unresponsive to his suggestion to enlarge the border crossing between Israel and Jordan at the Mandelbaum Gate in Jerusalem.

As the meeting drew to a close, Herzog had the impression that King Hussein was much more open and relaxed, and even took a personal interest in him and his family. Herzog suggested that the King might meet a member of the Israeli government, but it became clear that Hussein would prefer to maintain contact with him, and they agreed on methods of communication and a special code to arrange their future meetings. The King did agree to the appointment of a senior Jordanian representative who would be in regular contact with Israeli representatives.

At the end of the meeting Herzog again bowed and shook hands with the King. He joined Evron in another room where they waited for the King to leave. Except for the doctor and his secretary, who had given them coffee, no one had seen King Hussein with Herzog. Later, the doctor told Herzog that Hussein had left his bodyguards outside and entered alone. The doctor also reported that the King was extremely pleased with the meeting.

There were some immediate consequences. Herzog returned to Israel to report to Levi Eshkol, and Evron flew to New York to see Golda Meir, who was there for the opening of the UN General Assembly. She summoned the Ambassador, Abraham Harman, to join them and instructed him to take steps to implement the agreement between Hussein and Herzog. She herself met the US Secretary of State Dean Rusk, and recommended that America increase her economic aid to Jordan.[13] Nevertheless, when Jordan's Prime Minister, Abd al-Munim a-Rifa'i, made a speech at the UN on 1 October 1963, he rejected Golda Meir's call for direct talks between Israel and the Arab states.[14] Either he did not know about his King's secret meeting with an envoy of Israel's Prime Minister or it was not 'politic' to admit it.

An analysis of the discussion between King Hussein and Herzog reveals the king's motives for wishing to meet a senior Israeli representative at that particular moment. He clearly felt increasingly isolated in the Arab world, feared a new campaign of subversion by Nasser, and believed that Israel could help improve American attitudes towards Jordan.

The civil war in Yemen, where Nasser intervened on the side of the revolutionaries, had heightened Hussein's fear of Egypt. Hussein – together with the King of Saudi Arabia and with Britain's support – had helped the monarchist forces. But his air force commander and two of his pilots, who had been sent to help the monarchists, had defected to Egypt with their aircraft.[15] In spite of his concerns, Hussein had not been able to avoid joining the Iraqi-Syrian-Egyptian federation, which had been created in April 1963, thus reviving pro-Nasser sentiments in Jordan. For the first time in its history, the Jordanian parliament registered a vote of no-confidence in the government – that of Samir a-Rifa'i, the Prime Minister appointed by the King. Violent pro-Nasser demonstrations broke out in Jerusalem and Nablus, police stations were attacked, and the suppression of the outbreak left many casualties. When Jordan had reluctantly joined the federation, the royal Hashemite flag in East Jerusalem was replaced by one bearing the four stars of the federation. This was more than an exchange of one piece of cloth for another – the new federation was committed to the liberation of Palestine, conflicting with King Hussein's intention of continuing to rule over the West Bank.

In Israel, too, the creation of the federation had aroused anxiety. Prime Minister Ben-Gurion, who was about to retire, even wrote to the heads of leading governments to warn them against the new danger. (Ben-Gurion's worries were excessive – his fear that the federation represented a deadly threat to Israel was soon dispelled.) Israel and Jordan were, therefore, both opposed to the federation, even though Jordan had joined it. Both states wished to maintain the status quo in the Middle East in general and in Jordan in particular.

In fact, the federation did not last long – it was brought down by mutual accusations among the Arab leaders. But its very formation had increased Hussein's sense of isolation and must have prompted him to seek a secret route to Israel. It also intensified his bitterness towards the United States, who misread the situation in the Middle East and continued to cultivate Egypt's Nasser, despite her commitment to Jordan's territorial integrity.

This was the background to Hussein's historical move, which he had contemplated for some time. Without informing his immediate entourage, he had instructed his mother to establish a link with Israel and propose a high-level meeting.

After the meeting on 24 September 1963, Yaacov Herzog certainly had no idea that it would lead to a series of similar encounters – in Europe, at the Red Sea, and on the Israel-Jordan border – and involve a number of other Israeli and Jordanian figures. That meeting in London established Herzog as the main Israeli representative in the meetings with King Hussein, a position he would retain until his death nine years later.

The day Herzog met King Hussein in London was an historical day for Israel, and the start of a process which culminated in 1994, 22 years after Herzog's death, with the signing of the peace treaty between Israel and Jordan. The central figure during the crucial years of that process, the person whom Hussein regarded as more representative of Israel than any other, was Yaacov Herzog.

On 6 October 1963, less than a fortnight after his London meeting with King Hussein, Yaacov Herzog had another secret meeting with a senior figure from an Arab country officially at war with Israel. As soon as darkness fell, Yaacov went to Rome's Maronite College,[16] accompanied by a senior officer of Israel's Military Intelligence in civilian dress. Two cars were parked near the entrance[17] (their occupants were probably Israeli secret agents sent to provide security for the meeting).

Herzog and his companion were met at the door and taken to a reception room on the second floor. They passed a number of Arabs, some in clerical robes, who observed them intently. They were met at the top of the stairs by their host, who shook their hands very cordially. Patriarch Mowassi, head of Lebanon's Maronite church, led them into his office, where they conferred together for a long time.[18] The two Israelis looked around them. One of the walls was covered with a huge mural, encircled by a Hebrew verse from the Book of Psalms. But they had no opportunity to study it more closely, as the conversation with Mowassi was practical and urgent.

Unlike the meeting in London, this was not Herzog's first encounter with his interlocutor. He had met him before in the United States, when he was still Ambassador to Canada. Since his contacts with the Vatican in the early years of the State, Herzog had become well versed with Israel's relations with the Christian world. But the conversation with Mowassi was not religious – it was purely political, and its purpose was to achieve the maximum coordination between Israel and Lebanon's Christian community. Mowassi spoke frankly about the Nasserist movement in his country and the need for cooperation with Israel. From an adjoining room he brought two documents about the current situation in Lebanon and left one of them for Herzog. It was evident that showing these documents made the Patriarch extremely uneasy – 'he became very nervous, turned pale and sweat broke out on his forehead'. But he continued the conversation and even agreed to a move he had avoided at their previous meeting – to open discussions about full coordination with Israel.

Herzog and Mowassi surveyed a number of issues, the most prominent of which was Nasser's subversive involvement in the run-up to the Lebanese elections in 1964. They also discussed the position of President Shihab, whom Mowassi described as a weak person, manipulated by the Nasserist movement. They talked about the meetings of Christian families on the Israel-Lebanon border, the possibility of Lebanese neutrality in the Middle East conflict, as proposed by the Christian leader Pierre Gemayel, and agreed to maintain regular contact through a Lebanese political figure. Mowassi wanted to know if the senior officer he had secretly assigned to maintain contact with IDF officers had already done so. Herzog asked if it would be possible to increase the migration of Palestinian refugees from Lebanon to other countries, but Mowassi said frankly that it would be very difficult. However, he added, the refugees were already aware that Israel could not be forced to accept their return. He promised to try to apply his influence on some Lebanese newspapers to adopt a more balanced attitude towards Israel. And, like King Hussein before him, Mowassi complained bitterly about the US Administration's support for Nasser, saying he could not understand it.

There was no doubt that the Patriarch's keenness to meet the Israeli envoy stemmed from his fears for the Maronite-Christian community in Lebanon in the face of Nasserist expansion. The danger had increased since their previous meeting, and it impelled the Patriarch to seek extensive cooperation with Israel.

Before parting, Herzog and Mowassi concluded arrangements for future meetings and agreed on appointing political and military liaison people. Herzog presented the Patriarch with a gold watch inscribed, 'From your friend in peace'. The Lebanese was deeply moved and said that heaven was his witness that a sincere desire for peace drove him to try to bring Lebanon and Israel closer. But he evidently did not wish his relations with Israel to be in any way tainted by gifts. He agreed to keep the watch as a souvenir for the sake of peace, but urged Herzog not to bring him any more gifts.[19]

The Patriarch then took his guests to the top of the staircase, and they left, once again, accompanied by the stares of Arabs who surrounded them on all sides.

The following day Herzog also met Bishop Hakim, the spiritual leader of the Christian Arabs in the Galilee, who was staying in Rome, and had a long discussion with him about the Palestinian refugees of 1948. Hakim also reported to Herzog about meetings he had held with various Arab figures in Rome, about the seditious role played by Egypt's Ambassador to Lebanon, and about the prospects of establishing contacts with the Palestinian delegate at the UN, Ahmad Shukeiri, in return for money.[20] Herzog returned to Israel with some important political achievements, but only a few weeks later he was already planning another secret mission.

Early in November Felice Bellotti, an Italian journalist from Milan, arrived in Israel and met Yaacov Herzog and the director-general of the Foreign Ministry, Chaim Yahil. He told them that while travelling in the Middle East he had come across something to do with Israel – 'a highly confidential matter that he had not passed on to the Italian authorities'.[21] Herzog and Yahil were favourably impressed by Bellotti's 'sincerity and politeness', and by his astonishing information. The matter was so sensitive, that they decided not to reveal it to anyone except the Foreign Minister herself, Golda Meir. The only other person in on the secret was Dan Avni-Segre, a Foreign Ministry official of Italian origin, who had accompanied Bellotti during his short stay in Israel.[22]

Golda Meir told Herzog to continue cultivating the Italian journalist, who had in the meantime returned to Milan. Herzog instructed the Israeli consul in that city, Issachar Ben-Yaacov, to keep in touch with Bellotti, but did not reveal the nature of the journalist's information. Bellotti was to inform Ben-Yaacov when a certain person, whom Herzog dubbed 'the patient', would arrive in Milan, at which time a special emissary would be sent from Israel to meet him. The 'patient' was due in Milan in mid-December.[23]

But the picture changed when Dan Avni-Segre received a letter from Bellotti, informing him that the 'patient' had changed his plans and would be going to London instead.[24] Moving quickly, Herzog arranged through Bellotti to meet the 'patient' in London on 10 December. He and the Italian arrived in London on the 9th, and the meeting took place the following day in utter secrecy, at the house of a Jewish businessman, Alec Lerner, whose wife was the Israeli actress Dalia Penn.[25] Dismissing her servants, Miss Penn herself, who was not introduced, received her guests and served them coffee. Bellotti, who had arranged the meeting, was allowed to sit in on it, and the only other person present was General Meir Amit, the head of the Mossad (the Israeli overseas intelligence agency). There was good reason for the presence of the head of Israel's secret service – the 'patient' was none other than the personal envoy of the Imam of the Yemen, who wanted to make contact with the Israeli government.[26]

The 'patient' himself was the state minister for the monarchy in the Yemen's government, which was then embroiled in a bloody civil war. The Imam's monarchist forces were fighting against a republican rebel force which was openly supported by Nasser. Twelve Egyptian divisions had arrived in the Yemen to fight with the rebels and the Imam was determined to use all possible means to block the Egyptian assault. In his desperation, he turned to Israel.

At the start of the meeting, the Yemeni minister verified his identity by showing the Israelis his passport, and photographs taken of him by Bellotti on various official occasions – which lead to Herzog giving him a new alias, 'The Prophet'.

The meeting lasted two and a half hours. Herzog opened by expressing his appreciation for the 'staunch and courageous' stand of the Yemeni people in the face of 'Egyptian aggression'. The Yemeni minister responded by saying that his nation 'felt no hostility for Israel, and in the face of the attempt to crush its independence, was asking for Israel's friendship and help'. He said that Imam Badr himself (dubbed by Herzog 'The Priest') had personally sent him to establish links and cooperation with Israel.[27]

Amit and the Yemeni minister exchanged assessments of the conflict in the Yemen. 'The Prophet' revealed that his side was suffering a serious shortage of weapons. Military aid from Saudi Arabia had ceased six months earlier, while the French and British were providing a small amount at full cost. He then read from his notebook a list of the Yemen's requests to Israel for military assistance which included specific weaponry; financial aid in the form of gold coins – 'Maria Teresa' *reals* or British sovereigns; diplomatic help, mainly in the United States, to persuade the Americans to withdraw recognition from the republican regime and to support the monarchists, as well as diplomatic support from Israel's friends in the world; and direct assistance in the form of Israeli intervention, such as an attack on Egypt.

The Yemeni minister also said that the Imam was asking Israel to send two undercover military and political delegations to the Yemen as soon as possible. 'Wouldn't it be better if you sent us a delegation?' Meir Amit asked. The Yemeni replied that it would be difficult to send people out of the Yemen at that moment, but when Herzog asked him if he would be willing to pay a secret visit to Israel himself, he agreed at once, provided that it was a purposeful visit leading to practical arrangements with the Israeli government.

In return for Israel's military and political help, the minister added that the monarchist government would recognize Israel as soon as it won the war. He was prepared to sign such a commitment at once. But Herzog was not content with the promise and questioned the Yemeni at length about the possibility of other contacts in the Arab world through the Yemen's mediation – chiefly with King Feisal of Saudi Arabia. 'The Prophet' avoided committing himself on this matter, but stressed that once the Yemen recognized Israel, Saudi Arabia would follow, and possibly Jordan too.

Meir Amit undertook to obtain a prompt response on the military issue and left the meeting, while Herzog and the Yemeni minister went on discussing links and joint action. The minister was clearly under pressure – he revealed that he had travelled from the Yemen solely for the meeting with the Israelis, and would wait in London for their response. He promised to send coded telegrams to the Imam with all the questions presented by Herzog and Amit, and to bring his answer within 48 hours.[28]

Later, when the Yemeni minister left, Herzog and Amit discussed the Imam's amazing proposal and formulated their recommendations to the government. 'Despite the considerable uncertainty whether, in the final analysis, we shall actually benefit from this connection,' Herzog wrote, '... we should not miss this opportunity.'[29]

In their report to the government, the two recommended approving the Yemen's appeal for financial, diplomatic and public support, and inviting 'The Prophet' to come to Israel for further talks. As for military aid – they recommended supplying arms indirectly, training Yemeni troops in the use of arms and radio communication, but not risking the lives of Israeli soldiers.[30] In return, they suggested demanding that the Imam deposit a letter recognizing Israel after the victory. Herzog and Amit met the Yemeni envoy again before returning to Israel, and informed him of their government's favourable response. Then things began to move much faster than either side expected.

A week after the London meeting, towards the end of December 1963, 'The Prophet' arrived secretly in Israel and held a series of talks, coordinated by Yaacov Herzog, with members of the Mossad and the Foreign Ministry.[31] The Yemeni minister was informed that Israel would assist the monarchist forces in a number of ways. On the international and diplomatic front, Israel would support the Yemen in Western Europe and the United States, and even finance official representation in Paris for six months (Israel was willing to spend up to $25,000 for the purpose). Herzog and the intelligence services also agreed on regular contacts and exchanges of secret information with the Yemenis. Israeli arms sent to the Yemen would include English rifles, bazookas, anti-tank cannons, machine-guns, mines, explosives and ammunition. Both sides changed their original positions and agreed to dispatch delegations to each other's country – Yemeni troops would receive training in Israel, and an Israeli representative would be sent to the Yemen. The Yemeni minister also undertook, on behalf of the Imam, that if there were real cooperation between the two states, then as soon as the Egyptian forces left the Yemen and the Imam recovered control over his country, he would recognize Israel.

Early in February 1964, Herzog was summoned to Paris and London for urgent talks with Yemeni representatives. This time 'The Prophet' arrived in Europe accompanied by the Imam's uncle, Prince Abd al-Rahman Yahya,[32] and the two held meetings with Herzog and representatives of the intelligence community in France and England. 'The Prophet' brought Herzog a letter from the Imam himself, confirming the agreements concluded by his envoy in Israel. Guided by Walter Eytan and Yochanan Meroz – respectively Israel's Ambassador and minister to France – the Yemenis asked France to exchange ambassadors with their country. The British Aviation Minister, Julian Amery, played an active part in the proceedings, conducting his contacts with the Yemenis in cooperation with Israel, with Herzog and Shimon

Peres, then Israel's Deputy Minister of Defence.[33] The British government sent two representatives to Israel to coordinate the operation. Later some legendary figures from the SAS took part in aerial operations in cooperation with Israel, in support of the Yemen's monarchists.[34] Israel sent representatives to the Yemen, notably the veteran Mossad agent David Kron.[35]

This was the start of secretive and intensive cooperation between Israel and monarchist Yemen which lasted for several years, directed chiefly by Yaacov Herzog. Four years later, after the Six Day War, two Yemeni princes arrived in Israel, met members of the security services and again asked for financial help and arms to continue their fight against Nasser's forces. When the people in charge of those talks reported to the Prime Minister Levi Eshkol, Herzog told him about the meeting in 1963 in London, together with Meir Amit and the Imam's envoy. 'I recalled,' he noted in his journal, 'how doubtful Golda and [Yitzhak] Rabin had been in those days about the chances that the monarchists would hold out against the invading Egyptians for any length of time.'[36]

The next two years were among the most active and exciting of Yaacov Herzog's life. He kept up the ever-growing secret connection with the Yemenis; he negotiated with his Lebanese contacts; he met King Hussein again, and continued to play a central part in the shaping and implementation of Israel's secret Middle East policy. Most of what he did would not become publicly known for years. 'He relished those intrigues,' said his friend Avraham Avihai, 'being a member of the secret service, carrying out hush-hush operations ... he enjoyed it like a small boy playing hide-and-seek.'[37] His superiors had complete confidence in Herzog's considerations and moves, and they got him actively involved in further confidential activities, such as security discussions concerning Cyprus,[38] and contacts with Reza Pahlavi, the Shah of Iran, which were conducted mainly by the Mossad.'[39]

Nevertheless, Herzog spent most of his time dealing with official and public matters in his role as deputy director of the Foreign Ministry. Although these were not nearly as weighty as the tremendous work he was doing behind the scenes, he did not dismiss them and was equally dedicated to them. He invested tireless efforts in preparing and instructing the Israeli delegation to the UN; in advancing the initiative launched by certain Western governments for direct negotiations between the Arab states and Israel; and in repelling attacks on Israel on the subject of the Palestinian refugees. This, and the Arab arguments for the refugees' 'right of return', were in practice his exclusive responsibility, and he was Israel's main spokesman in all the discussions on this subject with representatives of foreign governments. He also continued to wire advice and instructions to his successors in the embassy in Canada, both on international matters and on relations with the local Jewish community; he dealt with current affairs in the Middle East, both in internal discussions and in detailed directives to Israel's representatives abroad, and with foreign diplomats visiting Israel; and he mediated and mollified Israeli diplomats abroad who came to him with diverse grievances against their superiors.

One of his main preoccupations with the Americans concerned the waters of the Jordan River, a matter he had been dealing with since the early 1950s. In 1963, Israel completed the construction of the national water carrier and was about to launch its operation, which called for an extensive public relations campaign throughout the world. At this time the Arab leaders met in Cairo and launched their own campaign and water diversion project, while warning Israel not to draw any water from the Jordan. Herzog prepared a well-argued information campaign, showing that Israel was pumping only the amount allocated to it by the 1955 Johnston Plan. He also explained that the countries containing the springs and tributaries that fed into the river – Syria, Lebanon and Jordan – had already drawn as much water as the Plan had allocated them. Only political reasons – namely, the Arab countries' refusal to acknowledge the agreement with Israel which they had previously approved – stopped the Arab leaders from officially sharing the Jordan waters with the Jewish state. As the date for the launching of the national water carrier drew near, Prime Minister Levi Eshkol and Foreign Minister Golda Meir delegated responsibility for all public statements on the water issue to Yaacov Herzog.[40]

With his usual discretion, Herzog kept his secret contacts with Jordan, Lebanon and the Yemen out of sight. Only very careful observation could have revealed the effect of his behind-the-scenes dealing with Arab leaders upon the positions he expressed to foreign diplomats. For example, in late October 1963 he recommended to an American diplomat called Jernigan that King Hussein's forthcoming visit to Washington be given the red carpet treatment. Yet because of the sensitivity of his contacts with the Yemen, he made no comment when Jernigan informed him that the US Administration favoured the establishment of a republican government in the Yemen, and that if the US government accepted the continued presence of the Imam, it would insist on curtailing his powers and replacing him with another Imam.[41] In June 1964, towards the end of the discussions with the US State Department on the subject of the Palestinian refugees, Herzog said, as though in passing, 'You might wish to consider more extensive development in Jordan. It's a crucial issue, and it's very unfortunate that you keep cutting your aid to Jordan year after year.'[42]

Herzog took part in organizing Levi Eshkol's visit to the United States in June 1964. He prepared the Prime Minister's speeches, drafted his public statements and communiqués, and sat in on 'countless consultations'.[43] He was also a member of the Prime Minister's entourage on that visit.

Yet Herzog was in the second rank of Eshkol's advisors, and did not participate in the Prime Minister's meetings with President Johnson and his advisors about truly decisive issues. At this time the United States was applying great pressure on Israel over the nuclear issue, demanding that the Dimona reactor be placed under supervision; the Administration also sharply criticized Israel's plan to acquire missiles.[44] In vain did Israel argue that the missiles were necessary in view of Nasser's acquisition of missiles, built by German engineers in Egypt. It had recently become known that German scientists and engineers in Egypt were building medium-range missiles for Nasser, and even trying to include non-conventional warheads. In fact, the discovery had led to a serious rift between Ben-Gurion and the head of the security services, Isser Harel. The latter had maintained that the presence of these scientists in Egypt was a grave threat, and that the weaponry they were building might kill thousands of Israelis, but Ben-Gurion had disagreed. Their close cooperation came to an end, and Harel resigned his position at the height of this crisis.

The massive US pressure on David Ben-Gurion and his successor Levi Eshkol concerning the nuclear issue eased temporarily after President Kennedy's assassination. But Lyndon Johnson did not let up, and sought to make the provision of new American tanks to Israel conditional upon Israel giving up the development of missiles.[45] In 1963, the United States dispatched spy planes to reconnoitre Israel's coast several times, probably in search of missile test bases. On several occasions these reconnaissance planes fired on approaching Israeli aircraft, but the Israelis did not return fire.

These issues – Israel's nuclear programme, her missiles and tanks – were the principal ones discussed by Eshkol on his visit to Washington. Herzog was by his side at all the official events, but did not take part in the high-level discussions between Eshkol, Johnson and their aides.[46] He did participate in the consultations Eshkol held with his entourage,[47] but was only partly involved in the lower-level discussions that dealt indirectly with the main issues.[48]

Eshkol won some major concessions during that visit – a formula was found to keep the Dimona reactor going, the supply of US-manufactured tanks to Israel was assured, and America eased pressure on Israel to abandon her missiles programme. The success of that visit was confirmed by remarks made by certain American participants in the discussions, who expressed disappointment and frustration that Israel had won so many concessions and had made almost none in return.

While Yaacov Herzog had not taken part in the high-level meetings, he remained the principal spokesman on the subject of the Palestinian refugees. A few days after Eshkol left Washington, Herzog returned there for thorough and difficult discussions with the heads of the State Department.[49] Here he fought firmly and intelligently against the officials' rigid, unreasonable and conservative positions, which revealed their naivety about the question of the refugees, and their limited comprehension of Middle East issues. But Herzog's main contribution to Israel's foreign and defence policy in 1963–4 lay in the secret contacts he had built up in Arab countries. In the course of 1964 he met senior envoys of monarchist Yemen several times, and strengthened the practical cooperation between the two states on security and intelligence. A year after his meeting with Archbishop Mowassi, he returned to Rome and met him again in the same place, and their cooperation developed even further.[50] There was added drama on this occasion, as it was on the same day that police in Rome airport freed an Israeli, Mordechai Lok, from a large chest in which the Egyptians had planned to abduct him to Cairo. Inevitably, some people saw a connection between Herzog's arrival and Lok's release.

But Herzog's greatest achievement in those years remained the relationship he built up with King Hussein. Their second meeting took place when relations between Israel and Jordan were quite tense. It surprised no-one that the Hashemite King's public pronouncements on Israel differed sharply from his confidential statements to Herzog, but from time to time he seemed to be going much further, and his declarations made the Israelis fear that he had abandoned his moderate stance. Prior to an Arab summit on water, held in Cairo in December 1963, Hussein announced in East Jerusalem that Israel was 'planning to steal the holy water of the Jordan river and to dispossess millions of Arab refugees from their homes'.[51] He also supported the creation of a joint Arab command, to include the Jordanian military, and visited Nasser and improved their relationship. His improved standing in the Arab world gave him self-confidence, and the atmosphere at his second meeting with Herzog differed from the first.

In late April 1964, Herzog heard that Hussein was going to London, and he at once flew there and contacted Dr Herbert. At his request the doctor telephoned the Jordanian Embassy and even spoke to the King, who agreed to meet Herzog. Then on 2 May, while Herzog was dining at his uncle and aunt's, he received a call from Dr Herbert saying that the King was on his way and expected to meet Herzog. It was 6.45 in the evening and Herzog thought he might not get a taxi at that hour. He didn't want to arrive late at the doctor's house, fearing that Scotland Yard men, who protected the King in London, would have taken up positions around the house and would question him. It was imperative to arrive before they did. Luckily, Yaacov's aunt offered to take him. He urged her to drive quickly and she did her best, hurtling at top speed through the streets of London. Herzog reached the house just before the King, who arrived on his own, leaving his Jordanian bodyguard in the car. Another car, packed with British detectives, also stopped in the street. (The following day the *Sunday Telegraph* reported that on the previous night King Hussein had suddenly left his hotel and driven to an unknown destination, while the Jordanian Ambassador in London had tried desperately to locate him ... A few hours later Hussein returned to his hotel from 'a drive out of town'.[52])

Herzog sensed the difference in King Hussein as soon as he saw him. In contrast to the anxious, insecure young man he had met in December, this was a staid and assured man of noble cast, his face determined and calm.[53]

Herzog bowed and they shook hands, exchanged some courteous words and sat down. Herzog spoke frankly, saying that he had often wondered, in the months since their first meeting, if it had been the start of a relationship based on a shared purpose, or a singular event without a sequel. 'I must confess that I had grave doubts. Nevertheless, my inner belief told me that we would meet again and that our efforts towards a common purpose would continue.' Hussein smiled but said nothing. Herzog added that their meeting had been kept strictly secret, and Hussein nodded in agreement.

They talked briefly about the King's recent visit to Washington, and Herzog 'made Hussein blush' by repeating the praise showered on him by his American hosts. They discussed President Johnson's personality ('A capable politician ... but his understanding of foreign affairs as a whole and the Middle East in particular is quite limited,' said Hussein), and the late President Kennedy. (Herzog observed that Kennedy had tried to bring peace to the Middle East, and Hussein said with a slight smile, 'Sometimes he adopted positions which you did not like.') Then they moved on to the problem of the waters of the Jordan. Their differences became evident immediately, though their exchange remained courteous and amiable. Herzog challenged Hussein's statements in the United States, that Israel's pumping of water from the Sea of Galilee had caused the Lower Jordan to become brackish. 'We haven't begun to pump,' Herzog said, 'but the water is becoming brackish because you have diverted the Yarmuk.' In reply, Hussein argued that his own engineers attributed the change only partly to the diversion of the Yarmuk, but mainly to the brackish streams that the Israelis were diverting into the Lower Jordan. Herzog repeated that neither the pumping nor the diversion had actually begun. Hussein responded in vague terms to Herzog's warning that diverting the sources of the Jordan beyond the amounts allocated to the Arab states by the Johnston Plan would be viewed seriously, 'and we shall consider ourselves freed from our commitment to be bound by the Johnston Plan'. Though King Hussein said that he aimed to keep the Arab limits within the agreed Plan, his remarks were not unequivocal, and Herzog returned to the issue three times, with growing firmness.

Herzog gave the King a detailed intelligence report about the situation in the Middle East, and analysed Nasser's latest moves. But in contrast to their previous meeting, Hussein defended the Egyptian President. 'You have to understand his position,' he said. 'Sometimes he acts impulsively and responds angrily to unwise statements or acts [by other countries].' He added that at his recent meetings with Nasser, the President had admitted that he had made mistakes in the past, but 'wished to put it behind him'. Hussein said that for the last few years he had been struggling to promote cooperation among Arab states, and put an end to the attempts of any Arab state to dominate the others. Now Nasser agreed with him, he said, because he had learned his lesson in Syria (Egypt's union with Syria had ended in a bitter falling out), 'and the Syrian lesson has left a strong mark on him'.

Hussein continued to defend Nasser on other issues. Herzog mentioned Egypt's re-arming and Nasser's missiles project. Hussein shrugged and said that without nuclear warheads those missiles were not a threat. 'Perhaps Nasser thinks that you yourselves are working on a secret weapon,' he said, hinting at Israel's nuclear and missiles programme. To which Herzog responded by saying, 'May I ask Your Majesty a straightforward question – is Nasser's ultimate aim war?'

Hussein hesitated a moment and replied, 'I think he doesn't want war.'

Hussein then presented a broad review of Jordan's foreign policy in the Middle East, and reiterated that he wanted to rein in the extremist Arab leaders. To strengthen the moderates, he said, he had suggested to the Shah of Iran that he engage his country in a broad framework with the Arab countries.

Herzog was surprised by this reference to the meeting between the King and the Shah – Iranian sources had given Israel the opposite impression, reporting that Hussein had urged the Shah to befriend Nasser and distance himself from Israel.

Altogether, Herzog was greatly impressed by the Hashemite King's calm, self-confident demeanour. He attributed it to his stronger position in the region, his rapprochement with Nasser and the lessening threat from his neighbours, including Syria. He only showed uneasiness when discussing Jordan's economic situation. He admitted that budgetary difficulties were preventing Jordan from developing as it should. His worried expression reminded Herzog of their previous meeting.

Yet it was in this area that Herzog had some good news for Hussein. He told him that Israeli representatives had asked several US Senators to use their influence with the State Department to stop cutting US aid to Jordan. Israel would also try to interest some private investment companies in Jordan's potential. He named one of the companies – C. A. of New York, which worked with General Electric. Hussein expressed great interest in the idea, and Herzog added, 'If you're approached by C. A. or similar companies, remember that it arose from our meeting, though my secret contact with you will of course never be mentioned in our preliminary talks with these companies.' Hussein nodded his appreciation. (Three weeks later, on 25 May 1964, King Hussein received a letter from the head of C. A., who proposed that his company take part in the development of Jordan.[54])

Herzog's attempts to raise the subject of the refugees got nowhere, and the dialogue ended with a discussion about a local land dispute in the area of Latrun. Herzog promised to take care of the problem, and indeed it was soon resolved.

Finally Hussein and Herzog discussed the venue of their next meeting. The King did not want to meet another, more senior, figure from Israel, and went back on his earlier promise to appoint someone to maintain contact with Israel. He would only discuss the site of their next meeting. 'Do you ever go to Eilat?' he asked, and when Herzog said yes, he went on, 'I'm often in Aqaba, so we are quite close.' Herzog riposted: 'Do you have a house in Jerusalem?' Hussein replied that he was building one.

'Well then, I could meet you there?'

Hussein grinned. 'Not yet,' he said.

When the meeting ended with handshakes and good wishes, Herzog summarized his impressions. In contrast to the tension and anxiety which the King displayed at their first meeting, he wrote, this time, 'Hussein was perfectly at ease, quite untroubled by the fact that this was his second meeting with an Israeli representative.' He believed that the reason was the change in Hussein's position in the region, which had occurred between the two meetings (September 1963–May 1964). 'He sat up straight, like a respected statesman receiving a representative from another state with which he has had some disagreements in the context of normal relations. The personal contact was also easier. More importantly ... he did not give a sense of being dependent, and maintained a certain distance.'

Dr Herbert, too, who had witnessed both meetings, was struck by the King's different demeanour. He said that the conversation seemed to him like a diplomatic negotiation, and that he thought Herzog had been rather harsh, especially on the subject of water. Herzog replied frankly that developments since the previous meeting 'compelled him to issue an implied threat'. Later he wrote, 'Now and then the atmosphere was tense, and given the doubts about Hussein's stand on the question of water I had to use a rather firmer tone.'[55]

'At our first meeting,' Herzog reported to his superiors, 'Hussein concentrated on securing his rule, in view of the threat against it from Nasser and the Baath, the danger these two forces represented in the region as a whole, and his difficulties in the international sphere. He spoke with anguish about the problem of the refugees and urged us to recognize the profound trauma that the past had left on the Arab psyche. In his isolation, he wished – though he did not say so – to hear us affirm that we were interested in his survival, and willing to use our influence in Washington and other places.

'This time he spoke as a participant, even one of the leaders, of a new move towards Arab unity. He depicted his regional policy as part of this process, and avoided all substantial reference to the Baath and the situation in Iraq and Syria. He defended Nasser, though in a superficial way. He spoke about the Yemen not as a place and opportunity to deal Nasser a heavy blow, but as an internal Arab problem needing a solution. He did not stress the problem of the refugees, but demanded that we show flexibility in the matter of Latrun, and seemed to be hinting that he would regard the problem of Latrun, however marginal, as a test of our attitude towards him.'

Herzog in fact recommended that Israel make a goodwill gesture towards Hussein, though he admitted that the meeting did not achieve much. Only the coming months would show to what extent the relationship could be developed further and where it would lead. Nonetheless, he considered that the secret contact with the King should be kept up, despite the rapprochement between Hussein and Nasser in the previous five months. 'The main value of the second meeting,' he concluded glumly, 'was that it took place.'[56]

An examination of Herzog's talks with Hussein, with the envoys of the Imam and the Lebanese leaders, reveals his strategic concept and diplomatic tactics. The main basis for his contacts with the Arab leaders was the Nasserist subversion – in Jordan, Lebanon and the Yemen, where Egypt was involved in actual warfare. Herzog hoped that the Nasserist menace would drive those who feared it into Israel's arms, which is why he kept warning against it, and was plainly disappointed when he saw Hussein tending towards a pro-Nasserist line. Herzog also used Israel's reputation of wielding influence in Western capitals to impress his interlocutors, and in certain cases, such as Jordan and the Yemen, he actually applied this influence in a material way.

A third issue which constantly came up in his secret meetings was American policy in the Middle East. Apparently all the conservative and pro-Western leaders he met complained bitterly about the misguided American policy of supporting Nasser, the Baath, the Yemeni republicans, and all the subversive elements in the region, instead of strengthening the stable, pro-Western regimes. This was clearly a correct assessment, as the United States' Middle East policy in those days was simplistic, unrealistic and misguided. (The US did, however, place great value on the survival of the Kingdom of Jordan, and during the 1960s even considered military intervention if Hussein's regime were toppled by his neighbours' subversion.) Herzog made use of this failing in American policy to mobilize American journalists and Senators in support of his secret friends in the Middle East.

Herzog's value in the eyes of his Arab interlocutors also lay in his ability to provide them with high-quality intelligence about the Middle East, sometimes even regarding their own countries. In return he pressured them to accept the main planks of Israel's policy – namely, that the Palestinian refugees would never return to what was now Israel; the importance of an agreement on the division of the Jordan waters; the need for further secret channels to Arab countries; and the goal of direct negotiations to achieve peace with her neighbours. Herzog repeated these principles at his second meeting with King Hussein in London, on 2 May 1964.

But on 28 May 1964, a few weeks after his meeting with Herzog, Hussein gave in to Egyptian pressure, and allowed the founding conference of the Palestine Liberation Organization (PLO) to take place at the Intercontinental Hotel in East Jerusalem. The conference lasted five days and concluded with a number of resolutions regarding the new organization. Three days later, on 5 June 1964, Israel activated the new national water carrier.

*

Dr Davis and Mr Charles

In London in December 1964, a surreal scene took place in a side room of Dr Herbert's surgery. Amid the greatest secrecy, an important figure from Israel was telling a fascinated dignitary about a political/security drama then gripping Israel. The speaker was Yaacov Herzog, the listener King Hussein of Jordan, and the subject the Lavon Affair.[57]

The third meeting between Herzog and Hussein took place a few days after the resignation of Prime Minister Levi Eshkol. This resulted from a dispute between him and his predecessor David Ben-Gurion about whether to appoint a judicial commission of inquiry to investigate the Lavon affair. Eshkol wanted to put an end to the affair and turn over a new leaf, but Ben-Gurion demanded a judicial inquiry, as recommended by the Attorney General. Eshkol's resignation was a shrewd ploy that won him popular support. A few days later he would form a new government and end the affair, at least for the time being.

Hussein had heard about the crisis in the Israeli government and at the start of their third meeting asked Herzog to explain what had led to it. Herzog told him that in 1954 there was heightened tension between Israel and Egypt – Nasser was threatening to destroy Israel and kept dispatching murderous fedayeen across the border. In response, Israel's Military Intelligence launched a number of operations, one of which proved disastrous. The question arose as to whether the officers involved in the operation had been authorized by Defence Minister Pinchas Lavon. It was an important question of moral responsibility and the degree of civilian control over the military. Ten years later, Herzog continued, the truth of the matter was still unclear. Eshkol's government had decided that the question was out of date, that it had been investigated many times and there was no point in launching a new inquiry. Ben-Gurion insisted that it was a question of justice at the highest level, and demanded the inquiry.

At this point Hussein broke his silence. 'What's the point or wisdom of returning to something that is past?'

'Most of the public in Israel agrees with you,' said Herzog, but added that Ben-Gurion's position was also supported by many, 'because of the reverence for him.' Ben-Gurion thought that another inquiry would strengthen the rule of law in Israel. He explained that Eshkol would solve the crisis in a few days, when he formed a new government. But, ever the diplomat, Herzog proceeded to speak highly of Ben-Gurion. 'I spoke about Ben-Gurion the man, his amazing physical and intellectual energy.' He said, 'Ben-Gurion is an exceptional person.'

Which Hussein echoed, 'Exceptional.'

As before, the meeting was held in great secrecy and with all possible security precautions. And as before, Herzog had flown to Europe several times in order to coincide with Hussein's visit. He had thought about possible meetings in Paris or Bonn, but at this stage they all took place in Dr Herbert's surgery.

Dr Herbert was especially pleased with the third meeting, and the warmth with which Hussein met Herzog. He told Herzog that he had feared the King would refuse to see him again, because of the rather sharp tone of Herzog's remarks in May.

The meeting was short and businesslike. 'Hussein clarified his attitude towards us on the main issues that were raised,' Herzog reported. In fact, some of the main questions that concerned Israel were clearly answered. Israel had received information that Iraq had set up a radar station and stores of weapons in Jordan, and Herzog asked if Iraqi troops would be allowed to enter Jordan. Hussein's answer was unequivocal: 'No foreign army will enter Jordan ... We're aware of the danger of foreign forces in our country. We're watching out for it very carefully.'

The other issue Herzog brought up had to do with the PLO and its leader Ahmad Shukeiri. Israel worried that the PLO, which had opened recruitment offices all over Jordan, might create an army 'that would endanger Hussein and the integrity of Jordan'. Hussein's answer was equally firm: 'There will be no recruiting in Jordan, and I shall not allow a single unit of Shukeiri's forces to remain in Jordan.' He added disdainfully that some units of the Palestinian army might deploy in Egyptian-administered Gaza, but not in his territory. He also dismissed Herzog's concern that the 8,000-strong Palestinian 'national guard' would be integrated as a whole into Jordan's Arab Legion. A small number of them would be integrated, the King said, but they would be dispersed throughout the armed forces.

Herzog and Hussein reached an understanding on the issue of the Jordan waters, the King emphasizing that his country was pumping from the river and its tributaries only the amount allowed it by the Johnston Plan. He also reassured Herzog about the entry of three brigades of his armed forces into the West Bank, stressing that they would only be deployed in defensive positions. 'What are you afraid of?' he asked jokingly. 'You know how strong you are!'

Herzog expressed concern that Hussein would acquire Soviet weapons, but the King assured him he would buy arms only from the West. 'In Cairo they tried to persuade me to buy Soviet arms, but I refused. I'll get arms from the West and prove that it is not necessary to rely on the Soviets in order to build up an army.' He confirmed the information that Jordan was about to obtain a small quantity of weapons from the United States.

As in previous meetings, Herzog surveyed the situation in the Middle East and also passed some important intelligence to Hussein, including the fact that the Egyptians were trying to recruit a Jordanian air force officer, whom he named. The King was grateful for the information. He also seemed satisfied with the arrangement that had been made, following their previous meeting, to solve the land dispute in Latrun, and pleased with Herzog's promise that Israel would continue to support him in Washington and in his efforts to obtain economic aid. Herzog informed him that the head of C. A., the large business enterprise that had contacted Jordan on Israel's recommendation, would soon be visiting Jordan.

Still, the two did not agree on every issue. Hussein continued to express an attitude of cooperation and trust towards Nasser; refused to be drawn into the question of future relations with Israel; refused to include more participants in their meetings, or to raise the level of Israel's envoys; he also objected to the IDF's planned march in Jerusalem on Israel's next Independence Day, 'because it would raise tension'. Herzog said it was needed because of the government's internal difficulties, to which Hussein replied, 'I also have internal difficulties.'

In the final analysis, the third meeting with Hussein was the most businesslike and productive. Herzog concluded that despite all that had happened in the 15 months since their first meeting, and despite Hussein's strengthened position, his rapprochement with Nasser, the creation of the PLO and Jordan's participation in the joint Arab command, 'there has been no change in Hussein's attitude towards us or in his basic assessment of the various forces operating in the region'.[58]

One point that Herzog did not raise at this meeting was that it might well be their last – because before it took place, he had received a surprising proposal that might change the course of his life.

13

Collapse

Rabbi Israel Brodie, Britain's Chief Rabbi, was greatly respected and admired by his community. His decision to retire from his post, towards the end of 1964, set off a profound religious and communal crisis. Latent disagreements between various groups suddenly surfaced. The leadership of the Jewish community in Britain was splintered, rival groups proposed various successors to the Chief Rabbi, and there seemed to be no hope of getting them to support a single candidate. What was needed was a popular and charismatic figure who could reunite the agitated community. The ideal candidate had to be highly prestigious, with exceptional religious and social qualifications, and unchallenged status. He would also, ideally, come from outside and not be identified with any of the rival groups. Sir Isaac Wolfson, one of British Jewry's leading figures, proposed the man who in his view combined all the desired qualities – namely, Dr Yaacov Herzog.

This was a startling idea, in spite of Herzog's undoubtedly brilliant Jewish and rabbinical antecedents. Yaacov Herzog had abandoned the rabbinic world many years before, though not stormily, like his elder brother, but in his usual gentle, good-natured way. He had not followed in his father's footsteps, as he had been groomed and expected to do, but had chosen to enter the world of politics. He had, in fact, remained a Jewish scholar, with extensive knowledge of religious subjects, and maintained close connections with the world of the Torah and of the great rabbis of his day, with whom he kept up an extensive and learned correspondence.

But he had come a long way since the days when he translated and interpreted the Mishnah and used to sign his letters 'Rabbi Yaacov Herzog'. Now he was altogether a diplomat, one of the best in Israel's foreign service. His diplomatic undertakings were a constant challenge to him, as well as a source of satisfaction and sense of mission. By now the corridors of Washington and London were more familiar to him than the rivers of Babylon ... In addition, he was deeply and addictively involved in building up a secret network of contacts with some of the Arab leaders who were known as enemies of Israel.

Early rumours about the surprising idea of inviting Yaacov Herzog to be Britain's Chief Rabbi reached Israel in the autumn of 1964. At first Yaacov did not react, and at his express wish the Jewish press in Britain avoided mentioning it. But in November, when Isaac Wolfson mentioned him by name at a meeting of the ad-hoc Committee to Elect the Chief Rabbi, the weekly *Jewish Chronicle* decided to go public.[1] Then Solomon Sassoon, another leading figure in the Jewish community, joined Wolfson and urged Herzog to accept the appointment.[2] Finally, in February 1965, Herzog heard that *The Times* was about to publish a news story about it.[3]

All at once, the idea took on substance. It was no longer an amorphous notion toyed with by some Jewish dignitaries, but a serious initiative backed by the leadership of British Jewry. Herzog had to consider the offer even before it was put to him formally. It meant turning his back on the political world he loved so much, and returning to the family path and the vocation chosen for him by his parents.

'You have no idea what the rabbinate means in our family,' his daughter Shira Herzog said years later.[4] Yaacov was the son of the Chief Rabbi of Ireland and of Israel, the grandson of an Orthodox rabbi in Paris, the grandson – on his mother's side – of the head of the rabbinical appeals court in London, and married to a descendant of a grand rabbinical family. It looked like the most natural destiny for him. But could he leave the political world, and abandon the most important developments in Israeli diplomacy: his crucial dialogues with King Hussein, the leaders of the Yemen, the heads of the Maronite church of Lebanon and the Kurdish rebels; turn away from relations with the United States, the problems of the Jordan waters and the nuclear issue?

The personal conflict involved his family, too. The two women in his life, his mother and his wife, who were both strong and intelligent, supported the idea wholeheartedly. For his mother this would have been the realization of her fondest dream, Yaacov's place at the pinnacle of the rabbinical world. The author of the initiative, Sir Isaac Wolfson, was a friend of hers and of her family, and she received his suggestion with pride and joy.

Pnina Herzog, too, viewed the position of Chief Rabbi of Britain as elevated and worthy. She felt that it would provide her husband with a fuller expression of his unique abilities than did the role of Israeli Ambassador or senior official at the Foreign Ministry. Yaacov was a prodigy, a man of exceptional gifts, and she felt that his distinctive personality was unfulfilled in most of the posts he had held so far. Here, at last, was a proposition that she felt was more appropriate to his personality and abilities.

Yaacov struggled with himself. It was not easy to resist Wolfson's pressure – Yaacov had been closely associated with him, and had at least once helped him out by giving a speech (for Israel Bonds).[5] It was difficult to turn down a close friend who was also a prominent figure, especially since he knew that he would be a good Chief Rabbi and could reunite the contentious Jewish community of Britain. But still he wavered, and consulted his associates. 'I advised him to accept,' said Dr Nahum Goldmann, the President of the World Jewish Congress, 'because for several years he would be one of the foremost leaders of world Jewry. This, in my opinion, was also important to Israel. Of course, he had to consider what was more important, his work in the Israeli diplomatic service or in the diaspora, and I advised him to accept [the proposal].'[6] Foreign Minister Golda Meir disagreed. 'He was lying in bed sick, and asked me to come and consult with him. My mind was set against it ... I thought he ought to stay in Israel. When we talked at his house I didn't see any inclination on his part to go for it. He and his wife also faced the question of taking the children out of the country. Then I saw that he was torn between his own will and a sense of duty ... I must confess that I left with a heavy heart.'[7]

During the winter and spring of 1965 the rumour spread throughout government circles in Israel. Finally, in May, there was an extraordinary session of the Chief Rabbinical Council in the United Kingdom, chaired by Sir Isaac Wolfson, President of the United Synagogue of British Jewry. The 36-member council resolved unanimously to offer the position of Chief Rabbi to Yaacov Herzog. They also decided to send a seven-member delegation to Jerusalem, to present it formally to Dr Herzog.[8]

At this time Yaacov was lying in bed at home, recovering from appendicitis. Only the previous week, replying to a question from a British correspondent about the rumours, he had stated firmly that he was 'not a candidate for the post of Chief Rabbi of England.'[9] But this time it was an official offer, made unanimously, no longer a rumour. The delegation delayed a little, because of Yaacov's illness, but eventually visited him at home, where he was convalescing. In addition to the dramatic delegation, the family had added its own persuasive arguments. Yaacov himself was well aware of the tremendous importance of the proposed post – the Chief Rabbi of Britain was an almost royal position, in more ways than one.

The delegation went to Herzog's house on 24 May and they talked at length. In the end he accepted – the decision was made. Herzog issued a statement saying, 'I am deeply moved by the honour of the committee's unanimous request. After much thought and inner struggle, I have decided to accept. Providence has led me from the path I have been following for many years back to the sphere of religious thought, the sphere which had always been the deepest core of my life.

'If I am appointed, it will be my privilege to serve the Jewish community of Britain and the Commonwealth, with its long and noble tradition. It will be a privilege to do this service in the land of great liberty, which has made and continues to make such a great contribution to the world and human civilization.'[10]

And so Yaacov Herzog resolved to renounce his career in the political world and exchange the diplomat's suit for the rabbinical gown. He informed Levi Eshkol and Golda Meir of his decision. The two expressed regret, but also sympathy for his motives. In the Ministry corridors some gossips whispered that no one tried very hard to dissuade him.[11]

Herzog's announcement was welcomed in the media. The daily *Jerusalem Post* described it as a 'partial repayment of Israel's debt to England's Jewry', and expressed the hope that Herzog's appointment would serve to build 'natural and strong links between the Jewish people's emergent tribes'. *Ha-Tzofeh* described Herzog's appointment as reinforcing the struggle against assimilation in the diaspora.[12] Yaacov's mother was ecstatic. 'She dearly wanted him to accept,' said Shira Herzog. 'It would have continued the dynasty. She didn't have to pressure him – she was inside him.'[13] Pnina Herzog flew to London, rented a flat and found a decorator. She also put the girls' names down for Hasmonean, a Jewish day-school, and returned with the necessary school-books in her luggage.

'We knew it was not like being an ambassador,' said Shira, 'but mother said it was a very important and honoured position. I was still a child, but I knew that an honoured position was a good thing.'[14]

And then Yaacov collapsed.

It was a psychosomatic collapse, with symptoms of acute backaches, exhaustion and debilitation. He did not recover after the appendectomy and his condition deteriorated.

Yaacov had made a decision and sincerely meant to carry it out, but he was mentally incapable of confronting it. He could not wholeheartedly renounce the political world and choose the rabbinical one. 'What it amounted to,' said his friend Ari Rath, 'was an elegant emigration from Israel, a lifetime position, or at any rate for five to ten years'.[15] But if Yaacov was having second thoughts, he was unable to alter his decision. He had already resigned from his government posts, he was awaited in London, and his family was proud of his new status. Torn between opposites and unable to cope with the fateful choice, he collapsed.

'It was a tremendous inner conflict,' said his brother, Chaim Herzog. 'He was very distressed at that time. Though he did finally accept the proposal from Britain, I'm not sure he was happy about it. He loved diplomatic work too much; he always wanted to be at the centre of things and was afraid to leave it. Perhaps his inner struggle about it made him fall ill.'[16]

Another member of the family believed that Yaacov collapsed when he went to England and realized that he did not want the position offered to him. 'They also expected him to dress in a certain way, and he didn't want that either.'[17]

Nobody, not even Yaacov himself, doubted that the collapse was psychosomatic. 'It was a combination of his own inner struggles,' said his wife Pnina. 'Yaacov himself told Professor Zondek [his personal physician] that the illness stemmed from his mental state.'[18] And it had to be treated accordingly. Professor Zondek ordered him to withdraw 'from everything', and promised that if he obeyed his instructions, he 'would recover full health and vigour'.[19] To do this Yaacov would have to leave the country for some time and settle in Geneva, where Zondek had a colleague, Professor Mack, a renowned specialist in internal medicine, who would look after him and restore him to health.[20]

Had the problem been merely physical, a complication following the appendectomy for example, this would have been strange advice. But evidently taking Yaacov away from Israel and the tremendous pressure he was under was essential to his recovery.

The decision to go to Geneva was made in mid-summer in 1965. Yaacov and Pnina Herzog left abruptly, in a manner both secretive and nervous. The girls were told that Daddy was ill, and they were to stay with their grandmothers, alternately with Grandma Herzog in Jerusalem and Grandma Shachor in Tel Aviv. They did not know what their father was suffering from, nor how long he would remain abroad. Before leaving for Geneva, Pnina went to London to see Sir Isaac Wolfson to explain to him personally that Yaacov's frail health prevented him from immediately going to England to take up the post of Chief Rabbi.

In Geneva, Yaacov settled at the house of his friends, the Bloomfield brothers, Canadian Jews who had just returned to Canada for a long period. Pnina remained with him. 'It was a very difficult time,' she said. 'Can you imagine what it was like, leaving the girls behind?'[21] Shira was 12 and Eliezra 10. 'It was just after my bat mitzvah,' Shira recalled. 'Suddenly he disappeared – for six whole months! They said he was ill, and the two grandmothers looked after us. I was awfully stressed, because our parents had suddenly vanished. I was also anxious about the future – what would happen to us?'[22]

In Geneva, Professor Mack was entrusted with looking after Yaacov. Some time later Yaacov wrote to his brother, 'I have passed some very difficult months, suspended between heaven and earth – "The Lord hath chastened me sore, but He hath not given me over unto death."' Yet even in the depths of this crisis, Yaacov's characteristic humour did not abandon him. 'Having peeped into another world, I can testify that this world of ours, for all its imperfections, nevertheless seems pleasant and interesting.' But he stressed that Professor Zondek's decision to send him to Geneva had saved his life – 'both by his diagnosis of my condition, and his insistence that I retire from everything'.[23]

There is no evidence that Yaacov received any psychological treatment while in Switzerland, but apparently the sojourn in remote, peaceful Geneva was in itself a cure. He was examined every fortnight, and the results enabled Professor Mack to tell Herzog 'how I am to proceed'.[24]

He saw no one except a few close friends, rabbis and intellectuals, who visited him. He read a vast amount and avoided thinking about his future. He wrote to his brother: 'I have not yet decided what I shall do after I return.'[25] This suggests that he had already made up his mind to reject the post of Britain's Chief Rabbi.

At first he hoped that he would shortly be himself again and be able to return to Israel, but weeks and months passed and his condition did not improve. 'He has grown very thin,' reported a member of the family.[26] In November he wrote to his brother that he would be back in a matter of weeks, but November passed, then December and January, and Yaacov had not yet emerged from the crisis.

The turning-point was an external event. In January 1966 Pnina Herzog, who had not left Yaacov's side, herself had an acute attack of appendicitis. She had to be hospitalized without delay, operated on and put into intensive care. Yaacov took over, hired a nurse to help look after her and assumed all the necessary responsibility. Being responsible for another person in distress forced him out of his crisis. Suddenly he was not the patient, surrounded by doctors and looked after by his devoted wife. Now he had to make decisions for her, worry about her health and run around the corridors of the Geneva hospital. He did it all very well – Pnina recovered, and so did he.

Later, Yaacov said to Pnina that having to look after her and make decisions about her treatment brought him back to himself. The image of the frail patient in Geneva vanished, and was replaced by the familiar personality of Yaacov Herzog.

Pnina understood which way her husband was leaning. She

realized that the Geneva interlude was in reality his response to the offer of Britain's Chief Rabbinate. Bravely and decisively, she set it aside and got in touch with Levi Eshkol, who was showing great interest in Yaacov's condition. Already in September 1965, when he first heard about Yaacov's illness, he sent him a 'get well' telegram.[27] Pnina Herzog responded with a personal letter, describing her husband's condition and stressed that Professor Zondek believed Yaacov would recover after a complete rest.[28] She also met the Prime Minister and discussed her husband's condition.

Towards the end of the winter, while still recuperating in Geneva, Yaacov received a surprising offer from the Prime Minister – to become his political advisor. Eshkol also hinted that in a few months' time, when Teddy Kollek left, Yaacov would succeed him in the post of director of the Prime Minister's office. And that is what happened.

Yaacov returned from Geneva, having officially turned down the post of Britain's Chief Rabbi. In March 1966 he became the Prime Minister's political advisor, and on 24 July that year he was appointed director-general of the Prime Minister's office, the most senior position he had ever held.

He wrote about it to his brother Vivian (Chaim) before leaving Geneva. 'Vivian helped him a good deal in those days,' said Vivian's wife Aura. 'Vivian saw that he was in distress, that he didn't want to discuss the matter with his mother, and the only person left to him was Vivian ... I knew that Vivian wrote to Wolfson and tried to calm the storm in London when Yaacov turned down the position. Vivian used his connection with Wolfson to help Yaacov discreetly, and didn't mention it to a soul.'[29]

After his return to Israel, Yaacov said to Aura, 'You must read Proust's *Remembrance of Things Past*,' and she wondered, 'What was in that book that helped him so much?'[30]

He did not explain it to his sister-in-law, but an answer lies in an entry in his journal, written a few months after the event.

Recording a conversation with Theodore White, an American-Jewish writer, he wrote, 'When I read Proust in Geneva, I learned about the clash between a person's present consciousness and the consciousness of his experiences, which affects his attitude. That is, even though the person knows that circumstances have changed, if his personality was formed in particular circumstances, he cannot easily free himself of their memory.'[31]

Evidently he understood that his agreement to become Britain's Chief Rabbi had stemmed chiefly from the circumstances in which his personality was formed, in the house of his father the rabbi, and that he'd had to fight to free himself of those past circumstances. Although the situation had changed, now his world was that of international politics and this was what dominated his thinking. (He said as much in a conversation with White about a different subject – the difficulties of mental transition in Israel. Speaking about the Israelis of his time, their attachment to slogans and ideas derived from their diaspora past, from the Soviet Revolution and its experience, Herzog noted that 'the Israelis are aware that the circumstances from which they came and the slogans they uphold are not relevant to present-day reality, but because the minds of the first ones were formed in particular circumstances, they find it hard to free themselves.' White, of course, was not aware that Herzog was also speaking about himself and his anguished struggle to free himself from his parental inheritance).

Shira could well understand the nature of the burden that brought her father down. 'He had chosen the political world at an early age, before he met my mother. But he was also the younger son, the chosen one, who had been brought up under his father's tutelage, in the rabbinic tradition, as a Talmudic scholar and a new scion of the dynasty. He was ordained as a rabbi, lived till the age of thirty in his parents' house, and was his father's squire ... Then his father died, and the next thing you know, he is offered the Chief Rabbinate of Britain!'[32]

His younger daughter, the quiet and intelligent Eliezra, diag-

Collapse

nosed the source of the crisis, which she regarded as Yaacov's parting from his father's image.[33]

'His native intelligence,' she said, 'was diplomacy, so the post of Chief Rabbi would have been wrong for him. Judaism and the attachment to the Torah came to him from his father. It is possible for one's native intelligence to overlap with one's father's heritage, but in Yaacov's case they were two worlds, side by side. I sense that his religious scholarship was his internalization of his father, while his native intelligence did not tend that way. To put it another way – perhaps if he'd had a different father, he would not have gone in for religious study at all, but only into diplomacy. So in the end it was a good thing he did not choose to follow a rabbinic career.'

Eliezra thought that Yaacov had agreed to take up the post of Chief Rabbi because he was still to a great extent living 'through his father's figure'. 'The life of a person,' she went on, 'is a journey to inner knowledge, to self-realization, and in that journey he leaves behind many conventions, leaves behind his father – and finds his inner self. The father continues to dwell there, but on a different scale.' Sometimes this inward look into the depths, this discovery of the self, costs dearly. 'The price can sometimes be physical injury. If the person does not find the answer within himself, his psyche may signal the difficulty by various physical means, and then he must listen to himself and follow what is the right path for him.

'The physical distress that afflicted him caused Yaacov to clarify to himself his true path in life. His illness was the crisis of that self-discovery. It was another stage in parting from the father figure. You internalize and depart – that is growing up.

'Through that crisis,' Eliezra observed, 'he discovered what he really wanted and who he really wanted to be.'

According to his younger daughter, Yaacov Herzog resolved his need for the 'other world' by making study of Torah and Judaism a hobby. Indeed, later he devoted every free moment to the study of Torah and Talmud, which would remain part of his inner world – but as an added occupation, no longer as a parallel existence rivalling the first. Thereafter he conducted a weekly Talmud study circle at his mother's house, and did it willingly and enthusiastically. But it would not be his main occupation.

In the spring of 1966 Yaacov Herzog returned to Israel, convinced this time that he had made the right decision. The rabbinate, as well as the crisis, were behind him. Herzog returned to the political world, this time by the front door.

14

A Time of Flourishing

When Yaacov Herzog entered the Prime Minister's office in Jerusalem it was the start of a period of unprecedented success and satisfaction for him. Only days before he had been 'suspended between heaven and earth', his world seemingly darkened, and here he was now at the hub of national affairs, on the bridge of the political ship, in a more significant position than any he had held before. Suddenly he was one of the most important people in Israel, into whose hands were entrusted internal and international matters of state, relations with other leaders in Israel and abroad, and the writing of major speeches, statements and declarations that voiced Israel's policies. He accompanied the Prime Minister on his journeys abroad and placed his vast political knowledge at his disposal. Senior figures, both Israeli and foreign, sought his company, his advice and assistance.

Working with Levi Eshkol was a new experience. Eshkol was a team person, and treated his aides as his equals. At first, however, Herzog had a problem — when asked for his opinion he would present the Prime Minister with a number of alternatives. 'He had difficulty making decisions,' wrote one of his associates, 'and considered and reconsidered everything, over and over, sharing his doubts with others.'[1] A friend of his, a much younger man, once said to him, 'Listen, Yaacov, I know these people, they're pragmatists. Eshkol wants your opinion, not the other 100 possibilities. Give him your opinion and have done with it.'[2] Herzog never quite mastered this method, but Eshkol took his wavering in good spirit. Herzog was not only a wise man who could give him intelligent advice – after all, he had been Ben-Gurion's advisor – but had come to work for him wholeheartedly, without ties to any party, including Ben-Gurion's newly-formed party Rafi.[3] 'He suited Eshkol perfectly,' remarked his friend Ari Rath. 'Eshkol had sound, healthy instincts, but his speech was awkward, except in Yiddish. He had a strong Jewish background, and enjoyed discussing Jewish subjects with Yaacov, and also sent him on many missions abroad.'[4]

As far as Eshkol was concerned, according to the writer Medzini, 'Herzog had been Ben-Gurion's right hand during the Sinai campaign, and if he was good enough for Ben-Gurion, he was good enough for him.'[5] But Eshkol was very fond of the Talmudic scholar in Herzog. Being a man of action, he felt that his conversations with the Jewish scholar were enriching his mind. He began to invite Herzog to his house every Saturday evening to hear his views about the latest events, and also to discuss Judaism. But since Yaacov tended to be wordy, Eshkol would begin by saying, 'Reb Yankel [Rabbi Yaacov in Yiddish], please don't start from Abraham!'[6] He also joked about Herzog's tendency to interpolate Judaism and the God of Israel into every subject at every conversation. 'Please, Reb Yankel,' he would say, 'God gets tired, don't drag him into everything!'

The American astronauts' landing on the moon prompted a profound discussion between them. Eshkol said they had got there thanks to human genius and technology, while Herzog insisted it was thanks to God. The argument went on till the small hours. 'It was fascinating,' said Miriam Eshkol.[7]

Soon, Yaacov rose much higher than was usual for a Prime Ministerial advisor or for the director-general of the Prime Minister's office. At cabinet meetings he sat beside Eshkol, as he had sat beside Ben-Gurion during the Sinai campaign. In his intelligent and courteous way he defused dissension among cabinet ministers and between them and the Prime Minister. He showed similar

A Time of Flourishing

skill in smoothing relations between the intelligence and the security services, and created a coordinating committee under his chairmanship.[8]

He was clearly pleased by the fact that the Prime Minister and his immediate circle listened to him. Eshkol treated him warmly, his appreciation unaffected by Herzog's Geneva episode, and made him his right-hand man. Herzog's pleasant manner, bright intelligence, avoidance of political intrigue and great gift for diplomacy made him a much liked and respected figure in Israel's leadership. Despite his rather strange personality, dress, accent, manners, way of addressing Eshkol as 'Mr Prime Minister', and other signs of his exceptional background, he got on with the rather rough-edged Israeli leaders of various political parties and won their trust. He was also personally liked by his colleagues – the chief of the Prime Minister's staff Adi Yaffe, Eshkol's military secretary Colonel Israel Lior, and Herzog's deputy in the Prime Minister's office, Ami Kamir. He was on friendly terms with the head of the Mossad, Meir Amit, though his relations with the IDF Chief of Staff Yitzhak Rabin were less than cordial.[9]

Herzog's notes about his conversations with Eshkol reveal that the Prime Minister accepted most of his advice – perhaps because of a certain similarity in their temperaments. Whenever Eshkol perceived a problem, Herzog would recommend consulting cabinet ministers, experts, party leaders and the like. Eshkol followed this kind of advice willingly, because it suited his way of doing things. He spent much of his time in consultation and discussion, and made his decisions in an atmosphere of harmony. One day, when Eshkol decided to address the conference of the Opposition party Herut – the first time an Israeli Prime Minister had appeared at such a conference – Yaacov, the inveterate conciliator, congratulated him warmly on the move. Reviewing certain passages in Eshkol's speech, he said that 'in view of the sensitive nature of the event, it would be best to show the draft to members of [Eshkol's] party. [The Prime Minister] immediately sent for Galili, and he and I went over it.'[10] On another occasion Yaacov suggested that Eshkol find out from his associates something to do with Ben-Gurion. A short while later he asked Eshkol if he had done so. Eshkol said he had 'forgotten'. Herzog urged him to consult without delay, 'and so he did'.[11] Yaacov Herzog, pleasant, calm and smiling, succeeded in getting his advice followed and his policy adopted, in more than one area.

It is doubtful whether he could have done this with Ben-Gurion, who generally made his own decisions.

Ben-Gurion himself continued to think highly of Herzog. A senior member of the Prime Minister's office met Ben-Gurion at the Knesset, where 'the Old Man' asked him about his work and pronounced, 'There's a good director-general in the office.'[12] Herzog, for his part, felt great admiration and affection for Ben-Gurion. He declined to take part in a public debate in Tel Aviv with Nahum Goldmann and Ben-Gurion on the subject 'The Jewish People, the Diaspora and the Nature of Jewish History'. He explained that he feared that 'there might be a sharp disagreement between me and BG on these issues. I have spoken to him for ages about them, and if there were a break between us it would make it difficult to keep up the dialogue in private.'[13] (Their differences had to do with the nature of the State of Israel and its people. Ben-Gurion wanted to create a 'New Israeli', untouched by the diaspora experience, to make Israel a nation of pioneers and warriors. Herzog believed that the spiritual component in the life of the Israeli people should be much more prominent. However, as Ben-Gurion also stressed the Jewish people's spiritual and moral distinction, the disagreement between them was, as Herzog's daughter Eliezra said, 'a matter of dosage'.[14])

Herzog was especially proud of his role in organizing the festivities in honour of Ben-Gurion's 80th birthday. 'I felt great satisfaction,' he noted, 'that I succeeded in making a contribution to the birthday festivities. I owe a great deal to BG, whose friendship for me has not diminished since I've been working with

A Time of Flourishing

Eshkol [who had had a bitter row with Ben-Gurion]. I was glad to be able to repay him in some way.'[15]

Herzog's admiration for Ben-Gurion displeased Eshkol, who commented to one of his aides after a discussion in which Ben-Gurion's name was mentioned, 'Your buddy [Herzog] makes me ill. He won't touch anything to do with Ben-Gurion ...' The same aide accompanied Herzog on a visit to Sdeh Boker (the Negev kibbutz where Ben-Gurion lived after retirement), and saw 'the Old Man' receive him with open arms. Later Ben-Gurion launched into a furious attack on Eshkol. 'I was stunned. I hoped Herzog would respond. When we left I said to Yaacov, "We work with Eshkol, we should stand up for him." I was hopping mad. But on the way back to Jerusalem he made me swear not to tell Eshkol about it. He kept saying, "Ben-Gurion is one of our national figures. We mustn't argue with him."'[16]

People from all parts of the political spectrum asked to meet Herzog. His presence gave them spiritual and religious inspiration, and his conversations moved from everyday issues to spiritual and intellectual ones. Thinkers and intellectuals alike sought his company and respected his views.

'[In the time of the Unity Government]* I worked with Yaacov every day,' said Menachem Begin, leader of the Herut Party, 'and came to know his unique gifts. To me he seemed above all a scholar of Jewish learning, one whose knowledge was both broad and profound. He knew his Judaism, but also had a very broad general education and an extensive knowledge of numerous subjects ... In almost every conversation I had with him – invariably political in nature, he would introduce a parable from the Mishnah or Talmud about our people's history, going back to Abraham.'[17]

It was the same in his talks with the President, Zalman Shazar, and many others. One day he went to see the Minister of Education, Zalman Aranne, to discuss the government information service, and soon after, they had moved on to discuss the world-

* Created during the crisis leading up to the Six Day War in June 1967.

to-come in Judaism. Herzog told Aranne that the Prime Minister of the Irish Republic, Eamon de Valera, had asked him about it. 'I told de Valera that in my opinion Judaism does not distinguish between this world and the next, and that by obeying the precepts and doing good deeds in this world one attains a sense of the next world, and that the difference exists only in the human imagination, because the body dies in this world, whereas in terms of eternity the soul persists for ever. This means that the difference between Judaism and Christianity is that Judaism puts emphasis on this world not as the vestibule to the hall, but as the hall itself. As the Sages put it, "One hour of precepts and good deeds in this world is finer than the entire world-to-come." After talking about it with de Valera I found hints to that effect in Maimonides' responsa.'[18]

When Herzog finished speaking Aranne took a piece of paper from his pocket and read a poem he had written the previous evening: 'My time is not my own and the next world continues for ever.' Herzog concluded what was supposed to be their discussion about the information service with the words, 'We were both amazed by the telepathy and Aranne said we should meet more often.'[19]

Herzog also impressed the writer S. Y. Agnon, whom he saw frequently, and their conversations ranged from Jewish law to literature and concentrated mainly on the writings of Joyce and Proust. Herzog's conversations with Jewish journalists and writers from abroad – such as Max Frankel of the *New York Times* and Theodore White, the author of best-selling books on the presidential elections in the US – also ranged from the nature of Judaism, the soul of the Jewish people and the conflict between Rome and Jerusalem, to sober evaluations of contemporary American leadership, comparisons between Kennedy and Eisenhower, the Vietnam war and many other subjects.[20] A conversation with Dorothy de Rothschild in London about creating a fund for Jewish education developed into a profound discussion on

A Time of Flourishing

'concepts of immortality'. Levi Eshkol took pride in having a man like Herzog at his side. 'It mattered to him that he had someone who could invite Isaiah Berlin and hear his views'[21] – that is, a man who could hold his own with some of the finest thinkers and intellectuals of his time.

It seemed impossible that, only a few months before, this active, smiling, self-confident man, had been broken and depressed, cut off from home and isolated in distant, chilly Geneva, with his career seemingly about to end.

The subject of the British rabbinate rarely came up, but when it did, he would avoid it in a few words. When Mrs de Rothschild visited Israel and he called on her, she said how sorry she was he had not come to England – 'but better not go into it'. Yaacov promised that some day he would explain it to her, and they left it at that.[22] Another time he tried to analyse his real reasons for declining to take part in the public debate between Nahum Goldmann and David Ben-Gurion. At the time he had noted that he did not wish to clash with Ben-Gurion on issues on which they disagreed. Now he wrote, 'Perhaps the reason I mentioned before was only a part of my hesitation, but the second and perhaps main part is that after what I've been through in the past year, I'm not yet mentally ready for such a public appearance.'[23] And while spending a holiday break at the Sharon Hotel he noted, 'I returned to the room so exhausted that I didn't have the strength to go down for evening prayers. Perhaps the memories of my last stay at the Sharon contributed to it.'[24]

Herzog recruited Deborah Bregman, who had been his secretary in Ottawa and had returned to the Foreign Ministry, to work with him at the Prime Minister's office. She tried to resist, saying she had to look after her little girl – she still remembered the backbreaking work in Canada, the nights and weekends, and did not think she could go through it again. But he told her that he had been ill and was not allowed to work hard. He would put in less than a regular working day, he said, 'I'll be a simple official.' Even before she formally consented, she was informed that she had been transferred to the Prime Minister's office. And indeed for a while Herzog's office worked at a reasonable pace, and Deborah even went home for lunch, 'But pretty soon we were back at the mad old pace of work.'[25]

The addition of another secretary, Frieda Sofer, did not much alleviate the burden. 'Herzog's bureau in the Prime Minister's office was the busiest of all,' said Deborah Bregman. 'Everyone wanted to meet him, everyone wanted to hear him speak on any subject at all, because it was an experience.'[26]

Yaacov was so absorbed in his work that he did not pay attention to his devoted secretaries. One morning, out of the blue, he surprised them. 'He came in one morning and asked one of them how she was and how was her mother, who was ill. Something had happened to Yaacov – he remembered to ask.'[27]

The secretaries were alarmed. What had happened to Herzog to make him take an interest in them? They reported it to Adi Yaffe, chief of the Prime Minister's staff. 'I went in to see him and asked, "Doctor, what happened?" Yaacov replied, "Pnina said I treat the secretaries badly, I don't show any interest. So when I went in ... I quickly asked those questions."'[28]

The special closeness between Yaacov and Pnina grew stronger over the years. She was a true helpmeet and a sound counsellor. She played an important part in his public life, both abroad and when he directed the Prime Minister's office. Their love was even warmer and deeper than before. 'How much more can one love?' he used to say to her, and his letters to her overflowed with intense love.[29]

Many people asked Herzog for advice or for help. Israel Galili came to him to complain that the Prime Minister had not given him the information portfolio, as promised. (Yet when the problem was not resolved, and Herzog began to worry that Galili would resign, the sensible Miriam Eshkol reassured him. 'Even if nothing comes of it,' she said, 'internal political considerations will

Above 1959—with President of Ireland, Sean O'Kelly and his wife.

Below 1960—with Levi Eshkol at the Herzogs' home in Washington before leaving for Ottawa.

Above 1960—en route to credentials ceremony in Ottawa.

Below Yaacov and Pnina at the credentials ceremony, Canadian Governor-General's residence.

Above 1963—receiving the degree of Juris Doctor from the University of Ottawa.

Below Montreal, January 1961—the Herzog-Toynbee debate.

Above October 1966—the Rothschild Prize ceremony, Pnina and Yaacov with Meyer Weisgal. At left Yigael Yadin.

Below Israel, 1963—with The Rt. Hon. John Diefenbaker and Mrs. Diefenbaker.

Above June 1966—with Ugandan President Milton Obote during Prime Minister Levi Eshkol's African tour. At right Uri Lubrani.

Below Canada, 1968—Left to right Israeli Prime Minister Levi Eshkol, Canadian Prime Minister Lester Pearson, Canadian Foreign Minister Paul Martin, Yaacov Herzog.

Above   The Jewish leadership conference, 1968—Left to right Nahum Goldmann, President of the World Jewish Congress, Yaacov Herzog.

Below   Left to right U.S. Ambassador to Israel, Walworth Barbour, Abba Eban, William Rogers, Yaacov Herzog, an American advisor, Golda Meir, Yigal Allon, Jospeh Sisco

Above Ceremony granting honorary citizenship to Lord Sieff, 1970—Left to right Yaacov Herzog, S.Y. Agnon, Dr. Helena Kagan, Professor Yosef Rivlin.

Below 1968—with President Zalman Shazar and Jerusalem Mayor Teddy Kollek at the opening of the Ramban synagogue in the Old City of Jerusalem.

23 February 1969—on the day of Prime Minister Levi Eshkol's death, outside his house.

Above   With Moshe Dayan.

Below   With President Shazar.

A Time of Flourishing

stop Galili from leaving the Prime Minister's office.'[30]) The Labour Party spokesman, Yossi Sarid, asked for his help in obtaining a study grant in the United States.[31] Rabbis asked Herzog to help them raise funds abroad. Ephraim Broide came to talk about the personality of the late President Chaim Weizmann. A representative of the Rothschilds came to Herzog to prepare the visit of Lord and Lady Rothschild. Members of Knesset and cabinet ministers unabashedly asked him to write their speeches. The head of the Jewish Agency asked Herzog for a list of the five most prominent Jewish figures in the United States . . .[32]

The pressure of work and intellectual pursuits again left Yaacov without much time for his family. 'After the lesson [the Talmud study circle he conducted at his mother's house] I went to see Shira in the play *Hannah Szenes*, but arrived late, so I'll see her in her second appearance next Wednesday', he wrote.[33] But the following Wednesday he did not have time either.[34] When his son Yitzhak was an infant, Yaacov turned up one day at the child's nursery school and swept him off to the zoo. 'I was in kindergarten,' recalled Yitzhak, 'but he must have thought he didn't have enough contact with me, so he left his work in the morning and we went to the zoo, to the lion and monkey cages. We were there a long time . . .'[35]

His relationship with his brother Chaim was warm and close, but Norma Bar-Moshe, his English-language secretary, thought Yaacov felt a certain sense of inferiority towards his elder brother. When Chaim came to see him at his office, Yaacov told him that he had almost 200 people working under him. 'He was obviously eager to impress him.'[36] According to Ari Rath, who was a friend of both brothers, there was a certain awkwardness in their relationship, because Chaim Herzog knew that many people thought Yaacov was the more intelligent of the two.[37] Yaacov did in fact impress everyone he met. A common misapprehension survived for years that Yaacov Herzog was not really the director-general of the Prime Minister's office, but chiefly a political advisor and

Jewish scholar, whom Eshkol liked to keep at his side and listen to. 'What a strange country,' marvelled a foreign journalist, 'where the Prime Minister keeps at his side a director of conscience and consciousness.'[38]

But Herzog was not occupied exclusively with matters of conscience and spirit. An examination of the documents, letters, minutes of meetings and his journal from that period, reveals that he was a very active director-general, that he operated concurrently in a variety of spheres, and that he actually ran the Prime Minister's office. He enjoyed it, too. Some matters did not interest him, such as discussions about development towns and certain other socio-economic subjects, and he left them to his deputy Ami Kamir or the economist Dr Yaacov Arnon. 'His main contribution to Eshkol's premiership lay in two areas,' said one of Eshkol's aides, 'foreign policy and the security services. In foreign policy he was a treasure-trove. He was amazingly knowledgeable about the international situation, societies, states, international forces. He was at home in all of it. The other sphere was the secret services. I don't understand what drew him, a religious man, an intellectual, to it ... But he really flourished in this area.

'Perhaps his most important contribution to Eshkol was the sense that he knew which were the right questions to ask.'[39] Herzog's influence on the information services, foreign relations and the secret services was powerful and pervasive. Eshkol trusted him completely, and often poured out his heart to him about the problems of his premiership. Herzog noted a conversation in which Eshkol said he 'didn't know what to do as Prime Minister, and would open a tobacconist's shop instead'.[40] The Prime Minister's trust in the director of his office was such that on several occasions Herzog actually gave interviews in his name![41]

He identified with Eshkol wholeheartedly. When he heard that Isser Harel was about to launch a new attack on Eshkol, Herzog hastened to telephone him and wish him a happy new year, even promising to come and see him soon, all in the hope of averting

A Time of Flourishing

the attack.[42] Above all, Yaacov remained faithful to his two self-imposed rules: one, not to take part in gatherings of a partisan nature; and two – which arose from his own personality – never to offer his superiors substantive opinions and advice concerning Israel's policies, but only practical advice about methods and how to implement their policies in the best possible way. 'I never understood it and never talked to him about it,' said Nahum Goldmann, the president of the World Jewish Congress. 'He was never ambitious, didn't want to be in the Knesset; I never saw in him the ambition to be a cabinet minister. He was afraid of public life, was too civilized to enter the mess of political parties ... He was always content to be in the second row.

'I often pleaded with him, saying you should have more courage, why are you so shy, why do you hesitate, you should be in the front rank of Israeli and Jewish leaders. Why be content to be a simple official, to give advice and implement it? I can't say what was behind it, you'd need a psychoanalyst ... He was so modest he never wanted to appear at all, became embarrassed when people complimented him ... I told him, you can fight, but he was content just to give advice, and he suffered greatly when [the advice] was not taken ... I said to him once, I wish you had more of the evil impulse. With the good impulse you can live like a monk or a *tzaddik* [righteous man] and study Talmud, but not in the public world.'[43]

At this time, Herzog began to keep a journal and even to collect the notes that cabinet ministers and senior officials exchanged during cabinet meetings. Unfortunately, his journal mainly recorded observations from the sidelines about what others were doing, rather than his own actions and thoughts. Herzog was very prudent and took great care not to reveal his true feelings and opinions in his journal, perhaps fearing that it might fall into the wrong hands. Rarely did he express his own views about individuals and events – and even then only by a mere hint. His journals were meant to be the raw material for a book he intended to write about his work for the Prime Minister, a book which would never be written.

A rather amusing offshoot of Herzog's appointment was a story in the Egyptian daily *Al Goumhouriya* (*The Republic*), stating that Herzog should be watched, as he had been appointed chief of Intelligence, which meant that Israel was 'preparing a new aggression against the Arab people'. The paper described Herzog's close relations with Eshkol and Ben-Gurion, as well as with 'Zionist Congressmen in Washington'.[44] The Egyptian paper probably got the idea from a cover story in the Israeli weekly *Haolam Hazeh* (*This World*), where the caption under Herzog's photograph read, 'Security Service Chief?' It linked Herzog's appointment as director-general of the Prime Minister's office to Isser Harel's resignation from his post as advisor on Intelligence.

Following this story in *Al Goumhouriya*, the chief of the security service, Yosef Harmelin, decided to include Yaacov Herzog in the list of VIPs under special protection. Herzog found himself in the company of Eshkol, Ben-Gurion and Eban, and though he thought it was 'all quite exaggerated', he seemed to enjoy it too.[45]

Despite his natural modesty, he enjoyed the compliments and predictions about his brilliant future, and noted them in his journal. He met Aviezer Wolfson, a nephew of Sir Isaac Wolfson, who complained about the government's attitude towards the system of religious public schools in Israel. 'When you are Prime Minister,' he said, 'this attitude will improve.' Yaacov expressed surprise at his 'strange remark', but Aviezer said, 'There must have been a reason why God prevented your going to London, and it will become clear.'[46]

Herzog entered the Prime Minister's office at a time of great tension in Israeli politics. A rancorous conflict had erupted between Eshkol and his predecessor David Ben-Gurion, which was rooted in the murky residue of the Lavon Affair. Ben-Gurion and his supporters had walked out of their historic political home, the Labour Party, and formed the Rafi Party in 1965, which ran in

A Time of Flourishing

that year's general elections. Rafi won ten seats in the Knesset and joined the opposition. Ben-Gurion criticized Eshkol in extreme terms and demanded his resignation from the premiership. Then a crisis arose in the Prime Minister's office as Ben-Gurion's 80th birthday approached. It was obvious that Eshkol would not visit Ben-Gurion to congratulate him on the day, but Herzog found a solution – President Zalman Shazar would do so. He himself went to the President to propose this, and easily obtained his wish. Their conversation soon turned into a dialogue between two scholars of Jewish history. 'As I was leaving,' wrote Herzog, 'I thought about the two opposite worlds in the President's soul – Habad (the Hassidic Lubavitch sect with which President Shazar had a special affinity) with its powerful historical Jewish feeling, and Russian socialism of the early twentieth century. It's doubtful that the President is able to bridge these two worlds, but lives in each of them separately.'[47]

And so did Yaacov himself – he too lived in two worlds, though now with a sense of wholeness and inner calm. It mattered to him that the world of religion and spirit should realize that he had not abandoned it. 'I was glad to receive your letter,' he wrote to Rabbi Saul Liberman in New York, 'and was moved by your contents that indeed I have not left the Tents of Shem [the world of Jewish learning]. As the Talmud in the Tractate of *B'rachot* says, "I am appreciated and protected by the testimony of a great man such as yourself." ... I hope to be able to devote myself more to the Torah.'[48]

As Menachem Begin put it, Yaacov was 'an admirer of the Jewish people'.[49] Indeed, they were always first in Yaacov Herzog's scale of values. Though himself one of the people, he seemed to be standing on the side, observing with amazement and appreciation the voyage of his people through the ages and their ties with the Land of Israel.

Herzog accompanied Levi Eshkol on his journeys abroad. The

Prime Minister's visit to Africa in 1966 was especially dramatic. One night when they were in Uganda, they received a message that a coup had taken place in Congo-Léopoldville (former Belgian Congo), and that Colonel Mobutu had seized power and had hanged some of the ministers. Eshkol wanted to consult with his aides and, for lack of a better venue, they gathered around the hotel swimming-pool in pyjamas and dressing-gowns. The late-night meeting resembled a bedroom farce. Finally they decided to proceed to Kinshasa where they met Colonel Mobutu, who was well aware of the kind of stories that were circulating among Westerners about the Congolese. Describing to Eshkol the bloody events of his coup and the execution of the leaders of the ousted regime, he said wryly, '*Nous les avons pendus, mais nous ne les avons pas mangés.*' Miriam Eshkol translated this for her husband: 'He says, we hanged them, but we did not eat them.' Eshkol muttered, 'You can tell him that in our country the leaders are eaten without being hanged first' – but she preferred not to translate this.[50]

One of Yaacov's most moving experiences took place when he accompanied Levi Eshkol on an official visit to France. He had heard that the writer Elie Wiesel was in Paris after a visit to the Jews of the USSR. At that time, Jews in the Soviet Bloc were cut off from the rest of the world and officially silenced. Little information about their situation reached Israel and the West. Herzog contacted Elie Wiesel and invited him to Eshkol's hotel. Wiesel was surprised, knowing that the timetable of the Prime Minister and his entourage was extremely pressured.

'Tell me!' Herzog said to Wiesel.

'Aren't you busy? Meetings, consultations . . . ?'

'Tell me.'

'I told him,' Wiesel recalled. 'I described my main impressions of the Jews who broke the silence, what I'd seen in Tbilisi and heard in Leningrad. I'd heard nightly whispering and singing in public, the prayers of latter-day *Marranos* [crypto-Jews, as during the Spanish Inquisition] and the bravery of heroes. Those wonderful young people who were discovering their roots, three generations after the Revolution. They were a miracle.

'Herzog listened with his whole being, looking deep into my eyes, as if trying to see what I had seen and the people who had seen me, over there, behind the Iron Curtain. Suddenly he broke in: "Wait. I think the Prime Minister should hear your impressions."'[51]

Herzog got Eshkol out of a meeting 'for a short break', and the three sat down together. The 'short break' lasted two, then three, hours. Eshkol cancelled all his scheduled meetings to hear more. The two men were deeply moved and stirred by Elie Wiesel's description of millions of Jews awakening and seeking their identity. Wiesel noticed that while Eshkol was bombarding him with questions, Herzog remained silent, withdrawn. 'I'd never seen him listening so intently,' he recalled. 'His silence was never so strange.'

Finally Eshkol asked, 'So what do we do?' A practical man, he wanted advice about how to help the 'Jews of Silence'. Noticing Herzog's silence, he said to him, 'Advisor, advise!'

Herzog said in a voice hoarse with emotion, 'Forgive me, Prime Minister, I can't think in practical terms just now. All that comes to mind is a phrase that may sound like rhetoric – Everlasting Israel.'[52]

Herzog's first criterion was always what is good for the Jewish people? Despite his close relations with the Vatican and the heads of the Christian communities in Israel, he avoided responding when the writer André Chouraqui, a member of Jerusalem's city council, asked him 'to help promote Christian tourism to Jerusalem, by means of a campaign aimed at international Christian circles.' 'I hesitated in this matter, for various reasons, including the status of Jerusalem,' Yaacov wrote.[53]

His attitude towards Israel's Arab population was also largely determined by Jewish considerations. One of his earliest initiatives in the Prime Minister's office had to do with the Arab minority. Talking to Shmuel Toledano, the Prime Minister's advisor on Arab Affairs, Herzog suggested closing the advisor's offices in Nazareth and Haifa, and not opening one in Beersheba. This was not prompted by concern for the Arabs or understanding for their predicament. 'On the one hand, the special treatment meted to the Arabs gives them the feeling that they are entitled to more than ordinary citizens, and on the other, when their demands are not met, they become disaffected.' He suggested that the advisor on Arab Affairs restrict himself to cultural activities, and that the security services keep him routinely informed about political developments among the Arabs. 'I told him that if he adopted this proposal, his name would be associated with the start of an historical process, instead of being the target of complaints and calumnies (these days five Arab members of Knesset from the Labour camp are attacking him because they say he refused to support their demands for various favours).'[54]

In his modest way, Herzog suggested to Toledano that he present the idea to Eshkol as though it were his own. But the canny Eshkol knew perfectly well who had thought of it. 'I had told the PM earlier that I'd talked with Toledano, and when Toledano said, "I suggest," the PM's eyes twinkled. The PM approved, of course.'[55]

The first serious crisis Herzog dealt with in the Prime Minister's office was the confrontation with Syria, following the gravest incident since 1963. On 15 August 1966, an Israeli boat ran aground in the Sea of Galilee, near the north-east bank which was in Syrian hands. The Syrians opened fire on the boat and sent up two MiG-17 fighter planes. One of the MiGs was shot down by Israeli ground fire, and the other by Israeli fighter planes. Then both Israelis and Syrians tried to retrieve the broken plane parts from the lake. The United Nations and the United States intervened, Syria threatened war, and tension rose in the Middle East.

A Time of Flourishing

The situation became even more charged the following day, when an Iraqi MiG-21 landed in Israel, its pilot having defected in an intricate operation organized by Israel's Military Intelligence and security services. Herzog was in the thick of it. On 16 August, with all political fronts in turmoil, he wrote a speech for David Hacohen to address the inter-parliamentary conference in Iran, took part in a continuous series of meetings at the Prime Minister's office, prepared a number of official statements, and also discussed with the Prime Minister and Meir Amit a plan to capture the Nazi criminals Martin Bormann and Heinrich Müller in South America.[56]

Another major problem, one that Eshkol had inherited from Ben-Gurion, was the discord with the United States concerning the nuclear reactor in Dimona. It took Israel's best diplomatic skills to conduct negotiations with the Johnson Administration on this sensitive issue, which aroused tension in Israel and disputes between her leaders.

Yaacov Herzog was at his best in all these crises. He arranged consultations at the Prime Minister's office, instructed the Foreign Ministry, briefed the press, and persuaded cabinet ministers – above all the Prime Minister himself – to accept his advice. His views were heard and he was at the heart of the consensus on the adopted decisions. One by one, the crises were resolved to his satisfaction. Throughout that summer of tension, on both political and military fronts he was conscious of the perfect coordination and understanding between himself and the Prime Minister.

There were also some moments of joy and pleasure – for example, the opening of the new Knesset building. 'A sight to behold!' he wrote. He was less delighted with the official speeches. 'The PM's speech that we went over in the past week wasn't bad. The Speaker's speech was pretty feeble. Mayor Kollek's speech was very strange, Goldmann's speech routine. The most balanced, beautiful and inspirational was that of Mrs de Rothschild, who was able to distinguish between the building of the Knesset and the concept of the Temple building ... Her speech was graceful and carried out magnificently. Everyone present felt her true aristocracy.'[57]

He especially relished the speech given by President Shazar, of whom he was very fond. 'He put on his hat and spoke like a Talmudic scholar,' he wrote, and concluded: 'Throughout the ceremony I sensed the difficulty of harmonizing Jerusalem and eternal Judaism, on the one hand, with the attempt to seem like any other nation. The people living in Zion has yet to find expression for the miracle of its time against the background of Jewish continuity through the ages.'

That evening, at a celebration dinner with a delegation from the US Congress, he made a short speech about relations between the United States and Israel, saying that 'not only friendship binds us, but above all a joint understanding of historical processes'. He was followed by US Congressman Case, speaking for the visiting delegation, who said, 'I can't compete with your statement, which verged on poetry.' Herzog was embarrassed – 'I blushed and felt uncomfortable.'[58]

He renewed contact with King Hussein, whom he had last seen more than a year earlier, and met him again in July 1966.[59] While he had been lying ill in Geneva, Golda Meir had met the Jordanian King in Paris.[60] Their meeting, which took place in the house of a French Jewish family, was warm and friendly. They spoke, among other things, about Golda Meir's memories of Hussein's grandfather, King Abdullah. At that meeting Hussein promised that the tanks he had recently bought from the United States would never cross the Jordan river or be used against Israel. (This promise was not kept as, in the course of the Six Day War, tens of American tanks were found on the West Bank.)[61]

Now that Herzog was well again, he became once more the liaison with King Hussein. (Golda Meir had resigned from the government and was elected Secretary-General of the Labour Party.) It is possible that Herzog's amiable understanding with Hussein led him to a false optimism about the future of the Middle East, and to a vision of peace based more on wishful thinking than on clear-headed analysis. 'We talked [he and Golda Meir] about the Middle East, and I repeated the vision that I used to express to her when she was Foreign Secretary, namely that the thinking of some of the Arabs has changed significantly, and that a determined endeavour will enable us to advance our penetration in the region, so that in a few years' time coexistence will become possible, such as exists between India and Pakistan, meaning that Israel will be relieved of being the regional leper. I presented the development of Dimona as a central adjunct to bringing about this change.'[62]

His hectic existence notwithstanding, he did have moments of sheer contentment. On Yom Kippur (the Day of Atonement) he attended prayers at his mother's house. 'My nephew Michael read the Torah, to the great delight of all those present, especially of his grandmother and the family. I led the closing prayer, which filled me with inspiration, and in my mind I stood – perhaps for the first time – before my Maker.'[63]

His work with Eshkol revealed Yaacov Herzog's capacity for observation and clear-headed assessment of people. He wrote about President Shazar with affection and respect, recognizing his traditional Jewish scholarship and his personal warmth. He described his friend Chaim Israeli as 'a dear man, a gentle soul, with whom I've been closely associated for many years'.[64] He remained a devoted supporter of Moshe Sharett, and was annoyed when a friend told him that on the eve of the Declaration of Independence, 'Sharett revealed to Weizmann his profound doubts and predicted a massacre of Jews. To which Weizmann replied that if Sharett was losing his head, he should keep it to himself and not involve the entire people ...' Despite his natural open-mindedness and his matter-of-fact attitude to history, Herzog rejected the story (which was in fact true), 'because when Sharett returned [to Israel] a few days before the decision was made, he voted in favour of independence, though it might have been BG's influence.'[65]

After meeting MK Shulamith Aloni, who was on the left of the Labour Party, for the first time, Herzog wrote: 'A dynamic woman known for her independent mind, who clashes with the religious representatives in the Knesset at every opportunity ... She is an inveterate Sabra [native-born Israeli], with a simple integrity that borders on unreserved intellectual honesty as well as crudeness – depending on your viewpoint – and this type is rarely burdened with mental struggles.'[66]

One of the few individuals whom Herzog criticized throughout his journals was Abba Eban. Passages expressing reservations or disagreements with Eban, who was then Foreign Minister, appear in the journals frequently and in many connections. In a dispute between Herzog and the Chief of Staff, Yitzhak Rabin, concerning Israel's international presentation of its case, 'the Chief of Staff said that his criticism was aimed at the Foreign Minister, and referred to his recent statement to the press ... I told him that in this matter I saw some reason in his argument.'[67]

His criticism of Eban extended to his wife Susie. When he called at Eban's house in early September for a political consultation, the maid served them tea and biscuits. Herzog noted wryly that 'Susie honoured us by coming in, in person, to check that everything was all right. I'd last seen her ... over a year ago, when I was suspended between heaven and earth and my world was turning dark. She hasn't changed since Washington and still keeps a distance, as though *noblesse oblige*.'[68]

He wrote critically about his talk with Eban. Eban was 'very nervous' because of a recent disagreement with the Prime Minister. In reality, his reason for speaking to Herzog was his desire to secure a central role for himself in the celebrations of Ben-Gurion's eightieth birthday. He claimed that 'the President had asked me to extract him from the pressures of BG's birthday

A Time of Flourishing

and to advise him.' Herzog's note shows that he did not believe Eban and put him in his place. 'Perhaps you talked to the President before I did,' he said, 'since it has been agreed that the President will visit Ben-Gurion in Sdeh Boker. It has also been decided that the government will congratulate Ben-Gurion in a forthcoming session.' Eban seemed surprised, and was probably hurt that he had not been asked to join the public committee responsible for the celebrations. Herzog wrote: 'I assume that the failure to invite Eban stems not only from BG's contempt for him, but also from the profound hostility between him and [Shimon] Peres.'[69]

On another occasion he recorded the exact words of Arieh Disenchik, the editor of the daily newspaper *Maariv*, about Eban: 'Disenchik speaks critically about Eban, and generally his standing among the insiders of the political establishment in the country has declined steeply – not least because of his boundless publicity-seeking – though his position in the general public remains strong. Disenchik quoted approvingly Goldmann's description of Eban – "an intelligent fool". He said that when Eban became Deputy PM, Disenchik asked him about his relations with Golda. Eban replied that his relations with Golda and Zalman Aranne were fine. The reason was, he explained, that all those years they'd hated Peres but couldn't say why, till he (Eban) came along and gave it the right expression ...' Disenchik had added that the first disagreement between Golda Meir and Eban arose in the course of her visit to the United Nations during the Sinai campaign. 'Eban then said to various diplomats that the new Foreign Minister had no political understanding whatever, but when they met her they got the impression that she was not devoid of understanding, and they talked in the corridors about the inaccuracy of Eban's description, so that it reached her ears. On the other hand, the tension between her and Peres, which increased to a much more serious degree over the years, stemmed from their conflicting assessments of the first visit to France to discuss the Sinai-Suez operation.

Golda concluded that the French would not go for it, Shimon gave the opposite opinion and BG accepted it, and this started the antagonism that got worse and worse ... Incidentally, this is Shimon's version about the source of the quarrel. These matters seem personal, but their repercussions have a significant impact on public affairs.'[70]

It is noteworthy that during the political campaign after the Sinai war, Herzog voiced sharp criticism of Eban's moves. These journal entries rarely expressed Herzog's own views; they mostly noted other people's remarks. But since he generally avoided gossip, it is obvious that the extensive repetition of Disenchik's criticism of Eban hinted strongly at his own views.

When Richard Nixon visited Eshkol, Herzog introduced himself to him and was showered with compliments by the future US President. But the flattery did not cloud Herzog's judgement. 'By and large the conversation was not very useful,' he noted. 'Looking at Nixon I understood the tragedy of this man who [had at that point] reached the second-highest position in the US and was a step away from the pinnacle. When you look at him you feel a certain distrust due to his sharp glances and his grimaces, and who knows, maybe he's not sincere.'[71]

After a public dispute with the president of the Zionist Federation, Nahum Goldmann told Herzog of his relief at his imminent retirement from the presidency of the World Jewish Congress. 'But his eyelashes [sic] showed how bitterly disappointed he was,' noted Herzog.[72]

Herzog had a rare fit of anger when Eshkol decided to hold a state funeral for Mrs Vera Weizmann, the widow of Israel's first President, who died in London in September 1966. In discussions with the Prime Minister and with Meyer Weisgal, the president of the Weizmann Institute, Herzog voiced his determined objection to a state funeral, since 'it is limited to very few public figures, and to the best of my knowledge, does not include the wives of

A Time of Flourishing

presidents. With regard to Mrs Weizmann it is especially inappropriate to go beyond an official funeral. She was a grand lady to her dying day, but she never became an integral part of Israeli society – she was in the East but her heart was in the West. She had grandeur, but it was not Jewish grandeur, and some say that to a large extent she prevented her late husband from expressing his popular sentiments ... I thought it would be more appropriate that Rachel Ben-Zvi, when she passes away at 120, should have a state funeral, than her predecessor, because Mrs Ben-Zvi experienced in her own flesh the travails of the national renaissance.'[73]

In the latter part of 1966, tension in the Middle East intensified. In September, Herzog and Rabin fell out sharply when the IDF weekly *Bamahaneh* published an interview with the Chief of Staff in which he uttered blunt warnings against Syria.[74] At the same time, the USSR made several moves indicating its increasing coolness towards Israel. One of these was the cancellation, also in September, of reciprocal visits by orchestras from both countries. In October, Soviet Ambassador Leonid Chuvakhin requested an urgent meeting with the Prime Minister, in which he accused Israel of amassing forces on its northern border. Eshkol categorically rejected the charge, but to no avail.[75]

Tensions also rose on the eastern front. In November, the IDF carried out massive retaliation in the Jordanian village of Samua, after a dozen fedayeen attacks which culminatied in the blowing up of an IDF vehicle and the death of three Israeli soldiers. The Samua operation escalated and led to a battle with the Jordanian army, in which a Jordanian 'Hunter' plane was shot down, many houses were bombed and scores of Jordanian soldiers and some civilians were killed. Furious demonstrations against King Hussein erupted in the West Bank, and the Hashemite regime appeared to be in danger, both from within and from a possible invasion by neighbouring Arab armies. Herzog was sent to London to convey a reassuring message to Hussein through Dr Herbert.[76]

In a consultation at the Prime Minister's office in December,

Herzog expressed the view that if outside forces were to enter Jordan and if Hussein's regime fell and he was assassinated, the United States would not blame Israel. But the tension soon evaporated. Hussein suppressed the internal opposition, Arab armies did not topple him, the Syrian front calmed down, and it seemed that the crisis was over. In reality, it was only postponed.

In February 1967, Herzog's third child was born – a son, named Yitzhak. Israel's entire leadership came to the *brith* (circumcision ceremony). At the time Herzog was busy with preparations for one of his most ambitious projects in the Prime Minister's office – a conference of Jewish businessmen and economists from all over the world, aimed at encouraging them to invest in Israel. During the first half of 1967, he travelled extensively in Europe and the United States, meeting Jewish leaders and magnates, rallying their support for the project.

The endeavour came to an abrupt halt on 15 May 1967, when Israel found herself in a political and military maelstrom that would lead to the Six Day War.

15

Six Days and a King

On 2 July 1967, at eight in the evening, King Hussein arrived at Dr Herbert's house in London. He instructed the British security guard who accompanied him to wait outside, and entered the surgery. Dr Herbert was unusually excited as he informed the King that Dr Herzog was in an adjoining room and wished to see him. Hussein agreed without hesitation.

A moment later they were facing each other. Herzog bowed and they shook hands, but both were obviously embarrassed. Both were under the powerful impact of the dramatic events that were still reverberating around the world and that had changed the Middle East for ever – the Six Day War had taken place less than a month earlier.

The crisis began on 15 May 1967, when President Nasser of Egypt moved some élite troops into the Sinai Peninsula and stationed them on the border with Israel. He had been given incorrect information, probably by the USSR,[1] that Israel was amassing forces on her northern border, and was probably intending to attack Syria. Nasser saw no reason to distrust the information, given the rising tension between Israel and Syria, which had seen a number of clashes, including air fights in which six Syrian MiGs had been brought down. Nasser's first move was cool and calculated, but things soon spun out of his control.

A mixture of miscalculations, conceit, pressure from the streets, and waves of incitement and demagoguery which spread over

Egypt and overflowed into other parts of the Arab world, compelled Nasser to escalate the confrontation until war with Israel became unavoidable. Some unfortunate moves by the UN Secretary General U Thant, America's wavering about her Middle East policy, and the reversal of France's policy towards Israel – all these persuaded the Arabs that Israel stood alone and would be unable to withstand a new threat. This deterioration led to the outbreak of war.

Nasser began by expelling the UN Observers who were stationed in the Sinai, the Tiran Straits and the Gaza Strip; then he closed the Straits to Israeli shipping and air traffic, concluded agreements of military cooperation and joint commands with Syria, Iraq and Jordan, and threatened Israel with a military assault that would end with her total annihilation (though apparently he did not actually intend such action).

Israel reacted by calling up her reserves and appealing to Western powers for help. France turned her back on Israel, Britain listened sympathetically, while the United States promised to create an international *ad hoc* force to break the blockade of the Tiran Straits. In Israel there was a widespread feeling that in a matter of weeks, perhaps days, a tremendous, life-and-death struggle would break out. The Prime Minister was indecisive and unable to persuade the government to take immediate military action; he preferred to go the distance with the US Administration. In the early stage of the crisis, he chose to exercise restraint, as advised by Herzog, who drafted him a moderate speech that did not challenge Nasser – but which did not prevent the Egyptian President from closing the Straits either.[2]

On 23 May, following the Straits' closure, Levi Eshkol asked Herzog for his advice. 'I replied: first, in my opinion he ought to send a message to President Johnson to ask for his assessment of the situation, without of course committing us to act in one way or another. Secondly, I said that since he will have to decide whether to go to war or wait, I thought such a decision should be taken in consultation with all the political parties, and suggested that he bring in the leaders of the Opposition.'[3]

Abba Eban was sent post-haste to meet the French President Charles de Gaulle, the British Prime Minister Harold Wilson and the US President Lyndon B. Johnson. A year earlier, Eshkol had forbidden Eban to meet President de Gaulle – for reasons that remain unknown – and only Herzog's pleading persuaded Eshkol to rescind the prohibition shortly before the crisis of May 1967.[4] Even while Eban was on this tour, questions were asked in the cabinet about what Eban had said in those crucial meetings, and about the accuracy of his reports. These questions came up repeatedly in the cabinet for months after the war, and Herzog quoted them in his journal.

The Chief of Staff Yitzhak Rabin collapsed under the strain and spent a day in bed. Internal criticism of Eshkol grew, and several senior figures, including the Chief of Staff, complained that he was being indecisive. Herzog, as always, defended him whole-heartedly.[5] Voices were raised in public calling for the Defence portfolio to be given to Moshe Dayan, the hero of the Sinai campaign, and the decision was finally forced upon the Prime Minister by his own party – stunning Yaacov Herzog.[6] Levi Eshkol gave up the Defence portfolio and entrusted it to Moshe Dayan, a member of Ben-Gurion's Rafi Party. A national unity government was formed, including the leaders of Gahal (the Herut-Liberal bloc which would later be known as Likud), Menachem Begin and Yosef Sapir.

Yaacov Herzog warmly supported this national unity government. He had earlier urged Eshkol to add the leaders of Gahal and Rafi to the ministerial defence committee. According to Menachem Begin, 'the first suggestion put to Prime Minister Levi Eshkol to invite the leaders of the opposition parties Gahal and Rafi to the meetings of the ministerial defence committee came from Yaacov. It was he who advised Eshkol to make this unprecedented move. This led the way to the formation of the national unity government.

'Yaacov's sound instincts told him that the crisis was serious, that it was not the problem of just one or another party, one or another government coalition, but that it was actually a matter of saving the nation ... [Consequently] in the last week of May, the Prime Minister invited us to join the first session of the ministerial defence committee ... After a few days there was a discussion about forming a national unity government. I know that Yaacov was instrumental in getting this proposal accepted both by the Prime Minister and by some of the senior members of the government.'[7] When the new government was formed, Begin embraced Herzog and thanked him warmly for his part in bringing it about.[8]

However, Herzog was not among those who called for military action, preferring instead to explore all political avenues. He misread the position of the Great Powers – early in the crisis he warned those who called for military action that if war broke out between Israel and Egypt, the UN Security Council would stop the fighting immediately. 'This time, unlike the Sinai [campaign], there will not be enough time to defeat the Egyptian army.'[9] He proposed a number of diplomatic moves to the Prime Minister, that could lead to an Anglo-American initiative to solve the crisis.[10] On 25 May, using the roundabout approach he sometimes favoured, Herzog suggested to Yitzhak Rabin that he ask Abba Eban to find out to what extent the United States was prepared to implement the written undertakings it had given Israel in the past.[11] On 30 May a proposal was made to send the head of the Mossad, Meir Amit, to Washington, to meet the head of the CIA and find out what America's real position would be if Israel attacked Egypt. At first Herzog opposed the idea and proposed a rather intricate diplomatic manoeuvre before agreeing to send Meir Amit.[12] (In fact, the outcome of Amit's visit to Washington was the government's decision to go to war.)

Herzog was gravely concerned about the prospect of war with

Egypt.[13] Speaking with Eliezer Livneh, who was involved in the ideologically hawkish wing of the Labour Party and was calling for immediate military action, he explained the alternatives facing Israel and asked, 'What happens if, when we attack, the Russians send assistance in the form of planes and missiles to the defeated Egyptian forces? ... ' He also stated that 'the war would be total, and there will probably be more civilian than military casualties'. But when Livneh asked him point-blank for his own opinion, Herzog sidestepped the question. 'I refused to express my opinion on which alternative should be followed, saying that I only expressed my opinions officially.'[14]

But though he supported a national unity government, Herzog was not in favour of giving Moshe Dayan the Defence portfolio, and suggested to Eshkol that he appoint Dayan as his military advisor.[15] Relations between Herzog and Dayan were cool, and it seems that Herzog did not know how to deal with this shrewd, rough-edged, charismatic fighter. Nevertheless, as his journal shows, he was not dismayed when Dayan became Defence Minister. 'Moshe Dayan sat at the opposite end of the room from the PM, beside the military maps. The PM has undergone a marked change. In the past fortnight his speech was hesitant and he seemed to be cracking under the burden of responsibility ... He seemed to lose his self-confidence, his eyes lost their usual brightness. His statements and instructions did not seem to emanate from his inner person but were a kind of conditioned reflex. Today was the first time that he stood straight and spoke clearly. Now and then he glanced at Moshe Dayan, and it seemed that the latter's presence inspired him with confidence, and his face suddenly filled out.'[16]

Once the national unity government was formed, it decided to attack Egypt. On 5 June, Israel's armoured divisions invaded Egypt, while her air force destroyed the air forces of Egypt, Syria and Iraq while still on the ground. Two messages were sent to Jordan – one through General Odd Bull, the chief UN Observer in the region, and the other through Colonel Daud, Jordan's representative in the Israeli-Jordanian armistice commission – asking King Hussein to stay out of the fighting. However, the King ignored the appeal; instead the Jordanian air force attacked Israel, and Jewish Jerusalem was heavily shelled by Jordan's artillery. Consequently, the IDF also went to war against Jordan, destroying her air force and defeating her forces in the West Bank. Later the IDF attacked Syria on the Golan Heights.

The battles ended six days later, with Israel victorious on all fronts. The IDF conquered all the Sinai Peninsula and positioned itself along the Suez Canal in the south and along the Jordan River in the east, while in the north it captured the Golan Heights. The whole of Jerusalem and the entire West Bank was now in Israel's hands.

Throughout the war Yaacov Herzog was at Eshkol's side, participating in most of the political and military consultations, and directing the tactical and diplomatic strategy from the Prime Minister's office. He presented the Prime Minister with evaluations and situation assessments; but being a civil servant, not an elected representative, he was neither asked nor tried to make policy.

There was an essential difference between his work with Eshkol during the 1967 war and his role at Ben-Gurion's side in the Sinai campaign. In 1956 he was never asked if he thought Israel should launch military attacks – he was placed in a situation, when Israel had already resolved to go to war, and was expected to deal with the political fallout from that decision. By contrast, in May 1967, he had to advise the Prime Minister not only on policy, but also on the fateful decision whether to go to war or not. Herzog was not an advisor on warfare – he was well-versed on the political front, and recoiled from a war that might cost numerous lives. Therefore his advice to Eshkol was for political rather than military action, and his part in the crucial decisions of June 1967 was consequently much smaller. But once the war had begun, he responded excitedly and thought that Israel should also conquer Amman.[17]

For Herzog, the capture of East Jerusalem was the fulfilment of a dream. When the fighting was over, he was the one to coin the phrase 'the city that has been reunited'. Shortly after the war, while praying at the Western Wall, he was spiritually and religiously moved. 'The splendour of antiquity and splendour of continuity,' he wrote, 'permeated the place as hundreds, if not thousands, of Hassidim and Eastern Jews prayed at the Wall and the gates of heaven.'[18] He felt that Israel's liberation of the city was an act of God, and viewed its reunification in spiritual and religious terms.

'The problem of Jerusalem,' he explained to an Italian visitor, 'is not essentially political, and to depict it as such is not only to diminish it but to change its very nature. Even among us Israelis many have still not fully grasped what happened to us on the 6th of June 1967. Do you imagine that we entered the Old City because Hussein drove us to it by attacking us, and that now it belongs to us by right of conquest? If that was the reason we could even give it back. Jerusalem experienced seventeen different conquerors, not one of whom lasted long, because each conquest was a temporary action. Jerusalem is beyond time, it belongs to the Scriptures – that is, to eternity. We must prevent history and geography from re-dividing it like another Berlin. That is the true meaning of the war of '67. We may withdraw from Sinai, Gaza and the Golan, and – to carry it *ad absurdum* – you might say that we could even make the Arabs a gift of Tel Aviv, Haifa, Beersheba, Eilat, the Negev and all of Israel, but we can never renounce the unification of Jerusalem. That's the one irrevocable thing. For two thousand years we remained Jews, God knows at what cost, not to create the State of Israel, but to restore Jerusalem to itself and its destiny. The victory was not achieved by the army in battle – it was given to us by God, who led us in a few decades from the camps of Auschwitz to Jerusalem.' The Italian friend noted: 'This was not the director-general of a ministry speaking, but a prophet.'[19]

Herzog's chief contribution to the dramatic aftermath of the Six

Day War was to renew contact with King Hussein. Their secret meeting on 2 July 1967 was one of the high points in Yaacov Herzog's political career. Yaacov at this time was at the zenith of his powers, a senior figure in Israel's government, and profoundly moved by the historical events he had just experienced at first hand. He was now facing a fateful interview with King Hussein, four years after their first meeting, and was entrusted with the tremendous responsibility of finding out from the Hashemite King if it was possible to make peace between their countries.

Herzog went to London on 26 June, and waited six days for the King to come from Jordan. Finally Hussein arrived, and on 2 July visited some of the war wounded in a London hospital, then went to Dr Herbert's surgery, to find Herzog waiting for him. This was their fifth meeting. Herzog now saw a sad, resigned man, who nevertheless did not express either bitterness or anger about his defeat. In Herzog's words, Hussein seemed 'both depressed and relieved ... He had lost the war and a good part of his kingdom, but for the first time he had real status in the Arab leadership, his loyalty to the Arab nation was no longer in doubt, his motives no longer suspect ... He was both gloomy and unconcerned, thoughtful yet conversational, both broken and hopeful.'[20]

Herzog began by assuring King Hussein that their contacts would remain as confidential as in the past. He also conveyed personal greetings from the Prime Minister and Foreign Minister: 'We understand the pressure he is under, and regret the loss of life and the suffering on his side.' Then he asked the King to 'clarify his thoughts' about the future.

Hussein began by speaking about the war. 'In your place I'd have acted the same way.' For the past few years he had understood that war was inevitable, given Israel's political and strategic difficulties. The Arabs had made great mistakes, he said, as he had warned them time and again. He, too, bore some responsibility, since he had not made sufficient efforts to impress his warnings upon the

Arab leaders. After the war he had proposed a summit to formulate a unified Arab position, but the Arab leaders had rejected it. Now he thought such a summit would soon be held, and if it failed to reach agreement, each state would be free to act as it wished.

Herzog was surprised by Hussein's presentation of events. 'We never intended to launch a war,' he protested. 'We didn't need it. For years we only prepared for an attack against us.' He also denied that Israel had intended to attack Syria, as the Arabs maintained. Then he described the chain of events that gave Israel the feeling that 'the noose was tightening around our neck'. Israel had no choice but to launch a defensive war. Nevertheless, he insisted that when the fighting had begun Israel had not intended to take military action against Jordan, and he spelled out the messages conveyed to Jordan on the morning of 5 June, which stressed that if Jordan stayed out of the fighting, Israel would not attack it.

'There are two main points that the Arab leaders have never understood,' Herzog went on. One, that all Jews are responsible for one another, and an attack on any Jew is seen as an attack on the entire people. 'We cannot live our lives in Tel Aviv or Jerusalem while farmers are being murdered on the border.' The second point the Arabs had failed to understand was the link between the people of Israel and their land. They saw the Jews as a nation of refugees, they regarded the Jewish national movement as an artificial, rootless creation, and failed to see that their return to the land 'represented the eternal link of the Jews to the Land of Israel'.

Hussein addressed first the circumstances that had led up to the outbreak of war. He revealed that a summit meeting in Morocco in 1965 had resolved to be ready 'within three years'.

'Ready for what?' Herzog broke in.

Hussein was nonplussed for a moment, then said, 'Ready to talk to you as equals.' It was obvious that the real meaning of the Morocco resolution had been to be ready to go to war with Israel in three years. Hussein also revealed the reason: 'It was estimated that within three years Israel would have non-conventional weapons.' During those three years it was necessary to strengthen the Arab armies, solve inter-Arab disputes and create a joint command. But this was not done. The operations of the 'Fatah' movement were also contrary to the summit decision to wait and prepare.

Hussein spoke bitterly about Israel's harsh policy towards Jordan when he was unable to prevent terrorists from crossing the border. 'Then came the Samua operation,' he said, noting that the Israeli attack had taken place only a few days after Israel had thanked him for acting to curb the terrorists. 'The Samua operation shook him,' Herzog noted. 'Our actions convinced him that to us there is no difference between Syria and Jordan, despite the fact that we ourselves announced that the command and control over "Fatah" were in Syria.' This left Hussein no choice but 'to draw his own conclusions'. When he visited Nasser, the Egyptian President persuaded him that Israel was preparing to go to war against Syria. 'As an Arab, I had no choice but to prepare.' Hussein firmly denied that the Arab states had had any intention of going to war against Israel. 'One of the great failures of the Arabs is the confusion between words and deeds.'

Hussein sounded defensive when he said that he had advised the other Arab leaders to act with moderation. He also stated categorically that Saudi forces had never entered Jordan, and only one Iraqi division had done so.

'But there were Egyptian commando units in Jordan,' Herzog interjected, 'and the Egyptian General Riad was given a command over Jordanian units.'

Hussein did not respond to this, but went on: 'Your message to General Bull reached me when our aircraft were already in the air. But even if it had arrived earlier, it wouldn't have done any good. My planes were sent to attack military targets, mainly air force bases, to restore the balance broken by your aerial attack on Egypt.'

'What about the shelling of Jerusalem?' Herzog asked.

Hussein seemed taken aback and retorted that he had instructed his forces to attack only military targets. He admitted that he had ordered them to seize Mount Scopus*, which overlooked strategic routes. 'I did not order the shelling of Jerusalem.' He said bitterly that in such a situation no one is ever in complete control of all the forces in the field. The shelling of Jerusalem, he went on, must have been a response by local forces to Israel's attack on Amman's airport. Hussein estimated that Israel had won thanks to three main factors: her air force, military intelligence, and troop mobility. Israel had demonstrated impressive organizational ability and the capacity to move forces from place to place at great speed. Israel's striking force in the air and on the ground was tremendous, he admitted, and the Jordanian forces had felt it. 'That's war,' he concluded sadly.

Herzog praised the Jordanian army 'which had fought bravely', and summarized: 'What is done is done,' he said. 'Now what about the future?'

King Hussein repeated that he was calling for an Arab summit, which he hoped would result in a unified Arab position.

'Our direct contact and friendship compel me to speak frankly,' Herzog said. 'Does Your Majesty seek unity in order to prepare a fresh aggression, or to make peace? This is a crucial question for us. With all respect, I must ask for a clear answer.'

Hussein hesitated a little. 'The extremists,' he said, 'have one way, I have another. I must tell you frankly' – here his voice became firm and strong – 'it has to be a peace with honour and nobility. When you spoke before about the historical link with the land – I have understood it for some time, but others haven't. It's the most difficult obstacle for the Arabs ... Not only have you rights – we also have rights. Don't drive us into a corner ... Be aware of our feelings, treat us with respect and understanding. The

---

* An Israeli enclave in Jordanian Jerusalem, under the terms of the 1949 armistice agreement signed between Israel and the Hashemite Kingdom.

region is now at a crossroad. I hope we choose the right path. So much depends on you.'

Herzog analysed the alternatives to peace, and elaborated on the idea that, following the failure of Nasser and the Syrians, it was time for the moderate Arab leaders to speak about peace. Hussein had spoken of peace with honour and nobility, but he must 'tell me formally that he is willing to start negotiations for peace'. So long as he did not say this, Herzog could not discuss any details of a peace settlement. 'I've been sent informally to find out Your Majesty's thoughts about it.'

Nevertheless, he outlined for King Hussein a number of ideas about a possible solution – an economic union between Israel and the Hashemite Kingdom leading to a confederation, with a joint effort to solve the problem of the refugees. With substantial foreign investment, and friendship between the two states, Herzog prophesied, the two countries could become 'the garden of the world'. He urged Hussein to call publicly, together with other Arab leaders, for peace with Israel.

Hussein did not refer to the West Bank and Jerusalem, and Herzog had the impression that he did not wish to hear Israel's position on the subject, preferring to leave it open. He tried halfheartedly to defend Nasser, saying, 'He's no longer the man he was, and after what happened Nasser will not decide the fate of the Arab nation.'

Herzog spoke about the dangers of a new confrontation and the implications of a new arms race which would accelerate Soviet penetration into the region and pose a tangible threat to King Hussein and other moderate Arab regimes. He voiced his amazement that Hussein had survived so many threats against his life. 'In 1958 I was told in Washington that Your Majesty was likely to be assassinated at any moment.' He described Hussein's survival as 'symbolizing the search for a new Arab destiny', and noted that, in contrast to Nasser and the Syrians, Hussein had developed a form of 'social progress rooted in Islamic tradition'. He spoke about the billions of dollars wasted on weapons and the heaps of smashed weaponry spread over six kilometres in the Mitla Pass in the Sinai. 'Will the path of aggression and tension remain the path of the Middle East, or shall we join hands to build a new Middle East?'

'Give me a little time,' said King Hussein. 'I shall not hesitate to press my views and make them public.'

As usual, at this stage of the conversation, Herzog summed up its main points. 'King Hussein seeks to organize a summit meeting in which to formulate a unified move towards making peace. If he does not succeed, he will feel free to act unilaterally with regard to Israel.'

Hussein nodded agreement and, in conclusion, he said he was grateful for the decision taken that morning by the Israeli government to allow the refugees who had fled to Jordan to return to their homes in the West Bank. Then they discussed technical details and agreed on a code for future contact. Hussein said, smiling, 'Perhaps there will be no need for secrecy, and we may meet openly.' He added that 'despite everything that has happened, my people are not bitter'.

They parted with a warm handshake.[21] Herzog hastened to report to Jerusalem that he had agreed with the King to wait for the outcome of the Arab summit – if one were held – and that Hussein would notify Israel, via Dr Herbert, if he was ready for peace negotiations.[22]

Their next meeting, however, was bogged down in complications. In mid-July 1967 the US secret services proposed that Israel arrange a meeting with King Hussein in Europe. The Americans were unaware of the secret Herzog-Hussein channel. Herzog advised Eshkol against the intervention of a third party in the negotiations with Hussein, and together with the Prime Minister, sought feverishly for a way to turn down the proposal. Luckily the Americans withdrew it, sparing the Israeli government a serious headache.[23]

In August, G., a Jewish friend of Israel, came to the economic conference in Jerusalem. He informed Herzog and Eshkol that he had talked with the Aga Khan, leader of the Muslim Ismailia sect, the son of Ali Khan and the American film actress Rita Hayworth, and one of the wealthiest men in the world. The Aga Khan, who lived in Switzerland, had told him that he had met the King of Jordan, who 'was willing to make a deal with the Israelis'. The Aga Khan offered his villa in Switzerland for a secret meeting between Israeli and Jordanian representatives. Herzog again advised Eshkol to sidestep the offer, and the Prime Minister agreed 'to stick to the traditional formula of saying we were willing to meet Hussein himself at any time he wished'.[24]

No sooner did G. depart, than another friend of Israel arrived – Julian Amery, the former British Minister of Aviation. The Amery family had been in Tory politics for generations, and was traditionally friendly with Israel. When Julian Amery was in the government, he had been involved with the Israeli operation in the Yemen, which Yaacov Herzog had coordinated. At that time Britain was actively helping the forces of the Imam in the Yemeni civil war. Amery was also a close friend of King Hussein, and soon after the 1967 war he was asked by the latter to explore Israel's peace terms.

Amery arrived in Jerusalem entrusted with this mission but, like the Americans, he was unaware of Herzog's secret meetings with Hussein. Hearing Israel's official response he said to Herzog he was 'surprised that we didn't understand that Hussein could not meet us'.[25] He also met the Minister of Defence Moshe Dayan, the Foreign Minister Abba Eban and the head of the Mossad Meir Amit, and held talks with Israel's Ambassador to London Aharon Remez.

From that point on, a prolonged imbroglio grew around the issue of meeting King Hussein, involving personal interests, rivalry among Israeli leaders, the selfish impulses of government ministers, as well as bureaucratic pettiness and continual external pressure.

It began with Eban's decision – which greatly annoyed Herzog – that it was he who should meet Hussein. On his way to the UN General Assembly in New York Eban, with the active help of Ambassador Remez, met Julian Amery and talked to him about such an interview with the King.

Herzog came to London in October and told Dr Herbert that the Israeli government was still waiting for King Hussein's reply to the question of negotiations following the Arab summit, which had already taken place. This was a discreet message to Hussein that the channel to Israel was still via the doctor and Yaacov Herzog. But while Herzog was in London, Julian Amery returned from Amman and reported that Hussein wished to meet Moshe Dayan. 'Charles said to Amery,' Herzog noted,[26] 'that Hussein wanted to meet Dayan, not to negotiate but to hear his views. He wants a soldier-to-soldier meeting, and regards Dayan as the soldier who beat him.'

Eban, whose relations with Dayan were fraught with distrust, immediately said to his colleagues that 'Hussein can't decide which of us will meet him.' Herzog reported Hussein's request to Eshkol, but the Prime Minister, who viewed Dayan with profound suspicion, did not approve of the Minister of Defence meeting King Hussein. When Eban saw Eshkol and Herzog in Jerusalem on 16 October, he expressed vehement opposition to a meeting between Dayan and Hussein. Speaking privately with the Prime Minister, Herzog said, 'I can't enter into political considerations, but knowing Hussein, it seems to me that Dayan is the most suitable person to meet him.' He added that there was another problem – Julian Amery had told him that 'Hussein said he has no interest in meeting Eban.'[27] But for once Eshkol rejected Herzog's advice and remained opposed to letting Dayan meet Hussein.

Eventually a consultation between Eshkol, Eban, Dayan and Herzog resolved that there would be no meetings with Hussein through Julian Amery's mediation. Eban supported the decision, arguing that Amery was sure to report to the British secret service or the government, while Dayan agreed because Israel did not know whether Hussein had asked Amery to arrange the meeting, or vice-versa. The problem now was how to tell Amery that there would be no meeting. The former minister was naturally deeply offended by the refusal.

Offers for mediation began to arrive from all quarters. The English-Jewish magnate Marcus Sieff met Hussein's brother Mohammed and reported to Herzog that the Algerian president Houari Boumedienne 'supported Hussein's policy of seeking a political solution'. Lord Rothschild confided to Herzog that 'it would be possible to arrange a meeting for him with Hussein.' In response, Herzog revealed his true opinion: 'Time is on our side,' he said. 'There's no hurry, the government has not yet decided. Any decision at this time could cause a crisis.' He advised Rothschild to let the matter rest. Herzog also said to Meir Amit that 'it is in our interest to put off the meeting with Hussein as long as possible'. Amit and Dayan concurred.[28] Herzog also insisted that any settlement 'should at least secure our historical rights in the West Bank'.[29]

In retrospect it seems that it was the Israeli government's policy in 1967 and the first half of 1968 not to make any moves in relation to King Hussein, both in order to gain time on the international front, and to avoid upsetting the national unity government. Herzog's own views were quite hawkish, as his natural propensity for negotiation and compromise was overcome by his religious and historical concept of the link between the Jewish people and the Land of Israel. He could not give up his dream of realizing the Jewish historical claim to the country, and the possession of ancient Jewish sites on the West Bank of the Jordan and in Jerusalem.

He became a fervent supporter of intensive Israeli settlement in the West Bank, arguing that it held the key to a future arrangement with Jordan, and he kept saying this to Eshkol.[30] He said much the same to Dayan. 'I firmly believe,' he said, 'that we should use the time to carry out extensive settlement, and that only in this way shall we eventually come to an arrangement with Hussein.'[31] In 1968 he said to Chaim Bar-Lev: 'Our biggest mistake was not using the time to carry out widespread settlement in the West Bank, because in my opinion that is the only key to an eventual accord.'[32]

This argument may seem strange if one assumes that Herzog was interested in reaching a peace agreement with King Hussein fairly quickly. Had he been in favour of Jewish settlement as a cynical ploy, as a warning to Hussein that if he did not hasten to make peace he would lose the entire West Bank, he would have allowed for the possibility of dismantling settlements – which he would not countenance. Nor could he have imagined that 'creating facts on the ground' would lead to a Jewish majority in the West Bank – he was far too clear-headed for such wishful thinking. In the author's opinion, his strong support for settlement arose from his deep messianic aspiration to use the victory of 1967 to renew the connection of the people with the land and to encourage the return of the Jewish people to their ancient homeland everywhere west of the Jordan River.

Perhaps Israeli policy at the time was mistaken, driven, as it was, by Dayan's vague dreams of annexation and Eshkol's fear that Gahal would withdraw from the unity government. Or, on the other hand, with Hussein still in shock over the loss of the jewel in his crown, and the other Arab states still stunned by their defeat, it might have been possible to persuade Hussein to make some concessions in return for Israel showing greater flexibility, and thus achieve an accord of sorts.

But no one was advocating this position, except an interministerial committee created by the Prime Minister after the war to study possible solutions on the Jordanian front. The committee consisted of Moshe Sasson and Shaul Bar-Haim from the Foreign Ministry, David Kimche from the Mossad, and Chaim Herzog from the Ministry of Defence. The committee was chaired by

Yaacov Herzog. It submitted a report on 20 July 1967, recommending negotiations with Jordan, and even seeking 'a mutual defence agreement to protect the kingdom of Jordan and deter an Arab invasion or a local revolution, by giving the IDF the automatic right to cross the Jordan River in the event of a hostile change undermining the peace accord.'[33]

But these recommendations were never adopted. They were too detached from the political realities in Israel and Jordan alike – no serious person could envisage a peace agreement between Israel and Jordan in which the latter would agree in advance to the entry of the IDF in cases of emergencies or unrest. It also seems that the recommendations were in conflict with Herzog's personal opinion on settlement, reflecting the bi-polarity of his thinking – moderate policies versus activist Zionism. It appears that the 1967 war removed Yaacov Herzog from Sharett's school of thought, which would continue to be supported by Abba Eban.

Not long after the war Herzog outlined his own peace plan. Its main points were: the Jordan River to be Israel's legal boundary in the east; the West Bank to be ruled jointly by Israel and Hussein; Israel, Jordan and the West Bank to become an economic union and a political confederation; Jordan to have special status in Jerusalem, which would remain reunified under Israeli sovereignty.[34] He also upheld Israel's 'historical link' to the West Bank, which he believed entitled her to build settlements throughout her territory. These were strong positions and remote from the dovish camp in Israel. The war had indeed changed Herzog's ideas. Not long after the war he met his friend Eli Eyal at a dinner in New York. 'Suddenly he said to me,' Eyal recalled, '"You know, I was brought up in the Weizmann and Sharett school of thought, but it seems they were mistaken." He thought that the crushing victory in the war had vindicated Ben-Gurion's activist school of thought.'[35]

On 1 November, Herzog again flew to London. The local correspondent of Israel's news agency 'Itim' recognized him at the airport, but accepted his explanation that he was on his way to Geneva in connection with preparations for the economic conference. King Hussein had arrived in London the day before, and when the doctor asked him if he would agree to meet Herzog, he accepted. But when Herzog arrived in London and asked Dr Herbert to arrange the meeting, Hussein unexpectedly refused without an explanation. Perhaps they would meet when he returned from New York, he said, 'but the question was, would there be anything to meet about?'[36] Interviewed by David Frost on the BBC that evening, the King rejected Prime Minister Levi Eshkol's public proposal that they meet either in Jerusalem or Amman. Herzog returned to Jerusalem empty-handed, leaving a message for Hussein through his doctor that the channel for negotiations remained open.

On 4 November, Herzog reported to the Prime Minister about his journey. 'When I told him that the lawyer [the code-name for Dr Herbert] also suggested that Dayan come to a meeting [with Hussein] the following week, and that I, as I've already said, think that it would be good for Dayan to do so, he did not respond. I sensed that the idea displeased him. I did not hesitate to criticize Eban. He talked intimately with Julian [Amery] before his journey to Amman, yet when Julian proposed a meeting with Dayan, Eban argued that Julian could not be trusted not to reveal the contact and its substance to the British government. The PM agreed that Eban's conduct was improper.'

It is evident that Herzog often distrusted Eban's statements and telegrams,[37] and did not hesitate to criticize him to Eshkol. This was an extreme and exceptional attitude in this otherwise gentle and reserved man. It is not altogether impossible, as some of their acquaintances have suggested, that there was a latent rivalry between them. They both sprang from the same Anglo-Saxon background, both were talented diplomats and brilliant speakers, both were at home in the intricacies of international politics, but Eban had risen in the hierarchy to the position of Foreign Minister and deputy Prime Minister, while Herzog's abilities had not been given their full scope. It is possible that Herzog's criticism of Eban, which continued for years and was expressed on many occasions, stemmed from his unhappiness about this state of affairs, and his inward feeling that had matters been left to him rather than Eban, the outcome would have been better.

Herzog was keenly interested in the reports about Eban's unfortunate journey to Paris and Washington on the eve of the 1967 war, and gathered testimonies that Eban had not spoken to Johnson as he should have, or that Johnson had failed to understand him. He also had several meetings with the author of this book, who argued in *The Longest Month*, published at the time, that Eban's reports to the government on his meetings with world leaders were inaccurate. In his journal Herzog also quoted a statement made by the French Foreign Minister, Maurice Couve de Murville, to Nahum Goldmann. 'Couve explained that the reason for General de Gaulle's anger [with Israel] was his impression that we would not attack, on the basis of which he had strongly urged Nasser not to attack either.'[38] Though Eban was not mentioned, it was obviously a reference to Eban's meeting with de Gaulle, in which the French President had explicitly warned Israel not to launch a war, to which Eban had replied in vague terms.

Herzog also recorded in his journal a conversation with his sister-in-law, Aura Herzog, who came to him on the eve of the war, 'to ask that the government be expanded, and not to pay attention to the comments of her relative A. E. [Abba Eban], which she considered to be unfounded, given his lack of contact with reality. At the time I advised her to speak with A. E. Now she told me that following our talk she had met her sister [Susie Eban] and expressed her concern. Aura argued that Rabin did not have the necessary daring, and that only Dayan could lead the army to victory. Susie argued that after the war he would become a dictator, and Aura replied that the main thing was to avert the danger. Susie then announced that she had presented herself before A. E. in a state of collapse, in order to get through to him, and had told him what people thought about his policy; she maintained that her words had had an effect.

'Aura also said that she was still worried about A. E.'s assessments. "He's a brain but not a man, and lacks character." She believes he cannot be changed.'[39]

Herzog's journal also hints at his disappointment that Eshkol refused to allow Dayan to meet King Hussein. This was one of the few occasions when the Prime Minister rejected Herzog's advice. One cannot help but wonder how things might have turned out had Dayan met Hussein at this stage of Israel's contact with the King. But Eshkol was bitter and suspicious about Dayan – he could not forgive him for taking the Defence portfolio from him, or for his rebellious behaviour during the Six Day War. Herzog sympathized with Eshkol's feelings, but he thought Eshkol had lost the Defence portfolio not because of Moshe Dayan's manipulations, but because of Rabin's weakness. After the war he was told by Moshe Zack, of *Maariv*, that Ben-Gurion had advised Eshkol not to appoint Rabin as Chief of Staff (in fact, the opposite was true). Herzog noted, 'Perhaps if Eshkol had listened to BG [not to appoint Rabin], he would now be wearing the victor's garland.'[40]

After the 1967 war, there were several occasions when Eshkol showed extreme hostility to Dayan. Herzog had to use all his skills to include the Minister of Defence among the persons named by the Prime Minister in a solemn speech at the Knesset after the war. (Herzog added, on his own initiative, the concluding words, '... thanks to the Lord and saviour of Israel,' and regarded this as the most significant amendment he had made).[41] Eshkol also tried to take responsibility for the Dimona nuclear reactor away from Dayan, because of his conduct in the war, particularly his unauthorized decision to attack Syria.[42] When the economic conference was held in Jerusalem, Eshkol did not want Dayan to address it, and Herzog noted in his journal, 'I compelled Eshkol to accept it,' because the conference organizers had said that 'it is unthinkable that the visitors will not meet Dayan'.[43]

In December, the hostility between Eshkol and Dayan began to threaten the stability of the government. It climaxed when Dayan advised the Rafi Party convention to return to the fold of the Labour Party, and declared that he would endeavour to ensure that 'Eshkol would not be Prime Minister and Pinchas Sapir would not be Minister of Finance'. The leadership of the Labour Party was outraged, and many of its members called on Eshkol to sack Dayan. A compromise was eventually found and Eshkol and Dayan met to settle their differences. At one of their preliminary meetings, only Herzog was present, and when he rose to leave, Dayan passed him a note saying, 'Yaacov, don't leave Eshkol alone with me.'[44] Herzog stayed, and saved the meeting.

Abba Eban fought openly against Dayan, and also tried to prevent Shimon Peres from being included in a public-relations delegation that set out after the war.[45] His campaign against Dayan and Peres was backed throughout by Finance Minister Sapir. Herzog's attitude towards Dayan ranged from criticism and disapprobation to appreciation and even admiration. He could understand Eshkol's feelings, because Dayan had repeatedly offended him, but he admired the talents of the Minister of Defence. 'Slowly but surely,' he noted, 'the Minister of Defence is creating facts in the West Bank in accordance with his basic policy. This development is due not only to his personality and standing, but also to the fact that he offers clear suggestions while showing firmness and flexibility.'[46] While on a tour of Sinai, Herzog was impressed, if somewhat astonished, by the visible adoration of Dayan shown by thousands of soldiers, national servicemen and reservists alike.

There was another reason for Herzog's opposition to Eban, and for his support for a meeting between Dayan and King Hussein. Eban was seen as a 'dove', and was disposed to make far-reaching concessions on the West Bank in exchange for peace. Herzog opposed such concessions and found himself drawn to the hawkish wing of the government – Israel Galili, Yigal Allon, Moshe Dayan, sometimes even to Menachem Begin. He was determined to prevent or minimize Eban's part in the negotiations with Hussein. In the course of 1968 he made many clever moves to ensure that the negotiations with Hussein would eventually be conducted not by Eban alone, but by Eban and Yigal Allon. He also agreed with Galili and Allon on positions to be taken in future negotiations with Hussein, on keeping a sharp eye on Eban during the talks, and on presenting their own ideas. On one occasion Herzog expressed his true motives behind his talks with Hussein – not the achievement of peace, which he did not believe in, but a tactical move designed to gain time and reassure the outside world. 'Eban and I disagree,' he said to Allon. 'While Eban believes there is a chance [of peace with Jordan], I don't believe in it. I consider [the talks with Hussein] to be purely tactical.'[47] He said the same to Menachem Begin. 'I'm in favour of continuing the contacts with Charles [Hussein],' he said when visiting Begin at home, 'though I'm sure nothing will come of it.'[48]

The brilliant victory of the Six Day War effected a reversal in Herzog's mind. In the first days after the war he still thought that 'it's quite possible that we're missing opportunities with every passing day'.[49] But in conversation with the editors of the liberal daily *Haaretz* in January 1968 he stated, 'In my opinion we should not change our position regarding the West Bank – that is, there is no need to say more to the Americans than we have already said. In my opinion, where Jordan is concerned time is on our side.'[50] He said to Eshkol, 'I'm still of the opinion that we should not be hasty regarding Charles, and since October [1967] I have been opposed to renewing contact with him, because I think time is on our side. I'm not saying break off the contact, but there is no need to make substantive progress, and the more time passes the better it will be for us.'[51]

Only his determination to avoid a clash with the United States restricted Herzog's hawkish position. That is why he favoured negotiation and the adoption of a moderate position before the world, while at the same time continuing to build settlements and creating facts on the ground. In consultations he would express willingness to come to an arrangement not only with the King, but with 'a thousand dignitaries in the West Bank', if they would accept Israel's demands on the occupied territories and Jerusalem.[52] It is doubtful whether Hussein would have continued to talk to Herzog with such seriousness and conviction if he had known his true opinions. The passions which animated Herzog regarding the Land of Israel also affected his political stance. Having previously avoided giving Eshkol advice with a definite political slant, Herzog now began trying to persuade him to accept his opinion. He supported the Jewish settlements and once provoked anger from the dovish ministers by placing the settlement in Hebron on the government's weekly agenda. In this matter, too, the moderate Eban seemed to him an obstacle, and he opposed him time and again.

Looking back, it is difficult to avoid the impression that Herzog was so elated by Israel's possession of the historic areas of Judea and Samaria that it overwhelmed his political judgement – as it did with Dayan, Galili and others. Rather than use his talks with Hussein merely as a tactic and a means of gaining time, Yaacov Herzog, with his luminous mind, should have realized that this was a unique, historical opportunity to make peace with Jordan after the Six Day War. Curiously, it was Ben-Gurion, the bold activist, who said immediately after the war, 'In exchange for true peace, all the territories, except Jerusalem and the Golan Heights should be returned.' But the leaders of the State did not agree, nor did Yaacov Herzog.

Eventually Amery's pressure proved effective – Herzog agreed to the former Aviation Minister's arranging a meeting between him and King Hussein at his London house. The two met there on 19 November 1967. They tried to keep their host from realizing that they had met before, but Hussein made a slip – he asked Herzog if he had stopped smoking ... Later Amery said to Herzog that the remark showed that the two had known each other for some time.[53]

After an exchange of courtesies and some general talk about the intentions of the USSR in the region, Herzog said to King Hussein: 'After the war we had the impression that Your Majesty supports peace and that you wish to persuade your Arab colleagues to adopt a similar approach. Several months have passed, and I have been instructed by the Prime Minister to meet you and ask you if you are ready for direct negotiations and a peace accord.'[54]

Hussein confirmed that he had tried to persuade his Arab colleagues to agree to settle the conflict. The Khartoum conference had 'adopted general directives to search for a political solution'. He had talked with Gamal Abd al-Nasser and they agreed on a political line based on the following principles: (1) an end to fighting in all forms; (2) recognition of the existence of Israel; (3) the evacuation of Israeli forces from Arab territories; (4) freedom of navigation for Israeli shipping in the Suez Canal and the Straits of Tiran; (5) a solution to the problem of the refugees. In reply to Herzog's question, he explained that the proposal was a package deal, and that the reference to solving the problem of the refugees meant a move to start the process of solving it. Hussein added that this was real progress on the part of the Arabs, and that even the extremists among them were giving Nasser and Hussein a chance to follow this line through. But with regard to direct negotiations, he said that in this matter 'it is not permitted to act separately, but only from an all-Arab agreement'.[55]

Herzog refused to concede on this point. Without direct negotiations and a peace accord, he said bluntly, Israel had no interest in the King's proposals. 'We won't negotiate with a UN intermediary, except on his facilitation of direct negotiations towards a peace accord'. He asked the King if he realized that 'there could be no move on our part without negotiations and a peace accord.' Hussein said he did, and promised to try to persuade other Arab leaders to agree to direct negotiations. Herzog now proceeded to the next stage, built upon the first. Assuming he could not obtain Arab agreement, would he consider independent negotiations with Israel? The King replied that he was thinking about it, and asked if Israel would give him back the West Bank.

'I'm not authorized to say anything about the West Bank,' Herzog replied. 'I was sent to listen rather than speak.' But he added that there were three schools of thought in Israel. 'One is that Jordan has no claim to the West Bank, which it ruled by virtue of an unrecognized conquest. Another maintains that Israel must come to an arrangement with the Palestinians ... The third argues that for the sake of peace we should seek a settlement with King Hussein. This last school of thought also considers basic questions about long-term security, and the question of Israel's historical association with the West Bank, or at any rate with parts of it. The government has not yet decided, and there is no point in discussing it so long as peace is not on offer.'[56]

Hussein responded that he had made it clear to his Arab colleagues that if the inhabitants of the West Bank asked him to negotiate on their behalf, he would do so – in effect, agreeing to direct negotiations. Herzog seized on this and proceeded to the next stage. He asked the King to say frankly if his approach to the issue of the West Bank was rigid. The King replied that it was flexible.

Herzog promptly drew a conclusion from that response: 'Can I then report that the King is willing to consider a harmonization of what he describes as his right to the West Bank with Israel's security requirements and her historical association with it?'

Hussein hesitated a little, then said, 'Yes.' Then, in response to Herzog's statement about the Jewish people's historical association with the land, he asked morosely, 'And what are the boundaries of the land?'

It was another attempt to elucidate Israel's position on the West Bank, and Herzog again avoided it, saying he was not authorized to answer the question. Hussein then made a significant statement. The issue of Jerusalem, he said, could frustrate all hopes. To which Herzog made no response at all, 'because I wanted to give him the impression that Jerusalem is not even a subject for discussion'.[57]

In effect, by steering the conversation without spelling out Israel's position, Herzog obtained Hussein's consent to direct negotiations with the aim of reaching a territorial compromise with Israel. As always, Herzog summed up their dialogue; it was a very significant summary.

'Let me summarize Your Majesty's statements as I shall report them [to the Prime Minister].

'(1) Regarding a settlement, he [the King] favours ... a package deal, an end to armed conflict, recognition of [Israel's] right to existence, evacuation [of occupied territories], freedom of navigation and the initiation of a solution to the problem of the refugees.

'(2) He [the King] understands that we shall say to the UN intermediary that we shall first demand direct negotiations and a peace accord.

'(3) He understands that without direct negotiations and without a peace accord we shall not make any moves.

'(4) He will do his best to persuade his Arab colleagues to agree to direct negotiations.

'(5) At the same time, he is interested in additional confidential clarification of a possible separate settlement with him, especially on our position regarding the West Bank. Following an additional meeting like this one in a few weeks, he will decide if he can enter into direct negotiations and a peace agreement.'[58]

'I urge you not to recognize a Palestinian entity,' Hussein remarked.

'Is that a condition I should include in the summary?' Herzog asked.

The King said yes.

That was the end of the meeting. Left alone with Julian Amery, Hussein said that it had been a 'most important conversation'. It was, indeed, the most important dialogue to date, and certainly one of the most significant in the entire series of talks with King Hussein. Herzog had once again demonstrated a rare ability to lead his interlocutor step by step to the sought-for conclusions, just as he had done with Toynbee in their great debate. It seems that on this occasion he succeeded in bringing Hussein closer to Israel's position, and to stating his readiness to negotiate openly and to sign a separate peace accord, including a territorial compromise in the West Bank. Had it been utilized properly, that meeting might have been a breakthrough.

A few hours after the meeting, King Hussein asked Dr Herbert to arrange another, urgent meeting with Herzog. The two met again the following day and discussed the tension in the Beth-She'an area, in the north of Israel, following a 'Fatah' terrorist action. But it seems that Hussein's chief motive in calling for the second meeting was to disengage Julian Amery from their exchange. He said to Herzog that their future meetings must be arranged through Dr Herbert, and they agreed on methods of avoiding Amery in the future. At the end of the meeting Hussein approved the summary they had agreed on the previous day.[59]

Those two meetings, on the 19 and 20 November 1967, concluded an important chapter in Yaacov Herzog's life – his exclusive access to King Hussein. Thereafter other Israeli figures took part in these meetings as well. Abba Eban met the Jordanian King in May 1968, Eban and Allon met him in September that year, and a month later it was the turn of the Chief of Staff, Chaim Bar-Lev. In October, November and December 1968 and in early 1969, meetings were held with various Israeli representatives, some on board a ship near Eilat and Coral Island, and some in

London. The pace of the meetings accelerated – between May 1968 and May 1969 there were some 25 meetings with King Hussein, with his advisor Zaid a-Rifa'i or with both of them, and Herzog, the pivotal figure in these contacts, was present at all of them.

Scores of messages were also relayed during that year between the Israeli Prime Minister – first Levi Eshkol, and after his death Golda Meir – and the King, largely due to the tension on the front line between Israel and Jordan. 'Fatah' attacks from inside Jordan intensified, and Israel responded massively – with an attack on the town of Karameh, the bombing of the town of Salt, shelling and raids, which more than once prevented planned meetings. Herzog was very active in initiating and wording the messages from Eshkol and Golda Meir to Hussein, and wrote most if not all the Israeli letters.

But although Herzog still took part in all the talks with Hussein and his advisor, he now played second or third fiddle. When, during that year, he met the King or Zaid a-Rifa'i at the King's request, he was under explicit orders not to negotiate but only 'to listen to what they have to say'. When the two met in August 1968, he was instructed 'to listen ... and prepare a high-level meeting with Hussein.' (The 'high-level' meeting of Eban, Allon and Herzog with Hussein took place about a month later.)[60] The same applied to Herzog's meetings with Zaid a-Rifa'i in London – the two met several times, and in some of their meetings – for example, at the end of September 1968 – Jordan gave her response to Israel's proposals as presented by Eban and Allon. The to and fro of negotiations passed to the politicians, and the relationship with King Hussein was no longer exclusively Yaacov Herzog's.

16

A Gift from Hussein

Shortly after the war, a secret committee was appointed to devise ways to encourage Palestinian emigration to neighbouring Arab countries. Herzog set up the committee, and Ada Sereni chaired it. Herzog believed that everything should be done to persuade Palestinians from the West Bank and the Gaza Strip to emigrate across the Jordan River, and favoured the idea of paying them to do so. (Eshkol was rightly sceptical about the practicality of the idea.)[1] In fact, Herzog had for years favoured the 'assisted emigration of Palestinians'. As far back as 1957, ten years before the Six Day War, he wrote to Yosef Nahmias, deputy director-general of the Foreign Ministry, 'No doubt you remember my conviction that one of our main political goals must be the thinning of the refugee population on the West Bank, for an obvious reason that needs no elaboration.'[2] The emigration of Palestinian refugees was one of the additional issues that Herzog became responsible for, after the 1967 war.

It was also he who conceived and organized the economic conference of Jewish business people from all over the world, to encourage them to invest in Israel. He had first thought of it during the recession of 1966 – he wanted to bring to Jerusalem the economic élite of the Jewish people, to enlist their know-how and later their capital for commercial enterprises in Israel and to help promote Israeli exports. He had begun to work on the project, but the events of May-June 1967 had intervened. 'In June 1967,' said Avraham Avihai, 'the Six Day War overturned everything. We understood that we would be dealing with a different Jewish people, a different world, a different State of Israel. Then Dr Herzog suggested to the Prime Minister that we should bring fifty to sixty captains of industry and top scientists from all over the world to Jerusalem. They came enthusiastically and left even more elated. The first economic conference took place in April 1968. The atmosphere was electric ... Hearing the Israeli national anthem, "Hatikvah", and the song "Jerusalem of Gold", these Jewish magnates from all over the world shed tears, such was their exultation! And it was due to Yaacov's vision that this was a time for change.'[3] The conference, organized by Herzog together with the American Jewish leader, Sam Rothberg, laid the foundation for Israel's advanced technological industry that would later place her in the front rank of industrialized countries.[4]

Herzog also promoted a conference in Jerusalem that brought together leading Jewish scientists, following which a centre for scientific aid to African and Asian countries was established in Jerusalem.[5] That year, he was also responsible for the festivities marking the 20th anniversary of the establishment of the State of Israel, and incorporated some of these conferences into the planned events.

Herzog also visited the Vatican and oversaw the new relationship between Israel and the Holy See, which had undergone a profound change now that all the Christian holy places were in the hands of the Jewish State. He was keenly aware of the symbolic, spiritual and historic significance of the new relations between the Christian world and Israel. Herzog went to the Vatican with Israel's Ambassador to Rome, Ehud Avriel. 'We drove into the Vatican with the Israeli flag fluttering over the car,' Herzog noted in his journal. 'The Swiss Guards saluted. I remembered my visit to the Vatican in September 1948, and thought about the developments since that time.'[6] Herzog and Avriel were met by a group of cardinals, and the occasion became engraved in Herzog's memory. 'The cardinals sat down,' he wrote. 'There was a big argument about the future of Jerusalem. I saw that something had happened to them. They tried to convince me that during the War they did save Jews and that in Rome, they saved the community. They wanted to give an impression of moderation. They were trying to move us.' (In his journal he noted, 'Cardinal del Aqua argued passionately that one day Pius XII called him and said that it was necessary to save the Jews of Rome, and that if it took money, the Cardinal had to raise it no matter what. Avriel and I did not react.')[7] 'I sat there and marvelled about the miracle that this tremendous fortress that dominates six hundred million Catholics, whose edict spans continents and nations – yet here the Old City of Jerusalem is in our hands and [the Church] does not protest. I don't know if it's pragmatism, or concern for their institutions, or worry that we may give preference to the Eastern churches – but it is a fact, an amazing one.'[8]

Herzog described his Rome visit to some foreign journalists. 'The tone of his voice,' wrote an Italian journalist, 'his shining eyes and slight flush showed that the rabbi's son felt at home in the Vatican.'[9] Ironically, it was in the Vatican that he felt most comfortable explaining Israel's position on Jerusalem. 'The Vatican,' he said, 'is the place where you see Jerusalem in the true light of awe and sanctity. Everywhere else we have to justify our case by explaining that we've been here for two thousand years, a valid but feeble justification, not in keeping with the greatness of the occasion. Only in the Vatican do they know that we're here because otherwise our existence would have been futile. This does not mean that the Church acknowledges the political and diplomatic implications of this fact.'[10]

When he returned to Israel, Herzog went to see the Greek Patriarch Benedictus who received him cordially and reminded him that if he wished to discuss Jerusalem with the Christian world, he, the 96th Patriarch of Jerusalem, was the right person to address. The first Greek Patriarch, he emphasized, was appointed in 451, centuries before the Church of Rome appeared on the scene.[11] That day Herzog was also received by the Patriarch of the Armenian church, who reminded Herzog of his assistance to the Armenian church after the establishment of the State of Israel.

Herzog wrote in his journal, 'I was profoundly moved by both meetings. We have come to the point that the Christian leaders, in dealing with Jerusalem and their [holy] sites, are scrambling to negotiate with us, and depend on our decisions. From being Christianity's object of scorn and a symbol of [divine] punishment for many generations, we have become those who can decide their rights in this city, to which they have clung for about as long as we have been exiled from it. What an historical reversal, what a closing of the circle.'[12]

He continued to write brilliant speeches for Eshkol and the senior cabinet ministers, but an ironic climax was reached when the US Administration asked him to write a speech for President Johnson, who was due to address a Bnai Brith conference.

During those years Herzog also travelled a good deal on speaking and fund-raising tours. Once he dined with his old friend, Isaiah Berlin, the renowned philosopher and essayist. They discussed the situation in the Middle East, and Herzog noted, 'I found him generally out of touch with the real political facts. A very complex man, a genius who has achieved universal standing. He plays down his Jewishness, probably to avoid damaging his standing in Western culture, yet his Jewish roots keep showing.'[13]

At home, Herzog was also involved with religious issues that came up in the cabinet. As a member of the committee charged with rebuilding the Jewish Quarter in the Old City of Jerusalem, he played an important part in the construction of the Western Wall Yeshivah, and was subsequently among the originators of the 'special-status' Yeshivahs, which combined military service and religious study. He led the efforts to reconstruct four ancient synagogues in the Old City. Another issue associated with religion in Jerusalem was the right of Reform Jews to pray at the Western

Wall. A serious clash between the Reform and Orthodox rabbinates was prevented at the last moment. Another issue which was debated in the government was the question 'Who is a Jew?', which arose when the High Court of Justice proposed the removal of the 'nationality' clause in the population census (in which the term 'Jew' appears under 'nationality' as well as 'religion'). Here, Herzog's religious feelings overcame all other considerations, and he fought against the proposal with all his might. He was relieved when the government decided to reject it, and wrote, 'It was a weight off my heart.'[14]

Nevertheless, Herzog's main occupation at this time was contact with King Hussein and his representatives. The meetings took place twice a month on average, and usually required meticulous preparation, travel out of the country, and coordination with the Foreign Ministry, Israeli Ambassadors, the Mossad, the IDF and the Prime Minister. The utter secrecy surrounding these meetings meant that only Herzog and a handful of aides could know about and report on the meetings.

Herzog coordinated these talks with the Prime Minister and the ministers Yigal Allon and Israel Galili, and on at least one occasion he and Allon had to make political moves to block an unwanted initiative by Abba Eban.[15] Herzog opposed Eshkol's decision that Eban should be the only cabinet minister responsible for the meetings with Hussein. Hearing this decision, Herzog talked to some of the central figures in the government and pulled strings with exquisite finesse. He talked to Galili, Allon, Begin and Golda Meir, obtained their support and urged them to put pressure on the Prime Minister, leading Eshkol to add Allon to the talks with Hussein. Herzog and Allon became allies in a unified, activist front in the dialogue with Hussein, blocking Eban's more moderate approach. In September, when Eban presented a declaration of principles to Eshkol and Herzog in preparation for a meeting with Hussein, Herzog enlisted Galili's help to block it. Even in the course of an actual meeting with King Hussein, whenever Eban made a suggestion he did not like, Herzog 'whispered to Allon that it was risky and that he should propose putting it off until all the clarifications had been made ... Allon whispered back that he did not wish to hurt Eban, and I should do it.' Herzog then intervened and quashed Eban's idea.[16]

Relations between Herzog and Eban deteriorated after the war, for both personal and ideological reasons. Eban had promised Herzog to ask the Prime Minister to relieve him of the post of director-general of his office, and appoint him Ambassador to Washington, to succeed Abraham Harman. They talked about it several times and Eban confirmed the understanding. Herzog was therefore astonished to hear from Moshe Raviv – Eban's bureau chief – and from Eshkol, that Abraham Harman was returning and that Eban had already talked to Yitzhak Rabin about appointing him Ambassador to Washington. In the meantime, rumours about Herzog's forthcoming appointment circulated in the Foreign Ministry, and one of its officials, Simcha Dinitz, even asked Herzog to consider him as his minister in Washington, once he was appointed Ambassador.[17] 'After so many conversations with Eban before the war,' Herzog noted bitterly, 'I was surprised not to hear from him when he returned from the US.' But Herzog never knew how to fight for his own interests and immediately gave in, even trying to convince himself that it was all for the best. 'In point of fact, I was not especially sorry, because despite the great challenges in the US, I can be immeasurably more effective here, especially in view of the new situation, but I was puzzled by Eban's lack of sincerity.'[18]

In spite of this, Herzog's reserved, even hostile, reactions to Eban's ideas with regard to Hussein arose mainly from political and ideological considerations. 'On Monday, 18 November,' he noted, 'I contacted Galili and Allon and proposed we meet to compose a draft for the PM with suggestions for the meeting with Ch. [King Hussein], to avoid things being said by Eban that conflict with the agreed line ... My main purpose was to prevent Eban from proposing a meeting with Rifa'i (the Jordanian Foreign Minister – not Zaid a-Rifa'i, the King's advisor) in New York, a point on which we've been at odds since the end of September...'[19]

'Eshkol's instincts were hawkish,' said Ari Avner, one of his aides. 'When he heard Eban's analyses he had a gut feeling of disagreement, but could not find the arguments to rebut them. Yaacov Herzog found them for him.'[20]

Altogether, Eban was treated with glacial disapproval by Eshkol's entourage. Pinchas Sapir telephoned Herzog 'to protest vehemently that a campaign of "blood-libel" was being conducted against Eban, that the PM's office must react sharply, and Eban must be given bodyguards to protect him from physical harm.' Herzog reported Sapir's protest to Eshkol, who promised to take action. But when Herzog informed Sapir about the steps that Eshkol meant to take, 'he argued that it was not enough, and attacked me in front of the Minister of the Interior, crying out that "you people around Eshkol are accomplices in the blood libel against Eban." Later we met in the Eden Hotel and I furiously rejected his accusation, and he implicitly apologized.'[21]

As Eshkol's trusted advisor, Herzog was also responsible for smoothing relations between the Prime Minister and others. One who needed constant reassurance was Menachem Begin, the leader of Gahal (later the Likud), who repeatedly announced to Herzog that it was time for him to withdraw from the government because of the on-going talks with Hussein. Herzog met Begin many times in his office, in Begin's house and even over dinner at his own house, to reassure him that the talks with Hussein were only preliminary contacts and that no agreement would be concluded without the approval of the government. On 27 October 1968, the cabinet discussed Eban's proposed reply to the UN mediator Dr Gunnar Jarring, which seemed to imply a willingness to make territorial concessions. 'As we left the cabinet meeting,' Herzog noted, 'Begin asked me if he should withdraw [from the government]. I replied that Eban's suggestions had not been

A Gift from Hussein

adopted, and I couldn't understand why he should withdraw.'[22]

On 20 November and on several other occasions Begin appealed to him and threatened again to withdraw, but Herzog pacified him repeatedly.[23] Indeed, as time passed, it became clear that a separate peace with Jordan was not likely. For a while, both sides toyed with the idea that Israel and Jordan would conduct formal negotiations through Jarring, the UN mediator, while maintaining their secret channels, but this did not materialize. Hussein accused Israel, with some justification, of dragging out the talks to gain time in the international arena. He also grew suspicious because of Israeli military operations against terrorist targets in his territory (such as the Karameh operation in March 1968), in some of which the Jordanian Legion had to intervene. The King rejected Israel's ideas of territorial compromise, and would have nothing to do with the so-called Allon Plan, as proposed to him by the Deputy Prime Minister. Israel also began to build settlements in the West Bank, aggravating Hussein's resentment.

The Israelis, for their part, thought Hussein was playing a double game – appearing in his talks with them as a passionate advocate of peace, but in reality recoiling from any open move in that direction, preferring to hide behind Nasser or the Arab League. Nasser was hoping that by 1970 he would have recovered his military strength sufficiently to drive Israel out of the territories occupied in 1967. Despite his repeated promises, Hussein was unable to restrain the 'Fatah' organization, which by now dominated large chunks of his country, and it appeared that some Jordanian army units cooperated with it in clashes against Israel. Hussein probably feared attacks by other Arab countries if he dared make a separate peace with Israel. But the main obstacle to advancing the negotiations was Jordan's refusal to make territorial compromises and renounce her sovereignty over Jerusalem.

For some time the Israeli government thought that it might be possible to overcome these obstacles by an exchange of territories – the Gaza Strip in exchange for the Jordan valley, plus some border adjustments; IDF bases in the West Bank in exchange for an Arab Legion camp not far from Haifa ... But the gap between the two sides could not be bridged. Hussein also ruled out Israeli military bases along the mountain range in the West Bank as a security measure. Israel rejected a priori any solution that would restore the West Bank, or most of it, to Hussein.

Though he was no longer in charge of the dialogue with Jordan, Herzog continued to steer it skilfully. The talks became a regular feature. Herzog and his Jordanian interlocutors – Hussein himself and Zaid a-Rifa'i – exchanged messages and arranged meetings through Dr Herbert. The meetings were held in London or in the Gulf of Aqaba. Dr Herbert reported to Herzog the comments made by the King before and after the meetings. Julian Amery returned to play an important role in the negotiations. He received direct reports from the Jordanian side about the talks and conveyed the reactions of the King and his advisor to the Israelis.

The two sides used agreed codes in their messages, and Herzog especially enjoyed inventing them. Most of the codes were taken from the world of medicine, as though the two sides were exchanging messages about medical examinations, treatments and prescriptions – on account of Dr Herbert's role in the contacts. One of the codes referred to King Hussein as 'the patient', Israel's Prime Minister was 'Zondek' – after the famous physician – Herzog was usually 'Davis' and Abba Eban was called 'Sheba', after another well-known physician.[24] In correspondence with Dr Herbert arranging times and venues of meetings, telegrams were replete with references to 'medical tests', 'medical consultations', 'prescriptions' etc.[25] After one meeting with Hussein, Herzog sent him a telegram saying, 'It is the opinion of the two physicians who examined him, and of the hospital director [the Prime Minister], that it would be useful to continue the tests.'[26]

In July 1968, Herzog agreed with the Jordanians to hold the next meeting at sea in the Gulf of Aqaba, after which King Hussein might visit Israeli territory. He telephoned Eshkol to say,

A Gift from Hussein

'I've found in London a fishing company that is willing to enter business dealings in the south. We have to combine two fishing companies, and the head of the fishing company will come to us, and we shall have to entertain him. I want someone to come here from the city where Yosef Cohen is mayor [Eilat], someone subordinate to Moshe [a reference to a senior Navy officer] who took the place of Yohai [the previous commander of the Israeli Navy].'[27] This report caused quite a headache in the Prime Minister's office, and irritated Eshkol, who would have preferred a plain telegram ...[28] When it was decided to meet at Coral Island, Herzog agreed with Zaid a-Rifa'i that as the Jordanian ship approached, the Israelis would signal 'Moussa' and the Jordanians would signal back 'Davis', Herzog's code name.[29]

Herzog's preliminary talks always led to meetings at higher levels, first with Eban and Allon, and much later with Golda Meir and Moshe Dayan. Levi Eshkol refused to take part in these meetings while he was Prime Minister chiefly because he feared shaking the precarious national unity government – which annoyed and frustrated the Jordanians. Sometimes Herzog had to invent excuses for Eshkol's absence from the meetings. 'At the last encounter, when I was in Charles' boat on the way from the meeting point [Coral Island] to him, the advisor said he supposed the PM would be at the meeting, and I replied that the PM was ill and unable to attend.'[30]

Moshe Dayan also refused, but for a different reason – Eshkol did not allow him to meet Hussein on his own, and Dayan refused to be included in a delegation, in which he would play second or third fiddle. A strange situation arose – Hussein admired Dayan and made efforts to meet him. He said as much in his talks with Herzog and in messages conveyed through friendly governments, such as the British government.[31] But Dayan persisted in his refusal. In a meeting with the Prime Minister in January 1969, Dayan stated frankly that he was 'unsuited to our tactic of gaining time'[32] – meaning, that he would not take part in the policy adopted by Herzog, Eshkol and Galili, of holding talks with Hussein mainly to gain time for Israel to establish herself in the occupied territories, rather than to achieve a peace agreement, which they thought was unlikely. Dayan also argued that if he met Hussein and told him what he himself thought about a possible accord (the annexation of Jerusalem and of extensive stretches of the West Bank), Hussein would break off all contact with Israel. Hussein had to content himself with sending his book, *My War*, to Moshe Dayan's daughter Yael, who had sent him two of her novels.[33]

This state of affairs changed when Golda Meir became Prime Minister, and decided to meet Hussein, whom she knew from a previous meeting. She also persuaded Dayan, who submitted to her authority, to come with her. On several occasions when Hussein was disappointed or disheartened, Herzog managed to prevent the suspension, or even the total breaking-off, of contacts. He also worded the messages that Israel's Prime Minister forwarded to Hussein via a different channel, generally Israel's Ambassador in the US, who was unaware of the secret negotiations.

Herzog liked nothing better than his secret dealings. He was conscious of the great importance of his connection with Hussein, with whom he developed a friendly personal relationship and enjoyed a special status shared by no other Israeli. The records of their meetings show that the King valued and trusted him. Once in a cabinet meeting, Herzog described his view of Hussein. 'In July 1967 Hussein decided – in his heart he had always thought so – that he wanted to make peace. I think there are several reasons for it: he is first of all an Arab, yet his British upbringing gave him some sense of realism. Secondly, he has his grandfather's heritage, though it casts a shadow on him in terms of security, but it is there. Thirdly, I think he's a civilized man who dislikes war as a way of solving crises.'

Whenever he left to meet Hussein, especially in the Gulf of Aqaba, Herzog would don a peaked cap, sometimes leisure

A Gift from Hussein

clothes, and tell his family he was 'going fishing'.[34] Pnina knew very well what this meant, and Shira guessed.

It was Herzog who reported to the government on most of these meetings which, from May 1967, were sometimes held as frequently as twice a month and were his main occupation. Many of the meetings required his flying to London a few days in advance and returning a few days later, or reaching London after a roundabout tour of Europe, where he appeared on behalf of the UJA (United Jewish Appeal) or other organizations, by way of cover. But more than once he was recognized in the airport or on the plane, and had to make up a cover story.

Once Arieh Disenchik, the editor of *Maariv*, told him that on Independence Day, 2 May 1968, he had met Pnina Herzog at a dinner in the Knesset 'and asked about me.' Pnina had replied that Yaacov had flown to Geneva on UJA matters. 'He was puzzled that as chairman of the 20th anniversary [committee], I should leave the country directly after the parade in the morning. He checked and found out that there were no flights to Geneva, and concluded that there was something very secret and urgent going on, and thought of London. That day I travelled to meet Ch., and Eban flew in the following morning.'[35]

In the course of the meetings there were sometimes amusing incidents and gripping adventures. Once at a Friday dinner at the house of Rabbi Gaon in London, his host told him that not long before he had been ordered by his doctor to rest for a few days in a sanatorium, and who should occupy the adjoining room but King Hussein himself! The rabbi's wife was very anxious – 'What if Hussein were assassinated and her husband accused?' Herzog smiled and said that it must have been between Wednesday, 31 April and Saturday, 4 May. The two went pale, and concluded that Israeli secret agents had been following the King. 'I couldn't explain to them,' noted Herzog, 'that Hussein stayed there [in the sanatorium] till Saturday, to cover a meeting with Eban and me.'[36]

In October 1968, after exhaustive discussions, and despite

Dayan's angry opposition, the government decided to send the Chief-of-Staff Chaim Bar-Lev with Herzog to London, to put Israel's defence positions before Hussein, Zaid a-Rifa'i and the Jordanian Chief-of-Staff (whom Bar-Lev had met before). As instructed by the Mossad, Bar-Lev wore a wig and dark glasses, which turned the journey into an ordeal. The heavy wig bothered him, he misplaced his immunization card and the airport authorities at Heathrow insisted on his getting a new photograph there and then. At the Clive Hotel, where he and Herzog stayed, he discarded the detested wig, but every time a chambermaid knocked on the door he leaped up and put it on. When he and Herzog walked over to the Cumberland Hotel, they ran into a group of Israelis, among them Shimon Horn (formerly director of the North and South America investments authority), who gave them odd looks. Herzog promptly led poor Bar-Lev to a darkened room where he stayed until the military attaché arrived to take him to lunch.

When Herzog and Bar-Lev arrived at Dr Herbert's surgery, the good doctor was alarmed. 'Whom did you bring here?' he snapped at Herzog. Bar-Lev removed the wig and the incident ended in hearty laughter, and Herzog promised Mrs Herbert to bring her a similar wig from Israel. 'Not only was he disguised,' Herzog noted, 'Bar-Lev also slouched a little as he walked and looked like a beatnik, and I can only guess what the Israelis who saw us at the Cumberland must have thought.'[37]

Bar-Lev was equally unlucky a year later, when he came to London to meet Jordan's new Chief-of-Staff. He arrived in the heavy wig and glasses, and was again acutely uncomfortable. Before leaving, while lunching with Herzog and the Israeli military attaché, he noticed a man looking at him suspiciously. He had no doubt that the man recognized him, and the military attaché informed him that it was the IDF chief cantor, who was spending the High Holy Days in London.[38]

A few days after the talks in London, Herzog met Zaid a-Rifa'i

A Gift from Hussein

on board a ship in the Gulf of Aqaba, and even visited the town of Aqaba.[39] Later he thanked Dayan for making the arrangements for his visit to Jordan, and Dayan replied that 'he was glad I came back safe and sound.'[40]

On one of his secret trips to London, he made arrangements to meet a-Rifa'i, and telephoned him from the offices of Lord Thompson, the owner of *The Sunday Times*. He introduced himself as Dr Davis, and asked if he should bring 'another doctor'. The English guard who overheard him was 'somewhat alarmed', and asked, 'Isn't your name Herzog?' Yaacov assured him that it was indeed his name and that he had misunderstood what he had said about Davis.[41]

On 19 November, there was another meeting of Israelis with the Jordanian King aboard a ship near Eilat, followed by another meeting at Coral Island, which was recorded by the Israelis. Another meeting took place at sea on board Hussein's boat, on 20 February 1969, with Hussein and Zaid a-Rifa'i representing Jordan and Allon, Eban and Herzog representing Israel. They sat in a small stateroom which seated only four, and a-Rifa'i had to hover over the others. As at previous meetings of the Israeli trio with Hussein, Herzog refused to wear a hidden tape-recorder, but Allon wore one. 'Allon wore it,' Herzog noted, 'and looked a little bloated about the lungs.'[42] (The recording failed. The Jordanians also attempted to record some of the talks.)

The Jordanians served their Israeli guests sandwiches with meat and eggs, and Allon said to Herzog, 'It's all right to eat Muslim food. It's kosher.' But Herzog was not convinced and did not touch the food. 'You can eat it,' Eban joked. 'Don't worry, I won't tell your mother.'

In the course of the meeting, Eban looked for a pen to make some notes, and Hussein offered him his gold pen, engraved with the Hashemite crown. After the meeting he gave it to Eban as a gift. Feeling he ought to give Allon something too, he looked around and gave him 'some kind of rifle.' In the next few days

Eban showed the pen around, and only under pressure from fellow ministers and his own office staff did he put it away, but the damage was done. 'I was asked by Harif and Tzimuki [journalists from the dailies *Maariv* and *Yediot Aharonot* respectively] why I had not received a gift,' Herzog noted.[43] Hussein made a point of correcting the 'omission' – at Herzog's next meeting with Zaid a-Rifa'i at the Dorchester Hotel in London, a-Rifa'i gave him a gold cigarette box, saying that 'Ch. was sorry that the last time, when he gave gifts to Eban and Allon, he had none to give me.'[44]

Six days after the meeting on board Hussein's boat, on 26 February 1969, Levi Eshkol died. King Hussein sent a letter of condolence to the Acting Prime Minister Yigal Allon, and expressed his hope of reaching a just and permanent peace between the two states.[45]

Golda Meir was chosen to succeed Eshkol as Prime Minister. Thus began the decline of Yaacov Herzog's career.

17

Decline

Things began to change in the Prime Minister's office as soon as Golda Meir was installed as Eshkol's successor, but Herzog failed to see the writing on the wall.

Herzog wrote a speech for her swearing-in at the Knesset on 16 March 1969, but 'she wrote a draft of her own,' he noted sadly, 'and consulted with Galili about wording and ideas ... By and large her speech contained nothing new ... I was sorry she did not accept my suggestion to include our assessments of the situation in the Middle East.'[1] Four days later, when he gave her the draft of a message to send to President Nixon, she set it aside. At first, he did not grasp that he had been discarded as chief speech and statement writer for the Prime Minister in favour of Israel Galili. 'The person with the most influence [in the Prime Minister's office] was Israel Galili,' wrote Dr Meron Medzini.[2] 'He had a sharp mind, was a natural debater and a master of the phrase. He was Golda's chief speech writer.'

Herzog knew Golda Meir well – he had worked with her for nine years, when she was Foreign Minister, yet evidently he did not always understand her. When she presented her government, he was puzzled that she did not say a word in praise of Yigal Allon, who had been Acting Prime Minister since Eshkol's death. Galili enlightened him. 'Galili explained that people of her generation were not accustomed to expressing appreciation and gratitude,' Herzog noted.[3] But he was impressed by the way she conducted the weekly cabinet meeting. 'This first business-like meeting revealed the firmness, grasp and leadership ability of the new PM, in contrast to her predecessor, who had always had difficulty reaching decisions.'[4]

Herzog soon lost his special place in the Prime Minister's office, and at the beginning of June he was once again offended, when the Prime Minister prepared for her trip to the Socialist International conference in England. The visit was to include a meeting with the British Prime Minister, Harold Wilson, but the British government decided that it would not be an official visit. 'On 1 June the PM informed me that since it was not an official visit, she did not think I should come ... I was sorry that despite the change in the status of the visit she did not see fit to include me, especially as she had accepted my proposal to meet the editors of *The Times* and *Sunday Times*, and speak at Chatham House and the association of foreign correspondents.'[5]

At first Herzog went on as before. He worked closely with the new Prime Minister, though he could not get used to addressing her as 'Golda', as she was universally called, any more than he could call her predecessor 'Eshkol', like everyone else. To him she was 'Madam Prime Minister', which made people titter. He continued his usual work and his talks with Hussein and his advisors, and still composed the messages to King Hussein. But after another meeting, in the company of Allon and Eban at Coral Island on 25 May 1970, 'direct contact came to a halt' for a long time.[6]

In everyday life nothing seemed to have changed. Herzog still sat at the Prime Minister's side in cabinet meetings and took part in the inner-circle consultations at her house. The political scene, the media and the general public still saw him as he had been for years – the Prime Minister's right-hand man.

But the change gradually became apparent. Eshkol had loved Herzog and was proud of him, enjoyed having him at his side and admired his rich knowledge of Judaism and the world. He also trusted him unreservedly. Golda Meir, however, had no affection for Herzog.[7] She did not care for intellectuals and scholarly types, and had no interest in conversing with him. She did not imagine that she might learn something from him, and he felt uncertain in her presence. 'Herzog admired Ben-Gurion, loved Eshkol and feared Golda,' said one of his colleagues.[8] 'Golda crushed him,' said a friend of his, 'with the help of her aides Simcha Dinitz and Lou Kedar.'[9] Herzog's friends and relatives point to Simcha Dinitz, who became head of the Prime Minister's office, saying that he conspired against Yaacov Herzog and did all he could to isolate and remove him.[10] 'Golda and Simcha Dinitz gradually hung him out to dry,' said his friend Ari Rath. 'They literally pushed him into a corner: they gave him a small room near the staircase, very far from the Prime Minister, where he sat physically and mentally isolated. They also passed most of the duties of the director-general to Simcha.'[11]

Dinitz himself, however, maintains the reverse is true – he was a friend of Yaacov, he says, and helped and supported him all the way. 'Golda didn't like him,' says Dinitz. 'She would call a meeting to discuss the United States and invite the director-general of the Foreign Ministry, someone from the Mossad, and myself. I'd say to her, "Mrs Meir, don't you think we should include [our] director-general?" and she would reply, "No, he's busy with other matters . . . "'[12] Dinitz admits that Herzog accused him of being responsible for leaving him out of the Prime Minister's meetings. 'I said to him, believe me, when I schedule a meeting I begin with the director-general.' But Herzog's associates reject this claim.

Yaacov Herzog loved his work, and was extremely sensitive to the possibility that someone might seek to edge him out. When he worked with Eshkol he made a point of meeting everyone who made a remark that could be seen as criticism. This was not a survival trait so much as a sign of his extreme sensitivity, and his desire to be on good terms with everyone. He was easily hurt by criticism, and on the rare occasions when unflattering comments appeared in the press about him, he hastened to respond.

For example, at a meeting in July 1968, incidents on the Jordanian border were discussed, and the question arose whether Israel should retaliate despite her close contact with Hussein. Dayan stated that the Jordanians kept acting against Israel – 'and every two weeks they talk to Yaacov Herzog'.[13] The following day Herzog went to see Dayan, 'because I wanted to clarify the comment he made yesterday, and get to the bottom of his thinking about contact with Charles'.[14] The conversation flowed easily, and it looked as if they had exchanged roles: Dayan was the moderate statesman, while Herzog expressed the 'Greater Land of Israel' ideology. Herzog asked Dayan if he would approve a peace accord with Hussein on the basis of the 'Allon Plan', and Dayan replied that if Hussein accepted it – which he thought was impossible – he, Dayan, would begin negotiating with him. Herzog said, 'Why should we be interested, if time is on our side? Should we give up a part of the Land of Israel in return for peace?' This conversation reassured Herzog regarding his relations with Dayan, though they never became warm or companionable. His notes about Dayan's acts and statements often imply uneasiness and criticism. After the emergency meeting when an El-Al plane was hijacked by 'Fatah' to Algeria, Herzog noted, 'Dayan's position and especially his way of speaking left an unpleasant impression on me.'[15]

A comment made by Pinchas Sapir also upset him. Deputy Finance Minister Zvi Dinstein told him that Sapir was opposed to his, Herzog's, suggestion to convene the economic council in February 1969, after the economic conference. According to Dinstein, Sapir had said that 'Herzog is driving everyone crazy about the Jews.'[16] Sapir said something similar to Chaim Israeli, and Herzog asked to see the Minister of Finance urgently. 'On Sunday, 15 September, during the cabinet meeting, we stepped outside and talked,' Herzog noted.[17] 'I asked him why he was attacking me, and he denied it. But he added that he couldn't understand why a man like me, with so much influence over the PM, was so easily upset by criticism. He went on talking about my influence over the PM, and repeated the argument he had made to me long ago, that in the critical moment on the eve of the war, it was I who broke the PM's resistance and made him agree to the appointment of Dayan as Defence Minister. I told him it was a lie and that I'd never spoken to the PM about it.'

Some people opposed Herzog on account of his political opinions, which grew more extreme after the war. Herzog noted what Zalman Aranne said to him, in Sapir's presence, that though 'generally I have a clear and balanced view of political matters ... I have become dazzled and divided about the West Bank due to the religious aspect, and that in these fateful months I'm the only one at the PM's side'. Sapir also said, though in a joking tone, that 'I've picked up the tendency to expansionism'.[18]

Herzog's unique position at Eshkol's side annoyed a good number of political figures. They were especially upset because he was not a political man, nor a member of a party or 'anybody's man' who could be manipulated. Some were displeased that, while being Eshkol's confidant, he could not be given assignments on behalf of the political party – something he avoided – nor be included in party-political consultations. At some point a number of cabinet ministers sought to have him dismissed from his post. Chaim Israeli told him in mid-September 1968 that 'he had heard from certain sources "at the top", that they plan to replace me as director-general of the PM's office roughly next spring, the idea being to bring Rabin back for the elections and I would replace him. They're willing to offer me the post of director-general of the Foreign Ministry. They feel it is unthinkable that at such a critical time in Israel, a man holding a key position at the PM's side is someone whom they cannot steer. The people in the plan are Sapir and Galili and apparently Golda, though the person who talked to her about it found her extremely cautious in her response.'

Herzog also noted that this story tied in with something a friend had told him that 'Mrs E. [Eshkol] had recently stated that I should go to Washington, since with the approaching elections it will be necessary to have someone at Eshkol's side who can be in close contact with the party.' The person named as a possible successor to Herzog was Ephraim Evron, who was then minister at the Israeli Embassy in Washington. 'Effi must have done a pretty thorough job while he was there,' Herzog added angrily.[19]

But Herzog's position with Eshkol was unassailable, and the Prime Minister himself made no mention of replacing his director-general. In April 1968 some people protested that Herzog had provoked a dispute in the government, in which Eban too was involved. Moshe Raviv, a senior Foreign Ministry official, came to Herzog's office 'and mumbled that I'm being blamed for last night's dispute. I said I couldn't stand such an approach, and asked him if he had been sent by the Foreign Minister or not, adding that I'd have to make it clear to the PM when I'm asked about it. He claimed he had not been sent by the Minister and came of his own volition. I was annoyed and told the PM, who replied saying that no-one had the right to intervene in his relations with the people who worked with him.'[20]

Eshkol had always given Herzog his full backing. But once Golda Meir became Prime Minister, the atmosphere changed. She did not seek to replace him but gradually undermined his position, and together with her team deprived him of the running of the Prime Minister's office, in which he had been so extensively involved. 'Golda didn't need him the way Eshkol did,' said a friend of Yaacov. 'She was herself an English speaker and did not need Yaacov for that. In foreign relations she was much tougher than Eshkol, and more of a natural leader. Also the kind of companionable conversations which Eshkol enjoyed, and that Herzog was so brilliant at, were not Golda's style at all. To her, Jackie Herzog was Ben-Gurion's former advisor, and we mustn't forget that she was chosen to be Prime Minister at the time when

Decline

her feud with Ben-Gurion was at its height ... Moreover, she needed an assistant, and Simcha Dinitz was devoted to her. Yaacov Herzog was not strictly an assistant. They didn't need someone like him, let alone a semi-prophet.'[21] 'That was the period of his decline,' said his brother Chaim Herzog. 'The other Prime Ministers loved him. She was different ... Perhaps because of his intellectual quality, or his religiosity.'[22]

Golda Meir discarded Herzog for several reasons. She had a long memory, and did not forget that it had been Herzog who proposed the collective resignation of senior officials in the Foreign Ministry in 1956, when Ben-Gurion decided to appoint her instead of Moshe Sharett. 'She never forgave [those who wanted to resign] for doing so,' wrote Meron Medzini, 'and in later years she paid them back.'[23] She also remembered Herzog's direct line to Ben-Gurion when he was serving as minister in the Washington Embassy.'[24] But Golda had other reasons, as well as old resentments. As Medzini put it, 'She preferred Simcha Dinitz and Lou Kedar because she didn't want to have to deal with new people, because she relied on them after years of close cooperation. She did not demand fertile minds or innovative ideas. She did not care for war-games. She did not care to examine problems from every possible angle. Her team had no intellectual pretensions. The only intellectual of the lot was Dr Yaacov Herzog, whose influence kept shrinking ... He served Eshkol and Golda faithfully, but his relations with Golda were correct, and lacked warmth on her part. Herzog had a brilliant mind ... His intellectual ability militated against him in Golda's bureau. He was slow to come to a decision and re-evaluated everything seven times, sharing his mental deliberations with others. Once he was asked to describe the difference between working with Ben-Gurion and Eshkol versus Golda Meir. He replied that with the first two he was able to share his concern for the future of the Jewish people in the next generation, and they listened to him attentively and patiently, whereas Golda would say, "Yaacov, I don't know what's going to happen tomorrow – how can I talk about the future of the Jewish people in generations to come?" She lacked vision and imagination for philosophical discussions, and regarded them as sterile mental exercises and a waste of time. So Herzog's influence waned and Dinitz's influence grew.'[25]

Herzog was left out of important meetings, including some that were clearly within his remit, such as sessions with the heads of the secret services. Golda dismissed the suggestions and ideas he put to her. King Hussein, when he wished to meet her, sent a message through Dr Herbert asking her to include certain messages in her speech at the Knesset. 'On 14 December, when we discussed the draft of the speech, I suggested to the PM to respond as favourably as possible, and proposed a certain wording. The PM was unwilling ... '[26] Relations with Hussein reached their nadir in early 1970, as Israel all but broke off contact with him, on account of the tension along the ceasefire lines and the activities of 'Fatah'. Hussein's repeated requests that Israel compose a document with proposals for a peace settlement were ignored. In London, Dr Herbert gave Hussein some records and books for learning Hebrew that he had asked Herzog to get him. Hussein thanked the doctor, noting, 'This may be the only tangible contribution to peace and cooperation that he and we are capable of.' He added that 'he did not see any point or purpose in continuing the talks with Israel, since after more than three years and dozens of meetings the chances of mutual understanding seem no better.' Because Golda was unwilling to continue the contacts at a high level, it fell to Dr Herbert to talk to Hussein and act as *de facto* intermediary between the King and the Israeli government. This caused Herzog great frustration.

But this was not the only area in which he felt increasingly frustrated – his position as the Prime Minister's chief advisor on international matters was also eroding. In September 1970, relations between King Hussein and the 'Fatah' organization in Jordan reached a crisis, and he sent the army into the refugee camps

Decline

where thousands of 'Fatah' fighters were killed. The massacre came to be known as 'Black September'. Syria was about to send its troops into Jordan, and the United States asked Israel to attack Syria on the ground and from the air. It was the first time that the US planned a military operation together with Israel. In the end the IDF's movements near the Syrian border were enough to deter Syrian forces.

During that crisis Golda offered King Hussein aid and even a shipment of food, and afterwards Hussein sent her a message of warm gratitude.[27] It would have been reasonable to expect Herzog to play a central role in tackling this crisis, in his capacity as political advisor, his long familiarity with Hussein, and as an expert on the relations with the United States. But he was not called upon to do anything, beyond some minor wording. He only accompanied Yigal Allon in October to a meeting with Hussein and Zaid a-Rifa'i.[28] Everyone around sensed that his days of glory in the Prime Minister's office were over. One of Yaacov's close friends spoke bitterly about it. 'Golda simply had no patience with him ... Her attitude towards him, and that of her close aides, was simply coarse. Some meetings they simply left him out, or if he was asked to take part, they would cut him off in mid-sentence. The Foreign Ministry officials who heard about it were scandalized. Even the Mapai leadership were angry with Golda about this.'[29]

'One day,' said a colleague, 'we put before Golda a proposal that was sent from abroad, to construct an industrial area between El Arish and Rafah [in north-east Sinai]. The plan, which certain people abroad had put together, was to employ tens of thousands of Palestinian refugees in workshops for dismantling boats, in tanneries, and other enterprises. We took it to Golda Meir, and she summoned a meeting with "our comrades", Labour Party Ministers. For the next half-hour Golda incited the participants to mock and ridicule us. What, we are responsible for the refugees? said one. What sort of crazy plan is this? said another. Golda treated Herzog as a complete nonentity. One of the "Arabists" also tore into me.

'I left the meeting and went to my office, feeling horrible. After a few minutes Herzog joined me. I said to him, "I'm leaving. Golda has shown that she despises us. I've nothing more to do here. But he tried for a long time to talk me into staying. He had recently been invited to become president of Bar-Ilan University, a highly respected position. I said to him, "Yaacov, take it! Leave this place!"

'He said to me, "I consider it my national duty to stay and contribute my experience to Golda."'

'I said, "Contribute what? She doesn't listen to you!"'[30]

The quiet, noble Herzog did not tell anyone about his private pain. This honest and decent man, so removed from conspiracies and personal plots, was caught in a frightful nightmare. He had dedicated himself and his abilities to the State, and was determined to serve the Prime Minister and achieve an understanding with her close associates. Having no personal political ambitions, he regarded no one as an enemy or rival. Even in the worst times, he tried to fulfil his duties as before. He toyed with the idea of Bar-Ilan, or a year at an American university. He suggested to his friend Chaim Israeli that they collaborate on a book about the Sinai campaign.[31] But compared with the post of director-general of the Prime Minister's office, 'he was offered only subordinate positions, and he had no chance of getting anything better.' Talk about him becoming a Knesset member for the Mafdal (the National Religious Party) was likewise unfounded.[32] Just as in 1965, when he was offered the Chief Rabbinate in England, but did not wish to leave the centre of action, once again his body suffered the consequences. He was afflicted with terrible backaches, and sometimes could not rise from his bed.

'I knew him as a close friend,' Nahum Goldmann recalled. 'He was a victim of his own career. He'd had a number of disappointments ... And being the kind of person who hesitates to come out

Decline

fighting, he suffered, and locked everything up in his soul ... I'd say he was not happy.

'To succeed in the political life you have to be quite pitiless. I urged him to fight back, to protest, to complain, and start a new career. But he couldn't do it. I remember saying to him once that he should learn from Moses, who when necessary was capable of cursing his own people and criticizing it harshly. His answer was, "Moses acted upon God's command, and who am I to emulate him?"'[33]

With hindsight, it seems obvious that this was the right moment for Yaacov Herzog to quit his position, but he was incapable of abandoning the work that had become the centre of his existence. As Avraham Avihai said, 'The need to be in the corridors of power had become an addiction.'[34] In 1971, Herzog went to the United States and stayed at the Waldorf Astoria in New York. He telephoned one of his former colleagues, who had retired from government service and was studying at a remote American university, and asked him to come to New York to meet him.

'This was my most emotional meeting with him,' the man recalled. 'When I saw him I was shocked – he was half his old self, sick and agonized. He said to me, "What do they want from me?" He told me angrily about the abuse he was subjected to by the personnel of the Prime Minister's office. He said to me, "You see, I'm a religious man, a believer, I feel I'm finished. I've no strength for this insanity, this undermining."'

'I persuaded him to have dinner with me, as he hadn't eaten for two days. I said to him, "Yaacov, just leave it. Take a vacation, go write your book about the Sinai campaign. (He wanted to write a book about it, as an example of a conflict between the United States and the USSR which had been resolved in our favour.) Go to Harvard for a year – they'll grab you!" But he refused. "I have to help Golda. She's an important person."

'When I returned to Israel and went to see him he was already lying unconscious in hospital.'[35]

On 9 December 1971 Shira Herzog was home. She was serving in the IDF, and had returned after six months in the outpost of Masu'ah. That year her father had fallen ill twice; he had serious back trouble and had spent some time lying in hospital in traction. He was suffering physically, and was frustrated at work.

'He talked to me about the presidency of Bar-Ilan University, but his dream was to be the Ambassador to the United States.' On several occasions she saw him lying on the floor to ease his backache. 'It made him feel worse, because the staff at the office did not accept him, and when he was ill he simply wasn't there.' Years later, Shira suggested that the back pains were psychosomatic, 'because he was feeling wretched.'[36] Nahum Goldmann commented, 'He swallowed every injustice done to him, and I suspect that this was one of the causes of the illness that shortened his life.'

He had returned only a few days earlier from a gruelling trip abroad, which had followed shortly after a secret meeting with King Hussein in Aqaba. He returned from Aqaba at 2 o'clock in the morning, said goodbye to Pnina, who waited for him in a Tel Aviv hotel, and three hours later flew to London. When he got there he fell ill and ran a high temperature, but was given a penicillin injection by a medical acquaintance, and proceeded to Canada, where he gave one of the best speeches of his life. 'He's crazy!' said his brother Chaim angrily. 'That year he went abroad 32 times. He was burning hot as he flew to address the Jews of Canada. He destroyed himself.'[37] He was exhausted and aching. He returned ill, and his doctor thought he had a bad case of flu. In fact, he must have been struck by some unidentified virus. Golda was about to leave for the United States to meet President Nixon, and Yaacov, despite his condition, wanted to join her. 'What a terrible tragedy,' he said to his brother Chaim. 'This is the first time she really wants me to join her. But now, when she really needs me, I can't do it.'[38]

'In the middle of the night we heard a thump,' Shira recalled.

Decline

'He'd got out of bed and probably stumbled and fell. Later they found that he had suffered a haemorrhage in his head, near the brain. My mother woke me to call for help.

'We phoned for an ambulance and he was taken to hospital. He was unconscious, but they couldn't get the stretcher up to the flat, so they took him down in a folding garden chair. I saw him hanging limply from the chair.'

Shira watched the shrunken, drooping form, his limbs dangling from the chair. 'To me, that was the moment he came to an end.'[39]

Yaacov Herzog went into a coma. He was operated on to stop the inter-cranial bleeding, but it seems an infection set in. Some speculated that the haemorrhage had begun earlier, and increased until it felled him. 'Nobody knows exactly what happened to Yaacov,' his brother Chaim wrote. 'We knew he'd had a stroke, and knew that he fell, but it was not clear which came first.'[40] He lay in bed for three months and it is doubtful if he recognized the members of his family around his bed. Once he stirred and mumbled something about the Jews of Russia, about opening the gates for Jewish immigration from the USSR.

That was the last time they heard him speak.

18

Epilogue

Yaacov Herzog died on 6 March 1972, 23 Adar 5732 by the Hebrew calendar. He was 50 years old.

He was mourned by the foremost figures of the nation, the leaders of the political parties, intellectuals and great religious teachers. Abroad, his passing was lamented by statesmen, rabbis from all movements, writers, thinkers and leaders of the Jewish people. In Jerusalem, he was mourned by the Greek Orthodox Patriarch, and special prayers were said for him in the Vatican. The President of Israel, Zalman Shazar, grieved: 'I found him in the twilight of my life, and he was for me a joyful discovery, a longed-for gift, sent to me from afar and from the depths of my spirit alike.'[1]

'One of the best, wisest, most charming and morally impressive individuals I have ever known,' said Sir Isaiah Berlin, one of the foremost thinkers of his time. 'Delicate and modest physically, his frail frame contained a fierce and firm spirit, armed with a sharp critical mind, subtle perception, infinite patience, and a treasure trove ... of orderly and precise knowledge, which made him into an intellectual "superpower" that repulsed anyone who would challenge it.'[2]

'This genius of Jewish diplomacy,' said Elie Wiesel, 'will be an example and a model for anyone who seeks to serve the State in its highest echelons. The Jew in him enriched everyone who met him, and to everyone he gave something of his devotion, something of his faith.'[3]

Epilogue

'For three years I worked with Yaacov and observed him,' said Menachem Begin. 'I learned much from him and our relationship became as close as possible between two people.' What Begin learned from him was that 'our nation is an unusual nation, it is truly a unique nation, and we can all take pride in being members of the Jewish people.'[4]

'All his life was a paean to the love of Israel,' said Abba Eban. 'Ancient Israel – and no one was more knowledgeable about every expression and every vestige of the people's creative spirit at the start of its history. Israel today – ever since he had a mind of his own and set out to serve the nation, Yaacov was concerned day and night with his people and the State, exercising his mind and his imagination to find a way out of every hardship to a space of security and contentment. Tomorrow's Israel – this was his worry, worry about existence and about the greatness of spirit, of quality and standard ... He knew the people's weaknesses and often spoke about them, but always with a smile, a smile full of compassion, forgiveness and boundless affection.'[5]

'He was the symbol of the great faith in our lives,' said Shimon Peres, 'and he would not have been this symbol if he were not its bearer, sometimes its creator. Many among us mourn Yaacov for what he might have been. I mourn him above all for what he was, and it is doubtful if there will be another like him. Because he really was a very great spirit borne by a man of modest manner, an immense faith that inhabited such a delicate frame, a very wise man who sowed wisdom and found wisdom everywhere and in every one, a good friend who was a wonderful colleague, a man who could pray and bless, sanctify and ponder, and act ... '[6]

Most moving was Ben-Gurion's outcry, expressed in a letter to Yaacov as he lay in hospital:

'I pray to the God of Israel that they will be able to cure you and make you well again. You have a great past, and I believe you have a still more important future ... There are not many men as important as you, and do not despair. Get well, Yaacov, the country and the Jewish people need you!'⁷

Bibliography and Sources

In writing this biography of Dr Yaacov Herzog, I have used mainly documents and other written material held in a number of archives – the State Archive (which contains Yaacov Herzog's private archive), the Haganah Archive, the Jabotinsky, Ben-Gurion and Levi Eshkol Archives, and a number of private archives. I thank the devoted workers in all these archives, who helped and guided me and my assistant, Nili Avnat, through their mazes. Israel Radio and IDF Radio gave me the complete transcripts of interviews with Yaacov Herzog and programmes about him. In some cases I received the uncut original interviews. Pnina Herzog provided me with the tapes of the debate between Yaacov Herzog and Arnold Toynbee.

I have also used many books, the most important of which are:

1. Avraham Avihai, *Prakim Be'toldot Yerushalayim Baz'man Hachadash* ('Yaacov David Herzog – His Life' in *Passages in the History of Jerusalem in the Modern Time*) a book dedicated to the memory of Yaacov Herzog, Yad Ben-Zvi and the Ministry of Defence Publishing House, Jerusalem 1981.
2. Chaim Herzog, *Derekh Hayim* (*Living History*), Yediot Aharonot, Tel Aviv, 1997.
3. Moshe Dayan, *Avnai Derekh* (*Milestones*), Edanim/Dvir, Jerusalem and Tel Aviv, 1976.
4. Michael Bar-Zohar, *Ben-Gurion: Biografiya Medinit,* Am Oved, Tel Aviv 1975–7 (3 volumes). (*Ben-Gurion,* Weidenfeld and

Nicolson, London, 1978).
5 Meron Medzini, *Ha Yehudiya Hage'a* (*The Proud Jewess*), Edanim/Yediot Aharonot, Tel Aviv, 1990.
6 Yaacov Herzog, *Am Levadad Yishkon*, Sifriyat Ma'ariv, Tel Aviv, 1975. (*A People That Dwells Alone*, Weidenfeld and Nicolson, London, 1976).
7 Meir Amit, *Rosh Berosh* (*Head to Head*), Hed Arzi, Or Yehuda, 1999.
8 Moshe Zack, *Hussein Oseh Shalom* (*Hussein Makes Peace*), Begin-Sadat Institute for Strategic Studies, Bar-Ilan University, Ramat Gan, 1996.
9 Abba Eban, *An Autobiography*, Random House, New York, 1977.
10 Moshe Sharett, *Yoman Ishi* (*Personal Journal*), Sifriat Ma'ariv, Tel Aviv.
11 Yaacov David Herzog, *The Mishnah*, Soncino Press, London--Jerusalem-New York, 1947.

Important information about Yaacov Herzog, his life and work, was provided by members of his family, friends and colleagues. I interviewed most of them personally, though some of the interviews were conducted by Nili Avnat, who helped me at all stages of the research.

The following list of interviewees is incomplete, since some of them asked not to be named:

The Herzog family: wife Pnina Herzog; children Shira, Eliezra and Yitzhak Herzog; sister-in-law Aura Herzog (wife of the late President Chaim Herzog) and her sons Michael (Mike) and Advocate MK (Bougie) Herzog.

Friends and colleagues: Yitzhak Navon, Shimon Peres, Chaim Israeli, Teddy Kollek, Miriam Eshkol, Isser Harel, Avraham Avihai, Ami Kamir, Dr Meron Medzini, Pinchas Eliav, Ari Rath, Ari Avner, Michael (Mike) Arnon, Shimshon Arad, Simcha Dinitz, Professor Irwin Cotler, Jean Halperin, Nathan Ben-Horin,

Bibliography and Sources

Malka (Ben-Zvi) and Alex Keynan, Norma Bar-Moshe, Deborah Bregman and Frieda Sofer (the three in a joint interview).

My thanks to all those individuals who agreed to give me an interview, particularly those whom I met several times and who provided me with access to documents and letters in their possession. The Publishers and I would like to thank Martin Gilbert for generously providing the three maps in this book, and Tim Aspden for his cartography. Finally, I am grateful to 'The Association for the Publication of the biography of Yaacov Herzog' for making this biography possible.

Notes

Chapter 1   In the Thick of War

1. Herzog diary, 26.10.1956.
2. Ibid.
3. Herzog interviews with Shabbetai Tevet, *Haaretz*, 4, 11 November 1966.
4. Ibid.
5. Diary, ibid.
6. Author's interview with Pnina Herzog, 10.2.2000.
7. Diary, 27.10.1956.
8. Ibid.
9. Diary, 28.10.1956.
10. Ibid.
11. Ibid.
12. Michael Bar-Zohar, *Ben-Gurion*, p. 1149.
13. Herzog background document, in English, entitled 'Sinai', undated.
14. Author's interview with Teddy Kollek.
15. Ben-Gurion diary, 27.12.1950.
16. Ibid., 16.5.1950, 25.8.1954.
17. Moshe Dayan diary, 3.4.1956, quoted in *Avnai Derekh*, p. 185.
18. Herzog diary, 28.10.1956.
19. Ibid.
20. Herzog interviews with Shabbetai Tevet (see note 3 above).
21. Herzog diary, ibid.
22. Herzog interviews with Shabbetai Tevet.
23. Personal letter to Gideon Rafael, 19.12.1956.
24. Ibid.
25. Herzog interview with Yaacov Reuel, *Jerusalem Post*, 8.10.1971.
26. Ibid.
27. Author's interview with Yitzhak Navon, July 1999.
28. Navon interview with Meron Medzini, Jerusalem, 15.10.1972, quoted in Avraham Avihai's 'Yaacov David Herzog – His Life'.

Notes

29 Interview with Pnina Herzog, ibid.
30 Herzog, 'Sinai', ibid.
31 Herzog interview with Yaacov Reuel, ibid.
32 Ibid.
33 Ibid.
34 Ben-Gurion diary, 7.11.1956.
35 Herzog, 'Sinai', ibid.
36 Ben-Gurion diary, 8.11.1956.
37 Ibid.
38 Herzog, ibid.
39 Herzog interview with Reuel, ibid.
40 Herzog interviews with Tevet, ibid.
41 Navon interview with Avihai, ibid.
42 Herzog interviews with Tevet, ibid.
43 Herzog voice recording, a radio programme in memory of Yaacov Herzog, Kol Israel, March 1977.
44 Herzog, 'Sinai', ibid.
45 Abba Eban, Herzog memorial programme, ibid.
46 Ibid.
47 Navon interview with Avihai, ibid.
48 Interview with Navon, ibid.
49 Navon interview with Avihai, ibid.
50 Ibid.
51 Interview with Navon, ibid.
52 Herzog, 'Sinai', ibid.
53 Navon interview with Avihai, ibid.
54 Ben-Gurion diary, 8.11.1956.
55 Letter from Walter Eytan to Herzog, 12.11.1956.
56 Ben-Gurion letter to Chief Rabbi Herzog, 11.3.1957.
57 Dedication to Yaacov Herzog on Ben-Gurion portrait, at Pnina Herzog's house in Jerusalem.

Chapter 2 Two Worlds

1 Interview on IDF radio, November 1969.
2 Chaim Herzog, *Derekh Hayim*, pp. 29–30.
3 Solly Steinberg, tribute to Yaacov Herzog, manuscript.
4 Avihai, ibid., p. 12.
5 Steinberg, tribute, ibid.
6 Letter to his friend Charles, 18.11.1935.
7 Interview on IDF radio, ibid. (see note 1 above).
8 Copy of Yaacov Herzog's speech, typed by his grandfather Shmuel on Hanukkah eve, 1933, probably from the boy's handwritten text.
9 Chaim Herzog, ibid., p. 19.

10 Ibid., p. 20.
11 Ibid., p. 21.
12 See *Ha'entzeklopedya Ha'ivrit* (*Hebrew Encyclopedia*), vol. 15, p. 352.
13 Chaim Herzog, ibid., and Avihai, ibid., p. 11.
14 *Encyclopedia Judaica*, vol. 8, pp. 422–3.
15 Chaim Herzog, ibid., pp. 22–3.
16 Chaim Herzog on memorial programme (see chapter 1, note 43).
17 Chaim Herzog, *Derekh Hayim*, pp. 24–6.
18 *Encyclopedia Judaica*, ibid.
19 Chaim Herzog, ibid., p. 27.
20 When the author visited Belfast in 1989 he was warmly received by the leaders of the Irish national movement in a safe-house on the street where the Herzog family used to live.
21 Chaim Herzog, ibid., p. 24.
22 Avihai, ibid., p. 12.
23 Ibid.
24 Radio interview with Chaim Herzog, March 1973.
25 Chaim Herzog, *Derekh Hayim*, p. 32.
26 Author interview with Pnina Herzog, 6.8.2001.
27 Chaim Herzog, ibid., pp. 32–3.
28 Ibid., p. 436.
29 Louis Hyman letter to Pnina Herzog, 1.9.1975.
30 Avihai interview with Dr Solly Steinberg, ibid., p. 13.
31 Hyman letter, ibid.
32 Herzog letter to Rabbi Joel Herzog, 1932, and response to Rabbi Shmuel Hillman, undated.
33 Herzog letter to Rabbi Herzog, undated.
34 Chaim Herzog, ibid., p. 34.
35 Letter from Rabbi Shmuel Hillman, 'to my beloved grandson', December 1934.
36 Herzog bar-mitzvah Hebrew speech, undated.
37 Herzog bar-mitzvah English speech, undated.
38 'A Racial Difference', Herzog handwritten essay.
39 Hubert Wine, speech at scholarship ceremony in memory of Yaacov Herzog, 17.3.1974.
40 Herzog draft of a letter to Clement Attlee, undated.
41 Avihai, ibid., p. 13.
42 Herzog draft letter to Attlee, ibid.
43 Interview with Pnina Herzog, ibid.
44 Herzog second draft of essay, 1936.
45 Herzog essay, 1936.
46 Herzog essay.
47 Herzog essay.
48 Herzog essay, untitled.

Notes

49 Letter to 'Jack Herzog' from Max Pemberton, head of London School of Journalism, 1.1.36.
50 Due to the sanctity of the Passover week the Chief Rabbi would not engage in activities that resembled his routine work. For Yaacov, however, while the first and last days of the holiday had similar restrictions to the Sabbath, the intermediate days were less restricted, so he could write.
51 Herzog letter to Rabbi Sasson, Passover 1936.
52 Chaim Herzog, ibid., pp. 24–5.
53 Herzog postcard to his aunt in Paris, September 1936.
54 Interview with Pnina Herzog, ibid.
55 Yair Sheleg, 'His Talented Brother', *Haaretz* Friday magazine, 25.8.1989.
56 Rabbi Herzog letter to Yaacov.
57 Ibid.
58 Ibid.
59 Chaim Herzog, ibid., pp. 47–8.
60 Rabbi Herzog letter to Yaacov.
61 Wine, ibid.
62 Interview with Pnina Herzog, ibid., and Herzog letter to his friend Shlomo, 1939.
63 Chaim Herzog, ibid., p. 56.
64 Ibid., p. 48
65 Herzog letter to Shlomo, ibid.

Chapter 3   War

1 Yaacov Herzog's letters to Chaim Herzog, 3.10.1946–26.11.1946.
2 Indro Montanelli, 'A day in Herzog's company in Jerusalem', manuscript, 29.2.1969.
3 Letter to Yaacov Herzog from his company commander, 6.2.1941.
4 Letter by Rabbi Louis Rabinowitz, Rabbi of British forces in the Middle East, to Yaacov Herzog, 10.7.1942.
5 For example, air tickets issued to Yaacov Herzog by the British armed forces, 12.2.1946, and a letter from the British army chaplain, Yaacov Lifshitz, addressed to 'Rabbi Yaacov Herzog' (Hebrew), 18.6.1944.
6 Avihai, ibid., p. 15. See also, Yaacov David Herzog, *The Mishnah*.
7 Draft of letter by Yaacov Herzog to the Paper Section, Dept of Light Industries, the British Mandatory Government, 22.9.1941.
8 Quoted in the Kol Israel memorial programme, March 1977.
9 Herzog, *Mishnah*, pp. vi–vii.
10 Yaacov Herzog letter to A. Meir, Israel Consul in Milan, 3.11.1953.
11 Ehud Avriel, letter to Pnina Herzog, 3.11.1975.
12 Letter of Chief Rabbi Herzog to the Vatican representative in Jerusalem, 22.12.1942; acknowledgement of its receipt by the representative's secretary, 25.12.1942; Yaacov Herzog's letter to the Vatican representative, 21.1.1943,

and its acknowledgement, 22.1.1943; letter from representative's secretary quoting the Pope, 30.1.1943; and others.
13 Ibid.
14 Saul Friedlander, *Pius XII and the Third Reich*, Knopf, New York 1966, pp. 222–3, 226–34.
15 Avihai, ibid., pp.17–18.
16 Professor Dan Laor, Tel Aviv University, Lecture in memory of Yaacov Herzog, 5.4.2000.
17 Ibid.
18 Ibid.
19 Eliezer Aliner, Kol Israel memorial programme, March 1973.
20 Yaacov Herzog's letter to Colonel Joseph Nelson, 12.2.1947.
21 Avihai, ibid., based on a tape of Yaacov Herzog's conversations with Rabbi Yehiel Weinberg in Switzerland, 1965.
22 Nahum Snapiri report, 'Summary of conversation with the little one', 21.10.1946, Jabotinsky Archive.
23 Ibid.
24 Alpen Reese letter to Pnina Herzog.
25 Ibid.
26 Unnamed tribute.
27 Ibid.
28 Yaacov Herzog's letter to his brother Vivian (Chaim), 26.10.1946, Chaim Herzog archive.
29 Letter to Vivian, 3.10.1946.
30 Letter to Vivian, 26.10.1946.
31 Letter to Vivian, 23.11.1946.
32 Letter to Vivian, 26.10.1946.
33 Ibid.
34 Letter to Vivian, 3.10.1946.
35 Letter to Vivian, 26.10.1946.
36 Ibid.
37 Snapiri, ibid.
38 The undated note was found among Yaacov Herzog's papers. It was probably slipped into his mailbox or smuggled somehow to the Chief Rabbi or his son.
39 Chief Rabbi's letter to High Commissioner, 24.3.1945.
40 Menachem Begin interview for memorial programme on Yaacov Herzog, Kol Israel, March 1974.
41 Minutes of conversation, in Yaacov Herzog's handwriting.
42 Chaim Herzog, ibid., p. 101.
43 Author's interview with Pnina Herzog, 24.12.1997.
44 Menachem Begin interview, ibid.
45 Chaim Landau interview for memorial programme on Yaacov Herzog, Kol Israel, March 1973.

Notes

46 Ibid.
47 Ibid.
48 Ibid.
49 Snapiri, ibid.
50 Interview with Snapiri, 19.8.1973; in Avihai, ibid.
51 Chaim Herzog, ibid., p. 100.
52 Ibid.
53 Unedited interview with Menachem Begin for memorial programme, March 1973.
54 Unedited interview with Golda Meir for memorial programme, March 1973.
55 Ze'ev Shek interview with Medzini in Avihai, ibid.
56 Herzog, abridged curriculum vitae.
57 Letter from Louis Rabinowitz, 23.3.43.
58 Chaim Herzog, ibid., p. 92.
59 Yaacov's letter to Vivian, 3.10.1943.
60 Yaacov's letter to Chaim, 26.12.1946 or 26.10.1946 (unclear), Chaim Herzog archive.
61 Ibid.
62 Author's interview with Aura Herzog.
63 Ibid., and author's interview with Mike Herzog.
64 Interview with Aura Herzog.
65 Yaacov's letter to Vivian, 23.11.1946.
66 Ibid.
67 Interview with Aura Herzog.
68 Elie Wiesel, 'Certain Meetings', tribute to Yaacov Herzog.

Chapter 4 The Secret Agent

1 Interview with Malka and Alex Keynan, 2.3.1998.
2 Ibid.
3 Ibid.
4 Boris Guriel, handwritten article about Yaacov Herzog with letter to Pnina Herzog, 22.6.1972.
5 Guriel, interview on Kol Israel, summer 1974.
6 Guriel, article, ibid.
7 Guriel, interview, ibid.
8 Interview with Malka and Alex Keynan, ibid.
9 Herzog's report to his superiors, undated.
10 Interview with Malka and Alex Keynan, ibid.
11 Ibid.
12 Herzog's report, ibid.
13 'Harno Report', conversation dated 25.11.1947, Israel Galili archive, Haganah archives.

14 Ibid.
15 Ibid., 28.11.1947.
16 Ibid., 30.11.1947.
17 Ibid., 11.2.1948.
18 Ibid.
19 Ibid., 15.2.1948, marked 'Top Secret – Read and Destroy'.
20 Ibid., 7.3.1948.
21 Ibid.
22 Ibid., 19.3.1948.
23 Ibid., undated.
24 Ibid., 22.4.1948.
25 Guriel, interview, ibid.; Teddy Kollek's speech at the *shloshim* (memorial service) for Yaacov Herzog, April 1972..
26 Interview with Malka and Alex Keynan, ibid.

Chapter 5 Redeeming Lands in Jerusalem

1 Rabbi Isser Zalman Melzer's letter of ordination of Rabbi Yaacov Herzog, 13 Nissan 5708.
2 Yair Sheleg, ibid.
3 Abba Eban, Kol Israel memorial programme, March 1973.
4 Yaacov Herzog's letter to the Intelligence Reserve Unit (IRU), 25.5.1954; letter from head of Military Intelligence, Binyamin Gibli, to the IRU, 20.5.54.
5 Letter from Minister of Religious Affairs to the director-general of the Ministry of Defence, 20 Heshvan 5711 (31.10.1950).
6 Letter from D. Weiss, director-general of the Ministry of Religious Affairs, to the Harry Fischel Institute, 4.7.1948.
7 Interview with Pnina Herzog.
8 Weiss letter to the Foreign Minister, 14.7.1948.
9 Ibid.
10 Letter from Walter Eytan, director-general of the Foreign Ministry, to D. Weiss, 22.7.1948, State Archive.
11 Zerach Warhaftig on Kol Israel memorial programme, March 1977.
12 For example, see the report of the department of Christian communities, 15–20.8.1948, State Archive; letter from Yaacov Herzog to Michael Comay, Foreign Ministry, 2.9.1948, State Archive.
13 Letter to UN Secretary General from the papal nuncio, Monsignor McMahon, 1949, as well as letters from other churches, quoted in Kenneth Bilby, *New Star in the Near East*, Doubleday, NY, 1950, p. 215.
14 Bilby, ibid., pp. 213–15, 224–5.
15 Tribute from Patriarch Benedictus, 21.6.1972.
16 Herzog letter to the Foreign Ministry, Middle East department, 2.12.1948, State Archive.

Notes

17 Bilby, ibid., p. 214.
18 Yaacov Yehoshua draft tribute, May 1973.
19 Ibid. (final draft), 29.5.1973.
20 Ibid. (first draft).
21 Bilby, ibid.
22 Benedictus tribute, ibid.
23 Herzog letter to Mike Arnon, 2.9.1953.
24 Ibid.
25 Yaacov Herzog, *A People That Dwells Alone* (Hebrew), p. 62.
26 Sheleg, ibid.
27 Yaacov Herzog's report on meeting with McMahon, 25.2.1951, in issue 238 of 'Information for Israel's representatives abroad', the Foreign Ministry, 14.3.1951.
28 Guriel interview, ibid.
29 Sharett telegram to Eytan, 21.10.1948.
30 Herzog letter to A. Meir, Israel's consul in Milan, 3.11.1953.
31 Sharett to the Knesset Foreign Affairs and Security Committee, 18.7.1949.
32 Avihai, ibid.
33 Kollek, ibid.
34 Warhaftig, ibid.
35 Benedictus tribute, ibid.
36 Yehoshua, first draft, ibid.
37 Ibid.
38 Report on visit of Greek Patriarch to Israel, issue 269 of 'Information for Israel's representatives abroad', the Foreign Ministry, 29.4.1951.
39 Herzog letter to Y. Zisser, Ministry of Religious Affairs, 15.11.1951.
40 Herzog letter to Deputy Minister of Religious Affairs, 18.11.1951.
41 Issue 494 of 'Information for Israel's representatives abroad', the Foreign Ministry, 14.5.1952.
42 Yaacov Herzog letter to Mr Kornikos, at the Ministry of Finance, 3.6.1952.
43 Avihai, ibid.
44 Sheleg, ibid.
45 Ibid.
46 Herzog, recorded interview on Jerusalem, Kol Israel, summer 1974.
47 Interview with Pnina Herzog. Excerpts from the conversation were also quoted in Herzog's report on McMahon's second visit, 19.10.1949, State Archive, and in Ehud Avriel's tribute, 3.11.1975.
48 Avriel, ibid.
49 Herzog note about Dr Weizmann, undated.
50 Guriel, ibid.
51 Ibid.
52 Appointment letter by Foreign Ministry, 26.10.1949.
53 Letter of consent from Minister of Religious Affairs, 14.6.1951; appointment letter from Foreign Minister, 21.6.1951.

54 Letter from director-general of Foreign Ministry to the Civil Service commission, 16.3.1952.
55 Sharett telegram, 26.11.1949.
56 Herzog letter to Archmandrite Narkysos, 10.9.1950.
57 Herzog letter to Dr Bergman, Ministry of Finance, 10.10.1949; see also Herzog letters to the Custodian of Absentee-owned Properties, November 1950, and to Gershon Avner, Foreign Ministry, 12.11.1950.
58 Herzog letter to Sharett, 23.8.1950.
59 'Eastern Churches' Opposition to Internationalization of Jerusalem': issue 128 of 'Information for Israel's representatives abroad', the Foreign Ministry, 16.10.1950.
60 Herzog letter to Mr Brin, head of Foreign Currency division in Ministry of Finance, 24.10.1950.
61 Herzog letter to minister at Israel Embassy, London, 1.4.1952.
62 Herzog letter to the Ministry of Welfare, 20.8.1950.
63 Herzog letter to director-general of Ministry of Immigration, 28.12.1950.
64 Herzog letter to Archmandrite Narkysos, 28 Elul 5710 (10.9.1950).
65 Avriel, ibid.
66 Ibid.
67 Foreign Ministry consultation on Jerusalem prior to UN debate, 5.8.1953.
68 Herzog report to Foreign Minister about discussions with McMahon, on 6, 7 and 11 November 1953.
69 Ibid.
70 Sharett handwritten letter to Herzog, 10.11.1953.
71 Foreign Ministry consultation prior to UN debate, 20.7.1953.
72 Letter from director-general of Foreign Ministry to the Civil Service commission, 16.3.1952.
73 Herzog letter to director-general of Foreign Ministry, 6.6.1952.
74 Herzog letter to Deputy Minister of Religious Affairs, 5.3.1953.
75 Draft of circular from director-general of Foreign Ministry, autumn 1952, no exact date; and circular 282 to Israeli diplomatic missions and heads of departments, 16.1.1954.
76 Herzog reports to director-general of Foreign Ministry, 22.3.1953, 24.11.1953.
77 Herzog report to director-general of Foreign Ministry and senior officials, 2.3.1953.
78 Herzog letter to Pinchas Sapir, 17.8.1953, and Sapir's response, 20.8.1953.
79 Circular from director-general of Foreign Ministry, 28.3.1954.
80 Herzog letter to A. Alon, 20.1.1954.

Chapter 6   At First Sight

1 Interview with Pnina Herzog, 24.12.1997; see also Tehilla Ofer's article, 'The Pearl in the Herzog Dynasty', *Maariv* weekend magazine, 8.9.1989.
2 Ofer, ibid.

Notes

3 Interview with Pnina Herzog, ibid.
4 Ibid.
5 Ibid.
6 Interview with Aura Herzog.
7 Benedictus tribute, ibid.
8 Interview with Yitzhak Navon, ibid.
9 Interview with Pnina Herzog, ibid.
10 Ibid.
11 James McDonald letter to Yaacov Herzog, 7.5.1952.
12 Ofer, ibid.
13 Ibid.
14 McDonald's letter to Shira Herzog, 20.5.1953.
15 Letter from President of Israel to the Attorney General, 8.7.1954; letter from Prime Minister and Foreign Minister to the Judicial Council, 18.7.1954; letter from Boris Guriel to the Judicial Council, 19.7.1954.
16 Herzog report to the Israeli Embassy in Washington, 13.3.1955.
17 Herzog letter to Moshe Dayan, 14.1.1955.
18 Ibid.
19 Herzog telegram to Eban and Reuven Shiloah, 14.3.1955.
20 Herzog telegram, 16.3.1955.
21 Herzog letter to Sharett, 15.4.1955.
22 Herzog letter to Eban, 20.4.1955.
23 Herzog letter to Sharett, 22.4.1956.
24 Sheleg, ibid., author's interview with Eli Eyal.
25 Sheleg, ibid.
26 Herzog letter to Eric Johnston, 27.12.1957.
27 Herzog report to Israeli Embassy in Washington, 2.1.1956.
28 Herzog interview on fifth anniversary of Sharett's death, Kol Israel, 1970.
29 Herzog letter to Eban, ibid.
30 Sheleg, ibid.
31 Moshe Dayan diary, 3.4.1956.
32 Author's interview with Yaacov Tzur.
33 Ibid.
34 Sharett diary, 3.4.1955, vol. 3, p. 894.
35 Ibid., 8.11.1955, vol. 5, p. 1293.
36 Ibid., 20.12.1955, vol. 5, p. 1313.
37 Herzog summary, 'IDF attack on al-Fatah bases on East Bank, Thursday 21.3.56'; written 22.3.
38 Handwritten and typed notes of conversation with Sharett; handwriting might be Sharett's. Undated. Yaacov Herzog's private archive.
39 Avihai, ibid., p. 27.
40 Interview with Pinchas Sapir.
41 Ibid.
42 Herzog interview, ibid.

43 Meron Medzini, *The Proud Jewess*, p. 235.
44 Herzog interview, ibid.
45 Ibid.
46 Golda Meir interview in Avihai, ibid.
47 Medzini, ibid.
48 Herzog interview, ibid.

Chapter 7   Acting Foreign Minister

1 Herzog diary, 2.3.57.
2 Herzog interview with Michael Brecher, in *Decisions in Israel's Foreign Policy*, London 1974, p. 283. Herzog assisted Brecher in writing this book.
3 Herzog telegrams to Meir and Eban, 22.11.1956; to Meir, 22.11.1956; to Eban, 29.11.56 and 30.11.1956, etc.
4 Herzog telegram to Eban, 5.12.1956; telegram to Israel UN delegation, 8.12.1956.
5 Interview with Medzini.
6 Herzog diary, 3.1.1957.
7 Ibid.
8 Ibid.
9 Dayan diary, 25.2.1957, quoted in *Story of My Life* [Hebrew], p. 328.
10 Herzog telegram to Eban, 24.12.1956.
11 Meir telegram to Herzog, 25.12.1956.
12 Herzog diary and documents, 7.1.1957.
13 Dayan diary, 3.2.57, quoted in ibid. [Hebrew], p. 328.
14 Rafael letter to Herzog, 8.2.1957.
15 Herzog letter to Rafael, 13.2.1957.
16 Herzog interview with Reuel, ibid.
17 Herzog interview with Tevet, ibid.
18 Herzog diary, 8.1.1957.
19 Ibid.
20 Herzog interview with Tevet, ibid.
21 Mordechai Gazit, 'David Ben-Gurion and the Gaza Strip in the Sinai Campaign' [Hebrew], *Yahadut Zmanenu*, vol. 13, 1999, pp. 75–104.
22 Herzog interview with Tevet, ibid.
23 Herzog diary, 2.3.1957.
24 Herzog interview with Tevet, ibid.
25 Herzog diary, ibid.
26 Ibid., interview with Reuel, and other sources.
27 Herzog diary, ibid.
28 Ibid.
29 Ibid.
30 Herzog briefing notes on the Sinai campaign, undated, p. 13.
31 Ibid.

Notes

32 Ibid., p. 12.
33 Ibid.

Chapter 8 Birds Over the Cedars of Lebanon

1   Abba Eban, *An Autobiography*, pp. 270–1.
2   Author's interview with Shimon Peres, 26.2.2001.
3   Ben-Gurion letter, 18.9.1957.
4   Bedell Smith letter, 14.11.1957.
5   Herzog letter to Navon, 20.5.1958.
6   Herzog letter to Israeli, 5.7.1959.
7   Herzog letter to Eytan, 13.10.1957.
8   Herzog letter to Eytan, 28.10.1957.
9   Herzog letter to Eytan, 25.11.1957.
10 Interview with Abba Eban, memorial programme, March 1973.
11 Ibid.
12 Herzog letter to Nehemiah Argov, 8.10.1957.
13 Herzog letter to Eytan, 13.10.1957.
14 Herzog report to the Foreign Ministry, 25.10.1957.
15 Ibid.
16 Ibid.
17 Herzog report to the Foreign Ministry, 18.11.1957; Herzog letter to Murphy, 18.12.57; Herzog letter to Eytan, 25.8.1958.
18 Herzog letter to Gershon Avner, in Foreign Ministry, 27.1.1958.
19 Interview with a colleague of Herzog, who wished to remain anonymous.
20 Interview with Meir; memorial programme, March 1973.
21 Ibid.
22 Comay letter to Herzog, 12.8.1958.
23 Herzog letters to Comay, 15.8.58, 22.8.58, 29.8.1958.
24 Interview with Meir, ibid.
25 Interview with Eban, ibid.
26 Herzog letter to Foreign Ministry, 30.5.1958.
27 Ibid.
28 Interview with Abba Eban, ibid.
29 Herzog memorandum to Dulles, 13.5.1958.
30 Herzog, ibid.
31 Letter from Dulles to Herzog, 20.5.1958.
32 Herzog letter, ibid.
33 Interview with Eban, ibid.
34 Author's interview with Ari Rath.
35 Herzog letter to Eytan, 28.10.1957.
36 Cohen letter to Navon, 20.11.1958.
37 Interview with Pnina Herzog.
38 Herzog letter to Shiloah, 28.10.1957.

39 Herzog letter to Foreign Ministry, 15.12.1957.
40 Herzog letter to Argov, 8.10.1957.
41 Herzog letter to Peres, 25.11.1957.
42 Herzog letter to Navon, 25.11.1957.
43 Interview with Navon in Avihai, ibid.
44 Minutes of telephone conversation between Herzog, Shiloah and Navon, undated.
45 Interview with Medzini.
46 Minutes of conversation between Dulles, Eban and Herzog, 3.8.58.
47 Herzog letter reporting his meeting with Iran's deputy Prime Minister, Dr Shapur Bakhtiar, 23.10.1959.
48 Author's interviews with Simshon Arad, Meron Medzini, and others.
49 Medzini, ibid., pp. 270, 273.
50 Sheleg, ibid.
51 Ben-Gurion's diary, 2.1.1960.
52 Ibid., 9.1.60.
53 Ibid.
54 Herzog report; interview with Shimon Peres.
55 Ben-Gurion diary, 15.1.1960.
56 Herzog report, 4.3.1958.
57 Ibid.
58 Ben-Gurion interview in the film *Ben-Gurion Remembers*.
59 Original drafts of officials' statements with Herzog's handwritten notes.
60 Herzog letter to Meir, 30.3.1960; interview with Arad.

Chapter 9   The Challenge

1 Author's interview with Irwin Cotler, 30.7.1998.
2 *Encyclopedia Britannica*, vol. 10, pp. 75–6.
3 *Hebrew Encyclopedia* [Hebrew], vol. 18, pp. 408–12.
4 Toynbee letter to a Canadian Jewish publication, unnamed and undated.
5 *Al Goumhouriyeh*, Cairo, 29.1.1961.
6 Herzog report to Foreign Ministry, undated.
7 Yotam, 'Reflections Following a Debate', *Davar*, 5.4.1974.
8 Letter to Judge Yehoshua Auerbach, 21.2.1961.
9 Ibid.
10 Herzog press.
11 Herzog telegram to Toynbee, 26.1.1961.
12 Letter to Israeli, 2.2.1961.
13 Yotam, ibid.
14 Toynbee telegram to Herzog, 27.1.1961.
15 Avihai, ibid.
16 Interview with Peres.
17 Interview with Cotler.

Notes

18 Interview with Pnina Herzog, 16.8.2000.
19 Ibid.
20 Avihai, ibid.
21 Levavi letter to Herzog, 29.1.1961.
22 Author's interview with a former Israeli ambassador, 28.12.1998.
23 Interview with Meir, memorial programme, ibid.
24 Author's interview with Eliezra Herzog, 14.9.2000.
25 Herzog letter to Israel's Consul in Atlanta, 13.3.1961.
26 Herzog letter to Yehiel Ilsar, Manila, 29.3.1961.
27 Herzog letter to Chief Justice Moshe Zilberg, 8.3.1961.
28 Herzog letter to Israeli, 2.2.1961.
29 Interview with Pnina Herzog.
30 Justus, *Maariv*, 1.2.1961.
31 Maxwell Cohen tribute, 'Yaacov Herzog in Canada'.

Chapter 10   The Duel

1 Interview with Pnina Herzog.
2 Interview with Irwin Cotler.
3 Ibid.
4 Justus, ibid.
5 Herzog letter to Zilberg, ibid.
6 Ibid.
7 *Jerusalem Post*, 17.2.1961.
8 Ben-Zvi to Yaacov Herzog, 8.2.1961.
9 Rachel Yanait Ben-Zvi letter to Herzog, 9.2.1961.
10 Eban letter to Herzog, 19.2.1961.
11 Meir telegram to Herzog, 3.2.1961.
12 Israeli letter to Herzog, undated.
13 Hirschhorn letter to Herzog, 19.2.1961.
14 *New York Times*, 1.2.1961.
15 Herzog letter to Israel's Consul in Atlanta, ibid.
16 Letter from Marvin Needleman, Public Relations Officer of the United Zionist Council of Canada, to Rebecca Vinograd of the US Zionist Council, 1.2.1961.
17 Arnon letter to Herzog, 13.2.1961.
18 Letters to Herzog and others, and interviews with the author.
19 *Panim el Panim* [Hebrew], 10.3.1961.
20 Elon letter to Herzog, 14.2.1961.
21 Herzog letter to Michael Elizur, 21.2.1961.
22 Herzog letter to Yaacov Rosenthal, 4.4.1961.
23 Herzog letter to Israeli, 2.2.1961.
24 Herzog letter to Arnon, 29.3.1961.
25 Yotam, ibid.

Chapter 11 The Absent Father

1. Diefenbaker interview with Medzini.
2. Interview with Pnina Herzog.
3. Author's interview with Deborah Bregman, 10.12.1998.
4. Paul Martin tribute to Pnina Herzog, 30.6.1972.
5. Interview with Bregman, ibid.
6. Herzog's speech, in memory of his father Rabbi Herzog, at Heichal Shlomo, undated.
7. Herzog interview with Eli Eyal, IDF Radio, November 1969.
8. Eban's speech at Herzog's *shloshim*, memorial service, 16.4.1972.
9. Author's interview with Shira Herzog.
10. Martin tribute, ibid.
11. Eban speech, ibid.
12. Shazar, speech at *shloshim*, memorial service, 16.4.1972.
13. Interview with Shira Herzog.
14. Ibid.
15. Martin tribute, ibid.

Chapter 12 Dr Davis and Mr Charles

1. Herzog report on his first meeting with King Hussein, 25.9.1963.
2. Ibid.
3. Ibid.
4. Moshe Zack, *Hussein Makes Peace* [Hebrew], pp. 40, 98 (1).
5. Ibid.
6. Yaacov Herzog's official appointment letter, 25.8.1963, and director-general's circular, 23.10.1964.
7. Zack, ibid., p. 60.
8. Herzog report, ibid.
9. Ibid.
10. Herzog report on his second meeting with King Hussein, 2.5.1964.
11. Herzog report on his third meeting with King Hussein, 19.12.1964.
12. Herzog report, 25.9.63.
13. Moshe Zack, ibid., pp. 65–6.
14. News agency reports, 2.10.1963.
15. Zack, ibid., p. 58.
16. Herzog report, 18.10.1963.
17. Ibid.
18. Ibid.
19. Ibid.
20. Ibid.
21. Herzog telegram to Issachar Ben-Yaacov, Israel's Consul in Milan, 12.11.1963.

Notes

22 Ibid.
23 Ibid.
24 Herzog telegram to Ben-Yaacov, 20.11.1963.
25 Author's interview with Meir Amit, 11.1.2001.
26 Herzog telegram to Chaim Yahil, 10.12.1963.
27 Ibid.
28 Ibid.
29 Ibid.
30 Author's interview with Dan Avni-Segre, 21.2.2001.
31 Herzog report, 14.2.1964.
32 Ibid.
33 Interview with Peres.
34 Interview with Amit, ibid.
35 Ibid.
36 Herzog diary, 3.9.1967.
37 Interview with Avihai.
38 Amit letter to Herzog, 15.10.1964.
39 Summary of consultation, Eshkol, Levavi and Herzog.
40 Letter from Cabinet Secretary Yael Uzai to Cabinet Ministers, the Chief of Staff and others, 18.12.1963.
41 Foreign Minister telegram to Israel Embassy in Washington, 31.10.1963.
42 Herzog Report, 17.6.1964.
43 Herzog telegram to Eytan, 10.5.1964.
44 Memorandum, 'The Americans' arguments concerning the missiles', Prime Minister's office, 1963–4.
45 Report by Israel Ambassador to US Abraham Harman, 22.1.1964, and letter from President Johnson to Eshkol, 21.2.1964.
46 Harman report, 1.6.1964; Mike Feldman report, 1.6.1964; Feldman report, 2.6.1964.
47 Report of Israel minister to Washington Mordechai Gazit, 3.6.64, and Gazit report, 4.6.1964.
48 Harman report on Kollek and Herzog's meeting with Averill Harriman, 3.6.1964.
49 Herzog report, 17.6.1964.
50 Herzog handwritten summary of meeting, 18.11.1964.
51 Zack, ibid.
52 Herzog report, 2.5.1964.
53 Ibid.
54 Letter from C. A. to King Hussein, 25.5.1964.
55 Herzog report, 19.12.1964.
56 Herzog report, 2.5.1964.
57 Herzog report, 19.12.1964.
58 Ibid.

Chapter 13 Collapse

1. Letter from William Frankel, editor of the *Jewish Chronicle*, to Herzog, 11.11.1964.
2. Sassoon letter to Herzog, 12.11.1964.
3. Telegram to Herzog from Israeli Embassy in London, 2.2.1965.
4. Interview with Shira Herzog.
5. Herzog letter and draft speech to Sir Isaac Wolfson, 20.1.1965.
6. Nahum Goldmann interview, unedited, memorial programme, March 1973.
7. Meir interview, memorial programme, ibid.
8. *Jewish Chronicle* wire service, 18.5.1965.
9. Ibid.
10. *Jewish Chronicle* wire service, 26.5.1965.
11. Interview with Ari Rath.
12. *Jerusalem Post* and *Ha-Tzofeh*, 25.5.1965.
13. Interview with Shira Herzog.
14. Ibid.
15. Interview with Rath.
16. Sheleg, ibid.
17. Author's interview with a close relative.
18. Interview with Pnina Herzog.
19. Yaacov letter to Chaim, late November 1965.
20. Ibid.
21. Interview with Pnina Herzog.
22. Interview with Shira Herzog.
23. Yaacov letter to Chaim, ibid.
24. Ibid.
25. Ibid.
26. Author's interview with relative, not for attribution.
27. Author's interview with Miriam Eshkol.
28. Pnina Herzog letter to Levi Eshkol, 11.9.1965.
29. Interview with Aura Herzog.
30. Ibid.
31. Herzog diary, 24.8.1966.
32. Interview with Shira Herzog.
33. Author's interview with Eliezra Herzog, 14.9.2000.

Chapter 14 A Time of Flourishing

1. Medzini, ibid., p. 383.
2. Interview with a colleague of Yaacov Herzog, not for attribution.
3. Author's interview with Chaim Israeli.
4. Interview with Ari Rath.
5. Interview with Meron Medzini.

Notes

6 Interview with Miriam Eshkol.
7 Ibid.
8 Herzog diary, 11.8.1966.
9 Ibid., 14.9.1966.
10 Ibid., 26.6.1966.
11 Ibid., 10.8.1966.
12 Ibid.
13 Ibid., 27.6.1966.
14 Interview with Eliezra Herzog.
15 Herzog diary, 2.10.1966.
16 Interview with a colleague, not for attribution.
17 Menachem Begin interview, unedited, memorial programme, March 1973.
18 Herzog diary, 1.9.1966.
19 Ibid.
20 Herzog diary, 28.6.67.
21 Interview with colleague, not for attribution.
22 Herzog diary, 31.8.1966.
23 Ibid., 6.9.1966.
24 Ibid., 28.9.1966.
25 Interview with Deborah Bregman.
26 Ibid.
27 Adi Yaffe interview, Avraham Avihai, ibid., p. 58.
28 Ibid.
29 Herzog letters to Pnina, and interview with Pnina Herzog.
30 Herzog diary, 10.9.1966.
31 Ibid., 5.9.1966.
32 Ibid., 23.8.1966.
33 Ibid., 27.6.1966.
34 Interview with Shira Herzog.
35 Author's interview with Yitzhak Herzog.
36 Author's interview with Norma Bar-Moshe, 10.12.1998.
37 Interview with Ari Rath.
38 Indro Montanelli, ibid.
39 Interview with colleague, not for attribution.
40 Herzog diary, 13.7.68.
41 Ibid., 9.9.1966.
42 Ibid., 14.9.1966.
43 Goldmann interview, unedited, ibid.
44 Herzog diary, 7.9.1966.
45 Ibid.
46 Ibid., 30.9.1966.
47 Ibid., 9.8.1966.
48 Herzog letter to Liberman, 9.2.1967.
49 Menachem Begin interview, unedited, ibid.

50 Interview with Miriam Eshkol.
51 Elie Wiesel, tribute.
52 Ibid.
53 Herzog diary, 31.8.1966.
54 Ibid., 1.8.1966.
55 Ibid., 10.8.1966.
56 Ibid., 16.8.1966.
57 Ibid., 30.8.1966.
58 Ibid.
59 Ibid., 31.7.1966.
60 Ibid., 11.8.1966.
61 Medzini, ibid., p. 295.
62 Herzog diary, ibid.
63 Ibid., 24.9.1966.
64 Ibid., 11.8.1966.
65 Ibid., 1.10.1966.
66 Ibid., 6.9.1966.
67 Ibid., 11.8.1966.
68 Ibid., 4.9.1966.
69 Ibid.
70 Ibid., 1.10.1966.
71 Ibid., 3.8.1966.
72 Ibid., 17-18.7.1966.
73 Ibid., 24.9.1966.
74 Ibid., 14.9.1966.
75 Foreign Ministry telegram, 12.10.1966.
76 Records of the Prime Minister's office, 13–14.11.1966.

Chapter 15   Six Days and a King

1 Herzog diary, 15.5.1967.
2 Brecher, ibid., pp. 374, 377.
3 Herzog recording, memorial programme, March 1977.
4 Herzog diary, 21.10.1967.
5 Ibid., 1.6.1967.
6 Ibid.
7 Menachem Begin interview, unedited, memorial programme, March 1973.
8 Herzog diary, 1.6.1967.
9 Ibid., 16–17.5.1967.
10 Ibid., 25.5.1967.
11 Interview with Yitzhak Rabin, in Avihai, ibid.
12 Herzog diary, 30.5.1967; and interview with Meir Amit.
13 Interview with Meir Amit.
14 Herzog diary, 31.5.1967.

Notes

15 Ibid., 30.5.1967.
16 Ibid., 1.6.1967.
17 Interview with Chaim Israeli.
18 Herzog diary, 14.8.1967.
19 Indro Montanelli, ibid.
20 Herzog's notes, 2.7.1967.
21 Ibid.
22 Entry on 'Charles', Herzog diary, 3.11.1967.
23 Ibid.
24 Ibid.
25 Ibid.
26 Herzog diary, 27.9.1967.
27 Ibid., and entry on 'Charles', ibid.
28 Entry on 'Charles', ibid.
29 Ibid.
30 Herzog report on Jordan (talks in London 16, 19 and 29 October 1968).
31 Ibid.
32 Ibid.
33 Memorandum of inter-ministerial committee, 'The West Bank, the Kingdom of Jordan, the Gaza Strip: Proposal for a Solution and Policy'.
34 Herzog diary, 26.7.1967.
35 Sheleg, ibid.
36 Entry on 'Charles', ibid.
37 Ibid., and various diary entries
38 Herzog diary, 25.9.1967.
39 Ibid., 7.9.1967.
40 Ibid.
41 Ibid., 12.6.1967.
42 Ibid., 15.6.1967.
43 Ibid., 9-10.8.1967.
44 A photocopy of the note and Herzog's diary, 21.12.1967.
45 Herzog diary, 18.6.1967.
46 Ibid., 16.8.1967.
47 Ibid., 14.7.1968.
48 Ibid., 20.9.1968.
49 Herzog personal memo to Eshkol, 11.6.1967.
50 Herzog diary, 28.1.1968.
51 Ibid.
52 Eshkol's consultation with cabinet ministers Eban, Allon and Dayan, 29.5.1968.
53 Herzog summary, 21.11.67.
54 Ibid.
55 Ibid.
56 Ibid.

57 Ibid.
58 Ibid.
59 Ibid.
60 Herzog summary of talks with Hussein and his adviser Zaid a-Rifa'i in London, 22 and 24 August 1968 (English).

Chapter 16 A Gift from Hussein

1 Herzog diary, 12.8.1967.
2 Herzog letter to Yosef Nahmias, 15.11.1957.
3 Avihai interview, memorial programme, March 1973.
4 Ibid.
5 Herzog diary, 19.7.1968.
6 Ibid., 30.6.1967.
7 Ibid.
8 Herzog, *Am Levadad Yishkon* [Hebrew], p. 62.
9 Montanelli, ibid.
10 Ibid.
11 Herzog diary, 18.6.1967, and his speech, 'Israel's Twentieth Anniversary', to the Religious Kibbutz Movement, June 1968.
12 Herzog diary, 18.6.1967.
13 Ibid., 24.9.1967.
14 Herzog summary, 'A Few Additional Points', November 1968.
15 Herzog summary, 'Charles', December 1968–end of August 1969.
16 Herzog notes, 'Additional Comments on the Conversation with Charles', 27.9.1968.
17 Herzog diary, 30.6.1967.
18 Ibid., 16.8.1967.
19 Herzog summary, November 1968.
20 Author's interview with Ari Avner.
21 Herzog, personal note, 'The International Situation from 4.2.1968–8.6.1968', p. 163, passage from 21.3.1968.
22 Herzog, personal notes.
23 Herzog summary, ibid.
24 Coded note in Herzog's handwriting.
25 Exchange of telegrams between Herzog and Herbert.
26 Herzog telegram to Aharon Remez, Israeli Ambassador in London for transmittal to Hussein via Dr Herbert, 4.6.1969.
27 Herzog diary, 20.7.1968 (entry mistakenly dated 30.7).
28 Ibid., 21.7.1968, 24.7.1968.
29 Ibid., 21.7.1968.
30 Herzog summary, 'Charles', ibid.
31 Hussein letter to Dayan, via British government, 21.6.1969.
32 Herzog summary, 'Charles', ibid.

Notes

33 Hussein letter to Yael Dayan, 'Strictly Private', 22.10.1968.
34 Interview with Shira Herzog.
35 Herzog summary, November 1968, ibid.
36 Herzog diary, 19.7.1968.
37 Herzog report, 'Jordan', ibid.
38 Herzog diary, 28.9.1969.
39 Herzog report, 'Jordan', ibid.
40 Herzog summary, personal notes.
41 Herzog summary, 'Charles', ibid.
42 Ibid.
43 Ibid.
44 Ibid.
45 Hussein condolence letter to Allon, via US Embassy, 27.3.1969.

Chapter 17   Decline

1 Herzog diary, 16.3.1969.
2 Medzini, ibid., p. 383.
3 Herzog diary, 17.3.1969.
4 Ibid., 18.3.1969.
5 Ibid., 1.6.69 (handwritten).
6 Herzog summary, 'Charles', ibid.
7 Author's interview with Simcha Dinitz.
8 Interview, not for attribution, July 2000.
9 Interview, not for attribution, August 2000.
10 Interviews with members of Herzog family and colleagues.
11 Interview with Ari Rath.
12 Interview with Simcha Dinitz.
13 Herzog diary, 31.7.1968.
14 Ibid., 1.8.1968.
15 Ibid., 5.8.1968.
16 Ibid., 19.9.1968.
17 Ibid., 15.9.1968.
18 Ibid., 6.9.1967.
19 Ibid., 15.9.1968.
20 Yaacov Herzog, personal notes, 'The International Situation Between 4.2.1968 and 8.6.1968', p. 163, passage from 7.4.1968.
21 Interview with Ari Rath.
22 Sheleg, ibid.
23 Medzini, ibid., p. 235.
24 Interview with Shimshon Arad and Medzini, ibid., p. 270.
25 Medzini, ibid., p. 383.
26 Herzog diary, 20.12.1969.
27 Hussein message to Meir, 26.9.1970.

28 Herzog summary re meeting with Hussein and a-Rifa'i, 3.10.1970.
29 Sheleg, ibid.
30 Interview with colleague, ibid.
31 Interview with Chaim Israeli.
32 Interview with Meron Medzini.
33 Nahum Goldmann tribute.
34 Interview with Avraham Avihai.
35 Interview with employee at Prime Minister's office, not for attribution.
36 Interview with Shira Herzog.
37 Interview with Aura Herzog.
38 Chaim Herzog, ibid.
39 Interview with Shira Herzog.
40 Chaim Herzog, ibid., p. 329.

Chapter 18   Epilogue

1 President Shazar, on the 30th day of Yaacov Herzog's passing.
2 Isaiah Berlin, tribute in *A People that Dwells Alone*, pp. 14–15.
3 Elie Wiesel tribute, ibid.
4 Menachem Begin, interview, memorial programme, March 1973.
5 Abba Eban address, *shloshim* memorial service, 16.4.1972.
6 Shimon Peres, address, anniversary of Herzog's death, February 1973.
7 Ben-Gurion letter to Herzog, 23.1.1972.

Index

Abd al-Rahman Yahya (Prince of Yemen) 240
Abdullah (King of Jordan) 77, 81, 193, 226, 286
Adams, Sherman 17
Adenauer, Konrad 170, 173
Aga Khan (Ismaili leader) 306
Agnon, S. Y. 274
Akiva (Rabbi) 219–20
Aliner, Eliezer 55
Allon, Yigal 315, 320–21, 326–7, 329, 335–6, 337–8, 340, 345
Aloni, Shulamith 288
Alsop, Joseph 126
Ambache, Aura [see Herzog, Aura]
Ambache, Susie [see Eban, Susie]
Amery, Julian 240, 306–8, 311, 316–17, 320, 330,
Amit, Meir 237, 238–9, 241, 271, 285, 296, 306, 308
Anderson, Robert 6, 121–2
Aranne, Zalman 26, 126, 273–4, 289, 341
Arazi, Tuviah 166
Argov, Nehemiah 1, 2, 7–9, 11, 113, 125, 135, 154, 165
Aristotle 91, 220
Arnon, Michael 212, 278
Arnon, Yaacov 278
Attlee, Clement 42–3, 56
Avihai, Avraham 37, 95–6, 179, 180, 241, 322, 347

Avner, Ari 328
Avni-Segre, Dan 236–7
Avrekh, Yeshayahu 178, 214
Avriel, Ehud 99, 113, 323–4
Azzam Pasha 184

Badr, Mohammed al-Mansur al- (Imam and leader of Yemen) 237–8, 306
Balfour, Arthur James 197, 199–201
Bar-Haim, Shaul 309
Bar Kokhba 219–20
Bar-Lev, Chaim 309, 320, 334
Bar-Moshe, Norma 277
Bedell Smith, Walter 154–5
Begin, Menachem 60n, 61, 62, 64, 125n, 126, 273, 281, 295–6, 315, 326, 328–9, 351
Beilin, Naftali Zvi Yehuda 108–9
Bellotti, Felice 236–7
Benedictus (Greek Orthodox Patriarch of Jerusalem) 91, 93, 96–7, 110, 324–5
Ben-Gurion, David 1–7, 10–12, 14–15, 17, 19–25, 29, 30, 37, 43, 60n, 64, 64n, 73, 75, 79, 81, 99, 100–1, 112–15, 120, 122–7, 129–33, 136, 138–40, 142–8, 153–4, 167–9, 170–4, 210, 216, 221, 232, 233, 244, 253–4, 270, 272–3, 275, 280–1, 288–9, 310, 313, 316, 339, 342–3, 351–2

Ben-Gurion, Paula 9, 130, 211
Benson, Ezra 159, 172
Ben-Yaacov, Issachar 237
Ben-Zvi (Keynan), Malka 71–2, 73–5, 85
Ben-Zvi, Rachel Yanait 211, 291
Ben-Zvi, Yitzhak 3, 23, 182, 210–11
Berlin, Isaiah 275, 325, 350
Bernadotte, Folke 64, 64n
Berry (US State Dept official) 160
Bevin, Ernest 60
Bidault, Georges 56
Bloomfield brothers 263
Bormann, Martin 285
Boumedienne, Houari 308
Bourgès-Maunoury, Maurice 8, 122
Bregman, Deborah 217, 275–6
Briscoe, Robert 37
Brodie, Israel 257
Broide, Ephraim 217, 277
Browning, Robert 161–2
Buber, Martin 76n
Bulganin, Nikolai 19, 22, 23, 28, 132
Bull, Odd 297, 302
Burns, E.L.M. 134–5

Cabot Lodge, Henry [see Lodge, Henry Cabot]
Cadogan, Alexander 184
Casaroli (Monsignor, later Cardinal) 103
Case (US Congressman) 286
Chamberlain, Neville 181
Chesterton, G.K. 230
Chouraqui, André 283
Churchill, Randolph 127
Churchill, Winston 52, 113, 200
Chuvakhin, Leonid 291
Cohen, Louise 163
Cohen, Maxwell 179
Cohen, Yosef 331
Coleridge, Samuel 42
Comay, Michael 160
Confucius 220

Cotler, Irwin 179, 209
Couve de Murville, Maurice 312

Daud (Jordanian Colonel) 298
Dayan, Moshe 8, 12, 113, 115, 131, 133–5, 137, 146, 149, 295, 297, 306, 307–9, 311, 312–15, 331–2, 335, 340–1
Dayan, Yael 332
de Gasperi, Alcide 56
de Gaulle, Charles 19, 70, 295, 312
del Aqua (Cardinal) 324
de Valera, Eamon 36–7, 52, 56, 274
Diefenbaker, John 176, 215–16
Dinitz, Simcha 327, 339, 343–4
Dinstein, Zvi 340
Disenchik, Arieh 289–90, 333
Duek, Moshe 165
Dulles, John Foster 10, 11, 26, 114, 115, 118, 123–4, 129, 133, 141–2, 145–8, 160–2, 163, 167–8, 171
Duran, Shimon ben Zemach 161

Eban, Abba 11, 17, 20, 21–8, 65, 87, 118, 121, 133–4, 136–8, 141, 143, 145–8, 153–4, 156–7, 161–3, 167, 168, 205, 211, 220–1, 222, 280, 288–90, 295–6, 306–7, 308, 310, 311–16, 320–1, 326–8, 330–2, 333–6, 338, 341–3, 351
Eban, Susie 26, 65–6, 288, 312–13
Eden, Anthony 14, 118
Eisenhower, Dwight 2, 3, 6, 7–10, 13, 18, 20, 21–3, 28, 65, 119, 121, 133, 139–40, 142–4, 148, 168, 170, 172, 274
Eitan, Rafael (Raful) 12
Elon, Amos 212
Eshkol, Levi 137, 144, 153, 227, 231, 241, 243–5, 253, 261, 265, 269–73, 275, 278, 280, 281–5, 287, 291, 294–8, 305–7, 309, 311, 313–15, 321, 322, 325–6, 328, 336, 338, 339
Eshkol, Miriam 270, 276–7, 282, 342

Index

Evron, Ephraim (Effi) 225, 231, 342
Eyal, Eli 118, 219, 310
Eytan, Walter 3, 29, 94, 106–7, 137, 155, 160, 163, 240

Feisal Al Hashemi (Emir) 197
Feisal (King of Saudi Arabia) 239
Felici (Monsignor) 103
Fishman-Maimon, Yehuda Leib 88, 92
Frankel, Max 274
Friedman-Yellin (Mrs) 61
Friedman-Yellin, Natan 61
Frost, David 311

Galili, Israel 75, 272, 276–7, 315–16, 326, 327, 337, 341
Gandhi, Mahatma 185
Gaon, Rabbi 333
Gemayel, Pierre 235
Gibli, Binyamin 87, 114
Goldmann, Nahum 259–60, 272, 275, 279, 285, 290, 312, 346–7, 348
Gottwald, Klement 56
Grewson (Goldwater), Molly 39
Gruner, Dov 61
Guriel, Boris 72–3, 75, 94, 100–1

Hacohen, David 285
Hakim (Maronite Archbishop of Galilee) 91–2, 103–4, 236
Halevy, Yehuda 211
Hamilton, Charles D. 7
Hammarskjold, Dag 16, 19, 21, 28, 131–3, 135–9, 149
Ha-Parhi, Estori 198
Harel, Isser 12, 122, 244, 278, 280
Harif, Yosef 336
Harkabi, Yehoshafat 12, 166
Harman, Abraham 169, 232, 327
Harmelin, Yosef 280
Hayworth, Rita 306
Henderson, Loy 158–9
Herbert, Emmanuel 225–8, 246, 250, 253–4, 291, 293, 300, 305, 311, 320, 330, 344
Herzog, Aura 26, 65–9, 110, 265, 312–13
Herzog, Chaim (Vivian) 3–4, 26, 31, 36–9, 40, 45–9, 58–60, 63–9, 73, 78, 88, 169, 218, 226, 262, 265, 277, 309, 343, 348–9
Herzog, Eliezra 155, 164–5, 263, 266–8, 272
Herzog, Elka 33
Herzog, Esther 33
Herzog, Isaac (Bougie) 67
Herzog, Joel Leib 33–4, 39, 40, 45
Herzog, Michael (Mike) 67, 287
Herzog, Miriam Leiba (née Sarowitz) 33
Herzog, Naphthali Hirsch 33
Herzog, Pnina 2, 57, 72, 96, 107, 108–12, 155, 164, 173, 179–90, 182, 213, 214, 223, 259, 261–5, 276, 309, 333, 348
Herzog, Sarah 35–6, 45, 66, 67, 75, 263
Herzog, Shira 112, 155, 221, 223, 258, 261, 263, 266, 277, 333, 348–9
Herzog Yitzhak 277, 292
Herzog, Yitzhak (Isaac) Halevi, Rabbi 1, 30, 32, 34, 35, 41, 44–6, 49, 50, 52–63, 65, 67, 69–70, 71, 86, 109, 153, 218–19
Hezekiah (King of Judah) 219
Hillman, Annie 59
Hillman, David 59
Hillman, Sarah [see Herzog, Sarah]
Hillman, Shmuel Isaac 35, 39, 40–1
Hirschhorn, Yehuda Halevy 211
Hitler, Adolf 84, 85, 187, 191
Hoover, Herbert 20–1
Horn, Shimon 334
Hughes (Monsignor) 53, 54
Humphrey, Hubert 173
Hussein (King of Jordan) 166, 167–8, 225–34, 241, 245–52, 253–6,

Hussein (King of Jordan) (*cont.*)
    286–7, 291–3, 298–9, 300–11,
    313–15, 316–21, 326–30, 332,
    334–6, 338, 340, 344–5, 348
Husseini, Abd al-Khader al- 80
Husseini, Haj Amin al- 77, 84
Huysmans, Camille 56
Hyman, Louis 39–40

Isaiah 94
Israeli, Chaim 154, 155, 177, 182, 213,
    218, 287, 340, 346
Israeli, I. S. 212

Jami'an, Emile 226
Jarring, Gunnar 328
Jernigan, John D. 243
John XXIII (Pope) [see Roncalli
    (Archbishop)]
Johnson, Lyndon B. 144, 173, 243–4,
    247, 285, 294–5, 312, 325
Johnston, Eric 119–20, 242, 247, 255
Joyce, James 274

Kamir, Ami 271, 278
Kaplan, Eliezer 81, 97
Kass, Shmuel 178
Katznelbogen (Rabbi) 35
Kedar, Lou 339, 343
Kennedy, John F. 173, 215, 216, 244,
    247–8, 274
Keynan, Alex 71, 72, 85
Keynan, Malka [see Ben-Zvi, Malka]
Khan, Ali 306
Khrushchev, Nikita 29
Kimche, David 309
Knowland, William 144
Kollek, Teddy 1, 6, 96, 113, 121–2,
    265, 285
Kook, Avraham Yitzhak Hacohen 45
Kotsker Rebbe (Rabbi of Kotsk) 56
Kron, David 241

La Guardia, Fiorello 56

Landau, Chaim 63
Lavon, Pinchas 113–14, 210, 253, 280
Lawson, Edward 3, 7, 9, 121, 134,
    139
Lerner, Alec 237
Levavi, Arieh 180, 225
Liberman, Saul 281
Lie, Trygve 183–4
Lior, Israel 271
Livneh, Eliezer 297
Lloyd, Selwyn 8
Lloyd George, David 200
Lodge, Henry Cabot 146, 147
Lok, Mordechai 245
Lurie, Arthur 3, 12, 125, 126–8, 225

Mack (Professor) 262–4
Macmillan, Harold 170
Magnes, Judah 76n, 81
Maimon, Yehuda Leib [see
    Fishman-Maimon, Yehuda Leib]
Maimonides 14, 158, 198, 274
Martin, Paul 217, 221, 223–4
McDonald, James 93, 111, 112
McMahon (Monsignor) 99, 104
McRory (Cardinal) 37
Medzini, Meron 126, 134, 169, 270,
    337, 343, 354
Meir, Golda 3, 12, 15, 19, 22, 64–5,
    126, 127–8, 132–3, 136–8, 146,
    148, 153, 159–61, 168, 169, 171,
    174, 181, 222, 226–7, 232, 236–7,
    241, 243, 260, 261, 286–7, 288–90,
    321, 326, 332, 336, 337–9, 342–7,
    348
Meiri, Menahem 162
Melzer, Isser Zalman 86, 87
Meridor, Yaacov 63
Meroz, Yochanan 240
Mobutu, Joseph (later Mobutu Sese
    Seko) 282
Mohammed (Prince of Jordan) 308
Mollet, Guy 5, 8
Moses (Prophet) 347

Index

Mowassi (Maronite Patriarch in Lebanon) 234–6, 245
Müller, Heinrich 285
Murphy, Robert 144, 159

Nahmanides 198
Nahmias, Yosef 322
Najar, Emile 3
Napoleon 84, 219
Nasser, Gamal Abd al- 3, 4–5, 115–17, 120–1, 123, 128–9, 149–51, 166, 168, 226, 228, 229–32, 235, 237, 244, 248–50, 251–2, 256, 293–4, 302, 304, 317, 329
Navon, Yitzhak 1, 2, 12, 15, 16, 23, 26–7, 110, 126, 155, 163, 165, 166
Nebuchadnezzar 194, 198
Nelson, Horatio 219
Nixon, Richard 132–3, 172–3, 290, 337, 348

Ovadiah of Bartenura (Rabbi) 50

Pahlavi, Reza (Shah of Iran) 241, 248–9
Penn, Dalia 237
Peres, Shimon 5, 8, 9, 12, 13, 19, 113, 122–3, 165, 241, 289–90, 314, 351
Pineau, Christian 8, 145
Pius XII (Pope) 53–5, 93, 324
Plato 220
'Prophet, The' (Yemeni Minister) 237–40
Proust, Marcel 265–6, 274

Qassem, Abd al-Karim al- 166
Qawuqji, Fawzi al- 79, 80, 83

Rabin, Yitzhak 241, 271, 288, 291, 295, 296, 312–13, 327, 341
Rabinowitz, Louis 65
Rafael, Gideon 3, 123, 124, 126–8, 141

Rashi (Rabbi) 35
Rath, Ari 143, 262, 270, 277, 339
Raviv, Moshe 327, 342
Reese, Alpen 56–7
Remez, Aharon 306–7
Renan, Ernest 185–6
Riad, Abd al-Munim 302
Rifa'i, Abd al-Munim a- 232, 328
Rifa'i, Samir a- 232
Rifa'i, Zaid a- 321, 328, 330, 331, 334–6, 345
Roncalli (Archbishop) 52–3, 95
Roosevelt, Franklin Delano 158
Rosen, Pinchas 149
Rothberg, Sam 323
Rothschild, Dorothy de 274, 275, 277, 285–6
Rothschild (Lord) 277, 308
Rowntree, William 11
Rusk, Dean 232

Sacharov, Chaim 78
Said, Nuri 166
Sapir, Pinchas 26, 107, 126, 138, 314, 328, 340–1
Sapir, Yosef 295
Sarid, Yossi 277
Sarowitz, Miriam Leiba [see Herzog, Miriam Leiba]
Sasson, Moshe 309
Sasson, Shlomo 44
Sassoon, Solomon 258
Scholem, Gershom 76n
Sereni, Ada 322
Shachor, David 109
Shachor, Eliezer 109, 155
Shachor, Frieda 108, 263
Shachor, Pnina [see Herzog, Pnina]
Shachor, Zalman 108–9
Shaltiel, David 72, 73, 75
Shamgar, Meir 62
Shamir, Yitzhak 62
Shapira, Moshe Chaim 2, 123–4
Sharett, Moshe (formerly Moshe

383

Sharett, Moshe (cont.)
  Shertok) 5, 6, 65, 75, 79, 81, 88, 89,
  94–5, 101, 103–4, 107, 110,
  112–16, 118, 119–23, 124–8, 222,
  287, 310
Sharett, Zippora 125
Sharon, Ariel (Arik) 114
Shaw, George Bernard 31, 230
Shazar, Zalman 221–2, 273, 281, 286,
  287, 350
Sheleg, Yair 46
Sherringham 72, 73–4, 75–85, 87, 167
Shihab, Fuad 235
Shiloah, Reuven 20–1, 75, 164, 166
Shitreet, Bekhor Shalom 91
Shmulevich, Matityahu 61
Shneerson, Mordechai 3
Shukeiri, Ahmad 236, 254
Sieff, Marcus 308
Silver, Abba Hillel 17
Snapiri, Nahum 60, 63, 65
Sneh, Moshe 84
Sobolev, Arkady 28
Sofer, Frieda 276
Steinberg, Solly 32
Stern, Avraham (Yair) 60n, 61
Symington, Stuart 173
Szenes, Hannah 277

Tamir, Shmuel 62, 284
Thompson, Lord 335
Thucydides 91
Timotheos (Greek Orthodox
  Patriarch in Athens) 97–8
Toledano, Shmuel 284
Toynbee, Arnold 175–83, 186–91,
  192, 194–8, 200–1, 203–11,
  212–14, 320
Toynbee (Mrs) 209

Truman, Harry 84
Tzimuki, Arieh 336
Tzur, Yaacov 123

U Thant 294
Unterman, Joseph 37

Vardi, Chaim (Dr) 93, 95
Vered, Yael 225
Vilna Gaon 158

Warhaftig, Zerach 90
Weisgal, Meyer, 290
Weiss, D. 89
Weizmann, Chaim 79, 93, 99–100,
  118, 190, 197, 199, 277, 287, 290,
  310
Weizmann, Vera 290–1
Wellington, Duke of 219
White [US minister] 1, 2, 121
White, Theodore 266, 274
Wiesel, Elie 282–3, 350
Wilkowsky, Yaacov David 34, 36
Wilson, Harold 295, 338
Wine, Hubert 42, 45, 47
Wolfson, Aviezer 280
Wolfson, Isaac 257, 259–60, 263, 265,
  280

Yaffe, Adi 271, 276
Yahil, Chaim 225, 236
Yehoshua, Yaacov 92–3, 96–7
Yohanan ben Zakkai 185, 219

Zack, Moshe 98, 121–2, 313
Zain (Queen Mother of Jordan)
  226–7
Zondek, Bernard 9, 262, 263